COMICAL MODERNITY

Austrian and Habsburg Studies

General Editor: Howard Louthan, Center for Austrian Studies, University of Minnesota

Before 1918, Austria and the Habsburg lands constituted an expansive multinational and multiethnic empire, the second largest state in Europe and a key site for cultural and intellectual developments across the continent. At the turn of the twentieth century, the region gave birth to modern psychology, philosophy, economics and music, and since then has played an important mediating role between Western and Eastern Europe, today participating as a critical member of the European Union. The volumes in this series address specific themes and questions around the history, culture, politics, social, and economic experience of Austria, the Habsburg Empire and its successor states in Central and Eastern Europe.

Recent volumes:

Volume 23
Comical Modernity: Popular Humour and the Transformation of Urban Space in Late Nineteenth-Century Vienna
Heidi Hakkarainen

Volume 22
Embers of Empire: Continuity and Rupture in the Habsburg Successor States after 1918
Edited by Paul Miller and Claire Morelon

Volume 21
The Art of Resistance: Cultural Protest against the Austrian Far Right in the Early Twenty-First Century
Allyson Fiddler

Volume 20
The Monumental Nation: Magyar Nationalism and Symbolic Politics in Fin-de-siècle Hungary
Bálint Varga

Volume 19
Tropics of Vienna: Colonial Utopias of the Habsburg Empire
Ulrich E. Bach

Volume 18
Sacrifice and Rebirth: The Legacy of the Last Habsburg War
Edited by Mark Cornwall and John Paul Newman

Volume 17
Understanding Multiculturalism: The Habsburg Central European Experience
Edited by Johannes Feichtinger and Gary B. Cohen

Volume 16
The Viennese Café and Fin-de-Siècle Culture
Edited by Charlotte Ashby, Tag Gronberg and Simon Shaw-Miller

Volume 15
Territorial Revisionism and the Allies of Germany in the Second World War: Goals, Expectations, Practices
Edited by Marina Cattaruzza, Stefan Dyroff and Dieter Langewiesche

Volume 14
Journeys Into Madness: Mapping Mental Illness in the Austro-Hungarian Empire
Edited by Gemma Blackshaw and Sabine Wieber

For a full volume listing, please see the series page on our website: http://berghahnbooks.com/series/austrian-habsburg-studies.

COMICAL MODERNITY

Popular Humour and the
Transformation of Urban Space in
Late Nineteenth-Century Vienna

Heidi Hakkarainen

First published in 2019 by
Berghahn Books
www.berghahnbooks.com

© 2019, 2026 Heidi Hakkarainen
First paperback edition published in 2026

All rights reserved. Except for the quotation of short passages
for the purposes of criticism and review, no part of this book
may be reproduced in any form or by any means, electronic or
mechanical, including photocopying, recording, or any information
storage and retrieval system now known or to be invented,
without written permission of the publisher.

Library of Congress Cataloging-in-Publication Data
Names: Hakkarainen, Heidi, author.
Title: Comical modernity : popular humour and the transformation of urban space in late nineteenth-century Vienna / Heidi Hakkarainen.
Description: New York : Berghahn Books, 2019. | Series: Austrian and Habsburg studies ; Volume 23 | Includes bibliographical references and index.
Identifiers: LCCN 2019012575 (print) | LCCN 2019016355 (ebook) | ISBN 9781789202748 (ebook) | ISBN 9781789202731 (hardback : alk. paper)
Subjects: LCSH: Vienna (Austria)--Humor. | Austrian wit and humor--Social aspects--Austria--Vienna. | Austrian wit and humor--History and criticism. | Vienna (Austria)--In literature. | Urbanization in literature. | Urbanization--Austria--Vienna--History--19th century. | Vienna (Austria)--Social life and customs--19th century. | Vienna (Austria)--Civilization--19th century.
Classification: LCC PN6222.A8 (ebook) | LCC PN6222.A8 H35 2019 (print) | DDC 808.88/2--dc23
LC record available at hdps://lccn.loc.gov/2019012575

British Library Cataloguing in Publication Data
A catalogue record for this book is available from the British Library

EU GPSR Authorized Representative
LOGOS EUROPE, 9 rue Nicolas Poussin, 17000, LA ROCHELLE, France
Email: Contact@logoseurope.eu

ISBN 978-1-78920-273-1 hardback
ISBN 978-1-83695-382-1 paperback
ISBN 978-1-83695-383-8 epub
ISBN 978-1-78920-274-8 web pdf

https://doi.org/10.3167/9781789202731

Contents

List of Figures	vi
Acknowledgements	vii
Introduction	1
1. Power and Space	25
2. Tensions with City Authorities	56
3. City out of Control	94
4. Knowing the City	134
5. Urban Types and Characters	179
Conclusions	247
Bibliography	255
Index	270

Figures

Figure 1.1 'Exhibition', *Figaro*, 30 October 1858.   38
Figure 2.1 Police officer in Josefstädter Exerzierplatz. *Kikeriki*, 25 May 1865.   60
Figure 2.2 New regulations for dogs. *Kikeriki*, 23 October 1862.   65
Figure 2.3 'A new method for taxing'. *Kikeriki*, 13 May 1888.   67
Figure 2.4 The numbering of houses. *Kikeriki*, 14 November 1861.   74
Figure 2.5 Padded suit for train travel. *Kikeriki*, 23 February 1865.   83
Figure 2.6 'The proper toilette for ladies', *Figaro*, 19 April 1879 / *Wiener Luft* No. 16.   84
Figure 3.1 'The condition of our streets', *Kikeriki*, 9 January 1876.   98
Figure 3.2 Rising above the chaotic city. *Kikeriki*, 26 December 1875.   102
Figure 3.3 'Ringstraße'. *Der Floh*, 9 May 1869.   104
Figure 3.4 Vienna is still Vienna. *Der Floh*, 18 March 1888.   105
Figure 3.5 'Revolution?' *Kikeriki*, 2 August 1885.   109
Figure 3.6 Vienna before and after its beautification. *Kikeriki*, 26 May 1864.   118
Figure 3.7 The loss of old trees. *Kikeriki*, 4 August 1864.   123
Figure 4.1 'From a distance – From close-to', *Kikeriki*, 19 April 1874.   138
Figure 4.2 *Kikeriki*, 8 May 1873.   142
Figure 4.3 *Der Floh*, 23 September 1877.   142
Figure 4.4 *Der Floh*, 24 November 1878.   142
Figure 4.5 *Kikeriki*, 6 February 1879.   142
Figure 4.6 A statue sketched by a short-sighted person. *Figaro*, 10 June 1882.   144
Figure 4.7 The monument of Archduke Karl (1860) at the Heldenplatz.   145
Figure 4.8 'In ten years', *Kikeriki*, 20 May 1869.   164
Figure 5.1 'The elegant Vindobona'. *Kikeriki*, 3 April 1873.   183
Figure 5.2 The Rotunde was the main site for the 1873 World Exhibition.   184
Figure 5.3 Flower girl on the Ringstraße. *Der Floh*, 28 March 1874.   218
Figure 5.4 'To live like a god'. *Der Floh*, 31 October 1886.   220

Acknowledgements

My interest in Viennese cultural history started a long time ago when I was studying theatre, film and media studies at the University of Vienna, but this book was written at the University of Turku in Finland. It originates from a study that was conducted in the PhD Programme in Popular Culture Studies (PPCS), funded by the Academy of Finland. The financial support of various foundations has enabled me to do the necessary research in Vienna. I am grateful to the Turku University Foundation, the Eino Jutikkala Fund and the Hollo Foundation for their financial support that enabled me to work in the Austrian archives and libraries. I would like to thank the staff of the Austrian National Library, Wienbibliothek im Rathaus, Austrian State Archives and Verein für Geschichte der ArbeiterInnenbewegung for their help and assistance. Illustrations from the humorous magazines are reproduced by courtesy of the Austrian National Library.

I am a cultural historian by training and I would like to offer my warmest gratitude to my supervisors for guiding me in my research journey that has led to this book. Hannu Salmi from the University of Turku introduced me to the nineteenth-century studies and provided me with scholarly advice, inspiration and encouragement. Riitta Laitinen, who, to my grief, passed away before this book was finished, has read numerous versions of my texts, providing insightful comments, and her ideas about space and spatiality have guided my work from the beginning. Anu Korhonen from the University of Helsinki has shared with me her expertise on the historical study of humour, and I am deeply grateful for her learned advice and deep analytical insight. I would like to offer my gratitude to my examiners Mary Gluck and Markus Reisenleitner, who together with Susan Ingram came to the public defence of my dissertation, providing invaluable commentary and encouragement.

Many of the main ideas for this study were gained during my research trips to Vienna. I would like to thank Christina Lutter and Karl Vocelka for inviting me to visit the History Department at the University of Vienna in 2013. Lutz Musner took time to offer some thoughtful comments and insightful critique for which I am very grateful. I would also like to thank Harald Robert Stühlinger for the opportunity to take part in the publication *Vom Werden der Wiener Ringstraße*. I wish to offer my gratitude to Sylvia Mattl-Wurm for the permission to reproduce material from my contribution to this volume. I am grateful to the staff of the Wienbibliothek im Rathaus and especially Gerhard Murauer for the collaboration.

I wish to offer my warm gratitude to the whole community of the Cultural History Department at the University of Turku for their impact in shaping this book. I would like to thank the board and members of the PPCS, Mirka Ahonen, Anu-Hanna Anttila, Alessandro Arcangeli, Martin Cloonan, Pertti Grönholm, Bruce Johnson, Marjo Kaartinen, Kari Kallioniemi, Maiju Kannisto, Ralf Kauranen, Kimi Kärki, Silja Laine, Maarit Leskelä-Kärki, Rami Mähkä, Paavo Oinonen, Mila Oiva, Heli Paalumäki, Petri Paju, Jörg Rogge, Panu Savolainen, Marc Schalenberg, Gregory Shaya, Deborah Simonton and Mari Tanninen for their criticisms, advice and intellectual stimulation. The two symposiums of the network 'Concepts, Practices and Narratives as Tools of Studying Cultural History' in Mainz and Verona enriched this project and I would like to offer my sincere gratitude to all participants of these meetings.

I would like to thank Chris Chappell, Soyolmaa Lkhagvadorj and Caroline Kuhtz from Berghahn Books, and the anonymous readers for their constructive comments. Keith Battarbee polished my English and I thank him for his invaluable advice in translating the German quotations into English. All the possible mistakes remain my own.

Without the help of my family and friends I would never have been able to start such an intellectual endeavour, or to bring it to closure. My husband Juhana Saarelainen has encouraged this project from the beginning, providing invaluable support during years of research and writing. I dedicate this book with all my love to my mother Marja-Leena Hakkarainen and to the memory of my father Erkki Hakkarainen.

Turku, February 2019

Introduction

> You know that city so unshakeable and still,
> Where no one treats your ears ill,
> Where not every breath of wind makes you wholly
> Nervous, furious and full of folly?
> You know that city?
> That way! That way
> I'd like to escape with the next express train!
>
> —'Moderne Ballade', 1886

This is the first part of a poem titled 'Modern Ballad', published in the humorous magazine *Der Floh* in 1886.[1] The author is, as in most humorous texts and pictures published in magazines like *Der Floh*, unknown. The signature below the ballad says only 'Ein Wiener' – a Viennese. Yet, although the identity of the writer of the 'Modern Ballad' is unknown, the contemporary middle-class audience would certainly have immediately recognized the lines parodied here; they come from one of the most famous poems by Johann Wolfgang von Goethe, 'Mignon's Song'.[2] However, Goethe's classic text, which refers to Italy, is here radically transformed. In the modern ballad, the speaker is longing for a city still and unshakeable, in order to take an express train to get there. This ironic paradox cannot be fully understood without the framework of humour.

This inquiry into popular humour in Vienna between 1857 and 1890 is an attempt to discover why the city and its urban life in the late nineteenth century generated so much laughter, and how humour was used as an interpretative framework with which to deal with the changing city environment. In Vienna in the second half of the nineteenth century, when the urbanization and transformation of the city space were making the city the opposite of still and unshakeable, popular humour flourished.

The growing capital of the vast Habsburg Empire was a place where a variety of different local traditions and nationalities merged and created a new kind of urban culture. In the suburbs, popular singers sang couplet songs that circulated in the city from mouth to mouth; in festivals outside the city border, the pre-modern carnival culture persisted.[3] Whereas in the suburbs and in the fringe areas of the city an oral popular humour flourished, in the bourgeois downtown humour expanded in literary forms. Thanks to modern printing technology, in particular, humorous magazines and satirical journals became extremely popular among the literate middle classes. The new urban bourgeoisie enjoyed puns about dim-witted street watchmen and jokes about a beggar and a millionaire meeting on the street, and were amused by cartoons of modern women cross-dressed as men and early comic strips on the horror of riding an omnibus on an ill-paved street (passengers bumping up and down), not to speak of riddles that bluffed the human eye: puzzle pictures and wordplay that fooled reason and opened up another kind of reality with ambivalence, fantasy and hidden meanings.

This book explores popular humour in the nineteenth-century city both as a mode of lived experience and as a discourse on urban life. I am therefore interested in the ways in which lived experiences and representations of the material city were interconnected and how they shaped each other. By examining the ways in which the urban environment and life in the city were discussed in various printed media such as jokes, puns and cartoons, my aim is not only to look at how urban life was represented in humorous accounts but to approach them as something that sprang from the lived experience in the city and sheds light on the complexity of everyday life in the transforming urban milieu. The present study focuses on the bourgeoisie's perspective on the city. The rising middle classes had a vital role in shaping Viennese intellectual and cultural history towards modernist culture, and I am approaching humour as a key to the urban imagination of the Viennese *Bürger*, unveiling the contradictions and ambiguities in the transition towards modernity. The central question of my study is: how was humour deployed in encountering and interpreting the experiences of urbanization and modernity? In order to answer this question, I ask what aspects of the transforming city were either seen or portrayed as comical or as a target for satire; how humour was used as a way to understand and negotiate change in the everyday environment, and to create meanings and identities in a situation when earlier spatial and social relations were falling apart.

The major theme of the study is the fundamental transition towards modernity in late nineteenth-century urban history. The modern city has been viewed as an emblem or epitome of modernity,[4] where the paradoxes and ambiguities of modernity became visible: a locus of fragmentation, discontinuation, movement, unfamiliarity and estrangement.[5] However, although the relationship between popular humour and modern urban culture has attracted academic interest in recent years,[6] the interconnection between nineteenth-century popular humour and modernity is a relatively neglected topic that has not yet been subjected to extensive close study. By exploring the comic press in Vienna, this study aims to widen our understanding of the various ways in which humour and laughter have been used in creating, understanding and inhabiting the modern world.

The notion of comical modernity carries with it a long historical tradition. Modernity's comical, absurd or amusing aspects have been dealt with, especially, by various clown figures, from Karl Valentin's cabaret performances in the 1920s Weimar Republic to Charlie Chaplin's *Modern Times* (1936) and Jacques Tati's *Play Time* in the Paris of the 1960s.[7] However, all these examples represent a full-blown, mature phase of modernity that resulted from the cultural rupture of the early twentieth century. The current study seeks to demonstrate that the 'modern' was encountered and processed through humour long before it became such a prominent feature in society and social debate. Furthermore, it explores alternative, divergent ways of understanding and interpreting modernity, which found their expression in the field of nineteenth-century popular culture, and popular humour in particular, but are missing from the dominant discourses surrounding modernity.

The concept of *modernity* is extremely ambiguous and has been defined in many ways. As Rita Felski has noted, this results from the fact that the term *modernity* has been used both as a thematic and as a periodizing term, and covers various intersecting cultural, social and philosophical strands. Because modernity has been associated with various complex historical processes, including urbanization, the expansion of capitalism and the emergence of nation states, different theoretical debates in the fields of historical research, political theory or literary studies tend to locate modernity at different places in time and address different aspects of it. Furthermore, as a periodizing term, *modernity* has been conceptualized in relation to other adjoining terms that seek to explain different features associated with it. The origin of the concept *modernity* has often been traced back to Charles Baudelaire, who used it in his essay *The Painter of Modern Life* (1864) to depict the transitory, fugitive and contingent experience of life. The concept *modernism* refers to various literary and art movements and schools in continental Europe and the United States, mainly in urban centres like Paris, Berlin or Vienna, which created a new kind of radical aesthetics that challenged existing traditions of representation and style.[8]

In addition to the rupture from traditional society and the emergence of self-reflective subjectivism, modernity is often understood in terms of a shift in temporal understanding. It has been defined as a new concept of time as a linear continuum, externalized as a rational belief in progress and as a sense of a radical break from the past. Furthermore, modernity is linked to *modernization*, meaning the rational organization of space and society, manifested most clearly in the city renewal projects across nineteenth-century Europe. The reconstruction of Paris by the prefect Baron Georges Haussmann, between 1853 and 1870, created a model for a new kind of modern city that was followed by architects and urban planners across Europe.[9] Thus, as Marshall Berman has suggested, modernity can be understood as a body of experience involving a radically new kind of understanding of both time and space.[10]

My research focuses on urban renewal in Vienna and the emergence of modern Viennese culture and experience. The time frame chosen for this investigation, starting in 1857 and ending in 1890, encompasses three decades in which the city space was rebuilt and transformed. In the late 1850s, the old city walls, which dated from the Middle Ages, were torn down, and an architectural competition was organized for a new layout for the city.[11] In the following three decades, on the site of the former city wall there arose the new main boulevard of the Habsburg Empire, the Ringstraße. It surrounded the old city centre, connecting it with the growing suburbs. The urban renewal reached its conclusion in 1890 with the unification of 'Groß-Wien' into one municipal entity, although the rebuilding of the city continued into the next century.[12]

The aim of the city renewal, introduced by Kaiser Franz Joseph in 1857 with his famous declaration 'Es ist mein Wille' (it is my will), was to create new kinds of urban space to meet the demands of a modernizing and industrializing society. The population of Vienna was increasing rapidly, from around 476,000 in 1857 to approximately 1,365,000 in 1890 and to over two million in 1910.[13] The emergence of urban mass populations created tensions in the capital of the Habsburg Empire, and urban planning provided a means to govern and control the growing urban crowd more effectively. In Vienna the situation was distinctly turbulent, since the immigrants moving into the city represented a range of different cultures and nationalities, which created tensions and conflicts in an era of rising nationalism. Consequently, the symbolic and representative function of city space became a priority in the construction of the Ringstraße. The city renewal project, which aimed to create Vienna as a strong capital for the vast heterogeneous empire, was also a political attempt to reshape and reinforce the imaginary of a uniform nation and its shared past.[14]

Moreover, as the historian Carl E. Schorske has famously argued, the construction of the Ringstraße reflected the rise of the Austrian liberal bourgeoisie, which gained political power in the Habsburg Empire and in the city of Vienna as the political system changed in the 1860s from an absolutist to a constitutional monarchy. Schorske suggests that as the liberals started to reshape Vienna to their image, the city space became a battlefield, a 'politically contested space', through which different groups in society tried to express their claims to power and their cultural values.[15] Due to this specific historical context, Vienna's renewal differed from the rebuilding of Paris or, say, Berlin or Rome in the nineteenth century.

This book aims to give a new perspective on the heyday of Austrian liberalism by demonstrating that humorous sources give access to the underlying uncertainties and contradictions of the liberal era. Investigating popular humour helps us to understand better the crisis of Austrian liberalism and its historical roots in the Ringstraße era. The starting point of my approach is the suggestion that popular culture, which has received less attention in previous studies on late nineteenth-century Viennese cultural history, can provide a new perspective for the understanding of that era. Investigating popular humour enables a bottom-up perspective on late nineteenth-century Viennese cultural history and the dominance of the liberal bourgeoisie, which has previously been studied predominantly in terms of intellectual history and high culture.

Instead of further investigating the much-researched Viennese high culture between 1890 and 1914, my study focuses on the preceding era of the *Gründerzeit*,[16] and looks at how the transformation of city space was discussed in contemporary popular culture during the actual rebuilding process. As Marion Linhardt has suggested in her study on the history of Viennese popular theatre and operetta, the rebuilding of the city shook the old spatial and social structures and brought into existence a new urban community that created and consumed popular culture.[17] I am suggesting that, especially in this period of urban transformation, the realms of the popular can capture and uncover aspects from the everyday life that are missing from 'higher' elements of culture. Furthermore, the aim of this study is to rethink the boundaries of the bourgeoisie and to demonstrate that the fields of bourgeois 'high culture' and vernacular 'popular culture' or industrial 'mass culture' were not as separate from each other as the previous understanding of the nineteenth-century history has assumed. Therefore, my aim is not to present popular humour as something separate from other aspects of Viennese bourgeois culture, but rather to gain a new perspective on this culture by analysing it through its humour, which can reveal something of the dynamics of cultural processes that otherwise are hard to uncover. I am suggesting that shifting our attention from the high aspirations and ideals of the bourgeoisie to the plane of the low and mundane world of humour offers a new kind of insight into issues that were repressed, silenced and avoided in the official culture.

The focus on humour also offers a new perspective on the emergence of Viennese modernist culture, which has been the grand narrative of the studies in Viennese cultural history since the famous volume of Carl E. Schorske, *Fin-de-siècle Vienna: Politics and Culture* (originally published in 1979). Schorske's thesis of the emergence of the modernist culture as a reaction to the failure of bourgeois liberalism and rationalism has fundamentally shaped our understanding of Viennese modernity. Schorske's central argument was that the next generation of the liberal bourgeoisie became alienated from their class and turned to the world of aesthetics and the psyche, turning their back on the cultural values of their fathers. Schorske argues that the building of the Ringstraße had a great impact on intellectual history at the turn of the century, since it expressed all those values that the next-generation modernists resisted and rejected, thus making Vienna into one of the core centres of ahistorical modernity, a legacy that still affects our day in a range of ways.

Consequently, late nineteenth-century Vienna has been seen as a 'birthplace of the modern world',[18] a 'laboratory of modernity'[19] where often contradictory cultural ideas and processes collided and intertwined. The historian Allan Janik sees Vienna as a place where a self-aware and reflective 'critical modernity'[20] took shape. Moreover, as many of the contradictions and paradoxes of the modern emerged in Vienna, they also generated new responses to a changing reality, from Sigmund Freud's psychoanalysis to Adolf Loos's modern architecture and Karl Lueger's antisemitism and xenophobia. Because of the profound and far-reaching impact that Viennese modernity has had on the intellectual, political and cultural histories of the twentieth and twenty-first centuries, understanding late nineteenth-century Vienna is still significant and vital for the understanding of our modern world.

The underlying thread in this inquiry is to pinpoint the relationship between popular humour and the modern experience, and to show that humour was not just a way of understanding and discussing modernity, but an integral part of it. The popular humour of the liberal bourgeoisie not only helped people to navigate in the ambiguous urban reality, but it also played an active part in shaping this reality. Thus, my research seeks to demonstrate the crucial contribution of humorous magazines in negotiating the city's new, *modern* character.

While Schorske's interpretation has profoundly shaped the understanding of the birth of modernity in late nineteenth-century Vienna, his thesis has also been subject to critical evaluations. Steven Beller emphasized in his study, *Vienna and the Jews 1867–1938: A Cultural History* (originally published in 1989), the strong Jewish impact on the intellectual history and cultural flowering of *fin-de-siècle* Vienna as well as more widely on modern culture and thought. One of the most important critical contributions to the Schorskean paradigm was the article series *Rethinking Vienna 1900*, edited by Steven Beller, which came out in 2001. As scholars have tried to achieve more differentiated ways of understanding the cultural history of Viennese modernity, the main critique of Schorske's interpretation has focused on the question of who the liberal bourgeoisie actually were, and what the terms 'liberal' and 'bourgeoisie' meant in the Austrian context.[21]

The present study explores the problem of the liberal bourgeoisie and its relation to modern culture by looking at the popular humour published in the liberal humorous magazines that were produced and read by both the relatively assimilated Jewish and Gentile middle classes.[22] Looking at what kind of humour these magazines produced, what they found funny and what they laughed at, can reveal crucial insights into the ways the Viennese *Bürger* gave meanings to themselves, others and the changing world around them. I suggest that looking at the humour of the Viennese bourgeoisie sheds light on the heterogeneity of this emergent social class, revealing its controversies and uncertainties in the internal discussion on the changing city. As shown in the following chapters, although a liberal worldview permeated both the lower and higher middle classes, they enjoyed different levels of power in political and public life. Even when constitutional monarchy was achieved in the 1860s, only the wealthier bourgeoisie were able to vote. The lower middle classes were excluded from the political process, but followed it in the press. As John Boyer has shown in his study on political radicalization in late nineteenth-century Vienna, the Austrian 'liberals' in power were actually not very liberal, or even illiberal, and the crisis of liberalism thus involved a larger alienation of the lower middle classes from liberalist politics and thought.[23] This study seeks to demonstrate that during the liberalist era, the humorous magazines were a central forum for the ongoing negotiation around a cluster of cultural and political values central to liberalist politics and its ambition to create a new kind of modern city.

In addition to offering a contribution to the debate in the field of Austrian and Habsburg Studies about late nineteenth-century Vienna that has continued since the 1970s,[24] my work also relates to the partly intersecting research traditions of late nineteenth-century urban history and historical research on the modern city. Although until recently popular culture has been a relatively neglected theme in the field of Austrian Studies,[25] there are, of course, numerous excellent studies on the interplay between popular culture and the city elsewhere, such as Vanessa Schwartz's *Spectacular Realities* (1999), which dealt with early mass culture in nineteenth-century Paris.

Cities and the urban environment were crucial for the emergence of mass popular culture, which in turn helped to fashion the experience of urbanity and modernity. The research tradition of modernity has emphasized the role of urban representations – texts and images in particular – in the constructing of modern experience. Representations of the modern metropolis guided the living in a new kind of urban environment, and shaped the meanings of the 'new' and 'modern' in society.[26]

For example, Peter Fritzsche's *Reading Berlin 1900* (1998) introduced the idea of the 'word city', and emphasized the idea of city as a text. Fritzsche suggests that 'in an age of urban mass literacy, the city as place and the city as text defined each other in mutually constitutive ways'.[27] Because the idea of city as a text has been so influential, many of the historical studies on the nineteenth-century city have emphasized its role as a discursive place. The main idea shared in most of these studies is that as new representative practices emerged to capture the fugitive and contingent nature of the city, they at the same time created a discursive environment that shaped the ways in which the city was observed, interpreted and understood.[28]

However, the role of humour in experiencing and making sense of the nineteenth-century city has been overlooked in the discussion so far. Although there were all kinds of humorous prints circulating in nineteenth-century cities, the special ways in which humorous, satirical or ironic representations dealt with urbanity and modernity have remained relatively unexplored. Nevertheless, humour has always been an integral part of human existence and it was an inseparable part of nineteenth-century urban reality. In fact, in the age of rapid social change, industrialization and urbanization, popular humour had a new significant role in constructing local urban identity. Humour, above all else, was understood to express a certain urban worldview and a way of life that was unique and authentic for the inhabitants of the city.[29] It was cherished with pride and comparisons were made between the senses of humour of inhabitants of different cities. For example, the local humour in Berlin, the *Berliner Schnauze*, was seen as conveying the wittiness of Berliners, who were quick at repartee,[30] whereas *Wiener Schmäh* by contrast expressed the Viennese mentality, which hid ridicule in politeness, and combined sarcasm and melancholia with light-heartedness or the famous Viennese *Gemütlichkeit*.[31] Thus, popular humour provided a significant discourse for urbanity, and using humorous publications as primary sources brings out aspects that cannot be found in other source material.

By examining popular humour, my aim is to bring a new perspective to the research tradition, which has emphasized the textuality and visuality of the city, but overlooked it as a material place. Since the 1990s, the spatial turn and the material turn have raised growing interest in the spatial and material aspects of culture. The theoretical thinking of the French philosopher Henri Lefebvre, especially, has turned focus onto the dynamics of space: how space is not merely a passive background for human action and container of social life, but something that is continuously produced by everyday spatial practices, abstract conceptions, symbols and imaginaries.[32] As Lefebvre argues, '(social) space is a (social) product',[33] which means that space is not only produced by the continuous flux of social life and its embedded power relations, but also gives structure to these, and guides how people live and give shape to their everyday experiences. I am approaching the urban renewal between 1857 and 1890 as a rupture in the previous spatial organization of the city, which made these underlying processes visible: that is, how space embodies knowledge, power and social relations. Because the construction of the Ringstraße was linked with several different ideological perspectives, the relationship between space and power is especially important for my study. As this study sets out to investigate popular humour as a discursive and interpretative mode for the negotiation of the transformation of city space, I am interested in how lived, conceived and perceived spaces are always mutually interdependent and how urban representations are always embedded in the material conditions in which they come to life. Because of modernity's interrelationship with the new (urban) spaces, my approach to modernity emphasizes its spatial aspect, and special attention is given to the interplay between the material city space and popular humour.

Viennese *Witzblätter*

During the years of the urban reconstruction, a large number of humorous texts and images emerged to comment on the new urbanity. In addition to humorous magazines and calendars, there were numerous books and booklets, with titles such as *Modernes Wien: Humoristische Federzeichnungen* (1859)[34] or *Wien und die Wiener aus der Spottvogelperspektive* (1873).[35] In the weekly *Witzblätter*, modern city life was depicted in countless jokes and cartoons with titles and captions like 'Strassengespräch', 'Im Tramway-Waggon', 'Wien vom Einst und Jetzt', 'Moderne Sitten', 'Grossstädtisches', 'Wiener Strassenfatalitäten', 'Moderne Jungfrau', 'Im Park', 'Fremde in Wien', 'Ode an das elektrische Licht', 'Die kranke Mode', 'Groß-Wien Hymne' or 'Zukunftstraum', published side by side seemingly at random, without any obvious connection with each other. These juxtaposed scenes from the city pointed the reader's attention to different parts of Vienna, from downtown to the suburbs, from the Stephansplatz out to Ottakring. However, the central part of the city, surrounded by the new Ringstraße, is clearly the major location for bourgeois jokes and cartoons. The humorous popular publications thus actively constructed their own 'imagined geography'[36] of Vienna, by mapping the city with humour and giving meanings to various material places in which the magazines were, again, read and understood. The material city and the imagined city were thus intimately interlinked, which means that they should be studied in interaction with each other rather than as separate entities.

This spatial approach to humour is new in the study of Viennese humorous magazines. Although there are excellent studies on the German satirical press and popular humour, which provide a valuable reference point for my study,[37] the Viennese humorous magazines of the *Gründerzeit* have gone relatively unstudied. Previous studies have included attempts to create a comprehensive overview encompassing all the various magazines and their writers,[38] or the focus has been merely on political caricature and satire,[39] or on a specific event such as the 1848 revolution,[40] or on specific motifs such as the image of Jews in cartoons and caricatures.[41] The question of the relationship between humour and modernity has not been studied before at this length, although Viennese nineteenth-century popular culture in general,[42] and the impact of the shock caused by modernity on vernacular oral humour in particular, have been discussed by the Austrian scholars Wolfgang Maderthaner and Lutz Musner.[43]

The main reason for the fact that studies of humorous-satirical journals and studies of the history of popular culture have taken such different paths in the past is that humorous magazines and satirical journals have not been considered as popular culture. They have rather been seen as part of the modern press, and therefore studied in the context of the history of the press and other printed media. Furthermore, because the major European humorous magazines targeted an educated middle-class audience, and were produced, for the most part, by professional journalists, artists and writers,[44] they have been seen as a far cry from the emerging mass popular culture of the lower classes. Because of the emphasis on 'serious' political satire, the diversity of the material published in the humorous *Witzblätter*, for example, has not been fully considered. Furthermore, precisely the elements that seem most 'popular', in the sense of being light, commercial, vulgar, mundane or entertaining, have mainly been overlooked or even smoothed away.

However, because the *Witzblätter* published all sorts of material, and took their topics from both high and low, they captured many aspects of everyday life that otherwise were neglected in the more official or mainstream discourses on the city. For example, the historian Ann Taylor Allen sees that humour documented aspects of everyday life that were considered too common, coarse or mundane to be treated by 'high' art; 'such popular materials as the Witzblätter', she suggests, 'can help the historian to understand one of the least tangible facets of social change – the concomitant development of perceptions, attitudes and values of people affected'.[45]

In this study I am following the idea that details of everyday life that might not have been considered newsworthy for the 'serious' daily papers can reveal hints about mental patterns and experiences that have otherwise been left out of the documentation.[46] Moreover, because humorous magazines did not hesitate to deal with all aspects of bodily experiences of the city, they often captured sensory experiences that are otherwise pushed into the background in nineteenth-century literature. Humorous accounts referred not only to visuality and seeing, but to feeling, hearing and smelling as well. Whereas the research tradition on modern urban culture has strongly emphasized the visuality and textuality of the nineteenth-century city, less attention has been given to other sensory bodily experiences of transforming cities.[47] By exploring the city from unexpected and unconventional perspectives, therefore, humorous magazines help to shed light on multiple aspects of everyday life that otherwise would remain unnoticed or hidden.

Most importantly, until now, no attention has been given to the fact that the humorous magazines also invited readers to send in their own material for publication. Although the editorial staff were mainly responsible for the contents of the magazines, the three humorous magazines discussed in this study – *Der Figaro*, *Der Floh* and *Kikeriki* – all published material from their readers, and paid small fees for the accepted contributions.[48] The jokes and cartoons were sent in under pseudonyms and published anonymously; hence, the 'Modern Ballad' mentioned earlier, with the byline 'Ein Wiener', may indeed have been written by an anonymous reader, 'a Viennese', who decided to try his luck with *Der Floh* magazine.

My approach for this study is therefore guided by the observation that humorous magazines were not merely read passively, but that readers also sent in their own jokes, puns and cartoons for publication. Furthermore, this awareness among the readers that some of the material came from their fellow citizens will probably have affected the ways in which the jokes and cartoons were read and understood. By inviting citizens to send in their own jokes, puns and cartoons for publication, the magazines enabled a forum for grassroots-level negotiation on current issues in an age of censorship. The anonymity of the great city was turned to advantage. Because the texts and pictures were sent in under pseudonyms and published anonymously, they reveal a debate that had the potential to bypass social hierarchies and limitations.

The popular humour studied in this book was always public in nature because it was printed and circulated in the city. In these humorous magazines, the 'popular' and the 'public' merged. On the one hand, they represented a new kind of popular culture, not only aimed at the new kind of mass audience, but also partly created by this audience, representing their ways of imagining and reacting to the surrounding reality.[49] On the other hand, the humorous magazines were part of the new kind of public sphere (*Öffentlichkeit*), providing the magazines with an effective site for public debate. My work therefore relates to Jürgen Habermas's theory that in the eighteenth century newspapers and other print media brought into existence a new kind of critical public sphere, which enabled individuals to share ideas in public. The nineteenth century led, however, to the commercial transformation of the public sphere and thus to the loss of its critical potential.[50]

The history of the nineteenth-century humorous magazines has often been interpreted as a transition from critical to commercial. In particular, the collapse of state censorships in the 1848 revolutions across Europe created a boom of humorous-satirical magazines that stemmed from the tradition of political pamphlets and caricatures. As the historian Mary Lee Townsend has argued, in the early nineteenth century humorous magazines became an important part of the political culture, because they offered means of dealing with politically, morally or socially delicate matters in an age of strong censorship. By the early twentieth century, the press had on the one hand gained more liberties, and on the other the publishing industry developed and expanded its range. Humorous publications turned into light reading, preceding many of the twentieth-century forms of popular culture such as comics, graphic novels, pulp fiction and even men's magazines.[51]

The period from 1860 to 1900 was the heyday of humorous and satirical magazines in Vienna. In 1860 there were only ten humorous magazines in the city; in 1866 the number was thirty, and in 1870 as many as thirty-four.[52] The statistics of the city of Vienna counted *Witzblätter* together with literary magazines and came up with even higher numbers in the 1880s: forty-four in 1882 and fifty-eight in 1884.[53] The humorous-satirical journals *Der Figaro*, *Kikeriki* and *Der Floh*, which constitute the main sources for this study, were the three most influential humorous magazines in Vienna. Unlike many of their rivals, these humorous magazines succeeded in surviving against hard competition, and continued publication long after the turn of the century.[54] *Der Figaro* and *Der Floh* are considered as liberal, whereas *Kikeriki* had started as liberal and progressive in 1861, but turned conservative-nationalist and antisemitic in the 1880s, a political U-turn that was related to the wider rise of antisemitism in Austria-Hungary in the late nineteenth century.[55]

In addition to this political turnaround, between 1857 and 1890 all of the magazines underwent many other changes, which parallel wider shifts in the publishing industry. The popularity of the humorous magazines is related to the changing reading habits in the nineteenth century. As the literacy rate increased and printing technology developed, reading was no longer restricted to elite culture, but became a popular activity.[56] Whereas in the first half of the century humorous magazines published lengthy, florid texts that took a long time to read, by the turn of the century texts had become significantly shorter. They also became independent from each other, which made it possible to browse through only parts of the magazine. The humorous magazines enjoyed mixing different text types, from jokes, anecdotes and lampoons to sarcastic poems and funny songs. Furthermore, the humorous magazines also rewrote various urban texts, such as newspaper articles and official bulletins, thus not only commenting on the transformation of the city but also creating discursive practices that both guided and tried to give meanings to the changing material environment.

In addition to an expanded range of text types, the humorous magazines also experimented with their visual appearance. In the late 1850s, the pages of the magazines mostly consisted only of text, but by the 1890s the *Witzblätter* had become more and more visual in character. The cartoons and caricatures published in the *Figaro*, *Der Floh* and *Kikeriki* almost without exception included both text and image. Precisely this collision of words and images has been seen as a major characteristic of modern mass culture. Whereas the nineteenth-century high culture separated words and images and kept them far away from each other, the new kind of popular mass culture enjoyed mixing words and images together.[57]

There were many different types of images, political cartoons and caricatures of famous public figures such as politicians, artists and socialites. Moreover, these magazines published pictorial narratives, which resembled early comics, depicting everyday incidents from the changing city, encounters in the over-crowded tramways, rendezvous in the parks, and other stories from the fleeting urban life. Although the birth of modern comics has usually been located in the 1890s in the United States, European humorous magazines also played a pivotal role in experimenting with narratives made of words and sequential images, which later developed into modern comics.[58] The present study thus sheds light on the history of visual culture and early comics outside the Anglo-American culture.

In addition to comics, cartoons and caricatures the humorous magazines contained yet another type of image: advertisements. The increasing impact of commercialism on the publishing industry was clearly to be seen in the growing number of advertisements published in the 'Inseraten-Beilage' supplements that sometimes had more pages than the magazines themselves.[59] Commercialism ran through the popular humour as well. Humorous magazines targeted as wide an audience as possible, and they constantly tried to widen their circulation. By the 1860s, the circulation of *Figaro*, *Floh* and *Kikeriki* had reached around twenty thousand each,[60] but the actual number of readers was probably substantially higher, since humorous magazines and satirical journals were often read in coffee houses.[61]

Because of the humorous-satirical magazines' association with coffee houses, censorship issues and political debate, earlier studies of nineteenth-century satirical journals and humorous magazines have predominantly focused on political satire and humour. The topics covered have also typically been ranked hierarchically on the basis of their political relevance.[62] Issues in everyday life are often considered non-political, and therefore less interesting. For example, in his study on French political caricature, Robert Justin Goldstein argues that in times of heavy censorship the magazines were 'forced' to deal with trivial, harmless themes from everyday urban life, which lacked the cutting edge of political satire and made the magazines more like entertainment.[63] This study seeks to investigate the material in a new way, across the old borders of 'political' and 'non-political', to look at how they explored gender, fashion, urban mores and habits, material spaces and everyday life in the changing city. Therefore, my work is guided by a holistic understanding of culture that has been one of the main aspirations in cultural historical study. Moreover, the school of thinking in cultural studies that argues that issues of power affect all practices of everyday life, and 'everything is political', has been an inspiration for my approach.[64] Because structures of power are to be found in all aspects of human life, there are no 'harmless' or 'insignificant subjects', but rather it is important to pay more attention to what kinds of themes were raised as topics of humour and reconsider the question of why this was so.

Theories of Humour

The study of a culture through its humour is unquestionably a challenging undertaking. Nevertheless, examining what people laughed at in the past enables one to approach the fabric of a culture that fashions the thoughts and actions of the people living in it. As the cultural historian Anu Korhonen has pointed out, far from being trivial, humour actually addresses topics that are meaningful to society. By revealing fundamental structural uncertainties and internal contradictions in a past culture, humour helps us to understand not only the cultural values, attitudes and ideas of the past but also the practices in which these ideas, values and attitudes were formed, questioned and negotiated.[65]

But what do we actually mean when we talk about humour? If *modernity* is an ambiguous and elusive concept, so is *humour*. In fact, it has been a phenomenon notoriously difficult to define and tackle. Humour is an integral part of everyday life and human experience, but an extremely difficult subject for academic research. It tends to elude rigid definitions and generalizing theories, and because scholars working in different disciplines apply different approaches to humour, there are several coexisting but partially incompatible terminologies in the field of humour research.

Originally the word *humour* derived from the Latin word *humores*, which referred to the four bodily fluids in ancient and medieval medicine. By the eighteenth century, in most European languages, humour had become a word that meant a certain mood or atmosphere; slowly it came to mean a playful attitude towards amusing things.[66] Humour has been defined as an attitude, a feeling, or a way of perceiving things comical, as funny or amusing.

The latter emphasis on the interpretative function of humour has its roots in history, as well. Whereas the word *humour* has traditionally been associated with notions of personhood, the word *wit* has a different origin that relates to concepts like knowledge, creativity and imagination. Wit is related to the German word *Witz*, which originally developed from the verb *wissen*, meaning 'to know'. Michael Billig comments that wit and humour were treated in the eighteenth century as distinctly different phenomena. The word wit referred to 'playing with words and ideas', whereas humour meant laughing at a person with a ridiculous, 'humorous' character. Accordingly, in eighteenth-century texts, wit referred to clever verbal sayings and an ability to put different ideas together, whereas humour stood for a laughable character. Moreover, eighteenth-century writers used words like ridiculous or ludicrous rather than humorous for the category of things that are comical or that might provoke laughter.[67]

The meaning of humour has thus radically changed in the modern period. The historian Daniel Wickberg has offered one explanation why the concept of humour became so widely recognized and significant in the nineteenth century: he argues that the idea of 'sense of humour' as a positive personal attribute did not emerge until the mid nineteenth century in the Anglo-American world. The rise of the modern formulation of 'sense of humour' as a positive attribute, which a person might or might not have, was closely related to shifting ideas of personhood and to the birth of modern individualism. The subjectivization of humour was related to the rise of the bourgeoisie in the nineteenth century, as they invented new ways of navigating between personhood and social order, shaped by the bureaucratic and commercial tendencies of the period.[68] The birth of the modern sense of humour thus corresponded to the birth of the modern individual, able to laugh at everything and look at the surrounding reality with ironical distance.

Thus, the popular humour studied in this book did not merely address the new and the modern in the city, but the humour itself was also modern in many ways, shaped by the historical processes described in the previous paragraphs. The Viennese journalists and writers called themselves 'humourists' (*Humorist*) in the new, modern sense, as self-conscious creators of laughter.[69] In addition, they used the words humour (*Humor*) and humorous (*humoristisch*) in a distinctively modern sense, to point to that which was potentially funny or comical. Humour was thus above all understood as a subjective faculty, a way of perceiving or interpreting urban reality.[70]

It is important to note that just as the meaning and valuation of humour has changed over time in the various European languages, similarly there have been different approaches in different periods to explaining humour. The classical theories of laughter – superiority theory, incongruence theory and relief theory – entail multifaceted theoretical discussions that examine humour from different points of view and seek to explain different aspects of it. The superiority theories are the oldest theories of laughter, deriving their roots in antiquity. On the basis of their observations, the Greek philosophers Plato and Aristotle suggested interpretations of humour that were later developed into a theoretical tradition. Basically, superiority theory suggests that the foundation of humour is a feeling of superiority: laughter thus depends on a sense of hierarchies, and on demeaning and degrading others. One of the most famous contributions to superiority theories was the idea of 'sudden glory' proposed by Thomas Hobbes (1588–1679), which suggested that the passion of laughter was an elevated feeling, a sudden sense of eminence triggered by the infirmity of others, or one's own former infirmity.[71]

Since the eighteenth century, however, incongruence and relief theories have challenged the superiority theories. Incongruence theories have often been associated with eighteenth-century coffee house culture and with the ideal of wit: they suggest that humour is based on the discovery of an incongruence – a contradiction or unexpected co-occurrence, for instance when two or more different ideas are suddenly combined in order to create a comic effect. Incongruence theories offer a different perspective on the origins of humour, not looking into the motives of the person who laughs, but seeking to identify the incongruous features in the world that provoke laughter. Incongruence theories thus emphasize the cognitive rather than emotional aspects of humour.[72]

The nineteenth-century relief theories, on the contrary, emphasize mental relief or a release of energy as the foundation of humour. Herbert Spencer (1820–1903), for example, saw laughter as a physiological phenomenon, related to the nervous system, the function of which was to release excess nervous energy. The relief theory has often been associated with the Viennese psychoanalyst Sigmund Freud (1856–1939), whose complex theory saw jokes as a way of expressing repressed feelings and thoughts. Freud had a vast impact on how jokes and humour were understood: they were no longer seen as trivial or innocent, but like dreams and unintentional slips of the tongue, giving expression to hidden desires and wishes repressed by the conscious mind.[73]

Consequently, all theories of humour tell something about their own age. Although humour research has tended to treat humour as a universal phenomenon, the historical approach to humour has stressed its historical nature. Humour and laughter are historically and culturally determined phenomena that are thoroughly embedded in the culture.[74] This makes them extremely interesting, but challenging, subjects of cultural historical study. The cultural historian Peter Burke has reminded us that like any other aspect of culture, the realms of the comical are constantly changing. On the one hand there is continuity in the form of tradition that enables us to get hints of what people of the past thought to be funny, but on the other hand there are changes that make humour from the past unfamiliar and even impenetrable to today's reader.[75]

Because the ways of understanding something as funny vary across place and time, what people of the past laughed at may not seem funny to us at all. Some jokes become totally incomprehensible. This raises serious questions concerning how the humour of the past can be understood. The historian Robert Darnton has argued that one has to recognize the different ways of thinking of the people of the past in order to 'get the joke'. He argues that historical research needs to pay attention to the things that seem most unfamiliar and alien to us, and to try to make them comprehensible and intelligible. Because humour is embedded in a different mindset or mentality of the past, it is a phenomenon in which the profound 'otherness' of the past is truly revealed.[76]

In this study my approach to past humour and my attempt to 'get the joke' is based on contextualization. The task of contextualization is threefold. First, it is necessary to map the social and cultural circumstances that fashioned the uses of humour. For example, in nineteenth-century Vienna, the strict censorship and the development of mechanical printing technology were factors that significantly affected the uses of humour.

Second, my analysis of humorous texts and images is based on disentangling the different contexts or meanings that these humorous accounts have fused together. My analysis does not follow any of the classical humour theories in an orthodox manner, but rather combines elements from all of them according to my own research problematique, that is, what I am trying to find out by reading the jokes. Therefore, humour's relation to social hierarchy and social control makes both superiority theory and relief theory relevant to my study. In addition, incongruity theory helps us to understand that humorous expressions often entail some kind of conflict. The central idea of this approach is that humour is based on interpreting unexpected contradictions or surprising combinations: meanings from different contexts that are put together in a strange way. Thus, the comical effect results from the collision of different associative worlds that are evoked by the joke. Reading humorous representations as historical sources thus requires a process of disentangling the different contexts or meanings that these humorous accounts combine, and setting them in a larger historical and cultural framework. In order to unravel this historical and cultural framework, I cross-read humorous accounts with various serious sources such as press articles, city planning documents and police reports held in the Austrian State Archives (Österreichisches Staatsarchiv).

Third, in order to unpack the ambivalent meanings of jokes and cartoons published between 1857 and 1890, it is valuable to consult contemporary nineteenth-century theories of humour. Because these theories were developed to explain the humour of their own age, they provide valuable analytical tools for understanding how Viennese humour was imprinted with the marks of its own time.

As the number of popular humorous magazines, joke books, comic almanacs and posters increased, the question of humour aroused significant academic interest.[77] Not only did the nineteenth-century theories of humour emerge as a response to contemporary forms of humour, but their approaches to the questions of what humour is and what functions it serves also tell much about their own age. In *Le Rire* (1900), the French philosopher Henri Bergson saw laughter as a form of social punishment against the mechanization of life. Sigmund Freud's analysis *Der Witz und seine Beziehung zum Unbewussten* (1905), which he started to develop as early as the 1890s, linked jokes to the human psyche, suggesting that they provided an outlet for subconscious conflicts and desires, much like dreams. In a later short essay called *Der Humor* (1927), Freud returned to addressing the characteristics of humour and the distinction between humour, jokes and the comical.

Freud's ideas are highly valuable for this study, which explores Viennese popular humour almost at the exact time when Freud started to formulate his theory of jokes. I have referenced Freud to gain a historical rather than a theoretical perspective, since this study approaches humour in terms of cultural history, not psychoanalysis. In particular, Freud's emphasis on the joke's power to express repressed wishes and unveil unresolved problems helps us to recognize how Viennese middle-class humour used strategies of disguising and transferring meanings, and often revolved around topics that caused anxiety in society.

Since Freud, there has been wide scholarly discussion in the twentieth century on the relation between humour and cultural anxieties. In the field of folklore and sociology, jokes have been treated as socially accepted outlets for taboo subjects. In contrast to the regulated forms of social communication, humorous expressions are able to reference issues that are forbidden or unspeakable in the cultural, social and psychological environment in which they are told.[78] Humorous expressions can thus shed light on the ways in which emotions, such as anxiety and nostalgia, were voiced during the urban transformation, and give access to various changes in the emotional culture of the Viennese *Bürgertum*, which led to a new kind of understanding of humour at the turn of the century.[79]

Elizabeth Wilson has noted that Freud's theories were rooted in the urban Vienna of his own time, when he focused on things that critics of metropolitan life feared, such as transformation, the trivial, the ugly and the strange. Freud's modern focus displaced traditional assumptions about what was significant and central, and emphasized the fragmentary and marginalized aspects of daily experience as keys to understanding the human mind.[80] Similarly, this study seeks to demonstrate that in popular humour, seemingly trivial or odd topics were actually evoking complex and profound cultural meanings.

In Viennese studies, the theoretical discussion has not only stressed the suppressive functions of humour and laughter, but acknowledged their innovative potential as well. The next-generation theorist Arthur Koestler, for example, who like Freud came from Austria-Hungary and had studied in Vienna, linked humour with creativity and the human capacity to create new ways of thinking that challenge traditional patterns of thought. In his famous study, *The Act of Creation* (1964), Koestler suggests that humour involves a creative instability that shakes the routines of thinking. This results from the fact that there is not merely one single associative context within which the humorous text or image is interpreted, but several. Because humour operates on more than one mental plane, understanding humour requires a double-minded mode of thinking, which Koestler describes with his famous bisociative model. Furthermore, Koestler suggests that the more sophisticated the forms of humour are, the more contexts they entail. Whereas simple jokes are based on one culmination between an introduction and a punchline, that is, incongruence between two contexts, the higher forms of sustained humour such as satire do not rely on a single effect but on a series of continuously colliding meanings.[81]

Because my work deals with encountering change and unfamiliarity in the nineteenth-century urban milieu, the basic contradiction between humour's ability to both create and resist change is important for my analysis. Although the question of humour's function in society, whether it aims at changing the world or enduring the world, had been under discussion long before the nineteenth century, the basic dilemma of humour's double-faced nature that can work both as a means of suppression and empowerment became one of the key issues in nineteenth- and twentieth-century theories. The most famous example is probably Mikhail Bakhtin's *Rabelais and His World* (originally published in 1965), a classic that celebrated early modern vernacular spoken humour and laughter as a subversive, liberating force that resisted the dominant official culture in a carnivalesque spirit.[82]

In my examination of humour in the context of modernity, an exploration of humour's creative and innovative potential (rebellious humour), versus suppressive and conservative tendencies (disciplinary humour), provides a key theoretical framework for the analysis of the empirical material in the first part of the study (chapters 1, 2 and 3), focusing on negotiations over the material city space. Furthermore, because the discussion on the transformation of the city was intimately linked with negotiations over the urban community and bourgeois class identity in the expanding metropolis, the second part of the book (chapters 4 and 5) highlights the role of humour in practices of exclusion and inclusion.

Notes

1. Kennst Du die Stadt so still und unbeirrt, / Wo Niemand Deine Ohren malträtirt, / Nicht jeder Windhauch, falscher Töne voll, / Dich ganz nervös macht, wüthend, wild und toll? / Kennst Du sie wohl? / Dahin! Dahin / Möcht' mit dem nächsten Schnellzug ich entflieh'n! Moderne Ballade. (Sehr Frei Nach Goethe) *Der Floh*, 10 October 1886. All translations are by the author and Dr Keith Battarbee unless stated otherwise.
2. Mignon's Song, 'Kennst du das Land', originates from Goethe's novel *Wilhem Meisters Lehrjahre* (1795–96).
3. Wolfgang Maderthaner and Lutz Musner, *Unruly Masses: The Other Side of the Fin-de-siècle Vienna* (New York, 2008), 79–81.
4. Ibid., 3. See also David Frisby, *Cityscapes of Modernity: Critical Explorations* (Cambridge, 2001), 4–5.
5. See, for example, Peter Fritzsche, *Reading Berlin 1900* (Cambridge, MA, 1998), 33, 43–45, 101; Frisby, *Cityscapes*, 2–5.
6. See especially Mary Gluck, *The Invisible Jewish Budapest: Metropolitan Culture at the Fin de Siècle* (Madison, 2016); Julian Brigstocke, *The Life of the City: Space, Humour, and the Experience of Truth in Fin-de-siècle Montmartre* (Surrey, 2014); Olivier Ratous and Martin Baumeister, 'Rire en ville. Rire de la ville. L'humour et le comique comme objets pour l'histoire urbaine contemporaine', *Histoire Urbaine* 2(31) (2011).
7. On Valentin's comedy, see further David Robb, 'Cities, Clocks and Chaos: A Modernist Perception of Time in the Comedy of Karl Valentin', in Susanne Marten-Finnis and Matthias Vecker (eds), *Berlin – Wien – Prag: Moderne, Minderheiten und Migranten in der Zwischenkriegszeit. Modernity, Minorities and Migration in the Inter-war Period* (Berlin, 2001), 76–79.
8. Rita Felski, *The Gender of Modernity* (Cambridge, MA, 1995), 9, 12–13.
9. David Harvey, *Paris, Capital of Modernity* (New York, 2006), 99–116; Vanessa R. Schwartz, *Spectacular Realities: Early Mass Culture in Fin-de-siècle Paris* (Berkeley, 1999), 3.
10. Marshall Berman, *All That Is Solid Melts Into Air: The Experience of Modernity* (New York, 1988), 15.
11. Marianne Bernhard, *Die Wiener Ringstraße: Architektur und Gesellschaft 1858–1906* (Munich, 1992), 23–33.
12. See further, e.g., Frisby, *Cityscapes*, 18–19, 168.
13. Josef Ehmer, 'Zur sozialen Schichtung der Wiener Bevölkerung 1857 bis 1910', in Gerhard Melinz and Susan Zimmermann (eds), *Wien–Prag–Budapest: Blütezeit der Habsburgermetropolen. Urbanisierung, Kommunalpolitik, gesellschaftliche Konflikte 1867–1918* (Vienna, 1996), 73–83, 75; Allan Janik and Stephen Toulmin, *Wittgenstein's*

Vienna (Chicago, [1973] 1996), 50; 'Bevölkerungsgeschichte', Wien Geschichte Wiki, https://www.geschichtewiki.wien.gv.at/Bevölkerungsgeschichte.
14. Irit Rogoff, 'Gustav Klimt, a Bridgehead to Modernism', in László Péter and Robert B. Pysent (eds), *Intellectuals and the Future in the Habsburg Monarchy 1890–1914* (London, 1988), 32–33; Carl E. Schorske, *Thinking with History: Explorations in the Passage to Modernism* (Princeton, 1998), 109; Carl E. Schorske, *Fin-de-siècle Vienna: Politics and Culture* (Cambridge, [1961] 1981), 24–62.
15. Schorske, *Thinking with History*, 115; Schorske, *Fin-de-siècle Vienna*, 24–25, 30–31.
16. The *Gründerzeit*, or 'the age of the founders', is a term used of the mid-nineteenth-century epoch both in Austria and in Germany. In economic history this epoch is marked by the *Gründerkrach*, a stock market crash that ended a period of economic growth in 1873 and led to an era of recession. However, the *Gründerzeit* can also refer to a longer cultural period preceding the *fin-de-siècle* years from 1890 onwards, and this periodization is used in the present study.
17. Marion Linhardt, *Residenzstadt und Metropole: Zu einer kulturellen Topographie des Wiener Unterhaltungstheaters (1858–1918)* (Berlin, 2012), 1–4.
18. Steven Beller, *Vienna and the Jews 1867–1938: A Cultural History* (Cambridge, 2003), 2.
19. Wolfgang Maderthaner, 'Von der Zeit um 1860 bis zum Jahr 1945', in Peter Csendes and Ferdinand Oppl (eds), *Wien – Geschichte einer Stadt: Von 1790 bis zur Gegenwart* (Vienna, 2006), 249–51.
20. Allan Janik, 'Vienna 1900 Revisited: Paradigms and Problems', in Steven Beller (ed.), *Rethinking Vienna 1900* (New York, 2001), 30–45.
21. See Beller, *Vienna and the Jews*, passim, especially 1–13; Steven Beller, 'Introduction', in Beller, *Rethinking Vienna 1900*, 8–11, 19; Janik, 'Vienna 1900 Revisited', 34.
22. See further Elfriede Schneider, *Karikatur und Satire als politische Kampfmittel: Ein Beitrag zur Wiener satirisch-humoristischen Presse des 19. Jahrhunderts (1849–1914)* (Ph.D. diss., Vienna, 1972), 47.
23. See further John W. Boyer, *Political Radicalism in Late Imperial Vienna: Origins of the Christian Social Movement, 1848–1897* (Chicago, 1981), 3–17; Janik, 'Vienna 1900 Revisited', 34.
24. See, for example, William M. Johnston, *The Austrian Mind: An Intellectual and Social History 1848–1938* (Berkeley, 1983): Janik and Toulmin, *Wittgenstein's Vienna*. The most extensive Austrian study of the Ringstrasse is the eleven-part book series *Die Wiener Ringstrasse – Bild einer Epoche* that was edited by Renate Wagner-Riegel and published in the 1970s.
25. As Mary Gluck has noted, Viennese modernism has been studied in isolation from popular culture. Overcoming this 'Great Divide' calls for a new cultural history that would 'no longer talk about high art or popular culture, but rather of different human responses to the problem of creating values and meaning in an unprecedented modern world, where such values and meanings are no longer given in existing social and religious structures'. Mary Gluck, 'Afterthoughts about Fin-de-Siècle Vienna: The Problem of Aesthetic Culture in Central Europe', in Beller, *Rethinking Vienna 1900*, 269.
26. Fritzsche, *Reading Berlin*, 1–11; Schwartz, *Spectacular Realities*, 2; Frisby, *Cityscapes*, 5–7, 23–26.
27. Fritzsche, *Reading Berlin*, 1.
28. See, e.g., Fritzsche, *Reading Berlin*; Frisby, *Cityscapes*. Cf. Henri Lefebvre, *The Production of Space* (Oxford, [1974] 1991), 7, 28.

29. Jan Rüger, 'Die Berliner Schnauze im Ersten Weltkrieg', in Thomas Biskup and Marc Schalenberg (eds), *Selling Berlin: Imagebildung und Stadtmarketing von der preußischen Residenz bis zur Bundeshauptstadt* (Stuttgart, 2008), 147; Mary Lee Townsend, 'Humour and the Public Sphere in Nineteenth-Century Germany', in Jan Bremmer and Herman Roodenburg (eds), *Cultural History of Humour: From Antiquity to the Present Day* (Cambridge, 1997), 200–203.
30. Rüger, 'Berliner Schnauze', 147–60; Townsend, 'Humour and the Public Sphere', 200; Ursula E. Koch, *Der Teufel in Berlin: Von der Märzrevolution bis zu Bismarcks Entlassung. Illustrierte politische Witzblätter einer Metropole 1848–1890* (Cologne, 1991), 33–35.
31. See further Lutz Musner, *Der Geschmack von Wien: Kultur und Habitus einer Stadt* (Frankfurt am Main, 2009), 13–15, 119–20; Maderthaner and Musner, *Unruly Masses*, 88, 135–36.
32. See further Lefebvre, *Production of Space*, 33, 38–40.
33. Original brackets by Lefebvre, *Production of Space*, 26.
34. *Modern Vienna: Humorous Quill Drawings*, by Carl Sitter (Vienna, 1859).
35. *Vienna and the Viennese from a Mockingbird's Eye View*, by Franz Masaidek (Vienna, 1873).
36. The term 'imagined geography' derives from Cameron Blevins, who uses it in deliberate reference to Edward Said's term 'Imaginative Geography' and Benedict Anderson's *Imagined Communities*. The construction of imagined geography describes the active social construction of space in representations, narratives and discourses by giving meanings to places and privileging specific meanings over others. See further Cameron Blevins, 'Space, Nation, and the Triumph of Region: A View of the World from Houston', *Journal of American History* 101(1) (2014), 123–25.
37. See Ann Taylor Allen, *Satire and Society in Wilhelmine Germany: Kladderadatsch & Simplicissimus 1890–1914* (Lexington, 1984); Mary Lee Townsend, *Forbidden Laughter: Popular Humor and the Limits of Repression in Nineteenth-Century Prussia* (Ann Arbor, 1992).
38. Ernst Scheidl, *Die humoristisch-satirische Presse im Wien von den Anfängen bis 1918 und die öffentliche Meinung* (Ph.D. diss., Vienna, 1950).
39. Schneider, *Karikatur und Satire*.
40. Ingrid Rasocha, *Die humoristisch-satirische Presse im Vormärz und während der Revolution 1848'* (Thesis, Vienna, 1990).
41. Julia Schäfer, *Vermessen – gezeichnet – verlacht: Judenbilder in Populären Zeitschriften 1918–1933* (Frankfurt am Main, 2004).
42. See, e.g., Musner, *Der Geschmack von Wien*; Linhardt, *Residenzstadt und Metropole*; Wolfgang Kos (ed.), *Wiener Typen: Klischees und Wirklichkeit* (Vienna, 2013).
43. Maderthaner and Musner, *Unruly Masses*, passim and 88–91.
44. For example, the editorial staff of the famous *Simplicissimus* consisted of renowned figures such as Rainer Maria Rilke and Thomas Mann. Allen, *Satire and Society*, 35.
45. Allen, *Satire and Society*, 4.
46. See further Taina Syrjämaa, *Constructing Unity, Living in Diversity: A Roman Decade* (Helsinki, 2006), 18.
47. See, for example, Bruce Johnson, 'Sites of Sound', *Oral Tradition*, 24(2) (2009), 462.
48. For example, *Kikeriki* paid 6 Kreuzer per line in 1862. Kleine Post der Redaktion, *Kikeriki*, 6 February 1862.
49. See Dominic Strinati, *An Introduction to the Theories of Popular Culture* (London, 2004), 3.

50. Jürgen Habermas, *Strukturwandel der Öffentlichkeit: Untersuchungen zu einer Kategorie der bürgerlichen Gesellschaft* (Neuwied am Rhein, 1965), 38–68, 193–98 and passim. On later critical interrogations of Habermas, see, e.g., Gregory Shaya, 'The *Flâneur*, the *Badaud* and the Making of a Mass Public in France, circa 1860–1910', *American Historical Review* 109(1) (2004), 42–43.
51. Townsend, *Forbidden Laughter*, 2, 13, 19–21.
52. Scheidl, *Die humoristisch-satirische Presse*, 135.
53. *Statistisches Jahrbuch der Stadt Wien. Die periodische Presse in Wien in den Jahren 1875-1884*. ANNO-elektronisches Lesesaal. Historische österreichische Zeitungen und Zeitschriften. Österreichische Nationalbibliothek (ÖNB).
54. Both *Der Floh* and *Figaro* continued publication until 1919, and *Kikeriki* until 1933.
55. There are various views on the political orientation of the magazines. For example, Erns Scheidl associates *Der Floh* with the Liberal Party, although it attacked in all directions. Scheidl, *Humoristisch-satirische Presse*, 168. Elfriede Schneider sees *Figaro* as a supporter of the Liberal Party, *Der Floh* as independent, and *Kikeriki* as democratic and nationalist, as it stood up against the upper-middle-class *Grossbürgertum* and the clerical faction, fighting for the 'little man'. Schneider, *Karikatur und Satire*, 46, 61, 259–60. Matthias Nöllke sees *Figaro* and *Der Floh* as liberal and *Kikeriki* as initially a radical and populist periodical that turned to antisemitism in 1881/82. Matthias Nöllke, *Daniel Spitzers Wiener Spatziergänge: Liberales Feuilleton im Zeitungskontext* (Frankfurt am Main, 1994), 65.
56. Townsend, 'Humour and the Public Sphere', 204–5; Allen, *Satire and Society*, 3–5.
57. Scott McCloud, *Understanding Comics: The Invisible Art* (New York, 1993), 138–49; Schwarz, *Spectacular Realities*, 2.
58. On the history of comics in Europe, see especially David Kunzle, *Father of the Comic Strip: Rodolphe Töpffer* (Jackson, 2007). Cf. Jens Balzer, '"Hully gee, I'm a Hieroglyphe": Mobilizing the Gaze and the Invention of Comics in New York City, 1895', in Jörn Ahrens and Arno Meteling (eds), *Comics and the City: Urban Space in Print, Picture and Sequence* (New York, 2010), 19–31. See also McCloud, *Understanding Comics*, 17–18.
59. In Germany humorous magazines were among the first periodicals that started to finance their publication by selling advertisement space for companies. They were thus leading the way to a more commercial media culture. Georg Jäger, 'Das Zeitschriftenwesen', in Georg Jäger (ed.), *Geschichte des Deutschen Buchhandels im 19. und 20. Jahrhundert*. Vol. 1. *Das Kaiserreich 1871–1918* (Frankfurt am Main, 2003), 386.
60. For example *Der Floh*, 16 May 1869 (20,000); *Kikeriki*, 9 April 1868 (25,000). The *Figaro* magazine did not publish its circulation figures like the other *Witzblätter*, but at the turn of the 1860s it promoted a calendar that was sold together with the magazine and had a circulation of 20,000. *Figaro*, 16 August 1857; 25 August 1860; 1 September 1860.
61. For example, Scheidl, *Humoristisch-satirische Presse*, 155–56.
62. It was this emphasis on politics that made the humorous-satirical magazine interesting for researchers, especially in the 1970s.
63. Robert Justin Goldstein, *Censorship of Political Caricature in Nineteenth-Century France* (Kent, 1989), 91–96, 111, 180, 261.
64. On the relations between approaches in historiography and in cultural studies in the German-speaking area, see further Christina Lutter and Markus Reisenleitner, 'Introducing History (in)to Cultural Studies: Some Remarks on the German Speaking Context', *Cultural Studies* 16(5) (2002), 612–13.

65. As Korhonen suggests, 'laughter is at the same time recognition of and reaction to cultural boundaries'. Anu Korhonen, *Fellows of Infinite Jest: The Fool in Renaissance England* (Turku, 1999), 23–24.
66. Daniel Wickberg, *Senses of Humor: Self and Laughter in Modern America* (Ithaca, 1998), 16–19; Jan Bremmer and Herman Roodenburg, 'Introduction: Humour and History', in Jan Bremmer and Herman Roodenburg (eds), *A Cultural History of Humour* (Cambridge, 1997), 1–2.
67. Michael Billig, *Laughter and Ridicule: Towards a Social Critique of Humour* (London, 2012), 61–65. On the *wit/humour* distinction, see also Wickberg, *Senses of Humor*, 57–64. Cf. *Witz/Humor* in Jefferson J. Chase, *Inciting Laughter: The Development of 'Jewish Humor' in 19th Century German Culture* (Berlin, 2000), 5–6.
68. Wickberg, *Senses of Humor*, 13.
69. Daniel Wickberg claims that the self-conscious creator of humour was not called a *humourist* until the mid or late nineteenth century; Mark Twain was one of the first humourists in this modern sense. Wickberg, *Senses of Humor*, 29.
70. In addition, the comical was strongly associated with unfamiliarity as the novelty of city life was encountered with humour that pointed out the strangeness and ridiculousness of modern urban life. According to the dictionary of Jacob and Wilhelm Grimm, the word comical (*komisch*) already had two meanings in the 1870s and it referred not just to the foolish but to the strange and unfamiliar as well. Jacob and Wilhelm Grimm, *Deutsches Wörterbuch*. Vol. 5. *Bearbeitet von Dr. Rudolf Hildebrand* (Leipzig, 1873), 1625.
71. Thomas Hobbes, *Leviathan* (Cambridge, [1651] 1997), 43. See also the passage on *Human Nature* (1650), cited in Wickberg, *Senses of Humor*, 48.
72. See further Billig, *Laughter and Ridicule*, 57–85. Today, incongruence theories are the most widely supported in humour research. There has been a lot of discussion about whether humour is simply dependent on the occurrence of incongruence, or whether it needs the resolution of incongruence as well.
73. On the theories of laughter, see further Billig, *Laughter and Ridicule*, 37–110.
74. Ibid., 87; Wickberg, *Senses of Humor*, 11–12; Bremmer and Roodenburg 'Introduction', 1–10.
75. Peter Burke, 'Frontiers of the Comic in Early Modern Italy, c. 1350–1750', in Bremmer and Roodenburg, *Cultural History of Humour*, 61.
76. Robert Darnton, *The Great Cat Massacre: And Other Episodes in French Cultural History* (New York, [1985] 1999), 77–78. See also Korhonen, *Fellows of Infinite Jest*, 12.
77. Cf. 'Man darf auch daran mahnen, welch eigentümlichen, geradezu faszinierenden Reiz der Witz in unserer Gesellschaft äußert'. Sigmund Freud, *Der Witz und seine Beziehung zum Unbewussten* (Frankfurt am Main, [1905] 2006), 32.
78. For example, Alan Dundes, *Cracking Jokes: Studies of Sick Humour Cycles and Stereotypes* (Berkeley, 1987), vii; Elliott Oring, *Jokes and Their Relations* (Lexington, 1992), x, 30–39.
79. Cf. William M. Reddy, *The Navigation of Feeling: A Framework for the History of Emotions* (Cambridge, 2004), 124–29; Peter N. Stearns, *American Cool: Constructing a Twentieth-Century Emotional Style* (New York, 1994), 1–9.
80. Elisabeth Wilson, *The Sphinx in the City: Urban Life, the Control of Disorder, and Women* (Berkeley, 1992), 86.
81. Arthur Koestler, *The Act of Creation* (London, 1964), 35–37. Over and above the logic pattern, humour depends also on an emotive effect. Koestler suggests that the switch from one associative context to another is emotionally charged. This means that although the

reason can switch from one mental matrix to another, emotions cannot follow this mental leap, thus creating a sensation of confusion that dissolves in a smile, sneer or laughter. Ibid., 58. The theory of Freud went even further and located in the release of excessive emotional charge the very core of the joke, whereas the logical mistakes, transitions and dislocations represented only the technique of joke by which the relief and gratification are achieved. Freud, *Der Witz*, 160–71 and passim.

82. Mikhail Bakhtin, *Rabelais and His World* (Bloomington, 1984).

Chapter 1

POWER AND SPACE

Censorship, Satire and the Public Sphere

> Serious people, serious times!
> No-one enjoys a joke,
> Many discomforts
> Threaten our poor Figaro.
> If he sings his bold songs,
> Will he soon be confiscated? –
> Please dear Prosecutor General,
> Please don't do it again!
>
> Figaro must make jokes,
> Because that's what God created him for;
> Making people laugh,
> Well, that's just his duty and profession.
> They who laugh fresh and honestly,
> Stay healthy and live until old age.
> Please dear Prosecutor General,
> Laughing is not dangerous to the state! ...
>
> —*Figaro*, 29 March 1890

This notion of laughter as a valuable and positive force, with a political meaning, was typical of the late nineteenth-century German-speaking countries.[1] Both in Austria and in Prussia and Wilhelmine Germany, popular humour often turned into blistering satire, aiming at improving society by attacking social ills and human errors. Precisely this tendency to target all kinds of social faults and problems has been seen as something distinctive for satire, which not merely springs from social reality, but also seeks to have a direct influence on it.[2] Since the *Vormärz*, satirical humour had constituted an important part of nineteenth-century political culture, and was used as a means of self-expression in repressive and authoritative societies where public discourse was strictly regulated. As Mary Lee Townsend suggests in the case of nineteenth-century Germany, 'the voice of the people had been stifled and forced to express itself through the ambiguities of humour and satire'.[3]

The somewhat daring poem in *Figaro*, defending laughter to the authorities, was published in 1890, when the Viennese had been struggling with censorship for more than three decades. It probably saw daylight only because by the end of the century the censors had started to loosen their grip. As this poem indicates, the humorous magazines *Der Figaro*, *Kikeriki* and *Der Floh* all had problems with the censors. Some issues were seized and never reached the public; several times charges were pressed against the magazines, which were then required under the Press Law to publish the rulings of the *k.k. Landesgerichte*[4] on the front page of the next number of the magazine. Collisions between humourists and the authorities happened quite frequently. The main causes for trouble were accusations of offending 'public peace and order' (*öffentliche Ruhe und Ordnung*) by defamation or anti-governmental tendentiousness.[5] Laughing was, indeed, seen as dangerous to the state.

Kikeriki had the most trouble with censorship. It is revealing that even the first issue of the magazine caught the eye of the censors, and at the very highest level: it was suggested to the Minister of Police himself, Freiherr Karl von Mecsery de Tsoor (1804–85), that the attitude of *Kikeriki* should be 'strictly monitored' in the future.[6] Soon after, in 1862, the 29-year-old Editor-in-Chief of *Kikeriki*, O.F. Berg (1833–86), was arrested for attacking individual members of the Catholic Church.[7] He ended up writing a book on his prison experiences.[8] The Editor-in-Chief of *Figaro*, Karl Sitter (1825–84), on the other hand, had already been sentenced in the 1850s to twenty-three years with a penal battalion in Bohemia for his writings in the Viennese humorous magazine *Der Punch*. After being reprieved by the Minister of the Interior after one year of servitude, in 1857 at the age of thirty-two he launched his new humorous enterprise, *Figaro*.[9] *Floh* also suffered under censorship, and for some time in 1869 had to be published from Pest because of difficulties in Vienna.[10]

Clearly the censors were afraid of what kinds of dangerous thinking, criticism or new ideas the humorous *Witzblätter* might stimulate in their readers. For example, in the case of *Kikeriki* in 1862, the court commented that the popularity of the magazine among the lower classes and its wide circulation made its offence even more severe: 'With people of inadequate reason, nothing is more dangerous than mockery'.[11] In other words, a humorous magazine that was popular among the less educated population should bear greater responsibility for its content.

Kikeriki was strongly identified with the Editor-in-Chief, O.F. Berg, who had already established himself as a comic writer and humorous journalist in the magazine *Tritsch-Tratsch* when he started to publish *Kikeriki* in 1861. Berg continued to work at *Kikeriki* until a significant decline in his health in the 1880s. He died in a mental institution in 1886. As early as the 1880s, *Kikeriki* had inclined towards antisemitism, but after 1898, under the new Editor-in-Chief, Friedrich Igler (Fritz Gabriel), it turned into a totally antisemitic magazine.[12]

The editorial staff of *Figaro* and *Der Floh* were more heterogeneous: Karl Sitter worked as the Editor-in-Chief of *Figaro* until his death in 1884, but he had many established journalists working beside him. The most famous of these was Friedrich Schlögl (1821–92), who was responsible for editing the *Wiener Luft* appendix that started to come out in 1876. Schlögl had become famous for his humorous stories, published in the book-length collections *Wiener Blut* (1873) and *Wiener Luft* (1876), and together with Eduard Pötzl (1851–1914) and Vinzenz Chiavacci (1847–1916) he is one of the best-known authors of the late nineteenth-century 'Wiener Skizzen'. This was a genre of humorous stories that evolved from the feuilleton sections of the press and focused on local events and phenomena, creating famous humorous characters such as Frau Sopherl vom Naschmarkt, a market wife from the old Vienna who comments on the new urbanity.[13] Chiavacci was one of the many prominent co-workers on *Figaro* along with others such as Daniel Spitzer, Ludwig Anzengruber and Fritz Mai, who worked there along with their other publishing activities. The most famous caricaturists on *Figaro* were Ernst Juch, Hans Schließmann and Theodor Zache. The latter two especially drew caricatures for the *Wiener Luft* appendix.[14]

Der Floh was founded by Joseph Frisch and Karl Klíč in 1869, and the first Editor-in-Chief was Joseph Braun, who also founded the humorous magazine *Der Bombe* in 1871 together with another *Der Floh* co-worker called, coincidentally, Carl Floh.[15] One of the most famous caricaturists on *Der Floh* was Ladislaus von Frecskay (Laci v.F.), and caricaturists like Theodor Zache and Karl von Stur, who worked for *Figaro*, published their work in *Der Floh* as well. *Der Floh*, which started publication a few years later than *Kikeriki* and *Figaro*, was famous for its visual impact, and it was the first Austrian magazine to publish cartoons and caricatures in four colours, following the European examples of *Punch Magazine* and *Le Charivari*.[16] In the late nineteenth century, the field of humorous magazines was very dynamic, and many journalists and caricaturists worked for several magazines at the same time. Furthermore, contributions were also sent in for publication by amateurs. Most of the images in the humorous magazines were published unsigned, and practically all texts were published anonymously, although journalists often also had their own fixed columns and comical characters.

Previous research has successfully charted the editors, journalists and cartoonists working on the humorous magazines, but the question of readers' contributions has not previously been studied.[17] The fact that the readers not only read the humorous magazines but also wrote for them probably did not make them any less suspect in the eyes of the authorities. But who were these authorities, and what kind of information is available about the readers of the *Witzblätter*? In order to understand the discussion in humorous publications on the transformation of the city, it is important to look into the social function of humorous magazines in late nineteenth-century Vienna. In the following I will give a short overview of the censorship in Vienna between 1857 and 1890, and examine the material from the readers' columns of the *Witzblätter* in order to find out what kind of people were reading, and writing for, the humorous magazines.

Censorship in the Habsburg Empire

Censorship was crucial in defining the limits for humour: what was permitted to be said aloud and what was prohibited. In Vienna, as in many other European cities, the revolution of 1848 was a significant turning point. For a short time, censorship was abolished and the printing press, flyers and pamphlets were brought to the streets. After the restructuring of the imperial power of Franz Joseph from 1848 onwards, censorship was re-established and the conditions of the press became very strict.[18]

Between 1801 and 1848, during the *Vormärz* period, when Austria was more or less a police state, the *Polizei- und Zensurhofstelle* was responsible for the strict censorship. The *Polizeihofstelle* was closed down on 23 March 1848, and the Emperor ordered the police to work under the Ministry of the Interior, until 1852, when a supreme police authority directly responsible to the Emperor was established.[19] From the 1850s, the highest police authority had a special department for the censorship of the press, which oversaw individuals who worked in the press: writers, editors, correspondents, booksellers, printers and lithographers.[20]

In the Habsburg Empire the key institutions of centralized power were the ministries, which worked directly under the Emperor, and during the neo-absolutist era, the *Ministerkonferenz* was the most important governmental body. In the 1860s, when the Austrian political system was in turmoil, the ministries continued to be the most powerful institutions.[21] As we will see in the following chapters, the Ministry of the Interior (*Innenministerium*), especially, held power not only over the transformation of the city space but also over the public discussion concerning the city space. The other key institution for the regulation of the public sphere was the Ministry of Police, which was responsible for censorship throughout the whole empire. The police headquarters in Vienna supervised the press in the capital city and reported to the Ministry of Police. Importantly, the police were responsible not just for censorship but also for the maintenance of the city. They also supervised street lighting, street paving, construction works and other practical matters in the city, which, as we will see in the following chapters, were also themes that provoked much humour.

Because of the fire at the Justizpalast in Vienna during the July Revolt of 1927, a great deal of the police authority's archive material has been destroyed and part of the surviving material is severely damaged. For example, because there are documents available only until 1867, there are no mentions of *Der Floh*, which started publishing in 1869. However, the remaining material indicates that the humorous magazines were frequently monitored, as the police strived to maintain 'public peace and order' (*öffentliche Ruhe und Ordnung*) in the empire.

The situation was, however, changing in the 1860s. In 1862 a new Press Law was enacted.[22] The Press Law of 1862 was the first piece of constitutional press legislation passed by the Emperor together with the parliament. Compared to the Press Law of the age of neo-absolutism it was more permissive, and in principle ended the pre-emptive censorship that had been in operation for all papers and magazines. However, in practice pre-emptive censorship still continued from 1862 onwards, as an advance copy of each periodical (*Pflichtexemplar*) had to be sent to the authorities either at least twenty-four hours before distribution or at the same time as distribution began.[23] This meant that although advance censorship was reduced under the new Press Law, some printed works were still pre-censored. The *Pflichtexemplare* were a significant means of monitoring the contents of the printed material.

The police reports shed light on the routines of censorship. Typically, the police found some incriminating material in the advance copy (*Pflichtexemplar*), and went to the printing house to make sure that no further copies were printed of that specific number. The police then made a house search looking for evidence in order to press charges. Sometimes the editors had time to destroy the evidence, as the Editor-in-Chief of *Figaro*, Karl Sitter, did in 1866 when the police came to search for manuscripts of issues 34 and 35, since they contained material that displayed, according to the report, a demeaning and mocking tendentiousness against governmental measures.[24]

The police monitored the press and reported to the Prosecutor General, who had the right to order numbers to be confiscated and to press charges against the magazines.[25] For example, *Der Floh* commented ironically on the situation of the satirical journals in Vienna: 'Comes out regularly every Sunday, that is, until it comes out no longer. Manuscripts returned only via the Prosecutor General'.[26] Furthermore, using advance copies, making house searches and destroying typesets of the composing machines were matters of routine as means of preventive censorship, especially during the Austro-Prussian War in 1866.[27]

All in all, the publishing industry was strictly regulated in late nineteenth-century Vienna. All publishers required a licence. In order to start publishing a periodical magazine, one had to be an Austrian citizen, legally responsible, without a criminal record, and resident in the place of publication of the periodical. When applying for a periodical publishing licence, the publisher and printer had to give notice to the Prosecutor General and to the local authorities of the proposed programme of the paper or journal and its date of publication. In addition, they had to provide their full names and their home addresses. Their names had to be printed clearly in each number of the printed work. Political activities or doubt about the character of the publisher could lead to the refusal of a licence.[28]

Censorship was intertwined with economic power. In addition to applying for a licence, until 1894 the publishers had to deposit a large bail (*Kaution*) in order to start publishing a periodical. All publications that dealt with political or social matters or religious issues in particular were required to deposit bail, the amount of which was determined according to how many people lived in the place of publication. The amount of bail was highest in Vienna: eight thousand Gulden.[29] The punishments foreseen included imprisonment from one to six months, or in most cases fines of up to two hundred Gulden.[30] Therefore, publishing activity required capital. Censorship supported the wealthy, since members of the lower classes simply could not afford to publish.

Publishing papers and periodicals thus demanded not just personal courage but also significant financial investment. Because of all this, in 1865 *Kikeriki* listed some 'useful addresses' for any incautious individual intending to start a new humorous magazine in Vienna: the police headquarters, the office of the Prosecutor General, the criminal court, tax office, prison hospital and lunatic asylum.[31]

Consequently, in the late 1850s, when the urban renewal started, critical voices were for the most part silenced, but by the late 1880s, when the new city space was almost finished, they were more likely to surface in the *Witzblätter*, expressing all the frustration boiling beneath the surface of the heavily regulated and supervised society. Like the *Figaro*'s poem dedicated to the 'dear' Prosecutor General, a poem in *Der Floh* titled 'The Muzzle' revealed heavy frustration at the situation, in which critical voices dealing with political and social issues were kept muzzled. The speaker of the poem would like to write a song that is 'sharp and fine', but cannot do so, because 'that sort of thing' leads to difficulties with the Prosecutor General. The only things one is allowed to write about are love and the weather, whereas topics like ministers and freedom are totally out of the question.[32]

The fact that more and more people could read and write in the expanding nineteenth-century cities caused problems for the censors. Not only did the number of readers increase, but the modern industrial print culture made it easier to reproduce and circulate printed publications. The new Press Law in 1862 was created to address the new means of mass production and technological reproduction. The text of the law used the term 'printed work' (*Druckschrift*), and covered not only the press but all 'mechanically or chemically reproduced products of art and literature'.[33]

Not only text, but especially the increasing number of images was seen as dangerous. Justin Goldstein suggests that censorship in France, for instance, was more sensitive to pictures in general, and especially caricatures, than to texts, because images were seen as having a greater impact on their audience. The power of images was seen to result from their ability to directly affect senses and emotions. Pictures addressed people's emotions, whereas words spoke to their intellect and reason. Thus, the pictures had an immediate impact that led to unconsidered actions, but words were contemplated with time and reason, and therefore their effect was delayed by a thoughtful process of considering the message. It was their immediate impact on the readers that made pictures so dangerous, as the French authorities stated in 1829: 'Engravings of lithographed images act immediately upon the imagination of the people, like a book which is read with the speed of light'.[34]

In addition, reading was often seen as something personal, whereas looking at pictures was collective, an activity of the masses. The dangerousness of images was fed by their customary public display on the streets; in the windows of bookstores, street kiosks and print sellers they attracted the urban crowd, which could easily start unpredicted mob action. Reading, on the other hand, was seen as an activity of individuals or small groups in private spaces, and especially in the sphere of the home.[35]

In Austria, unlike France, the street sale of newspapers and periodicals was prohibited.[36] There were only a limited number of kiosks, scattered all over the city, that were allowed to sell magazines. All magazine sellers required a licence, and newsboys were not permitted until 1922. In addition to prohibiting street sales, the legislation also dictated that all periodicals, including the humorous magazines, had to be subscribed to and distributed by mail (*Postzwang*) and were therefore only accessible to the general public through places like bookstores and kiosks, public libraries, reading clubs or coffee houses. Because of the taxes imposed on periodicals and the rigid subscription system, coffee houses became the most important places where the humorous-satirical *Witzblätter* were read. They were the centres both for cultural and for political discussion in late nineteenth-century Vienna.[37] Many of the readers' letters were sent by groups in a café or other public venue.

The Readers

In the readers' columns of *Der Figaro*, *Kikeriki* and *Der Floh*, there are many pseudonyms that refer to a group, which could be a reading group or a circle of regular customers at a café or an inn.[38] This reflects the fact that, as Robert Darnton and many other scholars of the history of reading have shown, in the second half of the nineteenth century reading was not just a significant social pastime, but in the growing European cities coffee houses took on an important role as centres for political discussion.[39] Pen names such as 'Kaffeehausleser' or 'Kaffeehausbesucher'[40] also indicate that the humorous *Witzblätter* were often read in coffee houses or local inns. If one did not want to subscribe to the magazine, this was the easiest – and cheapest – way to read them.[41] For example, a song of the Viennese Students' Union (*Wiener Studentenschaft*) in praise of *Figaro* states that students read the humorous magazine enthusiastically in Viennese cafés and inns. The song ends with a line promising that when the students have their doctor's degree, they will also subscribe.[42]

The editors were so taken by the song that it was published in the readers' column. The interaction between editors and their readers was actually an important part of the *Witzblätter*, and the responses published in the readers' columns reveal only the tip of the iceberg of material that readers sent in to the magazines every week. For example, *Kikeriki*, which had a circulation of twenty-five thousand, reported in 1879 that they had received in a short time 625 readers' letters and were obviously not able to answer all of them.[43] During the second half of the nineteenth century, all three magazines reported over and over again that they were overwhelmed by the massive number of readers' letters and unable to give individual answers to all contributors.[44]

The readers' columns reveal that people not only offered comments and suggested further topics, but also actually sent in all kinds of material, not just their own jokes and cartoons, but also themes, songs and ideas for new comic characters.[45] The jokes and cartoons were sent in under pseudonyms and published anonymously. In most cases the pseudonyms consisted only of the reader's initials, and possibly the name of a street, neighbourhood or city. There were also references to literary characters, and famous figures from the theatre and opera were used as pen names as well. In some cases, the pseudonym was based on a professional title such as clerk or officer;[46] in other cases some information about gender or ethnicity was given.

Of course, it is important to keep in mind that people may not have been what they claimed to be. Because the texts and pictures were sent in anonymously, people could pretend to be somebody other than they actually were. This was in fact quite common: many readers used fictional or fake identities when writing to the humorous magazines. Because the humorous periodicals were often subscribed via post to public places, such as coffee houses, the editors did not necessarily know who their readers were and who they were dealing with. In many cases the editors were themselves uncertain whether the readers were actually who or what they claimed to be. For example, in 1886 the editors of *Der Floh* wrote to the pen name 'Fräulein J.H.' that they did not believe that she was a sixteen-year-old girl but a 'regular copyist'.[47] The same happened with the pen name 'Zwei Mädchen' in 1872.[48]

So, information given by readers in their pseudonyms was by no means trustworthy. But this does not mean that it is not interesting. One of the main reasons for playing with identities and adopting fake identities was censorship. As seen earlier, when suspecting incriminating material, the police made house searches in the editorial offices and printing houses. It was dangerous to have written something incriminating with one's own name or to possess daring material.[49] Therefore, using pseudonyms and fake identities was a way of navigating the strictly regulated authoritative society.

Consequently, instead of giving full names or addresses, members of the educated bourgeoisie played with references to art, literature and high culture in general, thus at the same time hiding their true identity and emphasizing the bourgeois idea of *Bildung*. When the readers used street names in their pen names, they did not identify themselves with wealthy, respectable addresses, but rather with modest parts of Vienna and even with the suburban areas. There were only a few references to places near the city centre.[50] Much more often, readers' letters came from the outer parts of the city and from the suburbs. Bourgeois city districts outside the old city wall, which later became the site for the new Ringstraße boulevard, such as Wieden, Landstrasse, Josefstadt and Neubau or even Währing and Hernals, were often mentioned.[51] In addition, especially *Kikeriki*, which targeted the lower middle classes, received readers' letters coming from suburbs such as Simmering or Ottakring.[52] This indicates that the readerships of the magazines were quite heterogeneous. The fact that the humorous magazines published material from their readers made them an important forum for grassroots-level negotiation in society, where not just the city space, but also public debate concerning it was strictly regulated and monitored. Readers' letters provided a loophole in the system that regulated who was able to publish what in Vienna. The following sections will focus on how the jokes, cartoons and other humorous accounts dealt with the great project of redesigning the capital city and making it into a modern metropolis.

Designing New Vienna

'What is the definition of fantasy? – The question of the city expansion.'[53] This joke was published in *Figaro* in 1857, when the Viennese people had become aware that their city was about to be changed in a radical way. In the following year a major public architecture competition was held in order to find a new design for the New Vienna (*Neu-Wien*). During the year, alternative plans for the future city were presented to the Viennese people, who started to reimagine their city and orientate themselves to the change that was about to come. This section pays attention to the planning phase of the late 1850s, and to the architecture competition of 1858 in particular, and explores how humour was used as a way of imagining and discussing the new city.

In the second half of the nineteenth century, urbanization and a huge increase in population in Vienna created a need to reshape the city. As a solution, an architecture competition for the new layout of the city was held in 1858.[54] The competing plans suggested various different solutions for the urban renewal, called in German *Stadterweiterung*, literally 'expansion of the city'. The idea was to find a plan for how to extend the city beyond the old limits of the city wall and fortifications. There was a vast unbuilt area between the old city centre and the suburbs that had emerged surrounding Vienna, as newcomers flowed into the city from all over the empire. This space was to be taken into use, and in total eighty-five plans were submitted, offering their own designs for the future Vienna.[55]

The architecture competition attracted huge publicity, and discussion about what the New Vienna should look like became an important topic for the press, the main media in the late nineteenth century. The daily papers commented on the plans and made suggestions for how the New Vienna should look. In October 1858, *Die Presse* published an article 'Ueber die Neugestaltung Wiens', written by 'St.', in which the transformation of the city was seen as something that affected the city as a whole, and was going to reshape the lives of all of its citizens. The text started by noting that the plans had been displayed to the public now for fourteen days and that the exhibition had attracted great publicity:

> This involvement of the public is understandable. Who would not be interested to see and to hear from the visitors what the New Vienna is going to look like? In what manner will the extension of the capital for forty million inhabitants be executed? Where can the city locate its new City Hall? Where are we going to hear operas? How large will the new Burg- and Opera theatre be? Where are we going to go riding in future, take promenades, or cool down by the fountains in the summer? Where will the scholars have their rare books, the art lovers their works of art, the scientists their rocks, dried plants and stuffed animals? Where will our wives find their fruit, vegetables, geese and chickens? Where will the merchant display the treasures of his storehouses before his customers' eyes? Where will the butcher and the baker store their ice? Where will the Fiaker carriages find the shortcuts for their zigzag routes? Where are the young people going to dance and the children play? As you can see, everybody is affected by the city expansion.[56]

The idea put forward here is that urban planning, which was something that affected everyone, was made transparent in the exhibition. Everyone could come and see what kind of alternative futures for Vienna were on offer, and inform themselves about the process by reading the papers. As Harald Robert Stühlinger has pointed out in his dissertation on the planning process, the ideal of the public sphere impacted not only on discussion in the press, but on the history of urban planning as well, for architecture competitions had emerged after the French Revolution as the best solution to create new urban designs. The nineteenth-century ideology saw open competitions as the most suitable way to design and create urban spaces, because the evaluation happened 'objectively' and in public.[57] However, this was not the whole truth. The relationship between nineteenth-century urban planning and public debate was not as simple as this text suggests. Decisions were anything but objective, and they were made by only a few behind closed doors. Ordinary citizens had very little power over the transformation of their city space. In addition, the press was censored and operated under imperial regulation, which meant that people could not really trust what they were reading about the urban renewal in the papers.

The planning phase of the late 1850s took place during the period of neo-absolutism following the 1848 revolution, when censorship was extremely strict and there were only a few humorous-satirical magazines existing in Vienna, including *Figaro*, *Der Humorist* and *Hans Jörgel*. Only after the new Press Law of 1862 did the number of humorous magazines begin to increase. Moreover, the humour of the 1850s was much more veiled than in the following decades. Despite this, humour, and especially satirical humour, was a crucial way of dealing with the contradictions and uncertainties relating to the redesigning of Vienna. For example, the following joke, published in *Figaro*, was set in the exhibition site where the competing plans for the new layout of the city were showcased. Two strangers stop to discuss the plans:

> This plan with the motto 'Sustine et abstine', I said to a gentleman at the exhibition site, seems quite excellent to me.
> Oh, he objected, do you not see that it is quite unfeasible?
> Why?
> Because according to this plan, that house there has to be demolished.
> Why does that single house matter? I asked.
> Sir, that is my house, he said and left me in a rage ...[58]

The comicality of this particular example seems to spring from a sense of uncertainty in the face of radical change. Like the man who discovers at the exhibition site that his house might be destroyed by the urban renewal, the members of the Viennese public were not sure how the transformation of the city would mould their own lives. Furthermore, this example is a clear reminder that the rebuilding of the city was not a harmonious collective effort, as presented by the article in *Die Presse*, but depended on multifaceted negotiations of power. Not just the power over city space, but power over discussion in the press was a major source of tension in the 1850s. The relationship between urban planning and public debate was not simple, since information about the urban renewal project was controlled by the authorities. There was a great deal of cover-up and secrecy related to the actual decision making. At first, the intended urban renewal was kept secret, and silently prepared in the *Ministerkonferenz*, the most important governmental body, during 1857. Consequently, when there was no solid information but only rumours on whether the urban renewal was to be carried out or not, and how radical the transformation would actually be, the impatience at waiting for the change found its expression in wordplay such as this, published in *Figaro*:

Glacis Beautification
Beautiful is what is simple, simpler thus *more beautiful,*
So what happens is the most beautiful, that is the simplest thing: *nothing!*[59]

This example gives voice to a clear willingness to see the city changing and improving.[60] Humour expressed dissent with the prevailing order, masked in clever word games, which in their own way emphasized the feeling of lack of influence: words and actions did not meet. The slow bureaucracy was ridiculed as absurd and inefficient.[61] In addition to disapproval, the anticipation of change caused uncertainty. The sense of a lack of power in the face of the potential urban renewal found its expression in recurring concern for the little creatures of the city. Jokes and cartoons dealt repeatedly with the question of what would happen to the millions of happy mice if the old city was to be demolished.[62] The question about mice can easily be interpreted symbolically: what will happen to the citizens?

At the same time as *Figaro* was asking these questions in 1857, the *Ministerkonferenz* started to prepare clear guidelines on how the transformation of Vienna should be executed. This document stated in black and white what was to be demolished and what to be saved. This *Kabinettschreiben* served as an outline for the decree that Emperor Franz Joseph issued to the Minister of the Interior, Alexander Bach, on 20 December 1857. No information reached the newspapers until the declaration was published in the *Wiener Zeitung* on 25 December 1857. The imperial decree, 'Es ist mein Wille', was a clear declaration of power over the city space: Emperor Franz Joseph ordered the rebuilding, regulation and beautification of the capital of *his* empire and *his* future residence.[63]

Only after this official imperial declaration were extensive, ostentatious articles published in the press, celebrating the city's leap into a new era.[64] Moreover, according to the historian Elisabeth Springer, who has investigated the planning process in detail, the Minister of the Interior, Alexander Bach, was well aware of the importance of public opinion in a society in which the bourgeoisie now had more power than ever before. Minister Bach collaborated over a long period with the Editor-in-Chief of *Die Presse*, August Zang, and organized several series of articles in the paper to convince the public of the need to reshape the old city structure.[65]

Consequently, the article 'Ueber die Neugestaltung Wiens', which we encountered earlier, was actually not such an innocent curious examination of the ongoing planning process as it led readers to believe. In 1858, *Der Figaro* published a 'supplement' to this article, addressing the writer as 'Herr St. (!)'.[66] The exclamation mark in parentheses following the pseudonym 'St.' suggests that *Der Figaro* wanted to draw attention to the pseudonym. In the Austrian nineteenth-century public debates it was common for prestigious members of society to write to the papers anonymously under a pen name, but everybody knew all the same who was actually behind the text.⁶⁷ In this case, Elisabeth Springer suggests that 'St.' was probably a pseudonym for Valentin Streffleur, a high bureaucrat with an outstanding military career, a member of the jury for the architecture competition and several other commissions responsible for the urban renewal, who to top it all had himself designed one of the competing plans, No. 53, which he then discusses behind the disguise of a pen name.⁶⁸ It is thus clear that the press was not truly independent. Anonymity, in theory much appreciated for enabling members of society to have equal opportunities to take part in public discussion, was in practice used in a questionable manner in order to affect public opinion.

For the liberal bourgeoisie, however, such manipulation of public debate was highly offensive, for they had fought for the freedom of the press in 1848, and considered it the duty of every enlightened individual to obtain information, and stay informed on political and social issues. The satirical humour of *Figaro* thus attempts to unmask the fact that the political elite was not interested only in how to regulate the public space, but also in how to regulate public discussion of that city space.

So, whereas the more or less government-friendly daily papers displayed fascination and enthusiasm for the transformation of the city, these humorous and satirical comments reveal a much more critical standpoint on urban planning. And, because in the late 1850s urban planning was so firmly in the hands of the Emperor and his government, a critical standpoint on urban planning meant also a critical perspective on those in power. As seen in the previous section, the censors showed mistrust of *Figaro*, and issues were confiscated for reasons like 'demeaning and mocking tendentiousness against governmental measures'.⁶⁹ The critical edge on the process of designing a new Vienna becomes visible as a strong aim to unveil the rotten hypocrisy relating to the discourses on and practices of urban design.⁷⁰

The visuality of the humorous magazines also offered other possibilities for satire than verbal puns, wordplay and parody. Notably, the humorous magazines used urban plans as subtexts for their cartoons on the designing process. After the imperial decree had been published and the architecture competition begun, the *Witzblätter* started to publish their own humorous plans and suggestions for the future Vienna, as comments on the existing plans. The architecture competition worked as a contextual framework in which the humour became intelligible. It was assumed that the reader would be aware of the competition and able to understand references made to it.

For example, a cartoon from *Figaro* (Figure 1.1), published within the fourteen days during which the architecture exhibition was open in autumn 1858, portrays an exhibition of three plans that, according to the text, 'will not receive the first prize in the competition'.⁷¹ The reason these plans will not win is left to the reader to decide: whether they are too comical or absurd to be taken seriously,

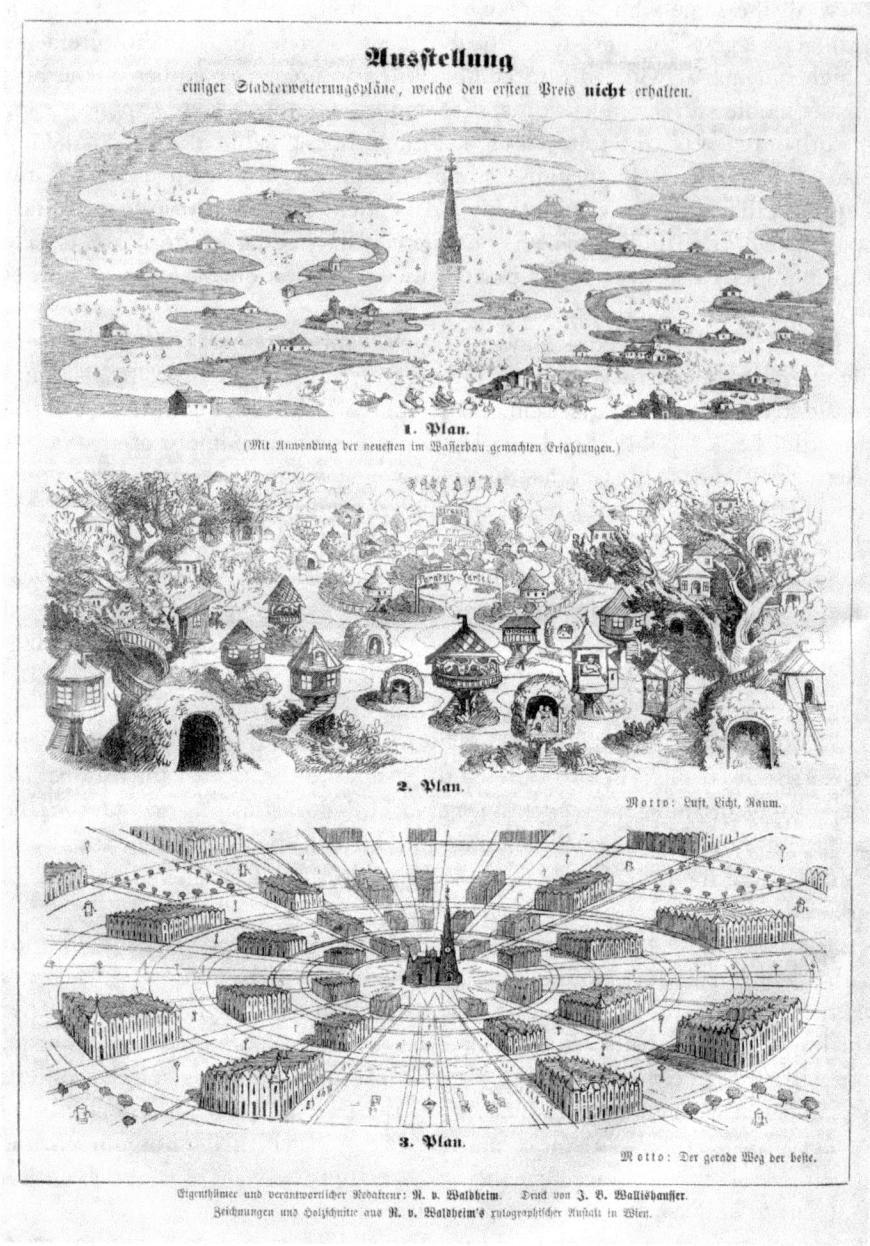

Figure 1.1 'Exhibition', *Figaro*, 30 October 1858. Source: Austrian National Library.

or that they portray possibilities for different kinds of societies that have no chance in the prevailing order.

In the first plan, Vienna is covered with water and only the top of St. Stephen's Cathedral (Stephansdom) is sticking out of the water. In the second plan, 'Luft, Licht, Raum', the city has been turned into a fantastical pre-modern village-like community. The texts in the middle of the image – 'Strauss' and 'Paradeis-Gartel' – refer to the composer Johan Strauss the Elder, and locate the image in the imaginary of the old beloved park in the Glacis area, which was extremely popular among the Viennese middle classes in the first half of the century. The third plan shows another extreme: an exaggerated modern rationalized space, which follows geometrical form. In all of these three plans, there is a clear tension between nature and technology, pre-modern and modern, industrial community and organic, 'natural' community. These tensions created humour that was very much related to nineteenth-century concerns and fears concerning modernity as well as to the enthusiasm and curiosity evoked by the novelty of the new era.

The process of making urban designs illuminates the very core of nineteenth-century popular Viennese humour: the imagination. Many of the humorous plans showed an alternative way of imagining the city. The humourists played with ideas that had been proposed in actual plans, and took them to extremes. For example, the motto 'Luft, Licht, Raum', which later became the guideline for modern architects,[72] inspired late nineteenth-century Viennese humourists to picture people living in tree houses – the very negation of modern urbanity.

The humorous plans were funny because they were impossible, for many reasons and in many ways. In fact, humour seemed to rise from the acknowledgement of recognizing the limits between the possible and the impossible. Since possible ideas and their realizations in society were defined by those in power, the notion of impossibility was encountered with humour: making fun of designing the New Vienna was an act of resignation and 'rising above' the lack of power by laughing in spite of all.[73] The alternative plans and comments on urban planning published in the humorous *Witzblätter* sprang from a complex situation in which enthusiasm, great expectations and wild imagination collided with dissent and frustration as the designing of the new city got under way.

Furthermore, the humorous alternative plans in the *Witzblätter* show how knowledge of the urban space was tightly interconnected with visualizations and representations of urban space. As Peter Fritzsche and Vanessa Schwartz have shown, in the nineteenth century texts and visual representations of the city were crucial in creating meanings for urban spaces. They guided how the city should be 'read' und understood.[74] Maps and layouts of the city, especially, were an important way of representing and claiming power over space. In Vienna, the final layout was published in 1860 as a prestigious poster loaded with symbolic meanings.[75] Therefore, it is hardly surprising that the humorous magazines chose urban plans and city maps as typical targets for mockery and parody.

In comparison with earlier urban renewals in Europe, instigated top-down by kings and other rulers, nineteenth-century citizens had access to more information than their predecessors. Thanks to the modern print culture, there was a new kind of publicity surrounding the process of redesigning and rebuilding the city. The press and other publications constantly reported the plans to the public and commented on how the renewal was proceeding. As the power relations changed in the empire, which was quite rapidly transformed from an absolute monarchy into a constitutional monarchy, the city space became a battlefield for representations of power, cultural meanings and political ideas.

Reorganizing Space in the *Residenz- und Reichshauptstadt*

The *Residenz- und Reichshauptstadt* Vienna was at the same time the seat of dynastic imperial power and a centralizing state capital. Towards the end of the century, as absolutist rule was replaced by constitutional monarchy, the latter function gained more and more significance.[76] In this section I investigate how this dual role affected both urban planning and humorous-satirical discussion on the transformation of the city. My aim is to demonstrate that modernity was encountered as a breakdown of the old structures of society. Moreover, these shifting power relations became visible through space and were discussed in terms of spatiality.

Urban renewal started out as an imperial enterprise to reflect the power of the neo-absolutist regime, but it was subsequently taken over by the bourgeoisie to express their own ideas and values. Carl E. Schorske divides the urban renewal process into two phases: the early imperial phase and the phase of ascendant constitutional liberalism, which started in the mid 1860s.[77] As seen in the previous section, in the first phase Emperor Franz Joseph authorized the demolition of the city wall and fortifications in 1857 and announced the architecture competition for the new layout of the city in 1858. The city expansion commission (*Stadterweiterungskommission*), which worked directly under the Emperor, was commissioned to oversee the urban renewal project.[78] However, at the same time as the city renewal went ahead, the political system was changing. The 1860s, especially, were a time of massive changes: Austria changed its constitution from an absolute monarchy to constitutional monarchy in 1867, when the Dual Monarchy of Austria-Hungary was born.[79] At the same time, the city of Vienna received municipal self-government.[80] Consequently, in the second phase, control over the planning of the Ringstraße project shifted from imperial interests to the interests of the liberal bourgeoisie, who had gained a dominant position in the City Council and embarked on building monumental buildings for institutions such as parliament and the university to express their values and identity. Vienna thus became, argues

Schorske, a political, intellectual and cultural bastion of nineteenth-century liberal politics and values.[81]

Schorske's famous phrase, the 'politicizing of aesthetics' in late nineteenth-century Vienna, highlights the representative function of urban space, as the city space became a battlefield, a 'politically contested space',[82] through which different groups in society sought to express their claims to power and their cultural values. Schorske argues that the urban renewal was above all a 'projection of values into space and stone'.[83] All the major institutions of the state and the city were now to be placed side by side along the Ringstraße boulevard, which surrounded the inner city, and all the monuments were built according to different historical styles. For example, the university commemorated the rise of humanism in the Renaissance, while the neo-gothic of the City Hall represented the ascendant town bourgeoisie. In order to understand the synthesis of the city space, one needed to move along the street from one building and one historical period to another.[84] The liberal city fathers focused above all on the visual impact and symbolic aspects of the architectural project of the Ringstraße, neglecting, for example, the social aspects of urban development.[85]

The Schorskean model has been criticized for assuming a coherent and homogeneous liberal bourgeoisie and neglecting the inner tensions within this social class.[86] Interpreting the Ringstraße as a middle-class space that enclosed the aristocratic city centre, taking it over both materially and symbolically,[87] ignores the inner tensions among the Viennese bourgeoisie. John Boyer's study of the political radicalization of the Viennese middle classes, for example, is based on a more detailed study of how the political system led to the dissent and alienation of the lower middle classes and to the rise of populist mass parties in the 1880s.[88] Similarly, the humorous magazines reveal the inner contradictions within the Viennese bourgeoisie, which did not simply position itself against the aristocracy in the construction of the new city space, but was also full of internal disagreement on the aims and priorities of urban planning. The humorous-satirical comments on spatial issues show how not only the physical space itself but also its representations became a battlefield between various interests. As the structures of power in material spaces were revealed through jokes, satirical writings and cartoons, these humorous representations also played an active role in creating immaterial meanings for the physical city space.

Representative Power of the State

Vienna had for centuries been the residence of the Emperor, but the shift in the political system in the second half of the nineteenth century radically diminished the power of the Habsburg dynasty. From the 1860s onwards, the Emperor and bourgeois city fathers struggled for power over the city space.[89] The historian Elisabeth Springer has observed that there was a basic contradiction between the ways in which the municipal leaders and the members of the imperial *Stadterweiterungskommission* and *Stadterweiterungsfond* saw the urban space. The members of the City Council focused on contemporary issues, and saw their main task as ensuring the interests of the citizens and especially of the privileged, who were entitled to vote in municipal elections. The powerful members of the Imperial Commission, however, represented the view of the Ministry of the Interior and the court, and emphasized the significance of Vienna as the residence of the Emperor and capital of the vast empire, with its tens of millions of inhabitants. Their goal was to create a strong capital for the vast and heterogeneous empire, and the representative function of urban space was seen as a means to hold the vast empire together. Their interest was therefore focused not on the present well-being of the citizens but on the future of the whole empire.[90]

The ongoing struggle over space and its meanings emerged in the Viennese *Witzblätter*, which paid much attention to the political and symbolic aspects of the urban renewal. *Der Floh*, especially, took a critical stand towards the representational power of the state, manifested in the reorganization of the city space. Humorous representations, such as jokes and cartoons, unpacked the spatial narratives that were embedded in the spatial composition of the Ringstraße programme, consisting of monuments, squares, statues and the street itself. For example, the following poem from 1869 illustrates how material places and immaterial meanings were always intertwined and how spatial rearrangements enabled people to discuss power relations and make political statements:

> It is said in our circles / That a worthy shelter / Is to be built for the imperial residence – / That the 'Burg' is to be extended.
>
> And certainly there will be no one / To contradict this aim, / For it is true, the gloomy Hofburg / No longer matches the greatness of the empire.
>
> Therefore build! Raise an edifice / Grand and handsome, worthy of our city, / A proud magnificent building, / Like none other in any capital.
>
> But consider one wish / Coming from the people's hearts, – / On which, – easily fulfilled, – / They set great value and significance.
>
> The people wish that the Emperor's home, / When it stands proudly to the sky, / No longer should be called the 'Burg', / But that you give it another name.
>
> Not 'Burg'! – In the sound of this name, / We think too easily of a 'fortress', / Absolutism, despotism, / Come to greet us from the past!
>
> This is not the Emperor's will! – The ruler / Who broke with rotten traditions, / And disregarding the voice of caution, / Spoke the proud words of freedom!
>
> He who has offered his reconciling hand / To his subjects for peace and settlement, / He has no need of a fortress / As a residence among his people.

For him the best castle is the love / Tendered to him by his realm; / The trust of his people is a wall / Through which no enemy spear can pierce.[91]

In talking about rebuilding and renaming the Hofburg,[92] the text actually offers a commentary on the current political situation, emphasizing the new constitutional role of the Emperor and making a clear break with the absolutism of the past. Although this poem is not particularly funny, in its poetic form and serious content, the context of a *Witzblatt* predestines it to be read in a framework of humour. As in many other cases of political satire, the realms of the comical are used as a strategy to talk about serious matters that were otherwise too delicate or explosive for public debate. Here the poem controversially demands that the rebuilding of the Emperor's residence should not just be a material renewal, but also a political one, a transition from the old order into a new more liberal era.

Der Floh's poem on the rebuilding of the Hofburg palace sums up the turmoil in the political system in the 1860s, as the old imperial power was breaking but many of the old structures of power still remained intact. The *Herrenhaus* represented the interests of the aristocracy, while the majority of the population remained outside all political decision making because of the rigid franchise. However, as seen here, despite its proud claims for constitutional freedom and critique of absolutism, the poem is highly conciliatory towards Emperor Franz Joseph. It ends with a celebration of the love and devotion of his royal subjects, who are presented as the best protectors of the Emperor: an ambivalent closure that could perhaps be read as a warning as well as a declaration of loyalty. In any case, it seems that the shifting power relations were an important context for understanding the humour around spatial issues. Satirical humour was a field in which the liberal bourgeoisie was able to challenge the old imperial power, which together with the Catholic Church had so long governed the city.[93]

In *Der Floh*'s poem, it is not only the construction but also the naming of the new palace that bears significance. The speaker of the poem pleads that the new residence of the Emperor should not be called 'Burg', because this name evokes associations of despotism and absolutism. This particular case presents just one example of the ways in which the humorous magazines paid attention to the practice of naming places as a way of exercising authority over them. Many jokes were based on playing with street names or place names and with the associations they evoked,[94] and this kind of humour, too, interrogated the power relations attached to space. It highlighted that naming was an act of power, which gave material places meanings and supported ideologies embedded in the spatial structures of the city.

In addition to humorous play on naming places, the architecture of the new monumental buildings on the Ringstraße was another important topic in the humorous magazines from the 1860s onwards.[95] As noted earlier, the renewal of the Hofburg was only one component in the vast project to create the Ringstraße as the modern Main Street of the empire: a *Prachtstraße* that would bring all the aspects of the city and state together in one spatial entity. The Votivkirche having been started already in the 1850s to celebrate the survival of the Emperor in a failed assassination attempt in 1853, numerous secular institutions of the city and the state were erected on the Ringstraße boulevard, which was ceremonially opened in 1865. The most famous buildings are the Opera House (1861–69), parliament (1874–83), City Hall (1872–83), the university (1877–84) and the Hofburgtheater (1874–88).

Discussion in the press closely followed the construction of these monumental buildings, but the architectural choices and symbolic meanings of different aesthetic styles were also addressed in humorous forums. In particular, the need of the middle classes to distinguish themselves from the aristocracy was clearly visible in the satirical humour. For example, in one poem from *Der Floh*, the new Opera House is heavily criticized as having been erected for the 'blue blooded' and not for ordinary (middle-class) citizens.[96] The Opera House was, in fact, subject to massive criticism, and contemporary public opinion turned against it. Humour and ridicule played an important role in this process. In addition to the Opera House repeatedly being mocked in the Viennese *Witzblätter*,[97] popular jokes circulated in other contemporary discourses. The building was mocked as a great defeat (*Königgräz der Baukunst*) and as a sunken chest (*versunkene Kiste*). The most famous song mocking the Opera House ridiculed the architects for having no sense of style.[98] The architects, Eduard van der Nüll and Sicard von der Sicardsburg, were devastated by the critique. The former committed suicide and the latter died soon after.

This heavy wave of criticism has often been associated with a new sense of power and self-understanding among the liberal bourgeoisie, who wanted to show off their own taste and their ability to read architecture and judge its aesthetic values. Humour on spatial issues presupposed an ability to read space, implying knowledge of the language of architecture and a tacit understanding of the symbolic hierarchies and meanings attached to urban planning.

These meanings and hierarchies were often turned upside down in order to create a comical effect. In many cases, jokes and cartoons were based on transforming something serious and sublime into the low and comical. For example, one cartoon from *Kikeriki* in 1869 criticized the slow construction works by portraying the unfinished university as a pile of garbage.[99] Another cartoon, from 1888, suggested for the new Burgtheater a comical decoration made of animal figures.[100] The language of architecture was used in various ways in both visual and textual gags that commented on society through statues and urban decoration.[101] In addition, humorous magazines played with the meanings associated with different sites in the city, highlighting the contrast between the city centre and the periphery of the suburbs. For instance, one comical plan suggested that the university and museums could be situated in Margarethen, far away from the city centre.[102]

This all shows that the middle-class humourists were well aware of the strong symbolic nature of urban space. Because the Ringstraße was above all a spatial narrative, intended to express power, meanings and values in spatial form, the humourists paid a great deal of attention to space and used it as a symbolic field that enabled them to comment on the immaterial meanings embedded in urban architecture. Discussing space was a way of negotiating the symbols and meanings attached to it.

David Harvey has written on Walter Benjamin's study of Paris and the Arcades project that Benjamin focused on representations, spectacle and phantasmagoria because people do not just live in a material world, but dreams, imaginations and concepts 'mediate the materiality in powerful ways'.[103] It seems that in late nineteenth-century Vienna popular humour was one way of mediating the materiality of the city. At the same time that the bourgeoisie were striving to achieve a new political status in society, the middle-class humorous magazines enjoyed playing with the immaterial meanings embedded in material spaces. Humour was used as a significant way of commenting on the ideas and power relations manifested in urban space. Because jokes and cartoons were able to give new meanings to the material world and, as in the case of the Opera House, undermine the message of the architecture and urban design, popular humour was an important tool for the middle-class struggle for new structures in social and political life in the late nineteenth century.

However, as discussed earlier, the power over urban space shifted decisively from the absolutist state to the liberal bourgeoisie, which held a majority in the *Reichsrat* (parliament) and in the City Council between 1861 and 1878. Consequently, the function of the humorous magazines shifted from external critique of imperial authority to internal critique of the City Council. At the same time, *Kikeriki*, especially, adopted a new perspective on the city as it increasingly aimed at revealing contradictions between the symbolic and material levels of urban spaces. As *Kikeriki* sought to adopt the role of defender of the unprivileged 'little people', it deliberately highlighted the materiality of the city, drawing attention to its spatial practices and the costs of the building projects rather than to their symbolic value. Accordingly, in addition to distinguishing themselves from the aristocracy, and demanding new civil rights and status in society, the middle classes engaged in internal discussion on the urban development and organization of spatial structures in the capital city.

Municipal Politics in the City

The liberals had the majority on the City Council (*Gemeinderat*) and dominated municipal politics in the city from the 1860s onwards. The two liberal mayors, Andreas Zelinka (1861–68) and his follower Cajetan Felder (1868–78), reshaped Vienna with several major urban projects such as the regulation of the Danube, the introduction of a new water supply system (*Wiener Hochquellenwasserleitung*), and complementing the Ringstraße project with the construction of the Stadtpark. In addition, hygienic conditions were improved by building a modern cemetery (*Zentralfriedhof*), and new forms of transport and lighting were taken into use. Many of the improvements centred around the desire to present Vienna as a modern metropolis at the World Exhibition in 1873, which will be discussed further in chapter 5.

The municipal franchise was based on taxed income and educational criteria. The City Council initially had 120 and then 138 members, divided into three classes (*curias*). In 1890 the system changed and a *Stadtrat* (consisting of twenty-five members) was established to direct the City Council.[104] The curia system divided voters into three categories based on their taxed income. The third curia was formed by those who paid at least ten Gulden (from 1885 onwards five Gulden) in tax, and the second and first curia represented those paying higher taxes. The first curia was particularly important, as it included the *Hausherren*, wealthier *Bürger* who owned apartment houses and rented them out to middle-class tenants. The conflict of interest between the *Hausherren* and their tenants was one important factor in the fragmentation of the Viennese *Bürgertum*.[105] Moreover, the majority of citizens were totally excluded from political decision making. In 1869, only 4.3 per cent of Viennese population were entitled to vote. In 1880, merely13.5 per cent and even in 1890 no more than 25 per cent of men over the age of twenty-four were able to vote.[106] Women and the lower classes were totally unrepresented in the political system.

The humorous magazines ridiculed the *Hausherren* and wealthiest *Bürger*, and defended the less privileged among the middle classes.[107] The sharp criticism of the City Council, which was a dominant feature in *Kikeriki* especially, also highlights the function of humour as a means of internal appraisal. The City Council was the most frequent target for condemnation in the *Witzblätter*.[108] One reason for this was that censorship was most strict when it came to criticizing the government led by the Emperor. The municipal politicians were easier and safer targets than, say, the members of the City Expansion Commission or the Minister of the Interior, Alexander Bach, who dominated the implementation of the urban renewal, especially in the early phase.[109]

On the other hand, the ridicule of the City Council reveals the significance of the humorous-satirical magazines as a forum for internal debate within the bourgeoisie. The next chapter will discuss in more detail this ridicule of the City Council in the Viennese *Witzblätter*. It is, however, necessary to note here that *Kikeriki*, in particular, focused in its critique on spatial arrangements and the cost of the building projects. Poor practical decisions by the architects and urban planners were ridiculed in many ways in the magazine.[110] Furthermore, comical alternative plans were used as a means to visualize everyday experiences and to comment on the material arrangements in the city.[111]

Mock plans and cartoons were a way for individuals to get their voices heard in public and to comment on the institutions that were in charge of redesigning and reorganizing urban space in Vienna. Moreover, the visual impact of the comical plans depended on the visual conventions of urban planning as a subtext for parodies. The humourists were attacking the City Council with its 'own weapons', acknowledging that the language of plans and maps was an important language of power when it came to reorganizing cityscapes.

Despite the public discussion around the rebuilding of the city, ordinary citizens had very little influence on the process. The majority of the middle classes were excluded from the making of municipal policy. Because the City Council represented only a minority of citizens, there was a growing gap between the *Groß-* and the *Kleinbürgertum*. The lower middle classes were frustrated by the fact that the City Council pursued only the interests of the capital owners and wealthiest Viennese *Bürger*.[112] This conflict of interest related to a general fragmentation of the bourgeoisie, which was no longer held together by the ideals and goals of the 1848 revolution. John Boyer suggests that the former ideal of the *Bürgertum* as the 'allgemeiner Stand' had been replaced by the idea of a middle class (*Mittelstand*) divided across a range of different social realities and political worldviews.[113]

The humorous magazines thus provided a forum for internal debate among the middle classes over managing and organizing urban space. After the early 1860s, the satirical critique was in most cases directed towards the city fathers and the City Council for not defending the interests of the lower middle class, in particular. Instead of playing with the symbolic aspects of the Ringstraße architecture, *Kikeriki*'s humorous writings and cartoons pointed out how the organization of the city affected everyday life here and now. Furthermore, *Kikeriki* also pointed out that not just experts and academics but also ordinary middle-class citizens had the potential to improve the urban space.[114] This was thus a demand for more influence over the city space. Accordingly, popular humour was one cultural sphere in which the gap between the wealthy bourgeoisie and the lower middle classes became visible.

In conclusion, spatial issues formed an important part of the material of the Viennese *Witzblätter* during the urban renewal. Between the early 1860s and 1890, the perspective shifted significantly from negotiation with the imperial authorities and power of the aristocracy in the 1860s to internal critique of the bourgeois-controlled City Council in the 1880s, as the costs of the monumental buildings and problems in city management became the dominant issues in the humorous-satirical press.

The different humorous magazines adopted, however, slightly different approaches to these spatial issues. *Figaro* and *Der Floh* played above all with symbolic meanings and the representative function of urban space, commenting on immaterial ideas and ideologies through their expression in space, and subjecting the power of the church and the aristocracy to particular ridicule. *Kikeriki*, on the other hand, repeatedly focused on the materiality of the city, and tried to unpack the contradictions between the symbolic and material levels of urban spaces. *Kikeriki*'s viewpoint highlighted the fragmentation of the middle classes; the lower middle classes, who had no vote and thus no influence on the *Reichsrat* or the *Gemeinderat*, criticized the liberal urban renewal projects through popular humour and satire. Both of these approaches, however, were based on using the new media of the press, and humour specifically, to comment on the politics of the material city.[115]

This chapter has investigated the relations between space and power in late nineteenth-century Vienna. The sections have covered three aspects that were crucial for the discussion of the transformation of Vienna in the contemporary humorous magazines: censorship, urban planning and political reforms, all of which impacted on the reorganization of the capital city of the Habsburg Empire. All these aspects were also interconnected with the shift in power relations in late nineteenth-century Austrian society after the liberal bourgeoisie gained a dominant position in both state politics and municipal decision making in Vienna in the 1860s.

The rise of the bourgeoisie caused turmoil both in the material city space and in the public debate around this transformation of space. Humour and laughter provided means to deal with this crisis. The humorous magazines *Figaro*, *Kikeriki* and *Der Floh* were deeply involved in the liberal pursuits for constitutional reform, civil rights and press freedom; they were all anti-clerical and expressed a liberal bourgeois *Weltanschauung* in their humour and satire, although *Kikeriki* inclined more towards the left-oriented, democratic side or the Liberal Party. Spatial issues and the urban renewal project were closely followed in the humorous magazines, because the reorganization of space was closely related to the creation of new political and social structures, ideas and identities in modernizing Vienna. Educated members of the middle classes were especially aware of the representative function of spaces. Space mattered, because it affected the ways in which things were organized, experienced and understood. The struggle over material spaces in the city was also a struggle over the immaterial meanings attached to these spaces. Accordingly, space was also a distanced way of talking about power relations and class structures.

Yet the middle-class perspectives on urban space were diverse and fragmented. *Kikeriki*'s humorous writings and caricatures, especially, document a new kind of self-understanding and self-confidence among the lower middle classes, expressing in satirical humour their ability to understand the city and manage it. Examining the humour on spatial issues also gives us insight into the ways in which the members of the middle classes perceived their relationship to public space, over which they had more power than ever before. This new responsibility for public space generated both self-confidence and uncertainty among the Viennese bourgeoisie. As we will see in the following chapters, the humorous magazines constantly needed to find a balance between a desire to improve and rationalize the city and a fear of its uncontrollable potential. This fear of the city was manifested in humour concerning all kinds of problems in urban life, from overcrowded trams to inadequate lighting of the streets. The following chapter, 'Tensions with City Authorities', looks further into the negotiations over the material city space between the urban authorities and middle-class citizens.

Notes

1. Ernste Menschen, Ernste Zeiten! / Niemand ist des Witzes froh, / Mancherlei Verdrießlichkeiten / Droh'n dem armen Figaro. / Singt er seine kecken Lieder, / Wird er konfiszirt alsbald – / Bitte thun Sie das nicht wieder, / Bitte lieber Staatsanwalt! // Figaro muß Witze machen, / Weil dazu ihn Gott erschuf; / Bringt die Menschen er zum Lachen, / Nun, das ist ja sein Beruf. / Wer da lacht recht frisch und ehrlich, / Bleibt gesund und wird auch alt, / Lachen ist nicht staatsgefährlich / Bitte, lieber Staatsanwalt! … Bitte, lieber Staatsanwalt! *Figaro*, 29 March 1890.
2. See further Susanne Schäfer, *Komik in Kultur und Kontext* (Munich, 1996), 28–30.
3. Mary Lee Townsend, 'Humour and the Public Sphere in Nineteenth-Century Germany', in Jan Bremmer and Herman Roodenburg (eds), *Cultural History of Humour: From Antiquity to the Present Day* (Cambridge, 1997), 200, 216. See also Ann Taylor Allen, *Satire and Society in Wilhelmine Germany: Kladderadatsch & Simplicissimus 1890–1914* (Lexington, 1984), 1–13.
4. The abbreviation *k.k. (kaiserlich-königlich)* referred to institutions in the Cisleithanien part of the Habsburg Empire, whereas *k.u.k. (kaiserlich und königlich)* referred to institutions in both parts of the empire.
5. 'Im Namen Seiner Majestät des Kaisers', *Figaro*, 11 July 1868; 'Preßprozess des "Figaro"', *Figaro*, 15 February 1868; 'Das k.k. Landesgericht zu Wien in Strafsachen an Herrn O.F. Berg', *Kikeriki*, 14 May 1868; 'Urtheil im Namen Sr. Majestät des Kaisers!' *Der Floh*, 10 March 1872. Violating common peace and order (*öffentliche Ruhe und Ordnung*) was a criminal offence under the law. Reichsgesetzblatt 1849–1918. Pressgesetz vom 17. Dezember 1862 IV Stück 8 Artikeln I–V.
6. An seine Excellenz Herrn Carl Freiherrn v. Mecséry de Tsór, AVA/II 2823/1861.
7. Sebastian Korabek, *Preß-Proceß des 'Kikeriki': Abgeführt vor dem k.k. Landesgerichte in Wien am 5. August 1862* (Vienna, 1862), 3–4.
8. O.F. Berg (pseudonym for Ottokar Franz Ebersberg), *Kikeriki im Arrest: Ernste und heitere Erinnerungen an meine Haft* (Vienna, 1863).
9. Elfriede Schneider, *Karikatur und Satire als politische Kampfmittel: Ein Beitrag zur Wiener satirisch-humoristischen Presse des 19. Jahrhunderts (1849–1914)* (Ph.D. diss., Vienna, 1972), 41, 50; Karl Vocelka, *K.u.K. Karikaturen und Karikaturen zum Zeitalter Kaiser Franz Josephs* (Vienna, 1986), 20–21.
10. See further Ernst Scheidl, *Die humoristisch-satirische Presse im Wien von den Anfängen bis 1918 und die öffentliche Meinung* (Ph.D. diss., Vienna, 1950), 169; Schneider, *Karikatur und Satire*, 50.

11. '... nichts ist bei vielen Menschen von unzureichender Unterscheidungskraft gefährlicher als der Spott.' 'Wir sind verhalten, Folgendes zu veröffentlichen', *Kikeriki*, 18 December 1862. See also Korabek, *Preß-Proceß*, 17–18.
12. See further Schneider, *Karikatur und Satire*, 45, 62.
13. See further Susanne Feigl, *Wiener Humor um 1900: Literarische Skizzen* (Vienna, 1986), 7–8.
14. Schneider, *Karikatur und Satire*, 51.
15. Because of the pseudonyms, information on the editors is partly contradictory. See Schneider, *Karikatur und Satire*, 69; Scheidl, *Humoristisch-satirische Presse*, 170; Alfred Estermann, *Die Deutschen Literaturzeitschriften 1850–1880: Bibliographien – Programme* (Munich, 1988), 191; Wien Geschichte Wiki, https://www.geschichtewiki.wien.gv.at/Joseph_Braun. It is possible that Joseph Braun (1840–1902) and Karl Klíč (1841–1926) used the names Joseph Frisch and Carl Floh as pseudonyms.
16. See further Scheidl, *Humoristisch-satirische Presse*, 170–72; Schneider, *Karikatur und Satire*, 69–70.
17. Previous research has focused solely on how the magazines tried to affect the opinions of their supposed readership, and neglected the fact that readers themselves actively took part in creating these magazines. Cf. Schneider, *Karikatur und Satire*, 234–40.
18. See further Markus Reisenleitner, 'Austria: To 1918', in Derek Jones (ed.), *Censorship: A World Encyclopedia* (London, 2001), 147–50.
19. Empress Maria Theresia had founded the Polizeikommission in 1749. Her son Joseph II turned the Polizeikommission into a secret state police that oversaw the whole state. The highest police authority was called Polizeidirektion from 1852 to 1859 and Polizeiministerium between 1859 and 1867; from 1868 the police came under the new, enlarged Ministerium für Landesvertheidigung und öffentliche Sicherheit and from 1870 the Ministry of the Interior (*Innenministerium*). Bertrand Michael Buchmann, 'Dynamik des Städtebaus', in Peter Csendes and Ferdinand Oppl (eds), *Wien – Geschichte einer Stadt: Von 1790 bis zur Gegenwart* (Vienna, 2006), 69–71.
20. G. Wolf, *Geschichte der k.k. Archive in Wien* (Vienna, 1871), 156.
21. Helmut Rumpler, *Eine Chance für Mitteleuropa: Bürgerliche Emanzipation und Staatsverfall in der Habsburgermonarchie* (Vienna, 2005), 329, 405–26.
22. Pressgesetz vom 17. Dezember 1862 (hereafter PressG 1862). As in Germany, no distinction was made between newspapers and other periodicals, and the same means of regulation that were aimed at newspapers also applied to magazines and journals. Cf. Andreas Graf and Susanne Pellatz, 'Familien- und Unterhaltungszeitschriften', in Georg Jäger (ed.), *Geschichte des Deutschen Buchhandels im 19. und 20. Jahrhundert*. Vol. 1. *Das Kaiserreich 1871–1918* (Frankfurt am Main, 2003), 416.
23. §17 PressG 1862.
24. Polizei-Ministerium. Bericht der k.k. Polizei-Direktion in Wien. Ein Beschlagname der No 34 und 35 des 'Figaro' betreffend. AVA/II 2033/1866.
25. On the changes within the censorship see further Catherine Horel, 'Austria-Hungary 1867–1914', in Robert Justin Goldstein and Andrew M. Nedd (eds), *Political Censorship of the Visual Arts in Nineteeth-Century Europe: Arresting Images* (London, 2015), 89–91.
26. 'Erscheint jeden Sonntag täglich und zwar so lange bis es nicht mehr erscheint. Manuskripte werden nur durch Staatsanwalt zurückgestellt', *Der Floh*, 16 May 1869.
27. Polizei-Ministerium. Bericht der k.k. Polizei-Direktion in Wien betreffend die Beschlagnahme der 31. Nummer des 'Kikeriki'. AVA/II 1994/1866.

28. §9–§12 PressG 1862. See also William M. Johnston, *The Austrian Mind: An Intellectual and Social History 1848–1938* (Berkeley, 1983), 49.
29. §13–§14 PressG 1862.
30. §33 PressG 1862.
31. 'Wegweiser für unvorsichtige, welche hier in Wien ein neues Blatt anzufangen gedenken', *Kikeriki*, 12 January 1865.
32. 'Der Maulkorb', *Der Floh*, 28 February 1886.
33. §4 PressG 1862. See further Thomas Olechowski, *Die Entwicklung des Preßrechts in Österreich bis 1918: Ein Beitrag zu österreichischen Medienrechtsgeschichte* (Vienna, 2004), 463.
34. Robert Justin Goldstein, *Censorship of Political Caricature in Nineteenth-Century France* (Kent, 1989), 2–3.
35. Ibid., 3. As Robert Darnton and other scholars interested in the history of reading have shown, in the modern era reading became both more extensive and a more private and personal matter, whereas pictures continued to be perceived as something accessible and understandable for a large number of people. See further Robert Darnton, 'History of Reading', in Peter Burke (ed.), *New Perspectives on Historical Writing* (Cambridge, 1995), 147–50.
36. §23 PressG 1862.
37. Graf and Pellatz, 'Familien- und Unterhaltungszeitschriften', 416–20; Johnston, *Austrian Mind*, 49. On Viennese coffee house culture, see further, for example, Harold B. Segel, *The Vienna Coffee House Wits, 1890–1938* (West Lafayette, 1993), 1–40.
38. See, for example, 'Genossen am Abendtische', *Figaro*, 24 March 1883; 'Tischgesellschaft in T.', *Kikeriki*, 18 September 1879; 'Die Herrn aus dem Dianasaal', *Kikeriki*, 30 January 1862.
39. Darnton, 'History of Reading', 151.
40. 'Kaffeehausbesucher', *Kikeriki*, 6 February 1879; 'Ein Kaffeehausleser', *Figaro*, 1 March 1890.
41. On the subscription system, see further Graf and Pellatz, 'Familien- und Unterhaltungszeitschriften', 418–21.
42. 'Lied der Wiener Studentenschaft. Briefkasten der Redaktion', *Figaro*, 27 May 1882.
43. 'Kleine Post der Redaktion', *Kikeriki*, 18 September 1879.
44. For example *Der Floh*, 28 July 1870.
45. 'B.F.D. Keine Post der Redaktion', *Kikeriki*, 12 December 1861; 'Xaverl. Kleine Post der Redaktion', *Kikeriki*, 16 January 1862; 'Schauspieler Z-tti. Kleine Post der Redaktion', *Kikeriki*, 12 June 1862; 'L. Goldschmidt. Kleine Post der Redaktion', *Kikeriki*, 23 January 1862; 'J.H-r.Nr.239. Kleine Post der Redaktion', *Kikeriki*, 22 June 1865. On readers' letters in the eighteenth- and nineteenth-century press, see further Uwe Hohendahl, 'Die Entstehung der modernen Öffentlichkeit im Zusammenhang mit der Entstehung des modernen Publikums', in Uwe Hohendahl et al. (eds), *Öffentlichkeit: Geschichte eines kritischen Begriffs* (Stuttgart, 2000), 12.
46. 'Geschäftskanzleien', *Kikeriki*, 12 June 1862; 'J.G.W. Ingenieur', *Figaro*, 29 September 1884; 'K.f. Offizier', *Figaro*, 10 November 1883; 'J.K. Staatseisenbahn', *Der Floh*, 10 April 1870.
47. 'Fräulein J.H. Feistitz. Correspondenz der Redaction', *Der Floh*, 23 May 1886.
48. 'Zwei Mädchen. Correspondenz der Redaction', *Der Floh*, 14 January 1872.

49. Polizei-Ministerium. Bericht der k.k. Polizei-Direktion in Wien. AVA/II 2033/1866; AVA/II 2055/1866.
50. See, for example, 'H. Schm. Spiegelgasse', *Figaro*, 11 February 1882; 'J.J. Bräunerstraße', *Figaro*, 10 May 1884.
51. E.g. 'Rennweg', *Kikeriki*, 14 January 1864; 'A.F. Praterstrasse Nr. 26', *Kikeriki*, 28 March 1864; 'E.S. Josefstadt', *Der Floh*, 17 April 1870; 'Karl K. Westbahnstraße', *Kikeriki*, 11 March 1877; 'J.W. Nordwestbahnhof and A.T. Quellengasse', *Kikeriki*, 18 September 1879; 'Fritz H. Favoritenstraße', *Figaro*, 23 December 1882. See also John W. Boyer, *Political Radicalism in Late Imperial Vienna: Origins of the Christian Social Movement, 1848–1897* (Chicago, 1981), 257.
52. 'Max R. in Simmering', *Kikeriki*, 27 January 1876; 'Ein Ottakringer and A. Pt. in Simmering', *Kikeriki*, 16 September 1880; 'Fr. K. Simmering', *Figaro*, 2 April 1881; 'E.W. Ottakring', *Figaro*, 21 May 1881.
53. 'Was versteht man unter Phantasie? – Stadterweiterungsfrage', Philosophische Lehrkurse, *Figaro*, 17 May 1857.
54. See further Elisabeth Springer, *Geschichte und Kulturleben der Wiener Ringstraße* (Wiesbaden, 1979), 77–148.
55. Ibid., 116. The seven best plans were also published later in 1859 as a book called *Die preisgekrönten Entwürfe zur Erweiterung der inneren Stadt Wien* (1859), edited by the art historian Rudolf Eitelberger von Edelberg. On the planning process, see further Harald Robert Stühlinger, *Der Wettbewerb zur Wiener Ringstraße* (Ph.D. diss., Zürich, 2013).
56. Diese Betheiligung des Publicums ist begreiflich. Wer ist nicht begierig, zu sehen und durch die Besucher zu hören, wie Neu-Wien aussehen wird? – In welcher Weise wird die Hauptstadt eines Reiches, das vierzig Millionen bewohnen, ihren Ausbau vollenden? Wo wird die Stadt den Palast ihrer Repräsentanz hinstellen können? Wo werden wir Oper hören? Wie groß wird das neue Burg- und Operntheater werden? Wo werden wir künftig spazierenfahren, lustwandeln, uns an der Kühle der Springbrunnen im Sommer erquicken? Wo haben die Gelehrter die seltenen Bücher, die Kunstliebhaber die Werke der Kunst zu schauen, wo die Naturforscher ihre Steine, ihre getrockneten Pflanzen und ausgestopften Thiere? Wo werden unsere Hausfrauen Obst, Gemüse, Gänse und Hühner finden? Wo kann der Kaufmann den Reichtum des Lagers dem Publicum vor Auge legen? Wo kann der Fleischer und Zuckerbäcker sein Eis einlagern? Wo werden die Fiaker das Zickzack ihrer Fahrten abkürzen? Wo werden die Jungen Leuten tanzen und die Kinder spielen? Man sieht, alle sind in der Stadterweiterung betheiligt ... 'Ueber die Neugestaltung Wiens. II. Die Austellung der Concurrenzplane', *Die Presse*, 28 October 1858.

   See also Springer, *Geschichte und Kulturleben*, 119–20; Marianne Bernhard, *Die Wiener Ringstraße: Architektur und Gesellschaft 1858–1906* (Munich, 1992), 30.
57. See further Stühlinger, *Der Wettbewerb*, 9–16 and passim.
58. Dieser Plan mit der Motto: 'Sustine et abstine', sagte ich gestern zu einem Herrn im Austellungslocale, scheint mir ganz vorzüglich zu sein. / So, erwiderte er, sehen Sie nicht, daß er ganz unausführbar ist? / Warum? / Weil nach diesem Plane jenes Haus dort niedergerissen werden muß. / Was liegt an einem einzigen Haus? Fragte ich. / Herr, das ist mein Haus, sagte er, und verließ mich erzürnt ... 'Auf der Ausstellung der Konkurspläne für die Erweiterung der Stadt Wien', *Figaro*, 23 October 1858.
59. Schön ist das Einfache nur, Einfacheres also ist *schöner*, Also das Schönste geschieht, nämlich das Einfachste: *Nichts!* 'Glacis-Verschönerung', *Der Figaro*, 11 January 1857. Original emphasis.

60. See also, for example, 'Erbauliches', *Der Humorist*, 17 August 1857; 'Stadterweiterung', *Der Humorist*, 13 August 1857; 'Wiens Herz-Erweiterung', *Figaro*, 3 January 1858.
61. 'Stadterweiterungs-Aphorismen', *Figaro*, 27 August 1859; 'Von den neuen Ringstrasse', *Figaro*, 7 July 1860; 'Die neue Ringstraße', *Der Figaro*, 23 June 1860; 'Mehrere Kastanienbäume auf dem Glacis', *Figaro*, 22 September 1860.
62. See, for example, 'Tagesordnung', *Figaro*, 4 January 1857; 'Baurummel', *Der Figaro*, 3 January 1858.
63. My emphasis. 'Allerhöchstes Handbillet vom 20. December 1857 an Seine Excellenz den Minister des Innern Freiherrn v. Bach', *Wiener Zeitung*, 25 December 1857.
64. See further Carl E. Schorske, *Fin-de-siècle Vienna: Politics and Culture* (Cambridge, [1961] 1981), 29.
65. Springer, *Geschichte und Kulturleben*, 86–87.
66. 'Ueber die Neugestaltung Wiens. Supplement zu den 'St.' Artikeln der Presse', *Figaro*, 21 April 1858.
67. See, e.g., Rumpler, *Chance für Mitteleuropa*, 306.
68. Springer, *Geschichte und Kulturleben*, 119–21.
69. Polizei-Ministerium. Bericht der k.k. Polizei-Direktion in Wien. Eine Beschlagnahme der No 34 und 35 des 'Figaro' betreffend. AVA/II 2033/1866.
70. E.g. 'Folgen der Stadterweiterung', *Figaro*, 24 January 1858. See further Heidi Hakkarainen, 'Aus der Nähe betrachtet. Figaro: Folgen der Stadterweiterung, 1858', in Harald R. Stühlinger (ed.), *Vom Werden der Wiener Ringstraße* (Vienna, 2015), 244–45.
71. 'Ausstellung einiger Stadterweiterungspläne, die den ersten Preis *nicht* erhalten', *Figaro*, 30 October 1858. Original emphasis. Cf. 'Zopfenberger's Plan zur Stadterweiterung', *Der Humorist*, 2 November 1858.
72. See also Harald R. Stühlinger, 'Inundationen, miese Luft und wenig Wasser. Berichte über den Stadtzustand aus dem Wien von 1858', in Stühlinger, *Vom Werden der Wiener Ringstraße*, 32.
73. Cf. Simon Critchley, *On Humour* (New York, 2002), 111 and passim.
74. Peter Fritzsche, *Reading Berlin 1900* (Cambridge, MA, 1998); Vanessa R. Schwarz, *Spectacular Realities: Early Mass Culture in Fin-de-siècle Paris* (Berkeley, 1999).
75. Allerhöchst genehmigter Plan der Stadterweiterung (Vienna: K. k. Hof- und Staatsdruckerei, 1860). Schorske suggests that the female figures in the poster symbolize the new liberal bourgeois 'Recht und Kultur' ideology embedded in the urban space: on the left, the spirit of art is dressing the city of Vienna (*Geschmückt durch Kunst*), and on the right the figures embody law and peace (*Stark durch Gesetz und Frieden*). See further Schorske, *Fin-de-siècle Vienna*, 31–33.
76. Carl E. Schorske, *Thinking with History: Explorations in the Passage to Modernism* (Princeton, 1998), 109–11, 129.
77. See further Schorske, *Thinking with History*, 108.
78. See further Springer, *Geschichte und Kulturleben*, 85.
79. This shift in power relations within the empire resulted largely from failures in foreign policy, especially defeats against Italy (1859) and Prussia (1866). The reign of the Liberal Party lasted in national politics from 1861 to 1878, and in Vienna until 1895, when the Christian Social Party took over and Karl Lueger was elected mayor in 1897. See, e.g., Schorske *Fin-de-siècle Vienna*, 31.
80. The *Gemeindeordnung* was introduced in 1850, and from 1861 the liberal bourgeoisie gained a new impact on city policy.

81. Schorske, *Fin-de-siècle Vienna*, 24, 30–31. See also Pieter M. Judson, *The Habsburg Empire: A New History* (Cambridge, MA, 2016), 280–81.
82. Schorske, *Thinking with History*, 115.
83. Schorske, *Fin-de-siècle Vienna*, 25.
84. Ibid., 33–36.
85. Wolfgang Maderthaner, 'Von der Zeit um 1860 bis zum Jahr 1945', in Csendes and Oppl, *Wien – Geschichte einer Stadt*, 195–96, 190. See also Wolfgang Maderthaner and Lutz Musner, *Unruly Masses: The Other Side of the Fin-de-siècle Vienna* (New York, 2008), 2–5, 52–55; Boyer, *Political Radicalism*, 196.
86. See further Steven Beller, 'Introduction', in Steven Beller (ed.), *Rethinking Vienna 1900* (New York, 2001), 2–18.
87. Schorske, *Fin-de-siècle Vienna*, 33.
88. See further Boyer, *Political Radicalism*, passim.
89. See further Johnston, *Austrian Mind*, 63.
90. Springer, *Geschichte und Kulturleben*, 196.
91. Man spricht davon in unsern Kreisen, / Dass man ein würdiger Asyl / Dem Kaiserhaus errichten werde.– / Dass man die Burg erweitern will. // Und sicher wird sich Niemand finden, / Der dieser Ford'rung widerspricht, / Sie ist gerecht, des Reiches Größe / Entspricht die düstre Hofburg nicht. // Darum baut nur! Das Haus erhebe / Sich stattlich, würdig unserer Stadt, / Es sei ein stolzes Prachtgebäude, / Wie keines bisher die Hauptstadt hat. // Doch einen Wunsch mögt Ihr bedenken, / Den Lang das Volk im Innern begt,– / Worauf, – obgleich er leicht erfüllbar,– / Es großen Werth, – Bedeutung legt. // Es wünschte, dass des Kaisers Wohnung, / Wenn stolz sie sich zum Himmel hebt, / Nicht 'Burg' mehr heiße, – das derselben / Ihr einen andern Namen gebt. // Nicht Burg! – Bei dieses Namens Lauten / An 'Zwingburg' denken wir zu gern, / Absolutismus, Despotismus, / Sie grüßen uns daraus von fern! // Das will der Kaiser nicht! – Der Herrscher, / morsche Traditionen brach, / Der Keine Rücksicht nicht beachtend, / Die stolze Freiheitsworte sprach. // Der selbst zum Ausgleich seinen Völkern / Die Herrscherhand versöhnend hat, / Der hat in seines Volkes Mitte / Nicht einer Burg als wohnhaus Noth // Ihm ist die beste Burg die Liebe, / Die ihm sein Volk entgegen bringt, – / Des Volkes Treu' ist eine Mauer, / Die kein feindlicher Speer durchbringt. 'Zum Umbau der Hofburg', *Der Floh*, 13 June 1869.
92. Although the planning of the extension of the Hofburg started in the late 1860s, the new Burg was not completed until the 1920s.
93. Cf. Boyer, *Political Radicalism*, 29.
94. See also, e.g., 'Eine Interpellation an den Gemeinderath!', *Kikeriki*, 16 January 1862; 'Die neuen Strassenbenennunge', *Kikeriki*, 9 October 1862; 'Wir schlagen der löblichen Häusernumerirungs-Kommission des Gemeinderathes folgende zeitmäßige Gassenbenennungen vor', *Figaro*, 16 August 1862; 'Veränderte Wohnungen', *Kikeriki*, 7 January 1864; 'Vorschlag zu neuen Strassenbenennungen', *Kikeriki*, 13 April 1865; 'Die Wiener Gassen, Straßen und Plätze', *Kikeriki*, 23 September 1877.
95. See, e.g., 'Häuser, vor denen man davonlaufen soll', *Der Floh*, 1 August 1869; 'Bei den Grundsteinlegung des Rathhauses', *Kikeriki*, 22 June 1873; 'Bei Anblick der neuen öffentlichen Gebäude', *Kikeriki*, 5 October 1873; 'In neuen Räumen', *Figaro*, 10 November 1883.
96. So ist vollendet nun der stolze Bau aus Stein / Und aufgerichtet prächtig anzuschauen / Steht dieser Tempel, ein renderd Zeugniß da, / Wie man auf Kosten unserer

Stadterweiterung / Ein Theater baut für 'Blaues Blut' allein! ... 'Prolog zur Eröffnung der neuen Oper', *Der Floh*, 9 May 1869.

97. See, e.g., 'Unglücksfälle', *Kikeriki*, 28 February 1867; 'Unser neuster Bau', *Der Floh*, 6 June 1869; 'Kikeriki im Neuen Operhaus', *Kikeriki*, 13 May 1869; 'Neueste Opernhaus-Schnaderhüpferl', *Der Floh*, 23 May 1869; 'Die Eröffnung des neuen Opernhauses', *Der Floh*, 30 May 1869.
98. 'Sicardsburg und van der Null, sie haben keinen Styl, Griechis, Römisch, Renaissance, Ihnen ist alles aas.' Cited by Karlheinz Roschitz, *Kaiserwalzer: Traum und Wirklichkeit der Ringstrassenzeit* (Vienna, 1996), 60–61. See also Bernhard, *Wiener Ringstraße*, 23–33.
99. 'Wie es bei uns mit den Neubauten vorwärts geht', *Kikeriki*, 10 June 1869.
100. 'Veränderungen in der Ausschmückung des neuen Burgtheaters', *Kikeriki*, 1 November 1888.
101. E.g. 'Architektonische Gegensätze', *Kikeriki*, 11 May 1879; 'Ein Gedenkblatt zum Abschied Wilbrands', *Der Floh*, 3 July 1887; 'Volkstheater', *Der Floh*, 29 April 1888; *Figaro*, 23 January 1886.
102. 'Lage der Öffentlichen Gebäude', *Kikeriki*, 23 January 1868.
103. David Harvey, *Paris, Capital of Modernity* (New York, 2006), 18.
104. Johnston, *Austrian Mind*, 63.
105. Boyer, *Political Radicalism*, 13, 15–16.
106. Maderthaner, 'Von der Zeit', 194–215. See also Allan Janik, 'Vienna 1900 Revisited: Paradigms and Problems', in Beller, *Rethinking Vienna 1900*, 34.
107. See, e.g., 'Moderne Architektur oder Verzweiflung eines Hausherrn von der Ringstraße', *Kikeriki*, 6 February 1871; 'Die Baugesellschaften und die Wohnungsnoth', *Kikeriki*, 25 December 1871.
108. *Kikeriki*, especially, attacked the City Council vigorously and criticized it for not being up to date with its task, managing the city. After publishing the humorous magazine for a decade, the Editor-in-Chief of *Kikeriki*, O.F. Berg, ran for the City Council, and was elected in 1870.
109. Schorske, *Thinking with History*, 109.
110. See, e.g., 'Die Demolierungswuth der Stadtverschönerer', *Kikeriki*, 10 May 1877; 'Das Ei des Kolumbus und unsere Stadtverschönerer', *Kikeriki*, 17 May 1877; 'Wienflussgegend – Phantasie und Wirklichkeit', *Kikeriki*, 8 December 1887.
111. 'Wie sie die Gehwege am Exerzierplatz praktisch angelegt haben', *Kikeriki*, 1 October 1863; 'Situations-Plan', *Kikeriki*, 29 September 1864; 'Die neue Stellwagen–Ordnung', *Kikeriki*, 1 June 1865.
112. Maderthaner, 'Von der Zeit', 194–96; Springer, *Geschichte und Kulturleben*, 162–63.
113. See further Boyer, *Political Radicalism*, xi, 1, 3–4.
114. 'Beweis, daß nicht blos Doktoren, sondern auch schlichte Bürger gute Einfälle haben', *Kikeriki*, 5 June 1881.
115. Cf. Jürgen Habermas, *Strukturwandel der Öffentlichkeit: Untersuchungen zu einer Kategorie der bürgerlichen Gesellschaft* (Neuwied am Rhein, 1965), 63–68.

Chapter 2

TENSIONS WITH CITY AUTHORITIES

Resisting Order

Rebellion against the control of the city authorities was visible in many ways in the Viennese *Witzblätter*. The humorous texts and cartoons often depicted comical encounters between authority figures and mischievous citizens. For example, in a poem called 'Ballad of the Street' ('Ballade von der Strasse'), published in *Der Floh* in 1884, a man is walking his little dog on the street. The dog is not wearing his muzzle, which is causing the man serious concern, and both of them are trying to escape the eyes of the street watchman:

> A little doggie creeps down the street,
> Looking distinctly troubled;
> A dejected gentleman follows behind –
> And a watchman follows them both.
>
> The dog is not wearing his muzzle,
> And that's what bothers his master;
> They both would like to escape
> The watchful eye of the guard.
>
> But alas, he is already in front of them,
> Frowning into his notebook;
> He writes down the doggie's address,
> And look – the gentleman's furious![1]

The speaker in the poem is watching this incident on the street as it were from a distance, dispassionately observing the emotions of the dog owner, which shift from despondency because his dog isn't wearing its muzzle, to fury when the watchman writes a report in his notebook. The watchman's officious enforcement of the regulations – against the dog – abruptly transforms the man's timid anxiety into anger. The very last word, 'furious' (*wüthend*) is the punchline: it unleashes the tension built up in the first two verses and reverses the emotions in the confrontation.[2] Alternatively, the ending can be interpreted from another angle: the man, previously discouraged and fearful, trying to escape the watchman's eye, now suddenly becomes angry when the watchman punishes his dog instead of paying attention to him, the animal's master. In any case, the feeling of anger and a sense of oppression play a vital role in this example, depicting a trivial incident from the streets of 1880s Vienna. The 'Ballad of the Street' is thus a good example of how humour relates not only to reason and intellect, but to emotions as well. In fact, emotions seem to play a vital role in humour relating to the new constraints of modernization.

Recent discussion on humour and laughter has increasingly paid attention to the relationship between humour and emotions such as aggression and anxiety. Scholars like Michael Billig and Daniel Wickberg have criticized humour research for overemphasizing the positive aspects of humour and neglecting the fact that humour often gains its power from the 'less worthy emotions', whereas it is precisely the negative feelings such as superiority, aggression, fears and anxieties that lie at the base of humour.[3]

Although early superiority theories already paid attention to the emotional ambiguity behind humour and laughter, the modern emphasis on the aggressive element of humour derives especially from Sigmund Freud's influence on humour studies. Freud emphasized the role of the nineteenth-century bourgeois culture of his time as a social force that affected the ways in which jokes worked in society. He argued that because modern social life would not function without constraint, the aggressive and sexual instincts that endangered social life had to be hidden and masked as something else. Freud saw jokes as a way of disguising inappropriate feelings such as aggression and expressing them in a more acceptable form. For Freud, this element of disguise was crucial. Jokes were a way to disguise inappropriate feelings and wishes not only from society, but from the self as well.[4]

Moreover, Freud developed his ideas about the relationship between humour and constraint even further by arguing that humour can be tendentious or non-tendentious, meaning that some jokes have a target or a purpose, while others exist simply for their own sake. Freud identifies three categories of tendentious jokes (*der tendenziöse Witz*): exposing or obscene jokes, aggressive (hostile) jokes, and cynical jokes. The aggressive type of tendentious joke, suggests Freud, functions especially as a means of rebellion and expressing critique towards those persons or institutions that have superior status or authority over others. The pleasure of joking lies in the brief escape from the constraint. In providing a means to criticize those in power, the aggressive tendentious joke thus offers emotional relief from the pressure of their authority.[5]

Freud's ideas pinpoint the important connection between satirical aggressive humour and the authoritarian culture of late nineteenth-century Vienna. As noted in the previous chapter, the humorous magazines saw the purpose of their satire as aiming to improve society by speaking the truth and exposing social ills and errors, one of which was the authoritarian control exercised by the authorities. The Viennese *Witzblätter* often targeted the city authorities as the butt of their humour when they criticized modern urban life for excessive constraint and the loss of citizens' freedom. *Kikeriki*, in particular, used the prohibition sign in its cartoons, in order to visualize the citizens' confrontation with the rules of the city.[6] In *Kikeriki* the prohibition signs both symbolized and were the rules, reminding people of the proper way to behave in the city space. These authoritarian messages were ridiculed in both cartoons and humorous texts. For example, in a cartoon published in 1863, the modern Adam is surrounded by the prohibition signs of the city: 'Adam had to observe only a single ban, and even this he transgressed. What would happen to him nowadays, where almost everything is forbidden?'[7]

Notably, in humorous representations the prohibition signs were often met with negative emotional responses, such as fear and anger. *Kikeriki*'s often repeated argument seemed to be that although rules may be a necessary evil in urban life, an excessive regime of over-authoritarian prohibitions deprives the citizens of their city, both physically and mentally.

From this point of view, popular humour offered a central means of negotiating the newly emerging boundaries of control and constraint in a modern society. Modernity meant not just the rationalization of space, but of living in that space as well. As the size of the population increased in the capital of the Habsburg Empire, more and more rules and regulations were introduced, with the aim of managing the urban masses and making life in the city better functioning and more controlled.

Next I will discuss two aspects of resistance to order that seem crucial for understanding the experience of modernity in the late nineteenth-century Viennese context. First of all, in the deeply authoritarian culture of the Habsburg Empire, resisting order and control by making fun of the authorities and their rules was not just a liberating act of rebellion, but also served as a means to express social critique in a situation where press freedom and the new structures of civil society were still under construction. Second, I would like to argue that, on a deeper level, humour expressed anxiety relating to the experience of becoming a member of an urban mass pervasively controlled by standards, rules and regulations.

Ridiculing the Police

It is striking how many jokes and cartoons in the *Witzblätter* relate to the police, street watchmen and other authority figures who were supervising and controlling everyday life in late nineteenth-century Vienna.[8] There was a huge number of jokes about the police officers and watchmen who tried to keep order in the city. Jokes about over-eager post office clerks and other civil servants were also popular among the Viennese middle classes.[9] This ridicule of the police and other authority figures was a reaction to the authoritarian culture in the Habsburg Empire, and it reveals the heavy frustration lying behind the highly bureaucratic Austrian society.

It is important to note that the police institution, especially, was an internal part of the repressive social structures that dated from the era of neo-absolutism. The Austrian police institutions underwent many changes between 1857 and 1890. At the local level, the police evolved from a military organization (*Militär-Wache*) into a civil institution (*k.k. Sicherheitswache*). In the *Gemeindeordnung* (1850) and *Reichsgemeindegesetz* (1862), the authority of the police was divided between two levels: the State Police (*Staatspolizei*), responsible for the security of the state, and the municipally governed regional forces (*Lokalpolizei*), who took care of local problems, such as crime and general security, and the maintenance of streets and other urban places. The local police in Vienna were in charge of traffic safety, preventing indecency, monitoring food supplies, taking care of the poor, and dealing with fires and accidents – even giving first aid.[10] The local police were thus a major presence in everyday Viennese life, enforcing the municipal laws in the city. Yet, because Vienna was first and foremost the capital city, and the residence of the Emperor, the State Police and military guards were in many ways visible in the city as well, although slowly losing their grip on parts of it as the old fortifications were torn down.[11]

Humorous scenes often portrayed rebellion against the authority of the police. Many jokes and cartoons pictured a situation where a watchman or police officer encounters citizens who are somehow violating order: by being drunk, walking on the grass, entering places they should not enter, or otherwise behaving improperly.[12] In most cases it is the officious and petty attitude of the authorities that is made the laughing stock: in vain the police and the city watchmen try to control everything that cannot be controlled.

For example, in a cartoon published in *Kikeriki* in 1865, a police officer is trying to keep the citizens from walking on the grass lawns next to the Ringstraße (Figure 2.1). His futile struggle is visualized by stretching and scattering his body as if he were about to explode in the effort to catch all the unruly citizens who are taking a short cut across the grass instead of walking along the footway as they should.[13] The perspective is, again, a distanced view from above. The police officer's struggle is seen from a bird's eye view, which makes the viewer

Figure 2.1 Police officer in Josefstädter Exerzierplatz. *Kikeriki*, 25 May 1865. Source: Austrian National Library.

all-knowing. Yet the bourgeois panoptic gaze[14] is not simple or coherent here; the cartoon plays with the gaze of the reader, as he or she has to turn over the page in order to piece together the fragmented body of the police officer.

Importantly, the place, Josefstädter Exerzierplatz, is pictured in this cartoon to the last detail: the names of the streets and buildings surrounding it are marked on the picture as if it were an official blueprint or plan. All this makes the joke very concrete. The joke is placed in a specific location in Vienna, and it comments on the use of this place. The cartoon thus does not make fun of the police in Vienna in general, but comments directly on the situation in the Josefstädter Exerzierplatz.

The Exerzierplatz, which later became the site for the Vienna City Hall (*Rathaus*) and new university building, belonged for a long time to the army,[15] which associates the site with authority and potential violence. The Exerzierplatz was used as a park for citizens in the 1860s, and *Kikeriki* often situated jokes on it, for example making fun of the impractical way in which the paths were arranged, which made it more than tempting to take a short cut over the grass.[16]

The example of the Josefstädter Exerzierplatz shows how humour often arises where it should not emerge, and comicality tends to relate to topics that are somehow inappropriate as a target of humour. 'We take pleasure', suggests Billig, 'at mocking things that should not be mocked'.[17] In this way, both acknowledging what is too serious and valuable to be laughed at, and yet laughing at it, humour both recognizes and challenges the limits of the prevailing order.[18] Joking about the police on the Josefstädter Exerzierplatz simultaneously represents a symbolic rebellion against the prevailing order, and the comic relief offered by these jokes is a response to the repression associated with the Exerzierplatz as a place and the military police as an institution. Jokes about the police thus reveal the heavy frustration that was boiling beneath the surface of politically and socially suppressed Austrian society in the 1860s.

This frustration had its roots, of course, well before the *Gründerzeit*, and it is important to note that there was a long tradition in Vienna of ridiculing the police in satirical songs and cartoons.[19] For example, a flyer called 'Policey-Ordnung' from 1672 mocked the police with subtle yet sharp irony, imitating the dignified and authoritarian discourse of the establishment in order to cloak discontent and hostility in words of praise.[20] The era of the *Vormärz* and the violence of the 1848 revolution raised intense resistance and hostility towards the military troops founded to fulfil the task of maintaining public peace and order in the monarchy.[21] Following the revolution, the *Militär-Polizeiwache* was a hated organization, the executor of state violence, which made house searches for weapons and forbidden publications and arrested those suspected of revolutionary activities.[22] The civilian *Sicherheitswache* (1869–1918) was the direct successor to the *Militär-Polizeiwache*, and its task continued to be the maintenance of the prevailing order and power relations in society.

In the case of the *Sicherheitswache*, the long tradition of state violence and political and social repression made the humour more aggressive, turning it away from playful banter to ridicule, which is often seen as a form of humour expressing hostility and serving as a means of social punishment.[23] Much of the *Witzblätter* material relating to the authorities falls into the category of ridicule. The late nineteenth-century humourists were aware of this hidden aggressive element in popular humour. O.F. Berg, for example, pointed out that there was a fine line between resisting order with laughter and potential violence. For instance, a note from Berg's *Kikeriki Diary* from 1870 reports an incident in the city when the crowd surrounding the *Sicherheitswache* on the Exerzierplatz starts to laugh at the police:

> For on this day, the Watch at the Exerzierplatz was laughed at and ridiculed by some people who had gathered there. The guardians of order were led to believe that they would face a tremendous beating if they were to try to intervene. A miserable experience, indeed. Many of those gentlemen who had gathered to pursue new, liberal laws, demonstrated that they have no respect for the old ones. They seek intellectual rights, and proclaim at the same time the law of the jungle! Fortunately, the healthy core of our workers took no part in the mockery of those men assigned for the protection of property and person, in the name of order and safety.[24]

The fact that, although the *Sicherheitswache* was a recurrent laughing stock in the *Witzblätter* such as O.F. Berg's *Kikeriki*, it was still seen as thoughtless and dangerous to actually challenge it – and the order it stood for – reveals the multifaceted and ambivalent nature of Viennese middle-class popular humour. As Michael Billig reminds us, rebellious humour might not necessarily have rebellious consequences, and can even have a disciplinary effect. Humour that might at first seem rebellious, subverting the serious world, might actually strengthen it. Billig refers to studies that find that jokes about powerful authority, for example in totalitarian regimes, may give an impression of rebellion, whereas they do not prevent living according to the rules and obeying the system. Feeling freed from the rules by laughter, people actually become more bound to them.[25] Here Billig comes close to the view of many relief theorists, who see the social function of humour as a safety valve. The very idea that humour gives the impression of undermining the prevailing order and challenging the authorities makes it a perfect tool for letting off steam, whereas the reality does not actually change.[26] Billig suggests that the mechanism of jokes is not based on letting out excess energy in order to release pressure in the system, but that the relief of rebellious joking comes from self-persuasion, when a clear conscience is achieved although nothing is actually risked. The popular humour of the Viennese middle classes was not intended actually to break the prevailing order, but to take pleasure in an act of resistance on an imaginary level.[27] The city of jokes was an imaginary city, a world upside down, in which it was possible to do and say things that were otherwise impossible or prohibited. In their imaginary encounters with the authorities, the subjects of control could have the last word, as in this example in which a laundry girl (*Waschmädl*) replies to the street watchman who objects to her pulling her cart on the pedestrian footway: 'Should I take a proper cab for my laundry instead?'[28] Carping at authority without actually resisting it, suggests William M. Johnston, was typical of late nineteenth-century Austrian culture.[29] The bourgeois *Witzblätter* were an important forum for ventilating dissent from and dissatisfaction with the authorities, but ultimately they did not challenge them. Resisting order in popular humour was, above all, an imaginative resistance, based on creating a boundary between the serious world and the world of humour.[30]

The world of humour, the Vienna imagined and portrayed in the *Witzblätter*, effectively resembled the scenery in a play, a comedy. It is revealing that the same kinds of characters, such as watchmen and police officers, appeared in the humorous magazines as in Viennese nineteenth-century theatre comedies.[31] A long tradition of fiction was constantly referenced and reawakened in the humorous publications, and this discursive tradition needs to be included in the framework in which the imaginary acts of ridiculing authority figures took place. Making fun of the authorities was at least potentially funny because it enabled the expression of aggression and frustration in a conventional, socially accepted way. The separation of the realm of the comical and the realm of the serious meant that resisting authorities was liberating, not because it was tolerated, but because it was prohibited and not possible in real life. Crossing boundaries in the world of humour did not mean that the boundaries were crossed in real life. However, the imaginary world of humour and the world of 'serious' reality were interconnected, but in a more complex way, and the humorous visions of resisting order did not just spring from the historical social reality but also actively shaped it, as the old authorities were challenged and undermined in contemporary popular culture. Ridicule of the police was symbolical resistance that attacked the authority figures on the plane of imagination. In this way, popular jokes and cartoons continuously tested sociocultural borders and practices in late nineteenth-century Vienna.

Rules, Regulations and the Standardization of Life

Resisting order meant more than resisting authority figures such as street watchmen and the police. They were merely the messenger, not the message. What was more unsettling was the internalizing of the disciplinary voice of authority.[32] Deep down, the humour seems to have been resisting a much more abstract and faceless standardization of life, which was part of the modernization process. The uncertainty caused by the new scrupulousness and punctiliousness that characterized modern life came out in the humour in many ways. For example, in one satirical text *Kikeriki* complained that passengers on the horse tramway who were lucky enough to get a seat were allowed to take with them as many packets as they liked, but those unfortunate ones who were forced to stand could not take packets with them, or would have to pay ten Kreuzer if they wished to do so. *Kikeriki* suggested ironically that in future other additional fees should be introduced, and provided a very precise price list stating how much extra passengers should pay if they brought an umbrella or smoked cigars or read papers during the ride.[33]

One of the new regulations, requiring dogs to be kept on a leash and muzzled, appeared frequently in the *Witzblätter*, as in *Der Floh*'s poem 'Ballad of the Street'. The constraint of dogs probably had symbolic elements, as the animals were often used to symbolize the people, and the muzzle was also an allegory for censorship.[34] Due to these symbolic aspects, the dog issue became a prime example of how the city government was trying to affect the individual lives of citizens and steal their freedom. For example, the humorous text shown in Figure 2.2 commented on the hunt for stray dogs in the city, which had taken on a massive scale; according to the magazine, sixteen thousand dog catchers were hunting down all the stray dogs in Vienna, and at the same time, pet dogs were also coming under stricter regulation. The magazine suggested new solutions for walking dogs: armour with a helmet that could be opened only after returning indoors, and special 'kites' for flying the dogs instead of walking them.[35]

The humour about the city's regulations for dogs is just one example of the many jokes and cartoons that dealt with the growing number of rules and regulations governing life in the city.[36] In many cases, the rules and regulation were used as subtexts, and the language of the authorities was parodied by taking it to ridiculous extremes.[37] The strategy of exaggeration was often adopted to highlight the absurdity of modern life, full of arbitrary rules and regulations, in this way suggesting that it was the rules and regulations that made the world absurd.[38]

The humour about the dog regulations is also a good example of how modernization was not something abstract or straightforward, but a complex process that affected the everyday lives of people in the city in multiple ways. The Viennese encountered modernity on the grassroots level of everyday experience as daily life in the city became more and more structured by the modern bureaucracy of city government.[39] A great number of new rules for the regulating of urban life were introduced during the *Gründerzeit*, and by the turn of the century directives and statutes existed for how to use the streets, how to deal with garbage, how to build new houses or plant new trees.[40] Ironically, it was the bourgeoisie itself which promoted the idea of law (*Gesetz*) as a foundation of modern civil society, instead of absolutist rule. Yet at the same time as the liberal bourgeoisie were succeeding in establishing the rule of law in both state and city government,[41] in their humour they expressed a certain uneasiness about this new way of life secured and controlled by regulation and legislation.

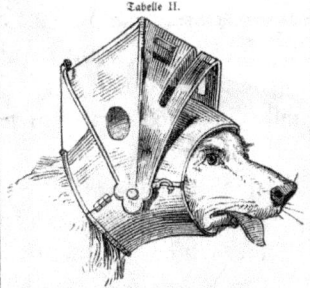
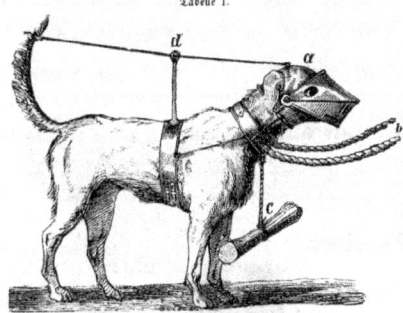

Figure 2.2 New regulations for dogs. *Kikeriki*, 23 October 1862. Source: Austrian National Library.

Humour relating to the new rules and regulations reveals how the modernization process involved a correspondence between radical shifts in society and culture and the inner mental processes of contemporaries living in this changing world. As Marshall Berman and other scholars of modernity have pointed out, the modernization of the late nineteenth-century cities also changed the inner worlds of their citizens, and the contradictions of the modern world resonated in the inner lives of contemporaries. Simultaneously, at the same time as the modern self was being shaped by vast social and political processes in the emergence of civil societies, nation states, mass political parties and modern print culture, the turn-of-the-century high culture retreated increasingly into the psyche, focusing on the inner worlds of the individual rather than social processes.[42] As Carl E. Schorske has suggested, rational man gave place to psychological man.[43]

From a cultural historical point of view, it seems crucial that jokes about resisting order came into existence in a specific historical and cultural context, and are not totally explained merely by hidden psychological sources; the inner processes of the mind are always interconnected with those changes in the outer world. I share the view of many historians and social scientists that humour is at root based on culture and society rather than the unconscious mind.[44] Instead of juxtaposing the inner self and culture, it would probably be more fruitful to ask how human beings react to the demands of the shared and social world at different points in time, and how they negotiate their place within the dynamic realms of culture. Moreover, if culture is understood as a way in which people create meanings for themselves, others and the world surrounding them,[45] humour can be seen as one way of exploring the constantly changing relationship between the self and the world.

In late nineteenth-century Vienna, constraint was a significant aspect of this relationship, associated with the new, contemporary or modern mores of urban life. The element of constraint emerged in many ways, often more implied than explicitly discussed. For instance, the cartoon from 1888 shown in Figure 2.3 comments on the news that the municipal authorities were planning to impose a new tax on signboards using the city airspace. *Kikeriki* was ready to take this initiative further in order to save the city from its financial misery:

> ... *Kikeriki* suggests that the air for the residents themselves should be taxed as well. That could certainly lift with one blow the financial plight of the city. I beg your pardon? This cannot be carried out? You are mistaken! It's quite easy! One would simply have to order the population to equip themselves with helmets, like divers in the sea. Everyone carries on his back a reservoir with his taxed ration of air – and a meter. Anyone found without this apparatus on the street is arrested as a tax dodger.[46]

The critique here is aimed in the first instance at the city collecting taxes from its citizens, and the strategy of exaggeration is again used to create a comic effect.[47] However, the cartoon, in which a whole bourgeois family is wearing air helmets, inhaling air that is taxed and measured precisely for their consumption, seems to express a more serious concern about and rebellion against becoming mere subjects of the city government, members of a law-abiding, tax-paying, anonymous urban crowd.

It seems that on many occasions the jokes about rules and regulations were a way of manifesting individuality. In this way resisting rules and regulations in popular humour often represented the individual's struggle against being a part of an urban mass.[48] Rules and regulations intended to improve life in the city, by controlling its growing population, shaped the everyday experiences of the

Figure 2.3 'A new method for taxing'. *Kikeriki*, 13 May 1888. Source: Austrian National Library.

Viennese in a deeply constitutive way, emphasizing the role of the citizen as part of a larger mass community rather than as an individual.

The rules and regulations were a way of teaching the individual to be part of modern society. The gradual but pervasive shift to modern society preoccupied contemporaries, who in arts and science tried to grasp and elaborate the far-reaching consequences of the changes of their own time. One of these endeavours was the new urban sociology, which explored how the urban environment affected social life.

Turn-of-the-century sociologists such as Ferdinand Tönnies (1855–1936) and Georg Simmel (1858–1918) emphasized the significance of urbanization for the emergence of a new kind of modern social interaction. In the 1880s, Tönnies formulated his famous distinction between *Gemeinschaft* and *Gesellschaft*, juxtaposing the new urban social structures with those of the vanishing traditional rural communities.[49] In the modern *Gesellschaft*, said Tönnies, the traditional bonds between individuals are broken; they are part of a rationally functioning society, but not of a community. This image of broken ties permeated turn-of-the-century discussions of the new urban way of life, often described in terms of growing anonymity, dispersal and 'atomization' of society.[50] Rules and regulations held this scattered society together and made it function. For example, Georg Simmel wrote in his famous essay *The Metropolis and Mental Life* how the large scale of metropolitan life requires accuracy, calculability and precision. Everything must be measurable, which prioritizes standardization over individuality.[51]

This tension between standardization and individuality was implicit in the background of many jokes dealing comically with the punctuality and regularity of city life. For example, in the text 'An important telegraph exchange between Frankfurt and Berlin', published in *Figaro* in 1858, the technological innovations serve no purpose but the exchange of trivialities: 'Berlin. (8 ¾ o'clock), slept badly (5 min. to 10 o'clock), nice weather today (¼ to 11 o'clock), painful corns, (15 min. later) fried cod for lunch'.[52] In this example, life has become both more exact and less meaningful. This humour about modern punctuality seems to suggest that the world was losing diversity and substance as the new technology made it smaller and more accessible.[53]

The theme of standardization was explicitly discussed in humour. For example, in 1884 *Der Floh* published this humorous text, an imaginary diary from the twentieth century written by an ordinary 'normal man':

> The normal human being (a diary from the 20th century) on 1 June.
> After I had slept normally during the eight-hour normal night's sleep, at the normal time, 7 o'clock in the morning, I left my normal bed, washed myself in the normal manner with normal soap, then clad myself in my normal underwear and my normal clothes and sat down, together with my standard four-person normal family, to the state-determined normal breakfast, which consisted of a cup of normal coffee and a normal bread roll. As normal, within a quarter of an hour, the meal was finished. Our normal maid, who at this time began her eleven-hour normal working day, cleared the table, cleaned the normal furniture and finally took my little son to the new normal school …[54]

After a normal day at work, the 'normal man' and his wife go to see a normal operetta full of normal nonsense, and get bored as usual. However, after returning home the wife falls abnormally ill and a doctor is called. The ordinary man ends his notes in the diary with a regretful acknowledgement that in order to be true to his nature and normal way of life, he will be forced to leave his wife if she does not recover in the normal time of nine days, five hours and twenty minutes.

Clearly, the text expresses ridicule of the political demands by the early Social Democrats for regulated working hours and a school system, which were current demands in the 1880s when this text was published. However, it also seems to express a deeper uneasiness about the norms and standards that permeate all aspects of life, from clothing to the arts and work. Furthermore, through the standardization of society, the individual is so radically changed that the men of the future have lost their humanity in obeying the rules and norms of modern life.

This text in *Der Floh* was only one example of many texts and pictures dealing with the standardization of modern life. One aspect of life where standardization was seen to manifest itself especially visibly was the city space, and many cartoons mocked the urban renewal for creating tedious (*langweilig*) places that all looked the same.[55] What is common to all these different kinds of humorous texts and images is that they saw standardization as a threat to individuality, and set out to unveil how cultural levelling was insidiously penetrating everyday life and thus slowly altering the way people think and act. Furthermore, this critique of norms and standards is based on the ability of humour to defamiliarize the familiar:[56] the life of the 'normal man' is presented as so normal that it becomes weird. The certainty of the normal is undermined by repetition and exaggeration, which shakes the basic presumptions of what is in the end normal.

This creative shaking of mental patterns was used not just as a way of exposing standardization but of resisting it as well. Jo Ann Mitchell Fuess has suggested in her study on the Viennese humourist Friedrich Schlögl (1821–92), who wrote for *Figaro* and edited the *Wiener Luft* supplement from 1876 onwards, that Schlögl saw humour as a counterbalance to the cultural standardization and levelling processes of his own time. Schlögl sees the ongoing cultural levelling (*Verflachung*) that resulted from the stiff and repressive official culture as signalling the loss of the individual and the future vitality of Viennese culture. Schlögl's point of view was nostalgic and reactionary; he saw humour as a bridge to the past, a way of reviving and maintaining the originality and creativity of Viennese intellectual potential by evoking people's wit and imagination.[57]

Thus, resisting rules and standardization through a framework of humour was meaningful because humour itself was seen as a counterforce to the cultural levelling of thought and action. Rising above the rules and regulations on the plane of fantasy was not mere escapism, but an act of wit and imagination. Furthermore, if wit and imagination were the very essence of the Viennese identity, then resisting order in humour was meaningful even if only imaginary. The creative and innovative potential of humour was based on the very act of shaking traditional patterns of thought and routines of thinking.[58] Humour, in this sense, was seen as a source of mental flexibility that challenged the standardization of life.

In the nineteenth century, this emphasis on humour's link to mental and social flexibility was actually a characteristic way of perceiving and evaluating humour. William Hazlitt (1778–1830) wrote that wit was the imagination inverted, testing the boundaries of knowledge. Arthur Schopenhauer (1788–1860) saw that witticisms juxtaposed different real objects and that the source of the ludicrous was always paradoxical, reflecting conflict between what is thought and what is perceived, and correcting over-rigid abstract categories of thought.[59] Perhaps the most famous idea, however, was the French philosopher Henri Bergson's (1859–1941), that humour and laughter were a way of resisting the mechanization of life and domination of rational thought, which, he argued, made people handle their new experiences in a rigid way, according to repeated familiar concepts. For Bergson, laughter was in the first place a social punishment, which aimed at maintaining the flexibility of society.[60]

In Viennese middle-class popular humour, the aggression and anxiety caused by the prevailing order were often turned into creativity, an imaginative flexibility that found ways to overcome the boundaries of control on the plane of fantasy. In the humorous visions, the imagination often transcended the limits of urban life and challenged the established order by creating solutions to existing situations that were otherwise impossible to change or impact.

In many cases these humorous fantasies of resisting order and control utilized a concrete motif of transcending the demands of the social world and looking at the city from high above, from a distanced perspective.[61] Although the limits of order in the city were challenged only on an imaginary level, it was not meaningless. The plane of fantasy was, in fact, a radical way of commenting on the shared social world, because it did not take it as it was, but suggested how it could be otherwise. The philosopher Simon Critchley has claimed that 'jokes, like fantasies and dreams, are acts of abstraction or distancing from ordinary life that reveal the shared structures of a common life-world'.[62] Late nineteenth-century popular Viennese humour thus reveals the shared 'stock of knowledge' and everyday practices that constituted the structures of their culture. Furthermore, suggests Critchley, humour contains a dynamic, creative element, because it does not merely reveal the structures of culture, but indicates how these structures could be improved or transformed.[63]

The historian Joan Wallach Scott has pointed out that modern historiography tends to look at the past according to an ideal of human rationality, thus ignoring the fantasies that have been an integral part of the ways in which the people of the past made sense of their world. Fantasy, like humour, is employed especially when encountering things that cannot otherwise be defined or understood. Furthermore, Scott reminds us that historical research itself has been coloured by fantasies that guide our understanding of history. Instead of denying or neglecting the role of fantasy in creating and understanding history, Scott argues, it should be taken into better consideration, and employed as a tool for historical research.[64]

When looking at the popular humour of the Viennese bourgeoisie, it is clear that fantasies and imagination were an integral part of experiencing the city. The plane of fantasy enabled them to deal with change in the city, and moreover made it possible to deal with things that were hard to define or understand rationally. Transcending the city by wit and imagination meant also transcending the rules and regulations that governed life in the city, by free mental leaps and jolts. Whereas exposure of the norms, rules and regulations was based on defamiliarization of the familiar, the overcoming of these rules often involved familiarization of the unfamiliar. In the imaginative city of jokes, it was perfectly normal to fly dogs as kites, inhale taxed air in a helmet or see an exploding policeman.

Yet the tensions with city authorities in the middle-class *Witzblätter* involved not just ridicule of the police and rebellion against rules and regulations that governed life in the city. Viennese late nineteenth-century popular humour did not just express a need to resist order but it also proclaimed a desire for order, punishment for violating rules or creating confusion and chaos in the city. Resisting order and desiring order, rebellion and discipline, were thus two sides of the same coin, mutually constructed in the bourgeois imagination. This major paradox in Viennese popular humour could be explained by the contradictory and inconsistent nature of modern urban life itself, which meant a perpetual struggle between order and disorder rather than the harmonious union of different elements of urban experience.[65]

Desiring Order

Despite the rebellious aspects of middle-class popular humour discussed in the previous part of this chapter, it was not that the bourgeoisie did not want order in city space; they just wanted better order. This desire was expressed by means of satire. The humorous magazines often dealt with various kinds of disruptions and problems in urban life: too dim gas light, crowds and traffic, accidents, lack of housing, collapsing houses and an unsafe urban environment.[66] The satirical humour had a clear target and a motive. The aim was to improve the city by criticizing the sources of disorder and punishing them with mockery and ridicule.[67] *Kikeriki*, especially, adopted an aggressive counterposition in municipal politics from the 1860s to the 1880s.[68] The main culprits of the disorder were seen as the City Council, failing to run the city in a proper way, and the new urban entrepreneurs, who were sacrificing the common good and safety just to make big profits.

The sense of increasing unmanageability of the city was related in the first place to the accelerating breakthrough of modern capitalism, as the liberals took charge in the City Council in the 1860s.[69] The social historian Wolfgang Maderthaner has drawn attention to how selective the liberal city fathers were in shaping the modern Vienna. They invested time and money in enterprises that were in their own interest and left those aspects of urbanization that did not fit into their own goals in the hands of the capitalist markets. What the liberals cared about, when creating their political legacy and self-image, were the monumental buildings on the Ringstraße, the improvement of hygiene, and education. The issues that were seen as less important in terms of political symbolic value, such as housing, traffic and the supply of gas for the lighting of the city, were solely in the hands of the free markets.[70]

Perhaps due to this arrangement, the aspects of the transformation of the city that were most affected by modern capitalism were also those repeatedly criticized in popular humour as chaotic and dysfunctional. As the previous discussion shows, middle-class popular humour had various functions and tendencies in late nineteenth-century Vienna, depending on the particular contexts in which the humour was used and interpreted. Censorship, political power relations and the highly exclusive electoral franchise, together with publicity in the press, formed a significant framework for satirical and disciplinary humour against the municipal decision makers. Ridicule of the City Council was a major feature of how the transformation of city space was discussed in the *Witzblätter* during the urban renewal between 1857 and 1890.

By focusing on the satirical critique of the liberal City Council, my aim is to continue the analysis of the dynamics and tension between resisting and desiring order, which is the topic of this chapter. The desire for order was intertwined with ideas of punishment and superiority, but rather than a sense of agency and potency, the satirical attacks seem to have their roots in a need for strong authority, which would protect citizens from the dangerous and uncontrollable city. Consequently, both rebellious humour and disciplinary humour originated from and were defined by the relation to the authorities, and their interdependent paradoxical existence reveals the Viennese *Bürgers*' contradictory relationship to the authoritarian culture of Vienna, which played an extensive role in shaping and conducting the late nineteenth-century urban experience.

Satirical Attacks against the City Council

The Viennese *Witzblätter* repeatedly demanded that the city fathers of the City Council should establish better order in the city and control and regulate the wild and uncontrollable capitalism. Popular humour adopted a significant disciplinary function, as it was used to criticize social ills and improve the city. It is important to note that the City Council was the organ on which the middle classes themselves had the most influence, although the majority of the population were excluded from participation in municipal politics. Consequently, the ridicule aimed at the City Council reveals that humour had much to do with internal discussion within the Viennese *Bürgertum*. What emerges as the main reason for ridicule is the idea that the representatives of the City Council seemed incapable of establishing better control in the city.[71] Often, the City Council and city fathers were publicly mocked in appeals for concrete improvements such as cleaning the dust from the streets:

When the rain covers
All the streets with wet dirt,
It gets carried into the houses
As a special kind of decorative art –
Anyone who ever has
Stepped on paving like this
Will shout aloud: Long live the City Council![72]

The Council's decisions were exposed as faulty or impractical, leading to more chaos instead of order in the urban space. In many cases the urban renewal was depicted as a poorly planned, absurd process.[73] One cartoon pictured the renewal of the city's pavements as a monotonous, unending project that is going nowhere and merely repeating itself.[74]

On the one hand, jokes exposed problems and flaws in everyday urban life, especially in regard to how the city renewal process was being planned and carried out. On the other hand, humour was used in order to comment on or criticize current political decisions on the municipal level. For example, the cartoon shown in Figure 2.4 comments on the city's plan to update the numbering of houses in Vienna: in order to make the city easier to navigate, the house numbers of each building of an entire street should be listed at the street corner.[75] The caption suggests that the new practice could lead to more chaos than clarity, as people won't be able to keep track of the long list of numbers:

… 'Please Sir, could you tell me – '
'Good heavens, darn it! Now you've made me go wrong, I don't know any more which line I was on, and I'll have to start my search for number 77 all over again.'[76]

In another example from the following year, 1862, when the new numbering system was introduced, the same joke is repeated with a slight alteration: two men meet on an empty street full of houses, which all look alike:

'Please can you tell me, where's house no. 20?'
'No. 20? – hm – Either over there round the corner, between numbers 632 and 37, or up there next to numbers 894 and 266.'[77]

Here, by exaggeration, order has turned into disorder. The standardization of space, which was much criticized in popular humour, has made the city into an unfamiliar place, where it is hard to find one's way around. The new house numbers are not helping at all; instead, they make the city seem like a labyrinth or a maze.[78]

The critique of the City Council expressed frustration and anger with the higher quarters that exercised power over reorganizing the everyday environment of citizens by remodelling material spaces and systematizing them in one particular order, which people had to learn and adapt to in order to navigate

Die neue

Häuser-Numerirung

welche für Wien beantragt ist, hat auch ihre Schattenseiten. Man beabsichtiget nämlich, am Eckhause jeder Straße alle Haus=Nummern derselben zur bessern Orientirung anzubringen. Daß dieß bei Straßen von größerer Ausdehnung mit bedeutender Häuseranzahl große Schwierigkeiten bieten wird, dürfte aus nebenstehendem Bilde hervorgehen.

„Sie, mein Herr — können Sie mir nicht sagen — — —

„„Himmel Sackerlot! Jetzt haben's mich irr gemacht, ich weiß nicht mehr, bei welcher Zeilen ich war und ich muß mein 77ger wieder von vorn zu suchen anfangen.““

Figure 2.4 The numbering of houses. *Kikeriki*, 14 November 1861. Source: Austrian National Library.

successfully in their urban surroundings. As we have seen, the municipal law gave the City Council authority over some aspects of Vienna, whereas the state still had influence over the city in its role as the capital. The municipal legislation especially addressed the use of public spaces and conduct in the city, and on a very concrete level it shaped life in Vienna as the city was transformed. Perhaps this emphasis on conduct in public, rather than on the representational function, opened the way for mockery and ridicule, because it resonated with the active agency of the Viennese and their direct contact with their everyday surroundings.

Laughing at the stupidity and incompetence of the City Council reveals the basic hierarchical nature of laughter, in this case scorn for incompetent politicians. The classical superiority theories, which had their roots in the classical philosophy of Plato and Aristotle, and dominated the understanding of humour until the eighteenth century, emphasized the connection between laughter and scorn.[79] According to the basic premise of the superiority theories, humour does not involve only frustration and aggression, but also feelings of gratification and a sense of superiority. The most famous example of this kind of theoretical thinking is Thomas Hobbes' (1588–1679) idea of 'sudden glory', a sense of eminence that arises from degrading others.[80] Superiority theories easily intertwine with the idea of the disciplinary function of laughter, which became crucial for the later modern understanding of humour. Before and to some extent also after Freud, the late nineteenth-century discussions on humour revolved around the idea of punishment, as humour was often described as 'playful judgement' or 'social punishment', attacking social ills and human errors and follies.[81] In the case of late nineteenth-century Vienna, the ongoing ridicule aimed at the City Council thus reflects the nineteenth-century understanding of humour as a political force that had serious, satirical purposes. However, what made the laughter about the City Council so enjoyable was probably also a sense of superiority, in the form of educated, intellectual middle-class 'besserwisserism'. Shared jokes on the stupidity and incompetence of the City Council constantly boosted the feeling that the Viennese middle-class audience would know better how to run and manage the city, although they had very little power over it.

This sense of superiority was based on a strong belief in reason: as in the case of the unending pavement works, the mistakes resulted from miscalculations and lack of intelligence. The underlying idea seemed to be that if the members of the City Council would just use their common sense more, the city would be more rational and make more sense. This belief in reason was linked to the belief in progress that was a major aspect of nineteenth-century rationalist liberal culture. Yet the increasingly dominant modern capitalism and free markets generated trends in urban development that challenged this belief in progress, showing that the logic of uncontrolled free markets did not necessarily lead to rationality and the common good for all, but to chaos and disorder. This was a profound paradox, which undermined the whole composition. In the liberal ideology, capitalism was thought to be based on the rational nature of man, delivering the common good to everyone, and Marxist ideas about class structures and relations of ownership and power were ignored. However, when looking at the world of humour, it becomes clear that the bourgeoisie struggled with the contradictions between their rationalist liberal ideology and their everyday experiences with the modern capitalism that was putting the city into a state of turmoil.

Three Sources of Disorder: Traffic, Building and Street Lighting

One aspect of urbanization in which the expansion of capitalism became visible was mobility. The construction of the Ringstraße created a modern boulevard with increasingly turbulent traffic, as the new means of mass transportation, the horse tramways and omnibuses, started operations at the same time as the urban renewal was in full swing.[82] The building of the Ringstraße thus changed the basic character of the city and opened it up for movement and traffic, which gave Vienna a new kind of 'modern' quality, shared with other nineteenth-century capitals and defined by continual flux and change.[83]

The horse tramway in Vienna started operations in 1865, and the number of tramway lines increased rapidly. By 1870 there were twenty-two kilometres of tramway lines in Vienna, and by the next year eighty kilometres. During the liberal era between the early 1860s and mid 1890s, the Wiener Tramway-Gesellschaft had a monopoly of the tramway lines, and in return paid the city 5 per cent of the total income.[84] The company thus had an extremely free hand in providing transfers for citizens. Only after the Christian Social Party took over in the City Council in the 1890s was the Wiener Tramway-Gesellschaft municipalized – a political move related to a larger strategy in which the Christian Socialists gained popularity by taking control over aspects of urbanization that had formerly been left in the hands of the free markets.[85] The rise of the Christian Social Party thus reflected the dissatisfaction boiling beneath the surface of the liberal era, as Karl Lueger and his followers promised to create much desired order in the city.

The traffic in the growing city was a phenomenon that was often dealt with in the *Witzblätter* during the *Gründerzeit*. The overcrowding of the horse tramway carriages, especially, was an aspect of late nineteenth-century Viennese urban life that was a constant topic of jokes in the humorous magazines for three decades from the 1860s to the late 1880s.[86] The overcrowding of the new vehicles was a result of the capitalist logic of urban development, in which private companies played a significant role in making the city work by providing transportation, delivering gas or building new houses. However, private companies such as the Wiener Tramway-Gesellschaft or the Imperial Gas Association, which provided gas for Vienna until the 1890s, operated in terms of business economy, which meant that they protected their own interests rather than taking responsibility for the design and maintenance of the urban development. This conflict of interests created the basic tension for disciplinary satirical humour, through which the Viennese could criticize these enterprises for making the city difficult and awkward to live in.

The monopoly position of these companies in street lighting and public transport was strongly criticized, and the overcrowded tramway carriages, especially, were a standard topic for caricatures for decades. The press of co-passengers competing for seats, squeezing and colliding with strangers, became a standard situation in humour regarding riding the tramway. The new lack of intimacy in modern mass transportation has later been associated with the new modes of living in a modernizing society, where strangers had to share confined spaces in urban surroundings.[87] In the Viennese humorous publications, the overcrowding of the tramways was above all attributed to the greediness of the company, which did not provide enough streetcars for the passengers, but made the poor horses pull overcrowded streetcars for greater profits.

In the 1870s the satire in the humorous magazines sharpened, as the struggles between the city and the tramway company became a standard topic for satirical writings.[88] These problems came to a head, not just because the population of Vienna was continuously increasing, but also because the foreign visitors expected for the World Exhibition of 1873 promised to bring the company significantly more paying customers. Moreover, The World Exhibition meant that the reputation of the city of Vienna was at stake, as the overcrowded tramways were not just a daily annoyance for the Viennese, but also a potential source of national shame.[89]

The satirical critique against the tramway continued after the World Exhibition. In 1875 the fare was raised from ten Kreuzer to twelve Kreuzer, which caused a wave of protest among the Viennese. In some of the humorous magazines from the end of July to early August 1875, the rise in fares was the dominant topic, with extensive exposure in *Kikeriki* and *Der Floh* and some in *Figaro*.[90]

> According to the new Tramway fare, adults are charged 12 Kreuzer and children 6 Kreuzer. There now arises the question of how much those 'fathers' have to pay, who were so childish to endorse this tariff.[91]

Because many citizens avoided the tramway after the fare increase, there were many jokes in which the emptiness of the tramway carriages was seen as an act of resistance:

> Tramway Director: Business going well now?
> Controller: The business no, but the public yes.[92]

In one case, Heinrich Heine's poem 'Leise zieht durch mein Gemüt' (1831) was transformed into a satirical song to mock the Tramway-Gesellschaft: the tramways are empty, and only the bells of the horses jingle merrily as they pull their carriages with no passengers.[93] The edge of the satire was directed above all at the greed of the Tramway-Gesellschaft, interested only in maximizing profits and neglecting the users and workers of the tramway.

In the 1870s, the suffering of the tramway horses came to symbolize capitalist exploitation.[94] As we will see later, in chapter 4 in particular, the personification of animals and urban places was one characteristic of late nineteenth-century

Viennese popular humour. Lending a voice to non-human figures such as buildings, places or animals was a way of commenting on the city from surprising and unexpected angles.[95] In the case of the horse tramway, a focus on animals enabled a distanced perspective on the economic inequality in Vienna, by looking at it from the perspective of the silent tramway horses.

Importantly, although the target of satire is here the capitalist greed of the company, the human suffering of the workers was to a large extent totally ignored. Perhaps because the tramway horses had gained so much attention in the bourgeois press, Dr Viktor Adler, founder of the Socialdemokratische Arbeiterpartei and editor of the weekly journal *Gleichheit*, made the famous comparison in 1889 between the tramway horses and their drivers, suggesting that the horses worked under far better conditions than the workers driving them.[96] However, jokes about the tramway horses indicate that the middle classes were unable to completely escape the encounter with urban suffering. The motif of animal suffering thus seems to fit Freud's idea that jokes provide a disguised form for unresolved conflicts of the mind. The transfer of meanings from human suffering to animal suffering might have provided an outlet for the anxiety and disturbance caused by urban misery, which was visible even in the prestigious parts of the city, or perhaps even more strikingly so there.

The motif of greed can also be seen in the discussion around other urban problems seen as sources of disorder in the city. In addition to the traffic problems, the construction sites for new buildings in the city were also often criticized in the humorous magazines. The *Gründerzeit* was an era of fast-paced building projects. Contemporaries spoke of a *Baurummel*, a hustle and bustle of construction, which was taking over the city.[97] In many cases, the construction companies were criticized as greedy and hasty, working solely in terms of fast profit. As a result, the new buildings were seen as unstable and unsafe, in danger of collapsing at any time and killing innocent inhabitants and passers-by.[98] *Kikeriki* especially criticized the prevailing 'modern' building practices,[99] where the term 'modern' refers to a lack of morality and decency.

Moreover, the contrast between the pompous and decorative facades and the reality inside the new buildings was often voiced in the humorous magazines.[100] The modern buildings were seen as embodiments of the hypocrisy characteristic of Viennese urbanization and urban planning at the time.[101] However, it might be good to note here that the *Witzblätter* were not entirely free of hypocrisy themselves. As yet another example of the Viennese ability to tolerate paradoxes and ambiguities, despite their sharp critical humour the humorous magazines published advertisements for the same construction companies and new building sites that in their jokes and cartoons they were mocking.[102] The level of commercialism, however, varied: *Kikeriki* had the fewest advertisements, whereas *Der Floh* sometimes had more space dedicated to advertisements than to humour.

In addition to hypocrisy, greed was also seen as a distinctively modern vice that flourished in the capitalist system and gnawed away at people's morality. According to the humorous magazines, greed made the city dangerous, because it led to immorality and irresponsibility by the companies. After disasters such as a house collapsing, the *Witzblätter* and other humorous-satirical publications were used as forums for public outrage and a demand for legal sanctions against those responsible for the devastation:

> … Against murder and manslaughter, against robbery and theft, or against all violations of law that have their origin mostly in effervescence of evil passions or moral depravity, little can be done; but transgressions against the safety of life that in most cases have their origin in negligence or greed, can effectively be curbed by strict laws. If the contractors knew that the lost lives, sacrificed by their guilt, would cost them not only a few months in prison, but also several thousand Guldens of money, then they would certainly go about their work a bit more cautiously and conscientiously …[103]

The idea here is that although crimes and all social ills that result from 'evil passions' cannot be totally avoided or controlled, those crimes that are motivated by money and big profits can be restrained by law. The implicit assumption here is that the capitalist need to make profits is seen as rational rather than passionate. Yet the problem of greed versus rationalism seems to have been at the core of middle-class humour about disorder in the city. What was unsettling was the idea that the City Council, which represented the bourgeoisie itself, might not actually have power over aspects of urbanization left to the free markets, and that the logic of modern capitalism might not be as idealist and straightforward as nineteenth-century liberalist ideology imagined; hence the idea that the entrepreneurs and their companies need to be controlled by the law, or otherwise they will bring the city into chaos.

One key symbol for this chaos was darkness. The third urban problem that attracted extensive discussion in the nineteenth-century Viennese *Witzblätter* was gas lighting. Jokes, satirical writings and cartoons about the lack of light were an important part of the repertoire of the humorous magazines in the 1870s and 1880s in particular.[104] Here again the theme of greed is highlighted, as well as the incapability of the City Council to control a private company that is vital for urban management. In the case of light, the main culprit for disorder was the British company Imperial Continental Gas Association, which provided gas for Vienna from the mid 1840s to 1902. Only at the beginning of the twentieth century were the gas lanterns slowly replaced by electric streetlamps.[105]

The lack of light provoked many jokes and cartoons during the *Gründerzeit*. Often, criticism of the City Council was intertwined with mockery of the private company, which was selling gas at such a high price that the city could not afford to provide more light, or failed in delivering it properly.[106] For instance, in the following joke, which combines German and English in a manner that cannot be fully rendered in only one language, the mayor of Vienna, Cajetan Felder, is ridiculed for failing in the negotiations for a new contract with the Imperial Continental Gas Association in 1875:

> Der Engländer: Sie sein the Lord Major of Wien?
> Dr. Felder: Oh Yes!
> Der Engländer: Ich kann nur sprek english, Sir. Thun Sie sprek english?
> Dr. Felder: Oh Yes!
> Der Engländer: Uill Sie thun unterschreiben uein Vertrag mit mir, Sir?
> Dr. Felder: Oh Yes!
> Der Engländer: Uill Sie thun geben gebunden in mein Hände, Sir?
> Dr. Felder: Oh Yes!
> Der Engländer: Uill Sie thun zahlen groß Pönale, uen Sie brek the Vertrag, Sir?
> Dr. Felder: Oh Yes!
> Der Engländer: Well, Uerde ich uider haben the Monopol auf fünfundvierzig Jahr, Sir?
> Dr. Felder: Oh Yes!
> Der Engländer: Well! Dann unterschreiben Sie?
> Dr. Felder: Oh Yes! (Nachdem er unterschrieben, lächelnd): Werden wir wieder so schlechtes und theures Gas haben, wie früher?
> Der Engländer: Oh Yes!
> Dr. Felder (erstaunt): Oh Yes?
> Der Engländer (nicht erstaunt): Oh Yes![107]

In another example, the poem 'On the Ring by Night' from *Der Floh* in 1869, the street watchman tries, in vain, to light the lanterns on the Ringstraße, which refuse to ignite. His frustration culminates in the final line, in which the man asks: 'Oh English Gas Company, why did you do this to us?'[108]

Street lighting was closely related to the tension between order and disorder in the nineteenth-century city. As Wolfgang Schivelbusch has shown, street lanterns were introduced by the absolutist regimes in seventeenth-century Europe in order to extend the order and control of the ruling power into the city space. Artificial lighting made the city more transparent and controllable for police surveillance. In Vienna, as in many other cities, public lighting was the responsibility of the police, whose aim, as seen in the previous chapter, was to maintain public order by protecting the city from revolutionaries, criminals and other forces that might create disorder in urban space.[109] Whereas light represented and created order, darkness was associated with disorder.[110] The late nineteenth-century humorous magazines were full of complaints about the lack of lighting, which made the city dangerous.[111] The desire for light as a desire for order thus had deep roots in the European context. Furthermore, there was a long tradition of satirical writings dealing with the fear of darkness in European cities. Schivelbusch notes that in seventeenth-century Paris, for instance, satirical verses emerged criticizing the dangers of the dark and uncontrollable city.[112]

Notably, the humorous magazines hardly ever commented that there was too much light on the streets, or criticized the city for being too bright.[113] On the contrary, the source of criticism remained almost without exception the lack of light. It is thus important to note that in the bourgeois Viennese *Witzblätter* the desire for light was very much intertwined with the desire for order. The humorous magazines did play with carnivalesque and rebellious aspects of darkness,[114] but the ultimate goal of the satirical humour was to improve the city lighting. Darkness was unruly and threatening.

In addition to the three major problems discussed in the previous paragraphs – overcrowded tramways, collapsing buildings and the lack of light – there were numerous other urban issues that were satirically attacked in the humorous magazines. In nineteenth-century Viennese popular humour, the city was in many cases portrayed as chaotic and dangerous, and all kinds of accidents, for example, were an important topic. In morbidly comical scenes, people were killed and injured in various ways by the hazards of the unpredictable and chaotic city environment.[115]

Humour thus provided one way of dealing with fears and anxiety arising from the uncontrollable nature of city life. The continuous movement and flux made the city dangerous, but even more threatening was the lack of moral values in the modern capitalism that was overtaking Vienna. Against the backdrop of the liberal *laissez-faire* mentality of the *Gründerzeit*, the era of city renewal appeared as an era of uncertainty, as the growing city was no longer cosy and familiar, but in many ways unintelligible and indifferent, ready to destroy its citizens in its great anonymity. The satirical humour expressed in its repeated disciplinary demands for order a desire for protection – and paradoxically, this desire was directed at the authorities, who were otherwise often mocked and ridiculed in the *Witzblätter* for their excessive control. Thus, the sense of intellectual superiority, so evident in the satirical dissent directed at the City Council, was linked to a range of emotional responses to disorder, such as fear and anxiety, which created an emotional need for protection in the great metropolis.

As the previous sections have shown, modern capitalism had a vast impact on how the physical city space was encountered and experienced in the second half of the nineteenth century. In concluding the argument that Viennese popular humour expressed not just rebellion against control by the authorities, but also a desire for order and security in the capitalist city, I would like to explore further one recurrent type of cartoon, featuring comical protective suits. Between 1857 and 1890, the Viennese *Witzblätter* offered numerous images of protective suits against the urban environment. There were suits against crowds, floods, railway accidents, runaway horses, falling flower pots and collapsing houses.[116] The shared component in these comical suggestions was the idea that the body needed somehow to be protected from its potentially dangerous urban surroundings. The suits formed a protective layer between the city and the person, thus emphasizing the vulnerability of the body. One explanation for these comical protective suits is that these cartoons were making fun of over-cautious emotional responses to the transformation of the city, but simultaneously they expose the vulnerable core in the bodily experience of Vienna under modernization, in which the city had become something unnerving, even terrifying.

What is striking in the images shown in Figures 2.5 and 2.6 is the contrast between hard and soft. In the first image (Figure 2.5), from *Kikeriki* in 1865, the caption says: 'Soon no one will dare to enter a train without such a padded suit'.[117] The man and his dog are comical in their cushioned suits, which make them look not only fat and clumsy, but also overwhelmingly soft, in contrast with the hard, black railway engine seen through the window. The soft padded suit is reminiscent of cushions, and suggests connotations of the private sphere and feminine sensitivity, in contrast to the masculine, modern machinery. In the adjoining image from the *Wiener Luft*, published fourteen years later in 1879, the idea is the same, but here the contrast between hard and soft, masculine and feminine, is turned upside down (Figure 2.6). A woman is wearing a hard, metallic suit reminiscent of the ancient torture device the 'iron maiden', with its cruel spikes turned inside out, to prevent other people from coming too close to the lady inside. The association with the torture device is most likely a deliberate reference, and it is a crucial element of the dynamics between anxiety and comic relief in this particular example. The caption states ironically: 'The proper toilette for ladies who want to watch the pageant undisturbed'.[118] The event referred to here is the silver wedding anniversary of Emperor Franz Joseph and Empress Elisabeth, which was celebrated by a spectacular pageant on the Ringstraße in 1879. In the cartoon the woman is holding eye glasses, which suggest active watching and participating in the city. On the other hand, the word 'undisturbed' (*ungestört*) and the spikes of the iron suit refer to the potential obstacles and inconveniences for women entering public spaces and taking part in mass events. The woman's iron suit also references anxiety about proximity and sexual danger, a fear of losing one's personal boundaries and intimacy in the crowds of the great city.

In fact, fear of touching (*Berührungsangst*) was one of the pathological conditions diagnosed in the growing nineteenth-century metropolises.[119] In contemporary medical debates, the city environment was seen as threatening not only the body, but the mind as well. Urban space as a source of spatial fears and mental conditions became a major theme in the discussion of modernity in the late nineteenth century. Doctors and early psychologists saw that change in the physical fabric of the city could cause mental disease. The fear of distance was especially related to the greater scale of the modernizing cities, and agoraphobia was first diagnosed in Berlin and Vienna in the 1860s. Furthermore, in the early discussion on agoraphobia, the fear of open spaces was associated with the anxiety caused by crowded and populated spaces.[120] The humorous protective suits

Tensions with City Authorities | 83

Jetzt wird man sich bald nur mehr in so einem gepolsterten Anzug' auf die Bahn wagen können.

Figure 2.5 Padded suit for train travel. *Kikeriki*, 23 February 1865. Source: Austrian National Library.

Die richtige Toilette für Damen, die den Festzug ungestört mit anschauen wollen.

Figure 2.6 'The proper toilette for ladies', *Figaro*, 19 April 1879 / *Wiener Luft* No. 16. Source: Austrian National Library.

can thus be understood to express a distressed response to the shifting sensory experiences of transforming Vienna.

As historical research has increasingly taken an interest in the historical nature of human emotions and senses, the dichotomy between hard and soft has been used in interpreting the sensual experiences of late nineteenth-century cities. The historian Hannu Salmi has used Alain Corbin's idea of 'the century of linen' to illustrate the ways in which industrialization changed sensory experience in nineteenth-century cities. Corbin suggested that linen underwear and domestic fabrics became so popular in the nineteenth century because they offered pleasure and softness as a counterweight to a sensory environment marked by urbanization and industrialization. The dichotomies between publicity and intimacy were related to the new significance of homes and family lives in the nineteenth century. In comparison to the noise, pollution and traffic of the outside world of the city, the home became a refuge for the private self, providing protection and care for the body.[121]

Although Vienna was far less marked by industrialization than, for example, contemporary Berlin or London, the urban renewal, rapid population growth and technological innovations clearly altered the citizens' sensory environment. The modernizing city, with its urban masses, created constantly changing sensory experiences of movement, crowds and artificial lighting; moreover, the Viennese lived for decades surrounded by rowdy and dusty construction sites for new monumental buildings and places.[122] Consequently, the protective suits can be seen as expressing anxiety regarding the body and sensory experiences in a changing city ruled by a new kind of economic order of modern capitalism.[123] The protective suits condense meanings relating to sensory experiences, manifested in the contrast between hard and soft, inside and outside, private and public, and the convergence of a desire for order with a desire for protection.

Consequently, the comical protective suits against the modernizing city draw attention to the innate relationship between space and the body. The bodily aspect of urban living has been a subject of growing interest in urban history. Even before the boom of the spatial turn and the rise of new materialism in the early twenty-first century, Richard Sennett investigated the relationship between the body and the city in the history of Western culture, and argued in *Flesh and Stone* (1996) that 'urban spaces take form largely from the ways people experience their bodies'.[124] Sennett's claim that the way people experience their own bodies shapes the urban form can also be understood the other way around: the urban form and spatial surroundings affect how people experience their bodies. This claim might seem less provocative and inspiring, but it is still worth explicating. The next chapter will continue this discussion by exploring how the transformation of the city was interpreted as a bodily experience in the Viennese *Witzblätter*.

Notes

1. Ein Hündchen schleicht die Strasse hin / Und scheint gar arg zu leiden, / Ein Herr geht muthlos hinterdrein – / Ein Wachmann folgt den Beiden. // Das Hündchen trägt den Maulkorb nicht, / Das scheint den Herrn zu drücken, / Gern möchten Herr und Hund entflieh'n / Vor jenes Wachmanns Blicken. // Doch ach, vor ihnen steht er schon, / Blickt in's Notizbuch brütend; / Schreibt drin des Hündchens Wohnung ein, / Und sieh' – der Herr wird wüthend! 'Ballade von der Strasse', *Der Floh*, 31 August 1884.
2. On the history and structure of jokes, see further, e.g., Daniel Wickberg, *Senses of Humor: Self and Laughter in Modern America* (Ithaca, 1998), 120–23.
3. Michael Billig, *Laughter and Ridicule: Towards a Social Critique of Humour* (London, 2012), 55; Wickberg, *Senses of Humor*, 186–96. The emphasis on aggression and anxiety derives from Sigmund Freud's influence on approaches to humour. A number of

psychoanalytical readings on jokes have been published in the twentieth century. One of the most famous is Alan Dundes' classic study in the field of folklore, Alan Dundes, *Cracking Jokes: Studies of Sick Humour Cycles and Stereotypes* (Berkeley, 1987). Many studies exploring incongruity in humour have on the other hand highlighted the multifaceted nature of humour and challenged the assumption that humour can simply be explained in terms of aggressive tendency. See Arthur Koestler, *The Act of Creation* (London, 1964), 51–58; Elliott Oring, *Jokes and Their Relations* (Lexington, 1992), 16–28.

4. Sigmund Freud, *Der Witz und seine Beziehung zum Unbewussten* (Frankfurt am Main, [1905] 2006), 123; Billig, *Laughter and Ridicule*, 98.
5. Freud, *Der Witz*, 119, 129. See also Billig, *Laughter and Ridicule*, 235. On jokes told in totalitarian societies, see further Christie Davies, *Jokes and Targets* (Bloomington, 2011), 213–52; Dundes, *Cracking Jokes*, 159–68.
6. 'Was in Wien unnöthigerweise verboten ist', *Kikeriki*, 17 September 1863; 'Gemeinderätlich-städtisches-kommunales-offizielles Stadt-Erweiterungs-Räthsel', *Kikeriki*, 14 January 1864; 'Merkwürdige Tafel auf dem Josefstädter Glacis', *Kikeriki*, 20 June 1867.
7. Der Adam hat nur ein einziges Verbot zu beobachten gehabt und sogar dieses hat er übertreten. Wie würde es ihn heutzutage ergehen, wo beinahe Alles verboten ist? *Kikeriki*, 15 October 1863.
8. See, for example, 'Die Weißen Riemen der Polizeimänner', *Kikeriki*, 7 September 1865; 'O, die Polizei ist klug!', *Der Floh*, 27 May 1888.
9. For example, 'Im Posterestante-Bureau', *Der Floh*, 19 July 1885.
10. Engelbert Steinwender, *Von der Stadtguardia zur Sicherheitswache: Wiener Polizeiwachen und ihre Zeit. 1. Von der Frühzeit bis 1932* (Graz, 1992), 123–24, 129, 131.
11. Ibid., 131.
12. 'Die öffentlichen Bauten in Wien', *Kikeriki*, 5 December 1867; 'Sicherheitswächter', *Figaro*, 16 November 1878 / *Wiener Luft* No. 46; 'Sicherheitswachmann', *Figaro*, 25 January 1879 / *Wiener Luft* No. 4.
13. 'Der Josefstädter Exerzierplatz und die dortigen Graspflanzungen', *Kikeriki*, 25 May 1865.
14. Ole Frahm notes that the early comics were often based on a bourgeois panoptic gaze over the city, which had become a dominant nineteenth-century way of perceiving urbanity. A distanced gaze from an elevated viewpoint promised control over the city, overcoming the controversies and contradictions of urbanity. Ole Frahm, 'Every Window Tells a Story: Remarks on the Urbanity of Early Comic Strips', in Jörn Ahrens and Arno Meteling (eds), *Comics and the City: Urban Space in Print, Picture and Sequence* (New York, 2010), 33. Chapter 4 will discuss further different modes of perceiving urbanity in early Viennese comics and cartoons.
15. The Josefstädter Glacis was used as a parade ground (*Exerzierplatz*) for the army. See, e.g., Carl E. Schorske, *Fin-de-siècle Vienna: Politics and Culture* (Cambridge, MA, [1961] 1981), 29, 39, 45.
16. 'Wie sie die Gehwege am Exerzierplatz praktisch angelegt haben', *Kikeriki*, 1 October 1863.
17. Billig, *Laughter and Ridicule*, 98. Billig continues by remarking that humour enables one to say things that are otherwise forbidden: it evades the restrictions of social life, permitting brief moments of shared freedom. Ibid., 154–56.
18. I follow here the ideas of Anu Korhonen, who has suggested that 'laughter is both resist-

ance of and reaction to cultural boundaries'. Anu Korhonen, *Fellows of Infinite Jest: The Fool in Renaissance England* (Turku, 1999), 24–25.

19. The police institution was related to maintaining order already in the early modern era. The German word *Polizey* originally meant 'good order' (*Gute Ordnung im Gemeinwesen*); the first institutionally organized officers of the peace in the city started work in the 1540s, and slowly evolved into the *Stadtguardia*. Günther Bögl and Harald Seyrl, *Die Wiener Polizei im Spiegel der Zeiten: Eine Chronik in Bildern* (Vienna, 1993), 13–14. See also Steinwender, *Von der Stadtguardia zur Sicherheitswache*, 122–23.

20. See further Bögl and Seyrl, *Wiener Polizei*, 16–17. On irony, see Linda Hutcheon, *Irony's Edge: The Theory and Politics of Irony* (New York, 1995), 11–12.

21. 'Aufrechthaltung der öffentliche Ruhe, Ordnung und Sicherheit.' See Steinwender, *Von der Stadtguardia zur Sicherheitswache*, 87, 93, 120. Bögl and Seyrl, *Wiener Polizei*, 27.

22. Steinwender, *Von der Stadtguardia zur Sicherheitswache*, 122–23.

23. Contrast aggressive ridicule and friendly banter. Billig, *Laughter and Ridicule*, 194–99. Billig argues that disciplinary ridicule usually functions to maintain social order, and rebellious ridicule to challenge it. Ibid., 202–35.

24. An diesem Tage wurde nämlich die Sicherheitswache am Exerzierplatze von Manchen der daselbst versammelt gewesenen Laute ausgelacht und zum Besten gehalten. Man ließ den Wächtern der Ordnung merken, daß ihnen eine ungeheure Tracht Prügel bevorstünde, wenn sie es versuchen wollten, einzuschreiten. Recht eine trübselige Erfahrung. Viele jene Herren, welche erschienen waren, um neue liberale Gesetze zu erreichen, bewiesen, daß sie keine Achtung vor den Alten haben. Sie begehren geistige Rechte und proklamiren gleichzeitig das Faust recht! Zum Glücke betheiligte sich der gesunde Kern unserer Arbeiter nicht an der Verhöhnung jener Männer, die zum Schutze des Eigenthums und der Person, im Interesse der Ordnung und der Sicherheit aufgestellt sind. 'Dezembertage, die sich Kikeriki schwarz angestrichen habe', *Tage-Buch des Kikeriki*, Vol. 1, January 1870, 6.

25. Billig, *Laughter and Ridicule*, 212–13.

26. For example, the historian Peter Jelavich has emphasized this idea of humour's relationship to politics in his study of the early twentieth-century Berliner cabaret culture. Peter Jelavich, *Berlin Cabaret* (Cambridge, MA, 1996), 34 and passim.

27. According to Freud, the element of gaining pleasure (*Lustgewinn*) is crucial for tendentious jokes. Freud, *Der Witz*, 115–16.

28. -Heda, 's Trottoir gehört nur für Fußgeher … -No - sitz i mit meine Washkörb' leich i an' Fiaker?! *Figaro*, 28 June 1879 / *Wiener Luft* No. 26.

29. William M. Johnston, *The Austrian Mind: An Intellectual and Social History 1848–1938* (Berkeley, 1983), 19.

30. Michael Mulkay, *On Humour: Its Nature and Its Place in Modern Society* (Cambridge, 1988), 1, passim; Wickberg, *Senses of Humor*, 170–72.

31. See, e.g., O.F. Berg, *Der Modeteufel: Posse mit Gesang in 3 Akten* (Vienna, 1860), 1–6.

32. See Billig, *Laughter and Ridicule*, 147.

33. 'Die Tramway-Gesellschaft', *Kikeriki*, 9 May 1870. See also 'Die neue Fiakertaxe. Eine Zukunftsszene', *Kikeriki*, 29 October 1868.

34. See further chapter 1.

35. 'Kikeriki weiß neue Maßregeln für Hundeverfolgung', *Kikeriki*, 23 October 1862; 'Sicherheitsmaßnahmen gegen Hundebiß', *Kikeriki*, 6 November 1862.

36. 'Nachtrag zur neuen Fiakerordnung', *Kikeriki*, 29 October 1868; 'Die Prater-"Verschönerungen"', *Kikeriki*, 17 April 1871; 'Neue Koder für die Tramway-Fahrten', *Figaro*, 19 July 1879 / *Wiener Luft* No. 29; 'Vorschläge', *Der Floh*, 15 November 1885.
37. For example, the statute requiring that all dogs should be kept muzzled in the city was parodied by exaggerating it: '1. Der Maulkorb darf dem Hunde auch bei der Nacht, wenn derselbe schläft, nicht abgenommen werden …'. (1. The muzzle may not be removed from the dog, even during the night when it sleeps.) 'Maulkorb-Verordnungen', *Kikeriki*, 13 June 1875.
38. 'Was verboten und was erlaubt ist', *Kikeriki*, 8 September 1864; 'Interessante Gegensätze zu den Wiener Verordnungen', *Kikeriki*, 21 June 1874; 'Formular eines Meldezettels', *Figaro*, 24 April 1875; 'Kundmachung', *Der Floh*, 25 September 1886.
39. Cf. Miriam B. Hansen, 'The Mass Production of the Senses: Classical Cinema as Vernacular Modernism', *Modernism/Modernity* 6(2) (1999), 60.
40. N. Oe. Landesgesetze, Bd. 2–5 (Vienna 1887–1897).
41. The Constitution of 1867 was the most important achievement of the bourgeoisie but there were a great number of other laws introduced as well, such as Organisation der Verwaltungs- und Gerichtsbehörden (1850), Gemeindegesetz (1850), Gesetz über Melde- und Paßwesen (1857), Gewerbeordnung (1859), Gesetz zum Schutze der persönlichen Freiheit und zum Schutze des Hausrechts (1862), Volksschulgesetz (1869), Gesetz über das Wasserrecht (1869), Reichssanitätsgesetz (1870), Gesetz über das Schulwesen (1871) and Gesetz über die Polizeiaufsicht (1873). Steinwender, *Von der Stadtguardia zur Sicherheitswache*, 118.
42. Marshall Berman, *All That Is Solid Melts Into Air: The Experience of Modernity* (New York, 1988), 147, 153–55, and passim; David Frisby, *Cityscapes of Modernity: Critical Explorations* (Cambridge, 2001), 2–3; Steven Beller, 'Introduction', in Steven Beller (ed.), *Rethinking Vienna 1900* (New York, 2001), 15.
43. Schorske, *Fin-de-siècle Vienna*, 4–5.
44. See Billig, *Laughter and Ridicule*, 236–43. See also Mulkay, *On Humour*; Wickberg, *Senses of Humor*; Korhonen, *Fellows of Infinite Jest*.
45. Cf. Hannu Salmi, *Nineteenth-Century Europe: A Cultural History* (Cambridge, 2008), 2.
46. Kikeriki schlägt vor, auch für die Bewohner selbst die Luft zu besteuern. Das könnte die finanzielle Misère der Kommune gewiss mit einem Schlage heben. Wie bitte? Das lässt sich nicht durchführen? Sie täuschen sich! Es geht ganz gut! Man müsste der Bevölkerung einfach gebieten, sich nach der Muster der Taucher mit Kopfhelmen zu equipiren. Jeder trägt auf dem Rücken sein Luftreservoir mit dem versteuerten Quantum – sammt Kontrolapparat. Wer ohne diesen Apparat auf der Straße betroffen wird, wird als Steuerdefraudant arrestirt. 'Eine neue Steuerungsmethode', *Kikeriki*, 13 May 1888.
47. In Vienna, citizens had to pay taxes to the state and to the municipality. The municipality received over half of its income from taxes, with other income coming from rents (*Mietzinse*). The lower classes had to pay relatively more taxes than members of the *Bildungsbürgertum*. Wolfgang Maderthaner, 'Von der Zeit um 1860 bis zum Jahr 1945', in Peter Csendes and Ferdinand Oppl (eds), *Wien – Geschichte einer Stadt: Von 1790 bis zur Gegenwart* (Vienna, 2006), 197.
48. This notion resonates well with Daniel Wickberg's argument that the modern sense of humour was essentially interlinked with new ideas of individuality, creativity and personality in the nineteenth century. On the other hand, Wickberg notes that the

self-objectifying capacity of the sense of humour makes it ideal for bureaucratic society, as it removes the conflict between internal and external sources of authority. Wickberg, *Senses of Humor*, 74–79, 107.
49. *Gemeinschaft und Gesellschaft* was published in 1887.
50. Frisby, *Cityscapes*, 5, 100–158; Johnston, *Austrian Mind*, 20; Dominic Strinati, *An Introduction to the Theories of Popular Culture* (London, 2004), 5–10.
51. Georg Simmel, *Suurkaupunki ja moderni elämä. Kirjoituksia vuosilta 1895–1917*, trans. Tiina Huuhtanen, ed. Arto Noro (Helsinki, 2005), 32. *Die Großstadt und das Geistesleben* was originally published in 1903.
52. 'Berlin. (¾ 9 Uhr.) schlecht geschlafen (5 Min. auf 10 Uhr), schönes Wetter heute (¼ 11 Uhr) Hühneraugenschmerzen, (15 Min. später) einen gebratenen Stockfisch zu Mittag.' 'Wichtiges Telegrafenwechsel zwischen Frankfurt und Berlin', *Figaro*, 12 May 1858.
53. Cf. Wolfgang Schivelbusch, *The Railway Journey: The Industrialization of Time and Space in the Nineteenth Century* (Berkeley, 2014), 33–44.
54. Der Normalmensch (Ein Tagebuch aus dem XX. Jahrhundert) Am 1. Juni. Nachdem ich während der achtstündigen normalen Nachtruhe normal geschlafen hatte, verließ ich zur normalen Zeit, um 7 Uhr morgens, mein Normalbett, wusch mich normalerweise mit Normalseife, hüllte mich dann in meine Normalwäsche und meine Normalkleider und setzte mich, gemeinsam mit meiner normalmäßig aus vier Köpfen bestehenden Normalfamilie, zu dem von Staate fixierten Normalfrühstück, das aus je einer Tasse Normalkaffee und einer Normalsemmel bestand. Normalmäßig, binnen einer Viertelstunde, war der Imbiß beendet. Unsere Normaldienstmagd, für welche in diesem Augenblicke der elfstündige Normalarbeitstag begann, räumte ab, säuberte die Normalmöbel und führte endlich mein Söhnchen in die neue Normalschule ... 'Der Normalmensch (Ein Tagebuch aus dem XX. Jahrhundert) Am 1. Juni', *Der Floh*, 22 June 1884.
55. See, for instance, 'Die Wiener Häuser sehen jetzt Eines aus – so wie das Andere', *Kikeriki*, 11 March 1868; 'Wir leben jetzt in einer wahren Bank-Zeit', *Kikeriki*, 25 February 1883; 'Wieder ein Stück altes Wien kassirt', *Kikeriki*, 29 May 1884.
56. Simon Critchley argues that in humour, as in anxiety, the world is made strange and unfamiliar. Simon Critchley, *On Humour* (New York, 2002), 41, 10–11. On the relationship between humour and anxiety, see also Dundes, *Cracking Jokes*, 4.
57. Jo Ann Mitchell Fuess, *The Cultural Crisis of Lower Middle Class Vienna 1848–1892: A Study of the Works of Friedrich Schlögl* (Lincoln, 1992), 6–10. Similar ideas of humour's empowering and creative function were shared by other humourists as well.
58. Koestler, *Act of Creation*, 91–93.
59. John Morreall, *The Philosophy of Laughter and Humor* (Albany, 1987), 59–82.
60. Henri Bergson, *Nauru. Tutkimus komiikan merkityksestä*. French original: *Le Rire. Essai sur la signification du comique* (1900), trans. Sanna Isto and Marko Pasanen (Helsinki, 1994), 28–35. See also Morreall, *Philosophy of Laughter*, 117.
61. See, for instance, 'Neuer Omnibusverkehr für Wien', *Kikeriki*, 30 June 1864; 'Mittel', *Kikeriki*, 5 October 1865; 'Das neue Stadtbahnprojekt', *Kikeriki*, 11 October 1888.
62. Critchley, *On Humour*, 80.
63. Ibid., 16, 86–87, 90. See also script theory: humour requires awareness of categories and conventions, and always contains pieces of implicit knowledge. These mental patterns and frameworks of thought and action are called 'scripts'. Jokes are often based on a sudden change of scripts, involving an element of surprise. Oring, *Jokes*, 9–13.

64. Joan Wallach Scott, 'Introduction: "Flyers to the Unknown". Gender, History and Psychoanalysis', in *The Fantasy of Feminist History* (Durham, 2011), 1–7.
65. See further Elisabeth Wilson, *The Sphinx in the City: Urban Life, the Control of Disorder, and Women* (Berkeley, 1992), 7–8.
66. See, for example, 'Wanderung durch die Strassen Wiens', *Tage-Buch des Kikeriki*, Vol. 11, June 1870, 171; 'Wiener Wasser-Melange Lied', *Der Floh*, 7 March 1886; 'Wassernoth in Wien', *Der Floh*, 19 September 1886; 'Strassenreinigung bei Nacht', *Der Floh*, 5 May 1889.
67. On satire in the nineteenth-century German-speaking area, see further Ann Taylor Allen, *Satire and Society in Wilhelmine Germany: Kladderadatsch & Simplicissimus 1890–1914* (Lexington, 1984); Mary Lee Townsend, *Forbidden Laughter: Popular Humor and the Limits of Repression in Nineteenth-Century Prussia* (Ann Arbor, 1992).
68. O.F. Berg used his magazine in order to run for the Council. He was elected in 1870. 'Kikeriki als Kandidat für den Gemeinderath', *Kikeriki*, 19 February 1863; 'Kikeriki im Gemeinderath', *Kikeriki*, 28 March 1870. See also 'Herr O.F. Berg', *Der Floh*, 27 March 1870.
69. The reign of the liberals lasted in the state from 1861 until 1878. However, in the municipality of Vienna their dominance lasted even longer, until 1895, when the Christian Socialists took power. The election of Karl Lueger as the mayor of Vienna was finally approved by the Emperor in 1897. Maderthaner, 'Von der Zeit', 193. See also Karl Vocelka, *K.u.K. Karikaturen und Karikaturen zum Zeitalter Kaiser Franz Josephs* (Vienna, 1986), 68–69, 76.
70. Maderthaner, 'Von der Zeit', 196.
71. Cf. 'Ordnungspolitik' was one of the main values of liberal city politics. See further Maderthaner, 'Von der Zeit', 215.
72. … Wenn der Regen alle Straßen / Ueberzieht mit nassem Schmutz, / Wird in Häuserln er gelassen / Als besond'rer Schmuck und Putz; / Wer je in ein solches trat, / Ruft: Hoch der Gemeinderath! … 'Wiener Straßensäuberungs-Hymnus', *Kikeriki*, 21 March 1889.
73. 'Die Demolirer im Neuthor', *Figaro*, 28 July 1860; 'Die neuen Park-Anlagen am Wasser Glacis', *Kikeriki*, 17 April 1862; 'Wiener Stadtverschönerung', *Kikeriki*, 3 July 1862; 'Stadtbauamtliches', *Kikeriki*, 10 September 1863; 'Was bei uns Alles geschehen muß bis Etwas geschieht', *Kikeriki*, 28 April 1864; 'An das löbliche Unterkammeramt!', *Figaro*, 3 August 1878 / *Wiener Luft* No. 31; 'An den Wiener Gemeinderath', *Kikeriki*, 23 May 1878.
74. 'Auf welche Art in Wien die Straßen in Einemfort gepflastert werden', *Kikeriki*, 8 October 1863.
75. See further Bertrand Michael Buchmann, 'Dynamik des Städtebaus', in Csendes and Oppl, *Wien – Geschichte einer Stadt*, 71–72.
76. 'Sie, mein Herr – können Sie mir sagen –' / 'Himmel, Sackerlot! Jetzt haben's mich irr gemacht, ich weiß nicht mehr, bei welcher Zeilen ich war und ich muß mein 77er wieder von vorn zu suchen anfangen.' 'Die Neue Häuser-Numerierung', *Kikeriki*, 14 November 1861.
77. 'Sie – ich bitt, wo ist denn hier das Haus Nr. 20?' / 'Nr 20? – hm – Entweder dort übers Eck, zwischen 632 und 37 oder oben in den neben 894 und 266.' 'Die Wiener Häuser-Numerierung', *Kikeriki*, 12 June 1862.
78. Cf. Wilson, *Sphinx in the City*, 3–4.

79. Morreall, *Philosophy of Laughter*, 3, 5–6; Critchley, *On Humour*, 3; Billig, *Laughter and Ridicule*, 38–39.
80. Thomas Hobbes, *Leviathan* (Cambridge, [1651] 1997), 43. See also the passage on human nature (1650), cited in Morreall, *Philosophy of Laughter*, 20. 'Passion of laughter is nothing else but sudden glory arising from some sudden conception of some eminency in ourselves, by comparison with the infirmity of others, or with our own formerly.' Michael Billig reminds us that the pessimist vision of Hobbes should be read in the context of his own time, the social and political turmoil caused by the English Civil War. Billig, *Laughter and Ridicule*, 6.
81. Freud, *Der Witz*, 25–26.
82. Whereas the traditional Fiaker horse carriages enabled the upper classes to move around the city to flexible destinations, the new horse tramways and omnibuses had fixed routes and timetables. The omnibuses, or *Stellwagen*, started to operate in the first half of the nineteenth century. The Neue Wiener Omnibusgesellschaft gained a monopoly position in 1873 when the different omnibus companies merged. It became one of the biggest such companies in Europe. See further Hans Roman Gröger, *Schienen für die Ewigkeit: 113 Wiener Straßenbahnstrecken aus dem Österreichischen Staatsarchiv* (Innsbruck, 2011), 20–21.
83. Schorske, *Fin-de-siècle Vienna*, 33–36; Rainer Hank, 'Topik und Topografie: Seelenlandschaft und Stadtlandschaft im Wien der Jahrhundertwende', in Manfred Smuda (ed.), *Die Großstadt als >Text<* (Munich, 1992), 226. Compare the transformation of Paris. See David Harvey, *Paris, Capital of Modernity* (New York, 2006), 107–16; Wilson, *Sphinx in the City*, 53; Berman, *All That Is Solid*, 148–64.
84. Johannes Sachslehner, *Wien: Geschichte einer Stadt* (Vienna, 2012), 236.
85. The Christian Socialists also ended the monopoly position of the British company, the Imperial Gas Association, and built their own gasometers in Vienna. Maderthaner, 'Von der Zeit', 215, 222–24.
86. 'Schon wieder eine Errungenschaft durch die Pferdebahn', *Kikeriki*, 30 July 1868; 'Die Ueberfüllung der Tramway-Waggons', *Kikeriki*, 24 June 1880; 'Zur Überfüllung der Tramway-Waggons', *Der Floh*, 18 May 1884; 'Vorschläge gegen die Überfüllung der Tramwaywaggons', *Der Floh*, 28 March 1886.
87. See further Harvey, *Paris*, 115.
88. 'Kommune und Tramway', *Kikeriki*, 21 January 1869; 'Zum Tramwaykrieg', *Der Floh*, 15 February 1885; 'Vom Tramwaykrieg', *Der Floh*, 22 February 1885; 'Aus der diplomatischen Correspondenz zwischen Tramway und Commune', *Der Floh*, 29 July 1888.
89. On the World Exhibition in Vienna in 1873, see further chapter 5.
90. 'Wenn sich zwei streiten, freut sich der Dritte', *Kikeriki*, 25 July 1875; 'Auf der Tramway', *Kikeriki*, 1 August 1875; 'Die Neuste Nutzen der Tramway', *Kikeriki*, 1 August 1875; 'Die Tramway', *Der Floh*, 18 July 1875; 'Pferdebahn-Skizzen', *Der Floh*, 25 July 1875.
91. Nach dem neuen Tramway-Tarif zahlen Erwachsene 12 Kreuzer und Kinder 6 Kreuzer. Es entsteht nun die Frage, wie viel jene 'Väter' zu zahlen haben, die so kindisch waren diesen Tarif zu befürworten. 'Arithmetisches', *Der Floh*, 18 July 1875.
92. Tramway-Director: Nun geht das Geschäft? Controlor: Das Geschäft nicht, aber das Publicum. 'Nach der Erhöhung der Tramway-Preise', *Der Floh*, 25 July 1875.
93. 'Frei nach Heine', *Der Floh*, 25 July 1875.

94. 'Melancholischer Ausruf eines Tramwaypferdes', *Kikeriki*, 1 August 1875; 'Monolog eines Ominibuspferdes', *Der Floh*, 18 July 1875.
95. See, for example, Eduard Pötzl's short story 'Gedanken eines Komfortablepferdes', in *Gesammelte Skizzen* (Vienna, 1907), 94–97.
96. Maderthaner, 'Von der Zeit', 224. The Socialdemokratische Arbeiterpartei started to consolidate the worker's movement in the 1880s.
97. 'Unser Bau-Rummel', *Der Floh*, 28 January 1872. See also 'Eine Alte und Ihre Jungen', *Der Figaro*, 22 March 1873.
98. 'So hat man früher gebaut – so bauen wir jetzt', *Kikeriki*, 12 May 1864; 'Die Ballade von der Bau-Kommission', *Kikeriki*, 7 March 1878; 'Vor'm eingestürzten Hause in der Kärntnerstrasse', *Figaro*, 20 August 1881 / *Wiener Luft*, No. 34.
99. 'Modernes Motto', *Kikeriki*, 10 May 1866; 'Modernes Bau(un)wesen', *Kikeriki*, 9 October 1887.
100. See, e.g., 'Moderne Bauspekulation', *Kikeriki*, 28 June 1888.
101. Cf. Wolfgang Maderthaner and Lutz Musner, *Unruly Masses: The Other Side of the Fin-de-siècle Vienna* (New York, 2008), 2–5, 52–55.
102. 'Bauplätze', *Der Floh*, 2 October 1870; 'Bauplätze', *Der Figaro*, 3 December 1870; 'Wiener Baugesellschaft', *Kikeriki*, 1 December 1872.
103. Gegen Mord und Todschlag, gegen Raub und Diebstahl, sowie überhaupt gegen Gesetzübertretungen alle, die ihren Ursprung zumeist in Aufbrausen der bösen Leidenschaften oder in moralischer Verkommenheit haben, läßt sich freilich nicht viel vorkehren; aber Uebertretungen gegen die Sicherheit des Lebens, welche in den meisten Fällen auf Nachlässigkeit oder Gewinnsucht basiren, können durch strenge Gesetze wirksam eingedämmt werden. Wenn die Herren Bauunternehmer wissen, daß ein durch ihre Schuld geopfertes Menschenleben ihnen nicht nur ein paar Monate im Gefängnis, sondern auch einige Tausend Gulden kosten wird, dann werden sie ganz sicher etwas vorsichtiger und gewissenhafter zu Werke gehen. 'Anläßlich der tragischen Katastrofe in der Maximilianstraße', *Tage-Buch des Kikeriki*, Vol. 18, 15 April 1870.
104. See, e.g., 'Die Wiener Gasfrage', *Kikeriki*, 20 September 1869; 'In puncto Beleuchtung', *Der Floh*, 13 December 1873.
105. Michaela Masanz and Martina Nagl, *Ringstraßenallee: Von der Freiheit zur Ordnung vor den Toren Wiens* (Vienna, 1996), 74. See also 'Private Gaswerke', Wien Geschichte Wiki, https://www.geschichtewiki.wien.gv.at/Private_Gaswerke.
106. 'Singspielhalle Flohrian', *Der Floh*, 4 July 1875.
107. 'Oh Yes, oder: Was dabei herauskommt, wenn ein Bürgermeister viele Sprachen spricht', *Der Floh*, 24 January 1875.
108. 'Bei Nacht am Ring', *Der Floh*, 16 May 1869.
109. Importantly, lantern smashing was often an important feature in urban uprisings and riots. For example, in the 1848 revolution in Vienna all the gas lamp-posts on the Glacis were smashed. Wolfgang Schivelbusch, *Disenchanted Night: The Industrialisation of Light in the Nineteenth Century* (Berkeley, 1995), 111–12.
110. Ibid., 83–89.
111. See 'Löblicher Gemeinderath!', *Kikeriki*, 14 May 1863; 'Die Beleuchtung der Ringstraße', *Kikeriki*, 22 November 1874. Cf. Harald Robert Stühlinger, *Der Wettbewerb zur Wiener Ringstraße* (Ph.D. diss., Zürich, 2013), 92.
112. Schivelbusch, *Disenchanted Night*, 84.
113. Ibid., 14.

114. See, for example, 'Wien ohne Gasbeleuchtung (Zukunfstbild)', *Der Floh*, 21 February 1875.
115. E.g. 'Wiener Straßenfatalitäten', *Kikeriki*, 19 December 1861.
116. See, e.g., 'Gehorsamste Anempfehlung', *Der Figaro*, 1 November 1857; 'Wichtig für alle Josefstädter', *Kikeriki*, 22 May 1862; 'Die neueste Wiener Sicherheits-Vorrichtungen für Spaziergänger (Vorschlag des Kikeriki)', *Kikeriki*, 11 June 1863; 'Neueste Erfindung des Kikeriki', *Kikeriki*, 25 March 1869; 'Kikeriki's allerneueste Erfindung', *Kikeriki*, 3 July 1871; 'Ängstlicher Phantasie-Bilder', *Der Floh*, 18 July 1875; 'Die Unsicherheit Wiens', *Kikeriki*, 27 January 1884; 'Sicherheitswachmann: Wo wollen sie hin?', *Wiener Luft* 1880 No. 35.
117. 'Jetzt wird man sich bald nur mehr in so einem gepolsterten Anzug auf die Bahn wagen können', *Kikeriki*, 23 February 1865.
118. 'Die richtige Toilette für Damen, die den Festzug ungestört mit anschauen wollen', *Figaro*, 19 April 1879 / *Wiener Luft* No. 16.
119. Anthony Vidler, 'Psychopathologies of Modern Space: Metropolitan Fear from Agoraphobia to Estrangement', in Michael S. Roth (ed.), *Rediscovering History: Culture, Politics, and the Psyche* (Palo Alto, 1994), 19.
120. See Camillo Sitte, *Der Städte-Bau nach seinen künstlerischen Grundsätzen. Ein Beitrag zur Lösung moderner Fragen der Architektur und monumentaler Plastik unter besonderer Beziehung auf Wien* (Vienna, 1889), 45–54; Vidler, 'Psychopathologies of Modern Space', 14–16.
121. Salmi, *Nineteenth-Century Europe*, 73–75. On the impact of nineteenth-century modern industrial capitalism on the shifting boundaries between private and public life, see also Richard Sennett, *The Fall of Public Man* (Cambridge, 1977), 11, 19–20; Harvey, *Paris*, 44.
122. See also Salmi, *Nineteenth-Century Europe*, 73.
123. Cf. Sennett, *Fall of Public Man*, 20, 27.
124. Richard Sennett, *Flesh and Stone: The Body and the City in Western Civilization* (New York, 1996), 370.

Chapter 3

CITY OUT OF CONTROL

Laughing at Chaos

The urban renewal in Vienna meant that especially in the early phase, from the late 1850s to the 1870s, large parts of the city were transformed into construction sites. The process of renewing the city structure was time-consuming and involved profound and radical construction works. Although the Ringstraße was opened in 1865, the city space was still far from finished. The vast monumental buildings along the boulevard were not completed until twenty years later. Before the new order could become established, many parts of the city felt unfamiliar and unstable, in a process of being transformed into something else.

This experience of the city as a chaos-like, uncontrollable space was depicted through the image of the human body. While living in this radically transforming space, the Viennese took pleasure from the comicality of the body having to adapt to the chaos-like city.[1] The bodily experiences of the changing space were a recurrent topic in the popular *Witzblätter*. For example, in 1865, the same year as the Ringstraße was opened, *Kikeriki* suggested that the German language should be updated for the city of Vienna. Instead of saying: 'Would you like to go to the city with me?', one should say: 'Would you like to fall into 13 holes and roll in 37 puddles with me?'[2]

Accordingly, bodily encounters with the changing city were repeatedly depicted in cartoons in which people staggered, fell, slid and stumbled in the capital of the Habsburg Empire.[3] The disorder of the city space affected actions in space, and made people lose control over their own body. Images of people falling down on the streets emerged repeatedly, not only in the *Witzblätter*, but could be depicted also in contemporary lithographs.[4]

The idea of losing control of one's body is, of course, deeply unsettling, which is why it has been linked to humour and comicality in many ways, especially in the bourgeois nineteenth century, an era that emphasized self-discipline and etiquette.[5] Henri Bergson suggested famously in *La Rire* (1900) that laughter is produced when a human being is momentarily transformed into a thing. Bergson argued that humour emerges from the idea of the mechanical encrusted onto the living; a man tripping and falling down on a street is an example of a comical situation where the source of humour is the idea of a human being turned into a mere object, not responsible for its movements and incapable of controlling them. Bergson offers a variety of examples of human beings as objects, from human cannonballs to clowns bouncing like rubber balls, which indicates that this kind of humour was common and popular in the late nineteenth century.[6] The philosopher Simon Critchley has pointed out in his book *On Humour* (2002) that this type of humour actually directs our attention to the dual nature of being, both being a body and having a body. Humour emerges, suggests Critchley, from the disruption in human existence when the material body suddenly takes precedence over the immaterial soul. Humour relating to the materiality of human existence thus arises from the painful revelation that human beings cannot entirely own or control themselves.[7]

Perhaps late nineteenth-century attitudes towards the body and sexuality explain why late nineteenth-century humour was so preoccupied with the material, uncontrollable body. Humour was frequently grounded in the aims of conceptualizing the body and controlling it.[8] As Critchley, among many other scholars discussing humour, reminds us, laughter often tends to reveal issues that people are troubled about or afraid of, relating thus more to feelings of uncanniness than pleasure.[9] In the Viennese *Witzblätter*, humour not only made the body visible, but also enabled a distanced, alienated perspective on it. In the context of humour, where the logic of the everyday world did not apply, and the world was made strange and unfamiliar, the Viennese could relieve their anxiety regarding the body but also explore its potential.

Humorous visions did not merely depict improper and embarrassing bodily movements, turning persons into thing-like objects unable to control themselves; there were also jokes envisioning more fantastic ways of using the city space that had become unrecognizable and unfamiliar due to the transformation process. For example, in the humorous text 'Neu-Wien' from 1874, the water mains pipes, which had caused trouble by repeatedly breaking, have now broken for good, so that there is water on the streets all the time, and everyone goes around the city in a swimsuit. The women have short hems like ballet dancers. During the winter the water is frozen and the government ministers and cathedral clergy are seen sliding to work over the ice.[10] Another example, a cartoon from 1871, suggested that in order to move in a blocked street, citizens should simply crawl through the water pipes lying on the ground, a triumph of mental and physical elasticity – at the price of losing one's dignity.[11]

These humorous visions of city life constantly adapting to exceptional situations were, of course, satirical attacks against the City Council and construction companies for causing the chaos. Yet, in addition, these jokes interrogate the conventions of using the body in urban space: what was proper and what was improper, what was normal and what was ridiculous. Laughing at comical bodily movements was a way of defining the cultural limits for actions in space.[12] Because all kinds of sliding and crawling in the city were abnormal and improper, it was also ridiculous. However, these ridiculous actions had an emancipatory or liberating element, and, in my view, they represent brief escapes from social norms and rules, expressing mixtures of curiosity and fright: what social life would and could be like if spatial order were not restored.

In order to understand the significance of these brief escapes, it is important to look at the rules that were being broken. Bourgeois late nineteenth-century Vienna was a society ruled by etiquette. All the studies on the cultural history of this era reiterate the multitude and rigidity of social rules that tied social life together and dictated how to act, dress and behave.[13] The higher one's rank, the more rules there were to follow in order to play the part in the right way. In the Hofburg, the etiquette of the Spanish Court regulated the life of the imperial family. The aristocracy imitated the court, and the *Grossbürgertum*, especially the bankers, industrialists and capital owners, tried to live up to the standards of the aristocracy by imitating their values and way of life in their new Ringstraße palaces. In the middle and upper classes, class identity was thus to a large extent performed by imitating the classes that were higher in the social hierarchy.[14]

Because of this characteristic, the Austrian liberal bourgeoisie has been seen as struggling with defining its class identity. Carl E. Schorske has suggested that, although the Austrian liberal bourgeoisie wanted to distinguish itself from the aristocracy by representing the values of rationality and order, in practice it had absorbed the aesthetic traditional culture of the aristocracy. Thus, although the members of the rising middle classes set out to distance themselves from the aristocracy by performing bourgeois values and way of life, they did this in a deeply aestheticized way, borrowed from the aristocracy.[15] The daily rhythm of the bourgeoisie went on from day to day and year to year with little variation, structured by visiting hours in the afternoon and the *Sperrstunde* (closing time) in the evening. Social status dictated what kind of carriage was proper to drive and how to interact with other members of the same class. The Viennese rules of politeness were especially sophisticated, with gentlemen always required to keep up gentlemanly behaviour (*Küss die Hand gnädige Frau*) and women to respond with chastity and grace. The fixed, aestheticized and mannered nature of Viennese everyday life has often been seen in terms of theatricality: William M. Johnston compares the social life of the bourgeoisie to a well-rehearsed play in which everyone was expected to know their part.[16] Carl E. Schorske has used the following quotation from Hugo von Hofmannsthal's *Rosenkavalier* as a distillation of how the late nineteenth-century bourgeoisie refined the niceties to a height: 'Und in dem *wie*, da liegt der ganze Unterschied'('And *how* one acts makes all the difference').[17]

The comical scenes in the humorous magazines, portraying a much more chaotic and, indeed, in a way, a much freer society, do not mean that the rules did not exist. On the contrary, the fact that the social rules and norms did exist and did play such a vital part in bourgeois everyday life helps us to understand why chaos and losing control had such vast humorous potential for the Viennese middle classes.

Furthermore, the significance of the city space as a place where these rules and norms were performed helps us to understand why it was considered funnier to fall down in the city, in front of other people, than at home alone. The fact that the city space was the stage for the public display of the self explains why so many caricatures dealt with losing control of the body in the city and so few, practically none, in the private sphere of the home. The city was a place to see and to be seen. It was part of the bourgeois public sphere, and entering the city meant entering the *Öffentlichkeit*. It was precisely this serious and dignified context that made the idea of failing to live up to it so funny. The sociologist Michael Mulkay has insightfully noted that humour not only arises from the serious world, but is also the precondition for the existence of the serious world, the only way to define and sustain that which is serious. The realms of humour and the realms of the serious are always mutually constructed.[18] As seen in chapter 1 not only was the idea of the public sphere highly valued by the bourgeoisie, but they also laid great expectations on the city renewal, with the aim of transforming Vienna into a glorious modern capital and emphasizing its role as the centre of power of the Habsburg Empire. Their laughter at chaos sprang from these serious tensions beneath the transformation process.

Moreover, it seems to me that the theme of losing control of one's body also unveils a deeper and more profound undertone running beneath the bourgeois aesthetic and performative way of life. Because control over one's body and one's actions was so important for successful participation in social life, the idea of losing this capability and turning into an object, a mere thing instead of a cultivated 'gebildeter Mensch', was profoundly radical and unsettling.

Because of the mannered and sophisticated way in which the members of the bourgeoisie used the city to express themselves, losing control of the body meant probably great embarrassment and was a source of anxiety. Thus, one explanation for jokes on falling in the city was that they provided some relief. The lens of humour was used as a distanced perspective that helped people to cope with inner disturbance and uncertainty followed by the encounters with the outer world that were somehow unexpected or uncontrolled. In fact, a great deal of humour was related to subjective bodily experiences with disturbing blocks or obstacles in the city: holes in the ground, pipes blocking the way,

Figure 3.1 'The condition of our streets', *Kikeriki*, 9 January 1876. Source: Austrian National Library.

pavements that made it difficult to walk properly, carriage rides that shook one to the bone.[19]

For instance, in the cartoon 'The condition of our streets' seen in Figure 3.1, the protagonist driving a Fiaker on an ill-paved street is bumped up and down: 'Immediately after stepping on board one is violently pushed, / then flung to and fro several times, / followed by a terrible crash; / until one finally gets out'.[20] The visual presentation of the cartoon highlights the subjective bodily experience: The disorder of the outer urban space brings the body into chaos.

This way of combining text and pictures to present a narrative storyline was something new in the humorous magazines, and represents a transition from the traditional German picture stories, *Bildergeschichten*, to modern cartoons in the second half of the nineteenth century.[21] What is also new is the idea that the protagonist is a rooster, an animal figure having adventures in the world of men. In fact, the Kikeriki rooster appeared frequently in the magazine, exploring the changing city and commenting on it. The rooster, a mascot of the magazine and a kind of self-portrait of its founder O.F. Berg, provided a distanced and critical perspective on the urban surroundings. However, it is clear that the rooster figure, with his silk hat and downtown adventures, represents a bourgeois perspective on the city.

This perspective puts the subjective experiences into their social context. The framework of humour turns subjective bodily sensations into public collective amusement. The bourgeois humorous magazines based their existence and their fun in the presumption that their audience had a shared city in which they had shared meanings and shared experiences. The cultural framework helped people to give meaning to private subjective experiences and share them with others. This explains some of the popularity of these jokes: the idea of chaos and losing control was tied to the cultural practices and mental patterns of the bourgeoisie as the negation of the real, serious order. Thus, chaos was funny.

However, it seems that their laughter at chaos was even more complex than that. As already seen in previous chapters, the Viennese Sigmund Freud, who developed his famous theory on jokes on the basis of the humour of his own time, emphasized the element of disguise as constitutive for understanding jokes.[22] Following Freud's understanding, therefore, instead of asking what these jokes tell us about the culture in which they were created, it may be more fruitful to ask what these jokes tried to hide about the culture in which they were created.

In addition to the prominence of social rules and discipline, the bourgeois culture of late nineteenth-century Vienna has often been described in terms of stagnation and inversion. As the historian Karl Vocelka has pointed out, those accounts in particular that looked back at late nineteenth-century Vienna from the perspective of the turmoil of the early twentieth century created a myth of Vienna in the age of Franz Joseph as a belle époque characterized by order and stability. In his novel *Der Mann ohne Eigenschaften* (published in three volumes between 1930–43), Robert Musil created the well-known concept of 'Kakanien' to describe this lost land of security, order and a predestined course of life. Musil's contemporary, Stefan Zweig, described in *Die Welt von Gestern* (1942) the late nineteenth-century Vienna as a world of security that was lost forever after the destructive phase of World Wars I and II.[23]

Yet although Vienna in the late nineteenth century was thus seen in retrospect as a place of order and security, behind the stability there were countless hidden tensions and conflicts that impacted on the cultural and political history of the Habsburg Monarchy.[24] Looking at late nineteenth-century Vienna through the *Witzblätter* such as *Kikeriki*, *Der Figaro* and *Der Floh*, it seems rather as if the opposite was true: tensions and conflicts underlie all the jokes, and security and stability are far in the background. The city of jokes was a city upside down, a 'verkehrte Welt' that emerged from the real city, reflecting its subterranean tensions and processes through humorous visions and interpretations of reality.[25] The world of humour was a place where the borders of the real world were shaken, a world of instability and incongruity. Perhaps due to this characteristic, jokes and cartoons seem to unveil experiences that tell more about a sense of rupture and insecurity than continuity and security.

Because the world of humour is unstable by nature, it cannot be taken as a one-to-one mirror of society. Nor can humorous accounts be understood as straightforward records of what Vienna looked or felt like during the urban renewal. Rather, the jokes and cartoons give us glimpses of the past experiences transmitted through the lens of humour. However, although the relationship between the real world and the world of humour is a complex one, the humour about chaos-like places and places that become unrecognizable and make people lose control over their bodies does draw attention to one important thing, that is, the city space as a source of uncertainty.

What seems to have been neglected so far is that although the cultural life of the *Gründerzeit* may have been stable and stagnant, the city space was at the same time in turmoil. The routines and social etiquette of everyday life may have gone on as usual, but the ground was moving, and this was something that was dealt with and captured by humour.

Witnessing the demolition and disappearance of old places in Vienna that had been there for centuries brought the Viennese middle classes into a new, transitory universe in which, in Marx's words, 'all that is solid melts into air'. Marshall Berman has compellingly suggested in his classic study with the same title that this quotation from the *Communist Manifesto* can be understood to capture some of the elusive essence of the experience of modernity.[26] The experience of modernity, argues Berman, was created by and resulted from a new way of seeing the world, the self and others: 'To be modern is to find ourselves in an environment that promises us adventure, power, joy, growth, transformation of ourselves and the world – and, at the same time, that threatens to destroy everything we have, everything we know, everything we are'.[27] The transformation of Vienna was full of this modern ambivalence. On the one hand, it was an act of creation, shaping a new kind of city for the future. On the other hand, the transformation process involved a great deal of destruction, and the annihilation of old spatial surroundings of everyday life. The experience of modernity came to life not just through entering new urban places but also by the destruction of old ones. Moreover, the Viennese did not just witness this destruction and recreation of city space, they lived through it. The transformation was experienced bodily, with all the senses, and through several decades of daily life. Therefore, jokes about the clumsy, comical encounters with the city turned weird remind us that the experience of modernity was not just an intellectual but also a bodily experience.

What is more important, the lived bodily experience of disorder in the city space meant facing the destructive side of development. As Berman has observed, the nineteenth-century bourgeoisie, absorbing liberal political values, were driven by a Faustian desire for constant growth, development and movement. The self-consciously monumental character of the bourgeois building expressed the seriousness and sincerity of bourgeois culture, which was dedicated to the ideal of order in politics and culture. However, argues Berman, there was a paradox that the bourgeoisie was reluctant to acknowledge: the willingness to destroy in the name of progress, to annihilate all that was solid and serious in order to keep the process of capitalist progress going.[28]

I am suggesting that the fugitive, elusive world of humour enabled one to process this profound paradox repressed in the official serious culture. Because jokes disguised and transferred meanings, instead of dealing with them openly, they enabled the accommodation of the ambivalence between progress and destruction, manifested in the Viennese urban renewal project. Freud saw jokes, dreams and slips of the tongue as means of dealing with unresolved problems, repressed by the conscious mind in the bourgeois culture. All of these phenomena are founded on a strategy of disguise or transfer in order to deal with issues that are too painful for the conscious mind. They all let the consciousness drop its guard and express denied wishes and unresolved problems in disguised form.[29] Following the Freudian understanding of jokes, they might at root tell of things that people try to conceal, in this case about the bourgeoisie's hidden fear of their own creativity: the image of chaos, often associated with creation myths and creativity, was also the emblem of destruction.[30] Laughing at bodies that fell in uncontrolled space tells of the sense of destruction, the dark side of the development.

Furthermore, it was the materiality of the body that linked people to the physical city space that was being demolished and rebuilt. Their humour about this city space that makes people lose control of their bodies seems to express a sense of feeling small and vulnerable in the face of progress. Although the mind and the reason might focus on the creation of a new city, the materiality of the body made it vulnerable to destruction. The laughter at chaos thus in fact seems to disguise anxiety relating to the transformation process. It was liberating and elevating because the idea of chaos was, at root, something terrifying.[31] Humour was a way of overcoming this dread.

Simon Critchley has pointed out that when Freud went back to discussing humour in his late essay *Der Humour* (1927), he made a distinction between

Figure 3.2 Rising above the chaotic city. *Kikeriki*, 26 December 1875. Source: Austrian National Library.

joke-work and humour, the former being linked to the economic side, saving nervous energy, and the latter being linked to the super-ego, which monitors the ego. Here, in late Freud, the super-ego of humour is not strict and authoritative, but friendly, offering guidance and consolation to the ego. This makes humour liberating, that is, elevating and uplifting – in Freud's term, *erhebend*.[32] Freud's idea of humour's function, as helping to overcome and transcend the conflicts and strains created by (modern) human existence, seems to give one explanation why so many cartoons, especially, contained the element of rising above the chaotic city by flying above it or by looking at it from an elevated point of view.[33] For example, in the cartoon shown in Figure 3.2, the Kikeriki rooster has invented balloons to carry himself above the chaotic street that threatens to break his bones.

The image of the flying rooster is almost a dream-like vision, reminiscent of Freud's analogy between jokes and dreams.[34] Hence, if the city of jokes is close to the city of dreams, it is interesting to compare Freud's idea of humour's uplifting function to his ideas of what it means to fly in dreams. According to Freud, dreams about flying are filled with pleasure, whereas dreams about falling express anxiety. Freud sees both dream types as originating from childhood games when the parents make the child 'fly' on their arms. This makes them involve a certain kind of childhood zeal.[35] Later on, in another chapter, perhaps not very surprisingly, Freud adds that dreams about flying and floating in the air are often associated with erotic and sexual pleasure. Yet Freud continues that the repressed wishes expressed in dreams can be more complex than they first seem.

In the extended editions of *Traumdeutung*, Freud further elaborates his analysis on the meaning of flying in dreams and gives one brief example of a tiny woman who had a dream in which she was floating in the air through the city so that she would not get dirty from the dust in the streets – a dream vision of transcending the disorder of the city, very similar to *Kikeriki*'s comical cartoon in which the rooster is flying above the dangerously chaotic street.[36] Thus, to laugh at chaos was to transcend it, to rise above it. The act of joking was in itself liberating and uplifting, because the lens of humour enabled one to look at the chaos from a distanced perspective, as if the city was looked at from high above.

My aim is not to develop a psychoanalytical reading or analysis of jokes, nor do I want to reduce the meanings of humour about falling and flying in the city to mere psychological processes. The purpose here is to pinpoint the relationship between collective anxiety, which had cultural origins and consequences relating to the transformation of urban space, and humour as a shared cultural response and solution to it, providing the means of taking distance to the chaos and controlling it.

In fact, the act of bringing chaos and disorder to the framework of humour was a way of controlling it. Because disorder was defined as belonging to the realms of the comical, it became the counterbalance of the ideal of serious order, which the bourgeoisie valued so highly. If the serious bourgeois culture of the *Gründerzeit* was defined by values of order and control, the world of humour was the world of political, social and aesthetic disorder. The theme of chaos was not limited to the comical images of living in a radically transforming city space, but extended more widely across all the realms of the comical. Because the sense of humour gave a distanced perspective, chaos could also become something to be enjoyed, because the framework of humour made the enjoyment safe.[37]

One illuminating example of how bourgeois humour was fundamentally linked to ideas of distance and control is the fact that in cartoons depicting comical chaotic scenes, the city is often seen from an elevated perspective.[38] For instance, in the cartoon shown in Figure 3.3, published in *Der Floh* in 1869, the Ringstraße is pictured as a chaotic place, full of accidents and simultaneous comic incidents, which probably results less from the fact that the Ring was a place of modern movement and traffic and more from the fact that it was funny to portray the prestigious main boulevard of the empire as a chaotic place, totally out of control.

However, although the image of the Ring is full of movement, simultaneity and fragmented events, reflecting the unpredictable nature of urban life, the vantage point is from above, transcending the disorder. The bourgeois humorous gaze on the chaotic city was also a panoptic gaze that tried to overcome the contradictions of urbanity by rising above them.[39]

Yet the number of cartoons like this radically diminished in the late 1880s, and in the turn-of-the-century cartoons the panoptic gaze has come down from

Die Ringstrasse.

Figure 3.3 'Ringstraße'. *Der Floh*, 9 May 1869. Source: Austrian National Library.

an elevated perspective to the street level.[40] This shift can be seen by comparing the previous cartoon with the one seen in Figure 3.4, which again portrays the Ringstraße and was published in *Der Floh* nineteen years later in 1888, the same year the Hofburgtheater, one of the last new monumental buildings, was opened on the Ring. Here the reader is no longer looking down on the city from high above, but is part of it. Moreover, although the city life is still comical, it is no longer portrayed as chaotic. On the contrary, everybody now seems to be in their place, and the caption poem below the cartoon heightens the sense of restoration of order as the winds let their master, the spring, know that Vienna and the Viennese are still the same, despite the wider streets and glorious new palaces:

> … Master, Vienna is still Vienna;
> And the jolly Viennese
> And the beautiful Viennese ladies
> Have taken our first breaths of wind
> Already for true spring itself.
> As soon as we had dried the streets,
> Broad between the towering palaces,
> In the pale sunshine,
> The people got up to their feet,
> And as if they were going to festivities,
> They flocked, dressed up in their best,
> Uncountable human waves,

Figure 3.4 Vienna is still Vienna. *Der Floh*, 18 March 1888. Source: Austrian National Library.

> Cheerful on the wide Ring.
> The trees were still bare and undecorated,
> But a lovely bloom of people,
> Women and many slender girls,
> Gleamed in the beam of sun
> As the men, like rapid butterflies,
> Hovered around them ...[41]

Here the well-dressed and well-mannered citizens are presented as the crown of the city. Their actions in space are graceful and mannered, celebrating the aesthetics and decorativeness of the bourgeois play. By the turn of the century, the city space increasingly became the scene of romantic encounters and flirting on the streets. It was portrayed as a place for strangers to meet, where one could see new urban figures such as the beggar and the dandy. As the images of chaos started to disappear, they gave way to scenes of encounters between different urban groups, classes and nationalities, a theme that I will examine further in chapter 5. The turn-of-the century visualizations of the city were often deliberately aestheticized, providing glimpses of urban mores and habits and of incidents from everyday life.

On the one hand, this profound change was related to a wider transition of humorous magazines in the early twentieth century from political satire to light entertainment. The growing interest in visualizing women, for instance, was related to the fact that the humorous magazines especially targeted the urban male public, preceding the later modern men's magazines.[42] On the other hand, the disappearance of chaos from the depictions of the city from the 1890s presumably reflects the fact that the great urban renewal was almost finished. The major turmoil was over. However, no matter how tempting it might be to interpret this change in terms of the establishment of a new spatial and social order after the chaotic phase of the urban renewal, it would actually be deceptive and incorrect to make such an oversimplifying analysis.

Rather than expressing a sense of stability, the absence of chaos in the humour could also be interpreted as a symptom of a crisis of the serious world. Whereas in the *Gründerzeit*, the 'age of the founders', the realms of order and disorder, the humorous and the serious, were separate and intact, even reinforced by the repeated images of chaos as comical, in *fin-de-siècle* Vienna these lines had become further blurred, leading to a merging of the spheres of the humorous and the serious. As the humorous became more serious, the serious became more playful.

The modern concept of a 'sense of humour' emerged, argues the historian Daniel Wickberg, in the late nineteenth century, as the rising middle classes came to value humour as a positive quality, which expressed a witty and amiable character and gave perspective and a sense of proportion. An ironical distance to the world, and the ability to laugh at everything and above all at oneself, became the distinctively modern understanding of humour.[43] However, the ability to laugh at everything did not mean that the serious did not exist. On the contrary, it was the sense of humour that enabled individuals to distinguish the serious from the comical and navigate between these realms without jeopardizing their counterbalance. Wickberg sees the nineteenth-century Anglo-American protestant culture as based on the separation of the spheres of the humorous and the serious. The serious world was the world of work, order and discipline, and the world of humour was the world of play, leisure and relaxation. The two spheres remained separate, as the world of humour enabled people to let off steam created by the tensions of the serious world. Thus, the world of humour did not undermine the serious, but helped to maintain it.[44]

However, in Catholic Vienna, where the serious world had already been ambivalent, the sphere of humour and the sphere of the serious did not remain separate but intertwined, leading to a crisis of the serious world, which is often described using Hermann Broch's (1886–1951) term the 'joyous apocalypse' (*fröhliche Apokalypse*).[45] Whereas the protestant culture was based on the dichotomy of work and play, sensuous Catholic aestheticism, merging with Jewish culture, did not value the serious in the same way, but emphasized the sensual, the beauty and wit. Moreover, as the historian Allan Janik has pointed out, in Vienna wit and humour were not isolated to the world of leisure and relaxation, but were essential parts of political life and literary culture. The Viennese were used to tolerating ambivalence in public speech and actions, and accepted a basic theatrical premise of bourgeois life – that people do not always mean what they say and say what they mean.[46] Thus, the collapse of the line between the humorous and serious realms of life was very much part of Viennese modernity, perhaps even one of the conditions for the breakthrough of the turn-of-the-century modernist movement. The grand narrative of the failure of liberalism has often been associated with the cultural crisis in which style, rhetoric and ironical distance replaced rationalism and serious political engagement. The leaders of the new mass parties such as Karl Lueger (1844–1910) successfully applied the art of wit and *Wiener Schmäh* to the masses. On the other hand, the breakthrough of modernism was also a collapse of solid meanings, and modernists such as Hugo von Hofmannsthal used the term *das Gleitende* to express the crisis of fixed meanings and stable structures. As turn-of-the-century Viennese culture increasingly turned to frivolous splendour, rejecting all serious thought, the turn-of-the-century Viennese modernists, the Secession movement and 'die Jungen', born during and after the urban renewal, turned away from politics to art, to the self and to the world of aesthetics.[47] Revealingly, it was the satirist Karl Kraus (1874–1936), an expert on humour, who at this point in time expressed the most profound concern for the crisis of the serious world and the decay of Viennese bourgeois culture: 'In Berlin things are serious but not hopeless; in Vienna they are hopeless but not serious'.[48]

The comical visions of the chaotic city published in the humorous magazines during the *Gründerzeit* were a way of controlling the sense of disorder and destruction. Laughter at chaos expressed anxiety, but it was creative anxiety, exploring the possibilities of disorder and overcoming the dread of destruction. Laughing at chaos defined it as comical, and thus laughter also helped to define and maintain the order of the serious world, which later fell into a severe crisis. In the next section, I will continue the discussion of the political meanings of disorder in city space by analysing jokes in which the chaos of the urban renewal was compared to the outbreak of a revolution.

1848 Revisited

During the city renewal, a group of tourists mistakenly takes a construction site for a barricade dating from the 1848 revolution.[49] An officer thinks that revolution has broken out and the proletariat is building barricades in the middle of the city; he commands his troops to prepare to fight, until it turns out that it is only the city engineer's office laying new pavements in the streets.[50] These cartoons, published in *Wiener Luft* in 1876 and *Kikeriki* in 1867, are examples of jokes in which the disorder of the unfinished city is somehow reminiscent of a revolution.

One specific type of making fun of the transformation of the city space was creating jokes in which the urban renewal was compared to a revolutionary situation. Humorous representations of how the transforming city was reminiscent of a revolution emerged in the 1860s when the construction works began, and gradually disappeared in the 1880s as the new city came closer to completion.[51] The tearing down of existing places, and the chaos of the construction sites especially, suggested the misrule and destruction of a revolution. For example, in one cartoon a group of men are standing on what seems to be a barricade made of loose cobblestones, pieces of pipes, cartwheels and broken barrels, and the caption reads: 'Paris? Barricades? Street battle? Gunsmoke? *Blousenmänner*[52] and *mitrailleuses*[53]? Oh no, but Vienna, broken pavements, water pipes scandal, endless dust, Slovaks and cracked pipes!'[54] The city renewal of Vienna was thus compared to the Fourth French Revolution, which had just taken place in Paris.

One obvious reason why the construction sites brought to people's minds images of urban riots and revolutions is that it was not long since there had been a revolution in Vienna. The city renewal began only a decade after the revolution of 1848, and the Viennese bourgeoisie still remembered what the city looked like when it was out of control. In addition, the bourgeois audience was well aware of the disturbance and unrest in other late nineteenth-century European cities, such as the founding of the Paris Commune in 1871.[55] These two things combined, it is no wonder that the disorder of the city space evoked the image of a revolution that lurked deep in the minds of the bourgeois audience.

These images of revolution, provoked by the disorder in the city space, illustrate how spatial order and control were intertwined with political order and control. In the historical context of post-1848 Europe, the demolition works, which involved tearing down houses and pavements, could create connotations of urban riots and revolutions (Figure 3.5).[56] The city space mirrored the society. As we have seen in the previous chapters, the spaces of the empire's capital, especially, were loaded with symbolic meanings. Architecture was a medium representing ideology and power. Public spaces in cities did not merely constitute the surroundings for the everyday bodily experiences of the people living there, but also embodied immaterial meanings and knowledge, thus guiding and governing the mental worlds of their inhabitants.[57] In other words, the city spaces structured the lives of citizens both physically and mentally. Thus, broken buildings, pipes and windows symbolized destruction and a threat to the prevailing order in the heavily regulated late nineteenth-century Viennese society.

Furthermore, all the nineteenth-century uprisings against the prevailing order across Europe took place in the physical city space. With industrialization, and the rising wave of nationalism, cities became the prime centres of political, economic and religious power, and they were also the main stages for uprisings

Figure 3.5 'Revolution?' *Kikeriki*, 2 August 1885. Source: Austrian National Library.

from below.⁵⁸ In the *Märzrevolution* of 1848, for example, the city space of Vienna became a battlefield, as the revolutionaries tried to seize the city by making barricades, breaking windows and gas lights, tearing up the pavements and throwing cobblestones.

The revolution was short but violent, demanding at least two thousand casualties. It started on 13 March 1848 and ended seven months later in October. In December of the same year, the eighteen-year-old Franz Joseph was crowned Emperor of the Habsburg Empire. He ruled for more than half a century, until 1916. The restoration of the power of the Emperor was sealed with violence as his troops suppressed the uprising and the revolutionary leaders were mercilessly killed, or arrested and executed.⁵⁹ Vienna saw no more urban uprisings in the nineteenth century; after 1848, the next time the army fired against citizens would be 1911, during the hunger revolts in the suburb of Ottakring.⁶⁰

The revolution of 1848 started as a bourgeois revolution that first erupted among university students. However, the lower classes, suffering in miserable conditions in the Viennese suburbs, then also joined the uprising, destroying factories, looting stores and attacking the authorities trying to control them.⁶¹ The radicalization of the masses leading to urban riots aroused unease and sheer fear among the upper and middle classes.

Fear of the lower classes was a clear source of anxiety for the Viennese middle classes. As the Austrian scholars Lutz Musner and Wolfgang Maderthaner have shown, in the bourgeois culture the lower classes were excluded and marginalized. The suburbs were associated with poverty, prostitution, criminality, sickness and lack of culture; they were the feared and desired 'Other' of bourgeois society. The workers of the Viennese suburbs surrounding the inner city thus represented both sexual desire and potential danger.⁶² The fact that the construction works for the urban renewal were often contracted out to Bohemian, Slovak or Polish workers reinforced the fear of an uprising from below. For example, in one cartoon an image of Slovak workers at the barricades in 1848 is juxtaposed with the urban renewal in 1864, highlighting the association with revolutionary destruction.[63]

Seeing workers demolishing the old city had a vast impact on the way in which the disorder of the urban space was interpreted. The haunting image of the revolutionary workers was the main reason the urban renewal was associated with revolution in bourgeois popular humour.

Consequently, commemorating the 1848 revolution further reinforced class borders and class differences. In 1898, a book titled *Fifty Years Ago: A Reminiscence of Vienna in 1848* (*Vor fünfzig Jahren: Erinnerungen an Wien aus dem Jahre 1848*), written under the pseudonym A. Rabus, gave a rare glimpse of a past that was already half a century away. While saluting the efforts of the bourgeois revolutionaries to gain political freedom,[64] the book distanced the bourgeois revolution from the claims of the underclasses. The message was clear: whereas the rebels of the inner city had noble causes, these middle-class revolutionaries had nothing to do with the anarchy and chaos that spread in the suburbs:

> At the same time it looked very different in the suburbs. While the Viennese people of the inner city risked their lives and offered their blood for their political rights and for the welfare of the whole empire, in the suburbs of Mariahilf, Lerchenfeld, Gumpendorf and in the adjoining settlements in Fünf- and Sechshaus, Neulerchenfeld, there gathered a mob and a proletariat of the most dangerous kind, who went plundering and stealing, destroying and burning through the streets.[65]

In the bourgeois understanding, the class division was clear: whereas the bourgeoisie had fought for noble causes, the workers had succumbed to violence without any higher aims than senseless rebellion, robbing and burning. This dual perspective on the revolutionary past, at the same time a source of pride for the liberal bourgeois self-understanding and a threat because of the potential danger of the underclasses, made it such an important topic for popular humour. Humour provided the means to deal with the ambiguity of what the 1848 revolution stood for. Dealing playfully with forbidden ideas about disorder and misrule and the delicate balance between fear and desire that they evoked was the fuel for the jokes about 1848. However, when the bourgeoisie played with these dangerous images of the possibility of a revolution, the resolution of the jokes was always the safe reiteration that it was in fact urban renewal and not revolution that was turning the city upside down. The old imperial power was not questioned but reinforced in city space.

The jokes and other humorous representations comparing the urban renewal with a revolution reveal how in late nineteenth-century Vienna the city space was a crucial site for negotiating the contested cultural memory of the *Märzrevolution* in 1848. In popular humorous publications, the places of the city still reminded readers of the revolution. In 1880, for example, the satirical book *A Humorous Travel Guide for Vienna and Its Surroundings* (*Humoristischer Fremdenführer für Wien und Umgebung*) depicted the old university building as a place where young students had once got heated up, but now were cooling down with ice-cream.[66] Although the present seemed to be tamed, old places such as the old university building were still reminiscent of the politically unruly past. In his short story 'How It Looked Back Then' ('Wie's damals aussah'), published in 1884, the famous humourist Vinzenz Chiavacci wrote about how the Glacis area had looked in 1855, when the traces of the 1848 revolution were still visible:

> On the front of the Burgtor gate the throats of the canons were still directed at the suburbs. Pyramids of cannonballs were piled up in front, as if at any moment it might be necessary to teach riotous crowds the logic of grapeshot. Those were some modest forget-me-nots from the year forty-eight. It did not, however, occur to the good Viennese to challenge the crude eloquence of these iron friends of order. They glanced curiously at these objects, which for seven years had no longer spoken, and then moved calmly onwards.[67]

In this story the Viennese encounter some reminders of 1848, but do not want to listen to their stories; they would rather leave the past behind, move on and forget. The urban renewal was, in fact, a process of collective forgetting. The old places, to which the memories of 1848 were attached, were demolished. The old university building, suggests Carl E. Schorske, was especially overshadowed by the revolutionary past, and between 1877 and 1884 it was replaced by a new building, situated on the spectacular Ringstraße, on the site of the former Glacis.[68] In this way, a site associated with the revolutionary uprisings was eliminated, and the university, which had been one of the starting points of the revolution, was symbolically linked to the authority of the Emperor by situating it on the Ringstraße, where all the central institutions of the state were located, surrounding the imperial seat in the Hofburg.

Thus, especially when the urban renewal first started in the 1850s, it was designed to demolish the memory of 1848 by tearing down the places that reminded people of it and by creating a new city structure that would celebrate the restoration of the power of the Emperor and prevent similar uprisings from reoccurring. The state authorities wanted to make the city more controllable. Vienna followed the model of the 'Hausmannization' of Paris, where wide straight boulevards were introduced, not only for aesthetic reasons, but because it was more difficult to build barricades on them than on the narrow twisty streets of the old city.[69] The army, in particular, emphasized the significance and necessity of the urban renewal as a means to protect the Emperor not from foreign enemies, but rather from rebellious royal subjects and revolutionaries.[70] Here again concrete material ends were intertwined with symbolic aspects. The reorganizing of the city meant also reorganizing its memories. By recreating the city, the urban renewal was intended to commemorate the survival of imperial rule from the revolution in 1848. As Carl E. Schorske has put it, the rebuilding of Vienna between 1857 and 1890 was 'post-revolutionary cultural politics through monumental building'.[71] Consequently, because the restoration of the power of the Emperor was the official narrative, expressed in spatial form in the city space, the memory of the revolution was risky and dangerous.

The events of 1848 were a sore spot for bourgeois society, something not to be spoken aloud. It was a memory that haunted the stagnant atmosphere of post-revolutionary Vienna. Much of the silence and repression of the memory of 1848 related to the violence, both during and after the uprisings, when the restoration of imperial power meant merciless executions of the revolutionary leaders. Former revolutionaries who had taken part in the events of 1848 were so afraid for their position under the neo-absolutist monarchy, and even under constitutional government, that they tended to protect themselves by turning their coats and hiding. The past was not to be discussed openly. The humourist Friedrich Schlögl, one of the key editors of *Der Figaro*, saw in this atmosphere of mistrust and uncertainty the main reason why bureaucratic standardization became such a dominant feature of Viennese society and the bourgeois mindset: the middle class exchanged their struggle for freedom and self-determination for *Kanzlei-Existenz*, security and safe jobs as clerks and civil servants.[72]

However, these same middle-class clerks and civil servants were the main readers of the humorous magazines that published jokes about 1848, which clearly shows that however much they tried, the Viennese bourgeoisie were not able to forget the revolutionary past. Unquestionably, humourists such as Schlögl were deliberately trying to remind their audience of the political ideals, such as press freedom, civil rights and a constitution, that had been so important for the 1848 generation. Furthermore, the readers themselves probably still had strongly mixed feelings about these touchy subjects that were hushed up in society. It is no wonder that precisely the issues that were not to be spoken about, the issues that were to be kept bottled in, came to the surface in humour.

Although I am not keen on interpreting jokes about 1848 solely in terms of Freudian theory, Freud's idea about how jokes at root express repressed thoughts seems to provide a fruitful way to interpret why the revolution of 1848 keeps coming up in middle-class humour. Freud argues that living in a society requires the repression of memory traces, desires and thoughts, which nonetheless keep on returning in disguised forms such as jokes, dreams and slips of the tongue. Moreover, Freud suggests that jokes do not just express repressed thoughts, but they also release the emotional energy that is normally used to hide these thoughts. This is why they provide such a relief in matters that cause anxiety.[73] This suggests that the popular humour both offered relief to the trauma, and yet sustained it, by constantly re-evoking the painful memory of the 1848 revolution.[74] Freud has used the term 'return of the repressed' to describe memory work in which nothing is forgotten, but only repressed, so that decisive early experiences return to the conscious mind in distorted or unrecognizable form.[75] Accordingly, although the memory of the revolution remained problematic, its modified comical form made the return of the traumatic experience tolerable.

Despite the fact that it is impossible to know how deep into the unconscious the roots of the humour about 1848 go, I find it safe to say that humour provided the means to ventilate the fears and desires relating to the year of the revolution. Reading the notorious humorous magazines, which were not well regarded by the authorities,[76] and possibly writing for them anonymously, could provide a safety valve for the constraints of *Kanzlei-Existenz*, the serious, regulated work in the machinery of the state bureaucracy that served to maintain the new prevailing order in society.

The ultimate achievements of the 1848 revolution – the new constitution and new liberties for the middle classes – were an important part of bourgeois identity, something to be silently if not openly proud of.[77] The liberal bourgeoisie felt a more or less hidden longing for the revolutionary year and for the political ideas that it stood for. For example, in 1873, *Kikeriki* criticized society, which had forgotten the noble causes of 1848, by juxtaposing the revolutionaries with the current Viennese, interested only in fashion and entertainment:

> 1848
> Huge excitement among the Viennese population because of the overthrow of Metternich's system. 200 students send a petition to the Emperor to end censorship; they demand freedom of teaching, public administration of justice, and parliamentary representation of the people. Large crowds gather to hear Fischhof's[78] speech.
>
> 1873
> Huge excitement among the Viennese population because of the annual Praterfahrt and spring fashions exhibited there. 20,000 slick dandies walk on the main avenue examining from time to time the dolled up ladies walking by. Large crowds gather to see when Geistinger[79] comes by in her carriage …[80]

Commemorating the 1848 revolution thus had a significant political meaning in late nineteenth-century bourgeois culture, and the humorous satirical publications were an important forum for commemorating the past and investigating its relationship to the present. Correspondingly, later in the 1890s the social-democratic humorous magazine *Glühlichter* commemorated the 1848 revolution from the workers' perspective.[81] Looking back at the revolution was thus an important part of the constant negotiation of the politics of memory and class differences in late nineteenth-century Vienna.[82] Furthermore, the processes of commemorating the 1848 revolution unveil not only the Viennese *Bürgertum*'s troubled relationship with the dangerous past, but even more so their uneasiness with the present. Jan Assmann argues that memories are never passively received from the past, but actively reinvented, modelled and reconstructed through the commemorating process in the present, which means that the present is constantly 'haunted' by the past.[83]

In the bourgeois *Witzblätter*, nostalgia for the revolutionary year emerged in the most haunting way in the poems and songs with titles like 'Märzlieder' published by *Der Figaro*, *Kikeriki* and *Der Floh* each March to celebrate the coming of spring.[84] Each March the cycle of the year evoked the memory of the *Märzrevolution*, and the *Witzblätter* reinforced this act of remembering by looking back at 1848: 'Anno forty-eight it was / Just as warm and beautiful, / A clear sky above, / in short, a regular spring. / These similarities in the weather / Remind us especially / Of the beautiful flowering / Of the ideal of liberty − …'.[85]

This welcoming of the liberation of spring after the long dark winter was a political metaphor for the desire to see the liberation of society.[86] The *Märzlieder* were not merely political statements veiled in nature symbolism, but also a way of commemorating the 1848 revolution, which was not officially permitted.

The way in which the *Witzblätter* held up the memory of the *Märzrevolution* each spring was also a way of creating hidden meanings and hopes for the future. The *März* stood for freedom. For example, in 1872, when *Floh* had to report that the *k.k. Landesgerichte* had sentenced the chief editor and publisher to prison, it added a poem called 'March' ('März') right underneath the report, celebrating the desire for freedom that will conquer in the end, despite all obstacles and repressive measures.[87]

The memory of the *Märzrevolution* was linked to the cycle of the year, and the coming of spring meant recollecting and revisiting the past. For the urban Viennese bourgeoisie, nature had a specific meaning: the trees and the many gardens of the city, and the Danube, which runs through it, were often portrayed as sites of memory and freedom. The following section investigates the anxiety about losing nature in the city. Jokes and cartoons about unruly and uncontrollable nature reveal a hidden anguish about the modernization process that was destroying the cyclical communion between the city and nature.

Unruly Nature

The change of seasons and the cycle of nature was a significant part of how the city was represented in the humorous publications. Spring was a political metaphor, as we saw in the previous section, but the seasons also gave structure to the whole of bourgeois social life, which was ruled by the Catholic calendar and etiquette. The beginning of the year was the time for great balls and Carnival, followed by Lent. The Praterfahrt on 1 May opened the summer. In July, the citizens hoped to escape the hot city into the countryside, which is why the summer was called the *saison morte*, the 'dead season' when nothing happened.

In autumn, everybody was back and the city streets again became places of encounter, to see and to be seen.[88]

Each year the *Witzblätter* made the same journey from January to Christmas, and each New Year they published poems that worked as ritual transitions from one year to the next.[89] Consequently, what was constantly recreated in the popular periodicals for decades was an image of urban life that was constantly changing in mutual correspondence with the time of year. The historian Ann Taylor Allen has noted that the cycle of nature was an important feature of the nineteenth-century periodicals, which followed the change of the seasons in their topics. Furthermore, Allen has suggested that by describing how the city lived and changed depending on the time of year, the periodicals also structured people's experiences according to the cycle of the year.[90]

The convention of understanding and representing the city in connection to the cycle of nature was the main reason why the urban renewal, which aimed at rationalizing the space and regulating nature, aroused so much resistance in popular humour. As Nicholas Green has argued, visions and discursive practices on nature were fundamentally interwoven into nineteenth-century bourgeois culture, and shaped the understanding of modern metropolitan urbanism.[91] In this section, my aim is to examine how nature in the city was interpreted and discussed through humour. The most important theme running through the humorous accounts relating to the relationship between nature and the city was the idea of losing control over nature. Phenomena like the disappearance of old gardens and the dying trees on the new Ringstraße impacted on middle-class urban life, challenged the established urban order and gave it new meanings. On the other hand, nature was the ultimate force that caused disorder in the city, and in this section my aim is to explore what jokes and cartoons about losing control over nature tell us about the experience of modernity.

The Lost Gardens

Not only was the temporal cycle of the year important for middle-class popular humour, but comical scenes were also often spatially located in urban nature. Reading the late nineteenth-century Viennese bourgeois humorous magazines over a timespan of more than thirty years, one cannot help noticing that not only the new monuments and the new streets, but also various parks and gardens frequently appeared as topics and scenes for jokes and cartoons.

This is probably due to the importance of the idea of nature in bourgeois ideology. The cultural historian Nicholas Green has observed that at the same time in the nineteenth century as Paris became a locus for emerging metropolitan modern capitalism, nature gained a significant role as a conduit of cultural power and identity for the bourgeoisie.[92] Similarly, in Vienna, gardens were an important part of the middle-class identity, places to perform bourgeois values and a way of life. Spending time in the natural environment, and naturalness, gained a new ideological and aesthetic meaning in the eighteenth century.[93] This was also a time when many new parks and green leisure areas were established in Vienna: the Prater in 1766, the Augarten in 1775 and Belvedere in 1776. The most spacious green area was, however, the Glacis area, a zone 365 metres wide between the city and the suburbs, for the most part unbuilt land, used as a place for leisure activities, especially for refreshing walks.[94] Ever since the sixteenth century, the Viennese *Bürger* had been accustomed to taking walks to the city walls and the surrounding green areas, and these *Landpartien* had become an inseparable part of the bourgeois way of life.[95]

The urban renewal interrupted this long tradition of interaction between the city and nature. It was centred on the Glacis area, destroying precisely those green areas that the citizens were so fond of. Thus, unlike in Paris or Berlin, the urban renewal in Vienna did not so much mean tearing down old urban structures, crowded city blocks with old narrow streets, but rather the elimination of nature from within the city. Perhaps due to this distinctive characteristic of Viennese nineteenth-century urbanization, modern and modernity were seen in popular humour to a large extent as the opposite of nature and the natural.

In the very early phase of the renewal process, there was already a narrative of leaving the gardens of a natural, traditional way of life and entering a comical, artificial and absurd modernity. For example, in the poem 'The lost Garden of Paradise' ('Das verlorene Paradies–Gartl'), published in *Figaro* in 1859, the loss of one of the popular parks on the Glacis was compared to the biblical expulsion from Paradise:

> … But all is vanity, and everything vain is ephemeral,
> And it has come to the time for 'the fall of Old Vienna!'
> And so we must leave the garden of innocence,
> Banished by the proposed 'Ringwall' snake
> Into the midst of newly planted chestnut-dryness,
> To finally, with ears blocked, 'face the sweat':
> To suffer the cleansing baptism of the Wasserglacis
> Carried out in the summer months, exactly between 3 and 4 p.m.,
> With a dust-removing hose from right to left …[96]

The narrative of entering comical modernity emphasized the break between the future and the past. This rupture was related to the prominent liberal *Gründerzeit* agenda to reshape the city. As discussed in the previous chapters, the bourgeois city fathers wanted to make growing Vienna safer and more controllable, and leave their legacy in improving the city. Regulating nature was one aspect of this mission.[97] Parks were an important part of the liberal bourgeois ideology and self-image: on the one hand they reflected the values of beauty and aesthetics, and on the other hand the mid-nineteenth-century bourgeoisie was already aware of the beneficial aspects of green areas for the health and recreation of citizens. For example, the liberal mayor Cajetan Felder (1814–94) stated that 'parks are the lungs of a megalopolis'.[98]

However, in popular humour the regulation of the park areas aroused extensive critical resistance. The new parks such as the Stadtpark and Volksgarten on the Ringstraße were juxtaposed with the old ones near the Glacis, such as the Paradeisgartl, destroyed in the urban renewal.[99] The new gardens like the Stadtpark, on the contrary, were mocked as artificial and bizarre.[100] The humorous representations thus constantly contrasted the new parks with the old ones, and contemporary artificial 'nature' with the lost green areas.

This yearning for a lost, liberating nature reveals the reactionary and anti-modernist vein from which much of the middle-class popular humour sprang. Yet a longing for nature had something very modern in itself. It is a good example of how late nineteenth-century anti-modernist attitudes emerged from modern experiences, and how resisting modernity acquired thoroughly modern forms of expression.[101] Furthermore, the contradiction between the lost 'real' nature and the modern 'artificial' nature opens up and intertwines with many other contradictions and paradoxes that were such an important part of late nineteenth-century Viennese culture: emotion versus rationalism, tradition versus progress, order versus disorder. Controlling nature was the ultimate act of controlling the city space, and thus a source of deep, structural insecurity, processed in humour.

One theme became the most visible symbol for the loss of nature: losing the shade of the old trees. An image of the city with no shade took on a major role in depicting the modern transformation of Vienna. In fact, over a timespan of nearly thirty years there were numerous different kinds of jokes and cartoons relating to losing the shade of the old trees. In 1864, for example, *Kikeriki* juxtaposed images of Vienna before and after its beautification (Figure 3.6), ironically suggesting that the city had been far more elegant before the renewal process. In these popular caricatures, the loss of the old trees had transformed the formerly beautiful and graceful city into something barren and comical.

The fact that the trees in the new parks were so young that for decades they gave no shade was a source of bitter humour – for decades.[102] *Kikeriki*, for instance, 'reported' in 1861 that the City Council had come up with new ideas to make the shadeless park on Franz Josefs-Quai more attractive and beautiful, including measures like obliging the four fattest members of the Council to stand in the park at noon in order to give shade to passers-by.[103] In 1884, more than twenty years later, *Floh* published the following joke on the same topic of the lack of shade in the Stadtpark:

– Just imagine, the thermometer in the city park showed 30 degrees in the shade.
– Impossible!
– But if I tell you …
– The 30 degrees I believe, but shade in the city park – impossible![104]

Figure 3.6 Vienna before and after its beautification. *Kikeriki*, 26 May 1864.
Source: Austrian National Library.

Why did these jokes emerge time after time? Didn't people get bored with them? Didn't the trees grow at all in all those years? This seems hard to believe. Although the planting of new trees was not very successful, and they had to be cut, pruned and replanted over the years,[105] the simple problems with city gardening do not entirely explain why the topic continued to entertain and preoccupy the Viennese audience for such a long time. Even more baffling is the fact that jokes describing the city as hot and unbearable without the cool shade of the old trees did not appear only during the summer months when the city was hot, but also in other seasons, when there was no connection between the immediate lived experience of the city and the jokes.[106] This leads to the conclusion that there was a symbolic layer related to the issue of losing the shade, which made it so important to the Viennese bourgeoisie.

The recurrence of one singular theme in many jokes over a particular period of time is often described as a joke cycle. Jokes and joke cycles are often seen as a modern phenomenon, characteristic of the era of mass media. In the field of folklore and social sciences, especially, there is a body of literature focusing on joke cycles and what they tell us about cultural anxieties and social contradictions in the environment that they spring from.[107] The folklorist Alan Dundes has suggested that where there is anxiety, there are jokes, enabling us to 'treat in fantasy what is avoided in reality'.[108] Dundes has also noted that joke cycles are always oral, although they may circulate in print as well.[109] Consequently, the printed jokes on losing the shade of the old trees may actually be only a small fraction of a larger Viennese middle-class oral joke culture from the period.

These late nineteenth-century Viennese jokes about losing the shade were not as homogeneous as the most famous twentieth-century Anglo-American joke cycles, such as the elephant jokes in the 1960s. Nor do they always follow the same structure; the forms of expression ranged from visual cartoons, humorous poems and merry tales to classic joke structures with an introduction and punchline.[110] However, the topic of losing the shade remained popular for a timespan of thirty years, which is why I suggest that these jokes tell us something crucial about the experience of the transforming city space.

Because the preoccupation with the loss of shade emerged so systematically and insistently, it seems symptomatic. Although the meaning of the loss of shade is elusive, there could be several explanations or possible interpretations to it. First of all, the loss of shade was clearly related to the lived experience of the city. The trees and old parks in the Glacis had been an important part of Viennese everyday life, but urbanization radically reduced and moulded the vegetation within the city. The jokes thus reference a real change in the city environment: in modernizing Vienna there were fewer trees giving any shade. Second, because nature was so important for the bourgeois ideology and self-understanding, the idea of the loss of shade was loaded with a cluster of symbolic meanings, making it a metaphor for more profound cultural change.

Accordingly, one explanation for this joke cycle is that the old trees and their shade were a way of observing time and temporality through space, as the trees stood for an organic attachment to the past. Thus, in the context of urban modernization, the idea of losing the shade of old trees seems to refer to a sense of a break with the past. Carl E. Schorske suggests that the *Gründerzeit* era was characterized by a strong culture of history, manifested most vividly in the historicist architectural programme of the Ringstraße. However, the transformation of urban space led to a profound sense of a break with the past, and a passage to ahistorical modernism came to define the cultural and political life of Vienna at the turn of the century.[111]

The jokes about the loss of shade thus seem to relate to a new kind of understanding of time and temporality. The old trees stood for an organic attachment to the past, whereas the young tree saplings clearly represented a new era with no connection to the past. Losing the shade of the old trees can thus be seen as a metaphor for losing the shelter of history and tradition, leaving people exposed to bare modern existence with no place to hide. Furthermore, in the world of art and literature, highly valued by the bourgeoisie, shade is traditionally strongly linked with the notion of identity.[112] Thus, a city without shade can be seen as an expression of a crisis of identity. The loss of shade was, in this way, not just a very profound part of experiencing the modern city, but also a wider symbol for the modern experience. It was an interpretation that through repetition became a convention that the Viennese middle-class audience could recognize.

The example of shade jokes shows that popular humour had a significant function in dealing with topics that were somehow meaningful to the late nineteenth-century Viennese audience. Humour is based on shared meanings and experiences, and, of course, it also actively shapes these meanings and experiences. What was important was the feeling of togetherness, as if the entire population of Vienna was standing in collective resistance against the changes that were taking place. In this way, the battle between tradition and modernity did not just boil down to the issue of the trees and parks in the city, making fighting for the old parks a way of resisting modernity, but the act of resistance was also a way of creating a collective Viennese identity. The collective resistance against the changes was the glue that held the imaginary community together.[113] Trees and parks were not just a link to history and tradition in general, but to their own past. The old parks had been the childhood playgrounds of the generation of middle-class men who now as adults faced the transformation of Vienna undergoing modernization. Therefore, in many cases nostalgia for one's personal past became intertwined with that for a shared past, the vanishing former Viennese way of life. The bourgeois (male) audience shared a feeling of loss, and collectively said goodbye to their childhood surroundings, as in the poem 'Abschied vom Wurstel-Prater' from 1890, in which the destruction of nature was seen as 'the modern goal'.[114]

In addition to childhood, the old shady parks were also associated with love and romance. They were repeatedly represented as the site of romantic encounters, enabling a small glimpse of freedom from the strict social etiquette. In one picture, for example, the Glacis is portrayed as a place of play and pleasure, with people lying on the ground, sitting on the grass, and kissing in the shade.[115] In humorous scenes, lovers meet under the green trees, and strangers exchange messages through the personal columns of the newspapers, and set up romantic meetings in the parks, leading to many mix-ups and misunderstandings.[116]

Regulating the parks and gardens had, thus, multiple aims and far-reaching consequences, and the discussion of nature was linked to ideas of morals and decency.[117]

Because the parks were associated with beauty, freedom, love and sexuality, the calculative regulation involved in creating the new parks was seen as threatening these values and emotions. Moreover, in the *Witzblätter*, the loss of the old environment also meant losing the inner worlds that it evoked. The old parks and gardens were an isle of bliss, the last forts of the traditional Viennese way of life, which modernization was insidiously intruding into by cutting down the old trees and with the rational arrangement of straight lines of new planting. Rational calculation was taming nature so much that it was destroying it.

Dead Trees on the Ringstraße

In addition to the parks and gardens, the theme of taming nature and the modern loss of shade appeared in another context: the Ringstraße. The Ring was not just the main street of the Habsburg Empire, but it was a boulevard. The idea of the boulevard was a nineteenth-century invention: the ideal of a wide spacious street with a line of trees and prestigious architecture that served a symbolic function more than anything else. European capitals competed in creating more and more impressive boulevards: Haussmann's Paris was famous for them, and the Unter den Linden in Berlin was the main rival of the Ringstraße in Vienna.[118]

Yet the project to mould nature to fit the prestigious image of the Ringstraße was the stumbling block for the urban renewal. When the old trees on the Glacis had been cut down to build the Ring, the new more delicate trees, such as plane and ailanthus (*Götterbäume*), did not survive in their modern urban surroundings, but died off, and the treeline had to be repeatedly replanted over the following decades.[119] Contemporary photographs show that the treeline on the Ringstraße was rather modest.[120]

Consequently, the one thing that was most often ridiculed in this proud modern boulevard was that it had no proper trees. In 1866, a year after the opening of the Ring, for instance, *Kikeriki* published a suggestion that before the new 'brooms' start to bloom, the supporting poles will develop pears.[121] What made the situation particularly embarrassing was that the Ringstraße was supposed to be the pride of the empire, something to show off to foreign visitors. This embarrassment created a multitude of jokes in which the treeless Ring was described by foreigners. In 1868, in the humorous book *Staberl als Fremdenführer*, written by Franz Masaidek, Herr Piefecke, a visitor from Prussia, describes the main street of the rival capital as follows:

> The first thing that catches the eye on the Ringstraße is – the dust. The bleakest disadvantage [in German: *schattenloseste Schattenseite*] of urban expansion is, as is well

known, the plane tree boulevards. Those poor plane trees that are not freed from their suffering by an early death should be provided with parasols next summer, to protect them to some extent against the horrible heat.[122]

Jokes about the dead trees on the Ring continued to emerge in the *Witzblätter* well into the 1880s, forming a parallel joke cycle to those jokes about the unshaded new parks.[123] The irony that the main street of Vienna, the pride of the empire, had not succeeded as a flourishing boulevard made the Ring comical, and this comicality was serious, because it undermined the whole spatial narrative that was otherwise so carefully and expensively constructed.

The comicality of the dead trees on the Ring reflected the observed contrast between the ambitious political architectural programme and the stunted nature next to it. Because of this contradiction, the jokes about dead trees on the Ring seem to exemplify the incongruence theories developed in the eighteenth and nineteenth centuries to explain the origins of humour. In these theoretical discussions, humour was seen to emerge in encountering and interpreting contradictions and paradoxes.[124] In the case of the Ringstraße, the symbolic meanings projected onto the city space created expectations of the serious, high and sublime, but the sight of the dead or stunted trees brought these expectations into an ongoing state of conflict. Because of these dead trees, instead of the experience of the Ringstraße being a coherent story of progress and power, there was a conflict, a counternarrative of the loss of control, which made the spatial environment so unsettling.

Moreover, the dead trees that did not survive in the new urban environment were, in my view, also a larger metaphor for industrialization, a theme otherwise neglected in bourgeois humour. There were, for example, no jokes or cartoons about the new factories in the suburbs. Partly, of course, this reflected the delayed industrialization of Vienna, which differentiated it from, for example, contemporary Berlin, which was living through an industrial boom in the second half of the nineteenth century.[125]

However, the persistent failure to deal with industrial development tells us, for one thing, that the bourgeois readers did not encounter many signs of industrialization in their everyday surroundings, and second, did not want to see or discuss the signs of industrialization further away. The only reference in bourgeois humorous discourse to the impact of industrialism in the everyday life of the Viennese middle classes were the dead trees: it was the new gas pipes, traffic and construction works in the city that most often killed the trees on the Ring.[126]

In the humorous magazines, this relationship between new technology, ongoing industrialization and the death of the trees was to a large extent ignored, and instead the city fathers, the City Council and other municipal institutions were held responsible for the damage. Still, I would suggest that although industrialization was never explicitly discussed, it was a source of tension behind the

Figure 3.7 The loss of old trees. *Kikeriki*, 4 August 1864. Source: Austrian National Library.

jokes about dead trees.[127] Viennese bourgeois humour about dead trees thus has its origin in wider social and cultural processes, and more specifically in the reluctance to see and acknowledge these processes.

This attitude seems very conservative or anti-modernist. However, reactionary humorous visions created to express dissatisfaction with the unnatural modern city were often in fact profoundly modern, not just because they were deeply ironical, but because this irony was used to imagine and portray things that were unprecedented and novel. For instance, in 1863 *Kikeriki* made the suggestion that because the young leafless tree branches gave the city a 'melancholy nature', various kinds of objects, like coffee pots, could be hung on them to cheer up the place.[128] Similar kinds of jokes were made recurrently over the years.[129] A year later, the magazine published a cartoon in which the formerly green treetops have been replaced by flower pots to give the citizens at least some enjoyment of greenery, since the old trees have been so murderously replaced and the new ones will not provide shade for another forty-five years (Figure 3.7).[130]

The words 'melancholy nature' seem to bear great significance. The idea of unnaturalness and melancholia went hand in hand. So did unnaturalness and comicality. As in the case of the picture shown in Figure 3.7, the comical was often something unnatural, and the unnatural was often comical.[131] Accordingly, comical modernity was often associated with the unnatural and artificial. Furthermore, these jokes express an awareness that behind the humour there was melancholia that was as impossible to hide as to mask living greenery with coffee pots or flower pots. Interestingly, these ironic solutions for improving the city seem to ridicule reason, which calculates and creates solutions for any problem, but ignores emotions. Flower pots are a 'rational' solution to the problem, but they do not feel the same. This basic contradiction between a rationalist and an aesthetic attitude towards urban space unveils a point of friction that has played a vital role in the discussion on late nineteenth-century Viennese cultural history.

Carl E. Schorske has famously argued that the two major strands in late nineteenth-century Viennese culture were the rationalist culture and the aesthetic tradition. These two strands came down from two long traditions of clusters of values and ideas, which stood opposed to each other: the rationalist tradition of the Enlightenment, and the Catholic Baroque culture of the Counter-Reformation. Both of these traditions survived, argues Schorske, to the second half of the nineteenth century, and metamorphosed to articulate two radically different modernisms. On the one hand there was the Viennese *fin-de-siècle* aesthetic culture, deriving from the Baroque emphasis on feeling, beauty and theatricality. The Enlightenment pursuit of ethics and truth, on the other hand, continued in the rationalist culture of the law, which was so constitutive for the self-understanding of the liberal bourgeoisie.[132]

Consequently, late nineteenth-century Vienna has been seen as a 'laboratory of modernity' in which these contradictory traditions collided and created new kinds of responses to the changing reality. The cultural flowering of Viennese high culture at the turn of the century has been seen as having been created by and resulting from this dynamic and volatile field, characterized by strong juxtapositions and oppositions such as the empirical natural sciences versus aesthetics, or rationalism versus culture of emotions (*Gefühlskultur*).[133]

The study of the humorous magazines and other popular literature shows that Viennese popular culture, too, was characterized by and preoccupied with the intersections of dissonant cultural processes and traditions that were somehow impossible to fit together. Popular humour was one way of sharing the ideas and emotions evoked by the dynamic field of crossing traditions and cultural processes. It was a way of exploring the paradoxical meanings of modernity. Because humour is based on recognizing and creating paradoxes and incongruences, it offered a significant means of dealing with contradictory worldviews and experiences. Furthermore, the issue of nature, especially, brings us right into the junction of rationalist culture and aesthetic tradition, which Schorske has seen as so definitive for late nineteenth-century Viennese culture.

The reason why the issue of nature was such a dominant theme in popular humour was that the two mutually opposite approaches to nature in urban space – the emotional/aesthetic and the rational – involved an unresolved conflict of desires and pursuits relating to how the green areas in the city should be arranged and taken care of. The comicality of the visions of modern and artificial nature seems to have emerged from the essential conflict between these two strands. The humorous form was able to give an expression to the major paradox of the time.

This chapter has explored cultural anxieties relating to the experience of modernity. Popular humour was a significant outlet for troubled experiences and memories relating to the change of the city. The three themes discussed in this chapter – chaos of the city, return of repressed memories and losing control over nature – were all discussed in the *Witzblätter* through powerful symbolic images: a falling body, a revolutionary barricade, a city without a shadow. The transfer and disguise of meanings into condensed images was a strategy to deal with distressing and problematic aspects of the modernization process. Consequently, in the analysis of these themes I have used Freud's psychoanalytical approach to laughter and humour as a signpost to understand the distanced and alienated language of the late nineteenth-century jokes and cartoons.

The conclusions of this chapter are not definite answers that comprehensively unravel the ambivalent meanings of jokes and cartoons, but rather analytical readings that offer cultural historical interpretations of and explanations for the baffling and repeated images of the Viennese *Witzblätter*, such as shadowless trees or chaotic street views. Yet there are, of course, other possible readings to these humorous expressions as well. In addition, the themes of this chapter overlapped with other matrices of contemporary humorous imagination. For instance, as we will soon see, the discussion on losing the old gardens was in fact part of a wider nostalgic discourse surrounding the vanishing *Alt-Wien*. The following chapters continue to investigate the affective and discursive elements of Viennese popular humour.

Notes

1. The topic of material chaos in the city was most dominant in O.F. Berg's *Kikeriki*, which was focused on the local issues of Vienna.
2. 'Wollen Sie nicht mit mir in die Stadt gehen?' 'Wollen Sie nicht mit mir in 13 Gruben fallen und in 37 Lacken herumkugeln?' ... 'Reform der deutschen Sprache für Wien', *Kikeriki*, 6 April 1865. See also, for example, 'Die Stadterweiterungs-Komission des Figaro', *Figaro*, 17 May 1862.
3. 'Eine Morgenpromenade mit Hindernissen', *Tage-Buch des Kikeriki*, Vol. 5, 5 March 1870; 'Wiener Straßen – Annehmlichkeiten', *Kikeriki*, 11 December 1871; 'Manche Straßen Wiens', *Figaro*, 25 January 1879 / *Wiener Luft* No. 4; 'Ein wahrer Schrecken', *Figaro*, 1 October 1887 / *Wiener Luft* No. 40.
4. Wien 1, Ringstraße. Josefstädter Glacis: Prekärer Zustand der Wegverhältnisse zur Zeit der Stadterweiterung. Lithographie um 1865. Digitale Sammlung ÖNB Bildarchiv und Grafiksammlung. The author of the lithograph is probably the caricaturist Vinzenz Katzler. See Elisabeth Springer, *Geschichte und Kulturleben der Wiener Ringstraße* (Wiesbaden, 1979), 631.
5. See especially Sigmund Freud, *Der Witz und seine Beziehung zum Unbewussten* (Frankfurt am Main, [1905] 2006), 115–16.
6. Henri Bergson, *Nauru: Tutkimus komiikan merkityksestä*. French original: *Le Rire: Essai sur la signification du comique* (1900) (Helsinki, 1994), 12, 44–52, 61. On Bergson's

anti-materialist philosophy, see further Michael Billig, *Laughter and Ridicule: Towards a Social Critique of Humour* (London, 2012), 128–31.
7. Simon Critchley, *On Humour* (New York, 2002), 41–43.
8. See further Daniel Wickberg, *Senses of Humor: Self and Laughter in Modern America* (Ithaca, 1998), 173–78, 184. Cf. Carl E. Schorske, *Fin-de-siècle Vienna: Politics and Culture* (Cambridge, [1961] 1981), passim, especially 208–78.
9. Critchley, *On Humour*, 56–57.
10. 'Neu-Wien', *Kikeriki*, 25 October 1874. For similar comical visions, see, for example, 'Pferde-Eisenbahn-Verbesserung', *Kikeriki*, 2 November 1865.
11. 'Dem Kikeriki ist es nach längerer Nachforschung doch gelungen, eine Passage für die Bewohner der mit Röhren, Erdhaufen, Scheibtruhen u.s.w. total verlegten Mariahilferstraße aufzufinden. Sie brauchen nämlich bloß durch die neuen Wasserleitungs-Röhren zu schliefen!' 'Die Röhrenlegung auf der Mariahilferstraße', *Kikeriki*, 22 May 1871.
12. Cf. Anu Korhonen, *Fellows of Infinite Jest: The Fool in Renaissance England* (Turku, 1999), 23–24.
13. See, for example, Allan Janik and Stephen Toulmin, *Wittgenstein's Vienna* (Chicago, [1973] 1996), 42–49; William M. Johnston, *The Austrian Mind: An Intellectual and Social History 1848–1938* (Berkeley, 1983), 116–19; Michaal Burri, 'Theodor Herzl and Richard von Schaukal: Self-Styled Nobility and the Sources of Bourgeois Belligerence in Prewar Vienna', in Steven Beller (ed.), *Rethinking Vienna 1900* (New York, 2001), 107–9.
14. Johnston, *Austrian Mind*, 34–40; Schorske, *Fin-de-siècle Vienna*, 6–7. Cf. Wolfgang Maderthaner and Lutz Musner, *Unruly Masses: The Other Side of the Fin-de-siècle Vienna* (New York, 2008).
15. Schorske uses the terms 'culture of Word' and 'culture of Grace' in his famous thesis to describe the two most important strands in late nineteenth-century Viennese cultural history. Schorske, *Fin-de-siècle Vienna*, 14–17. Cf. Steven Beller, *Vienna and the Jews 1867–1938: A Cultural History* (Cambridge, 2003), 174, 184.
16. Johnston, *Austrian Mind*, 116–19. On the theatrical nature of Vienna's public life, see also Allan Janik, 'Vienna 1900 Revisited: Paradigms and Problems', in Beller, *Rethinking Vienna 1900*, 35; Beller, *Vienna and the Jews*, 174, 184. Cf. Hannu Salmi, *Nineteenth-Century Europe: A Cultural History* (Cambridge, 2008), 77–80.
17. Original emphasis and English translation by Schorske. Carl E. Schorske, *Thinking with History: Explorations in the Passage to Modernism* (Princeton, 1998), 127. Cf. Steven Beller, 'Introduction', in Beller, *Rethinking Vienna 1900*, 14.
18. Michael Mulkay, *On Humour: Its Nature and Its Place in Modern Society* (Cambridge, 1988), 1. See also Wickberg, *Senses of Humor*, 170–218.
19. 'Ansicht der "Pflökeln" auf dem Exerzierplatz', *Kikeriki*, 8 October 1863; 'Seitdem in Wien so viel gebaut wird', *Kikeriki*, 15 September 1864; 'Wenn's vielleicht einmal Zeit haben?', *Kikeriki*, 11 February 1864; 'Was bei uns alles geschehen muß, bis Etwas geschieht', *Kikeriki*, 28 April 1864; 'Ringstraßen-Kalamitäten', *Kikeriki*, 8 April 1869; 'Als die ehrsamen Schildner ein großes Loch ausfüllen wollten', *Figaro*, 20 February 1869; 'Wiener Gasflammen', *Figaro*, 6 January 1872; 'Wiener Straßengenüsse', *Figaro*, 17 June 1882 / *Wiener Luft* No. 24.
20. Gleich nach dem Einsteigen verspürt man heftige Stöße, / man wird hierauf noch einige Male hin- und hergeschleudert, / welchen einen fürchterlichen Krach folgt; / bis man endlich aussteigt. 'Der Zustand unserer Straßen', *Kikeriki*, 9 January 1876.

21. Jens Balzer, '"Hully gee, I'm a Hieroglyphe": Mobilizing the Gaze and the Invention of Comics in New York City, 1895', in Jörn Ahrens and Arno Meteling (eds), *Comics and the City: Urban Space in Print, Picture and Sequence* (New York, 2010), 19–23; David Kunzle, 'The Voices of Silence. Willette, Steinlen and the Introduction of the Silent Strip in the *Chat Noir* with a German Coda', in Robin Varnum and Christina T. Gibbons (eds), *Comics: Word and Image* (Jackson, 2001), 3–6. See also Scott McCloud, *Understanding Comics: The Invisible Art* (New York, 1993), 17–18, 138–49.
22. Freud, *Der Witz*, passim, especially 115–16. See also Billig, *Laughter and Ridicule*, 141–61.
23. Stefan Zweig, *Die Welt von Gestern: Erinnerungen eines Europäers* (Frankfurt am Main, [1942] 2005), 15, 19–20. See also Karl Vocelka, *K.u.K. Karikaturen und Karikaturen zum Zeitalter Kaiser Franz Josephs* (Vienna, 1986), 7–8; Johnston, *Austrian Mind*, 30–31; Janik and Toulmin, *Wittgenstein's Vienna*, 13. Cf. Salmi, *Nineteenth-Century Europe*, 8.
24. Various studies in the cultural history of late nineteenth-century Vienna have emphasized the contradiction between cultural inertia and the avant-garde, between conservative institutions and innovative radical openings, in various aspects of culture that emerged despite – or because of – the rigid official atmosphere. See further Johnston, *Austrian Mind*, 396–99.
25. Cf. Critchley, *On Humour*, 1; Peter Berger, *Redeeming Laughter: The Comic Dimension of Human Experience* (Berlin, 1997), x.
26. See further Marshall Berman, *All That Is Solid Melts Into Air: The Experience of Modernity* (New York, 1988), 87–129.
27. Ibid., 15.
28. 'The pathos of all bourgeois monuments is that their material strength and solidity actually count for nothing and carry no weight at all, that they are blown away like frail reeds by the very forces of capitalist development that they celebrate.' Berman, *All That Is Solid*, 99. See also 90–105.
29. On the similarities between joke-work and dream-work, see Freud, *Der Witz*, 121. See also Billig, *Laughter and Ridicule*, 145–46.
30. See, for example, 'Figaros Stadterweiterungsplan', *Figaro*, 23 October 1858; 'Chaos', *Figaro*, 25 December 1869; 'Zweites Concert neuer Musik', *Figaro*, 15 October 1859; 'Wiener Gasflammen', *Figaro*, 30 September 1865; 'Der Behördenstyl', *Kikeriki*, 21 July 1864; 'Das Riesenmikroskop im Josefstädter-Theater', *Kikeriki*, 6 July 1873.
31. Cf. Janik and Toulmin, *Wittgenstein's Vienna*, 42.
32. Sigmund Freud, *Der Humor* (Frankfurt am Main, [1927] 2006), 254. See also Critchley, *On Humour*, 95; Wickberg, *Senses of Humor*, 90–91.
33. See, for example, 'Neue Omnibusverkehr für Wien', *Kikeriki*, 30 June 1864; 'Die Planken auf dem Paradeplatz', *Kikeriki*, 21 January 1872.
34. Freud worked on his books *Traumdeutung* (1899/1900) and *Der Witz und seine Beziehung zum Unbewussten* (1905) partly simultaneously, although he published the former five years before the latter. One of his major arguments was the analogy between jokes and dreams. See further Elliott Oring, *Engaging Humour* (Champaign, 2003), 27; Billig, *Laughter and Ridicule*, 14.
35. Sigmund Freud, *Die Traumdeutung* (Leipzig and Vienna, 1899/1900), 187–88.
36. Sigmund Freud, *Traumdeutung*, 3. vermehrte Auflage (Leipzig and Vienna, 1911), 204.

37. Cf. William F. Fry, 'Humor and Chaos', *Humor. International Journal of Humor Research* 3–5 (1992), , 219–220, 228–231; John Morreall, 'Enjoying Incongruity', *Humor. International Journal of Humor Research* 2(1) (1989), 4–5, 11–13.
38. See, for example, 'Ringstrassen-Corso', *Die Bombe*, 5 March 1871; 'Der Prater-Corso', *Kikeriki*, 15 April 1877; 'Ringstraßenbilder', *Wiener Caricaturen*, 27 January 1881.
39. The panoptic gaze has been seen as a dominant nineteenth-century way of perceiving and visualizing urbanity. A distanced gaze from an elevated viewpoint promised control over the city, overcoming the controversies and contradictions of urbanity. See further Ole Frahm, 'Every Window Tells a Story: Remarks on the Urbanity of Early Comic Strips', in Ahrens and Meteling, *Comics and the City*, 33.
40. See, for example, 'Nach den Festtagen', *Der Floh*, 15 May 1881; 'Frühlingsbilder', *Figaro*, 16 April 1892 / *Wiener Luft* No. 16.
41. … Herrscher, Wien ist Wien geblieben; / Und die Wiener, die fidelen, / Und die schönen Wienerinnen / Nehmen unser erstes Wehen / Schon für regelrechten Frühling. / Kaum daß wir die breiten Straßen / Zwischen ragenden Palästen / Nur ein wenig aufgetrocknet, / Bei noch mattem Sonnenscheine / Fuhr's den Leuten in die Beine, / Und als ginge es zu Festen // Strömten, festlich angezogen, / unzählbare Menschenwogen, / Fröhlich nach dem breiten Ring. / Kahl und schmucklos noch die Bäume, / Aber holde Menschenblumen, / Frauen und viel schlanke Mädchen, / Schimmerten im Sonnenstrahle, / Von den raschen Schmetterlingen / Aus der Männerwelt umschwebt … 'Ringstraßen-Frühling', *Der Floh*, 18 March 1888.
42. Andreas Graf and Susanne Pellatz, 'Familien- und Unterhaltungszeitschriften', in Georg Jäger (ed.), *Geschichte des Deutschen Buchhandels im 19. und 20. Jahrhundert*. Vol. 1. *Das Kaiserreich 1871–1918* (Frankfurt am Main, 2003), 493–96. Later the Secession movement had a strong impact on the visual style of *Der Floh* magazine in particular. See, e.g., 'Fin de siècle', *Der Floh*, 1 January 1899; 'Wiener Skizzen', *Der Floh*, 22 January 1899; 'Frauentaktik', *Figaro*, 18 February 1899; 'Secession', *Der Floh*, 2 April 1899.
43. Wickberg, *Senses of Humor*, 170–218, especially 212.
44. Ibid., 172.
45. Johnston, *Austrian Mind*, 391–402.
46. The emphasis on wit and eloquence has been seen as a result of the impact of the Catholic Counter-Reformation on the Viennese mentality. Janik, 'Vienna 1900 Revisited', 35–37.
47. Schorske, *Fin-de-siècle Vienna*, 4–5 and passim; Beller, *Vienna and the Jews*, 176–77; Lutz Musner, *Der Geschmack von Wien: Kultur und Habitus einer Stadt* (Frankfurt am Main, 2009), 11–14, 119–20.
48. See further Marjorie Perloff, *Edge of Irony: Modernism in the Shadow of the Habsburg Empire* (Chicago, 2016), 21. See also Johnston, *Austrian Mind*, 122.
49. 'Wien in der Fremdesaison', *Figaro*, 5 August 1876 / *Wiener Luft* No. 32.
50. 'Auf dem Stefansplatze', *Kikeriki*, 3 October 1867.
51. Excel file held by the author.
52. German name for a group of revolutionaries in Paris.
53. French machine gun.
54. Paris? Barricaden? Straßenkampf? Pulverrauch? Blousenmänner und Mitrailleusen? O Nein, sondern Wien, Pflasteraufritzung, Wasserleitungsscandal, endloser Staub, Slovaken und zersprungene Röhren! *Kikeriki*, 29 May 1871.

55. See, for example, 'Friedrich Schiller und die Pariser Commune', *Kikeriki*, 5 June 1871. On the history of nineteenth-century urban revolutions in Paris, see further David Harvey, *Paris, Capital of Modernity* (New York, 2006), 59–89, 311–40.
56. Revolution? Nein – aber so dürfte es in Wien drei Jahr' hindurch aussehen, wenn das Pflaster in allen Straßen wegen der Gasleitung aufgerissen wird. *Kikeriki*, 2 August 1885.
57. Henri Lefebvre, *The Production of Space* (Oxford, [1974] 1991), 10–11. Beatriz Colomina has suggested that in its ability to mediate meanings and patterns of thoughts, architecture should be understood as a mass medium. Beatriz Colomina, *Privacy and Publicity: Architecture as Mass Media* (Cambridge, MA, 1998), 14–15.
58. Maderthaner and Musner, *Unruly Masses*, 61.
59. See further, e.g., Karl Vocelka, *Geschichte Österreichs: Kultur-Gesellschaft-Politik* (Munich, 2011), 198–205.
60. There were, however, workers' riots in the suburbs in the 1860s, 1870s and even more from the 1880s onwards as the struggles of the urban underclasses became centrally organized with the emergence of a democratic mass party. Maderthaner and Musner, *Unruly Masses*, 7, 95–96.
61. See, for example, Vocelka, *Geschichte Österreichs*, 198.
62. Maderthaner and Musner, *Unruly Masses*, 58–61.
63. 'Im Jahre 1848 haben die Slovaken die Barrikaden erstürmt und die Erde gleich gemacht – und jetzt machen sie's selber! 'Unterschied zwischen 1848 und 1864', *Kikeriki*, 25 August 1864. See also 'Wiener Straßen-Annehmlichkeiten', *Kikeriki*, 11 December 1871; 'Beim Rathausbaue', *Kikeriki*, 17 November 1872; 'Die Kroaten in Wien', *Kikeriki*, 17 August 1884.
64. Although the major claims of the liberal bourgeoisie – constitutional government, freedom of the press and a National Guard (Nationalgarde) – were not achieved in 1848, by the end of the century the absolutist regime had been replaced and Austria had a new liberal constitution and a free press.
65. Um dieselbe Zeit sah es aber in den Vorstädter anders aus. Während das Wiener Volk in der inneren Stadt für sein politisches Recht und für das Wohl des Gesammt-Reiches sein Leben wagte und sein Blut zum Opfer brachte, sammelte sich in den Vorstädten Mariahilf, Lerchenfeld, Gumpendorf und in den daran angrenzenden Vororten Fünf- und Sechshaus, Neulerchenfeld und Umgebung der Pöbel und ein Proletariat der gefährlichsten Art zusammen, und zog plündernd und raubend, sengend und brennend durch die Straßen. A. Rabus, *Vor fünfzig Jahren: Erinnerungen an Wien aus dem Jahre 1848* (Würzburg, 1898), 8–9.
66. Julius Neidl, *Humoristischer Fremdenführer für Wien und Umgebung* (Vienna, 1880), 14.
67. Auf der Plattfäche des Burgtores dräuten noch die Kanonenschlünde nach den Vorstädten. Kugelpyramiden waren davor aufgehäuft, als gälte es jeden Augenblick, aufrührerischen Scharen die Logik der Kartätschen beizubringen. Das waren so einige bescheidene Vergißmeinnichte aus dem Jahre achtundvierzig. Den guten Wienern fiel es aber nicht ein, die plumpe Beredsamkeit dieser ehernen Ordnungsfreunde herauszufordern. Sie beguckten neugierig die Dinger, die schon sieben Jahre nicht mehr zu Wort gekommen waren, und schritten beruhigt weiter. Vinzenz Chiavacci, *Geschichten aus Alt-Wien* (Vienna, [1884] 1973), 27–28.
68. The new university building was designed by Heinrich von Ferstel (1828–83). See further Schorske, *Fin-de-siècle Vienna*, 38–41.

69. Schorske, *Fin-de-siècle Vienna*, 24–33. On the effects of the 1848 revolution on the cultural history of Paris, see further Harvey, *Paris*, passim, especially 2–19.
70. The vast unbuilt belt between the suburbs and the inner city protected the court and the upper classes. Therefore, in the 1850s the army tried to keep this place for itself for military use. Schorske, *Thinking with History*, 106; Maderthaner and Musner, *Unruly Masses*, 32.
71. Schorske, *Thinking with History*, 106–8. See also Springer, *Geschichte und Kulturleben*, 1, 78.
72. Jo Ann Mitchell Fuess, *The Cultural Crisis of Lower Middle Class Vienna 1848–1892: A Study of the Works of Friedrich Schlögl* (Lincoln, 1992), 71–72. On the world of security of the officials, see also Johnston, *Austrian Mind*, 45–46.
73. Freud, *Der Witz*, 131–33.
74. Cf. Jan Assmann, *Moses the Egyptian: The Memory of Egypt in Western Monotheism* (Cambridge, MA, 1999), 25.
75. Sigmund Freud, *Moses and Monotheism* (Hertfordshire, 1939), 197–205.
76. See further the section 'Censorship, Satire and the Public Sphere' in chapter 1.
77. On the impact of the 1848 revolution on the late nineteenth-century German liberal movement in the Habsburg Monarchy, see further Pieter M. Judson, *Exclusive Revolutionaries: Liberal Politics, Social Experience and National Identity in the Austrian Empire, 1848–1914* (Ann Arbor, 1996), 1–10.
78. Adolf Fischhof (1816–93) was one of the leaders of the 1848 revolution in Vienna.
79. Marie Geistinger (1836–1903) was a famous actress and an operetta singer.
80. 1848. Große Aufregung unter der Bevölkerung Wiens wegen Umsturz des Metternich'schen Systems. 200 Studenten richten eine Adresse an den Kaiser um Aufhebung der Zensur; sie bitten um Lehrfreiheit, öffentliche Rechtspflege und Volksvertretung. Großes Gedränge, um den Reden Fischhof's zu hören. / 1873. Große Aufregung der Bevölkerung Wiens wegen der Praterfahrt und den dabei zu Tage tretenden Frühjahrsmoden. 20 000 geschniegelte Modegecken spazieren in der Hauptallee auf und ab und zu mustern die vorübergehenden aufgedonnerten Damen. Großes Gedränge, wenn die Geistinger angefahren kömmt. 'In den Märztagen von 1848 und 1873', *Kikeriki*, 16 March 1873. Cf. 'Eine historische Paralelle', *Der Floh*, 21 March 1869.
81. See, for example, 'Die Brüder. Eine Erinnerung an die Märztage 1848', *Glühlichter*, 8 March 1890; 'Politische Zurückschau auf den Monat März', *Glühlichter*, 5 April 1890.
82. On the politics of forgetting and remembrance, see further Assmann, *Moses the Egyptian*, 8–9.
83. Ibid., 9, 25, 27.
84. See, for example, 'Der März, er ist gekommen!', *Kikeriki*, 1 March 1863; 'März-Lied', *Figaro*, 6 March 1869; 'Am ersten April', *Der Floh*, 4 April 1869; 'Zum 13. März', *Figaro*, 15 March 1873; 'Im März 1874', *Kikeriki*, 12 March 1874; 'Märzlied', *Figaro*, 15 March 1884.
85. Anno achtundvierzig war es / Auch so warm und auch so schön, / 's gab ein Firmament, ein klares, / kurz ein Frühlings-Phänomen. / Diese Witt'rungsähnlichkeiten / sie erinnern uns zumal / an die schönen Blütezeiten / Von dem Freiheits-Ideal … 'Schöne Märztage (Eine Reminizenz)', *Kikeriki*, 9 March 1882. See also 'Der 13. März war wiedergekommen', *Figaro*, 18 March 1882.

86. The metaphor of winter as a symbol for political repression was well known in the German satirical tradition. The most famous example is Heinrich Heine's *Deutschland: Ein Wintermärchen*, which he wrote in 1844 in exile in Paris.
87. 'März', *Der Floh*, 10 March 1872.
88. When the Ringstraße was finished, it became a place where the crème de la crème of society met, as in a fine salon. Marianne Bernhard, *Die Wiener Ringstraße: Architektur und Gesellschaft 1858–1906* (Munich, 1992), 32; Springer, *Geschichte und Kulturleben*, 622–26.
89. See, for example, 'Zeitgemäßes Herbstlied', *Kikeriki*, 1 October 1868; 'Im schönen Mai', *Figaro*, 13 May 1875; 'In der Junihitze', *Der Floh*, 21 June 1885; 'Saison-Beginn', *Der Floh*, 6 September 1885; 'Wien im Schnee', *Der Floh*, 17 January 1886; 'Frühling', *Der Floh*, 4 April 1886; 'Herbstliches', *Der Floh*, 14 October 1888; 'Winterlied', *Der Floh*, 6 January 1889.
90. Ann Taylor Allen, *Satire and Society in Wilhelmine Germany: Kladderadatsch & Simplicissimus 1890–1914* (Lexington, 1984), 4.
91. See further Green's study on nineteenth-century bourgeois culture in Paris. Nicholas Green, *The Spectacle of Nature* (Manchester, 1990), especially 11–13.
92. Ibid., 12–13.
93. Cf. Robert Rotenberg, *Landscape and Power in Vienna* (Baltimore, 1995), 84–87; Michaela Masanz and Martina Nagl, *Ringstraßenallee: Von der Freiheit zur Ordnung vor den Toren Wiens* (Vienna, 1996), 80–85.
94. There were altogether 129,736 hectares of green area outside the city walls. The Glacis was also used for military purposes, but as much as 64.8 per cent of the area was used as a public park. See Kurt Mollik, Hermann Reining and Rudolf Wurzer, *Planung und Verwirklichung der Ringstraßenzone* (Vienna, 1980), 63–65; Masanz and Nagl, *Ringstraßenallee*, 5, 57–59.
95. Masanz and Nagl, *Ringstraßenallee*, 65.
96. … Aber eitel ist Alles und alles Eitle vergänglich, / Und erfüllt ist die Zeit des 'Sündenfalles von Alt-Wien!' /Und so müssen wir denn hinaus aus dem Garten der Unschuld, / Umgepeitscht von der projektirten Schlange des 'Ringwalls,' / Mitten hinein in die neugepflanzte Kastanien-Dürrniß, / Um zuslezt, 'in des Angesichts Schweiß,' mit zerstommelten Ohren, / auf dem 'Wasserglacis' die Reinigunstaufe zu leiden, / Die in den Sommermonden, genau zwischen 3 Uhr und 4 Uhr, / Vom staublöschenden Schlauch noch rechtshin und linkshin ertheilt wird. 'Das verlorene Paradies–Gartl. Letzter Gesang', *Figaro*, 1 October 1859. On the interpretation of this poem, see also Springer, *Geschichte und Kulturleben*, 217–18.
97. See also Heidi Hakkarainen, 'City Upside Down: Laughing at the Flooding of the Danube in Late Nineteenth-Century Vienna', in Deborah Simonton and Hannu Salmi (eds), *Catastrophe, Gender and Urban Experience, 1648–1920* (New York, 2017), 157–76.
98. Schorske, *Fin-de-siècle Vienna*, 26.
99. The Volksgarten was extended in the urban renewal to the Ringstraße, and the 65,000 m^2 Stadtpark was opened in 1862.
100. See, e.g., 'Plan für den Wiener Stadtpark', *Figaro*, 14 December 1861; 'Wiener Punschlied', *Kikeriki*, 8 October 1863.
101. The sociologist David Frisby and the historian Sandor Békési have both drawn attention to the way that the anti-modernist movements and nostalgia for lost traditions

were a constitutive part of the modern project, which was characterized by an ongoing dialectic between tradition and progress. David Frisby, *Cityscapes of Modernity: Critical Explorations* (Cambridge, 2001), 18, 168–82; Sandor Békési, 'The Attraction of Heimat: Homeland Protection in Vienna around 1900, or the Preservation and Reform of the City', in Arnold Bartetzky and Marc Schalenberg (eds), *Urban Planning and the Pursuit of Happiness* (Berlin, 2009), 72, 76. See also Musner, *Geschmack von Wien*, 188–94.

102. 'Die beiden Riesen', *Kikeriki*, 25 September 1862; 'Der Stadtpark wird dem öffentlichen Vergnügungen vergeben', *Kikeriki*, 1 January 1863; 'Wir haben immer Malheur!', *Kikeriki*, 13 June 1867; 'Die Vindobona und ihre Gartenanlagen', *Der Floh*, 18 July 1880; 'Bei der Hitze', *Der Floh*, 10 July 1881; 'Kurzgefaßte Geographie von Wien', *Figaro*, 28 May 1887 / *Wiener Luft* No. 22.

103. 'Park am Franz Josefs-Quai', *Kikeriki*, 7 November 1861.

104. – Denken Sie sich, der Thermometer im Stadtpark hat 30 Grad im Schatten gezeigt. / – Unmöglich! / – Aber wenn ich Ihnen sage … / – Die 30 Grad will ich Ihnen ja glauben, aber Schatten im Stadtpark – unmöglich! 'Aus den Tagen der Hitze', *Der Floh*, 20 July 1884.

105. On the difficulties in planting new trees in Vienna, see further Masanz and Nagl, *Ringstraßenallee*, 96–126.

106. For example, 'In Angelegenheiten des Wiener Stadtparks', *Kikeriki*, 5 March 1863; 'Wiener Punschlied', *Kikeriki*, 8 October 1863; 'Schubert und Zelinka im Wiener Stadtpark', *Kikeriki*, 6 March 1879.

107. See, e.g., Alan Dundes, *Cracking Jokes: Studies of Sick Humour Cycles and Stereotypes* (Berkeley, 1987); Elliott Oring, *Jokes and Their Relations* (Lexington, 1992); Christie Davies, *Jokes and Targets* (Bloomington, 2011).

108. Dundes, *Cracking Jokes*, 4.

109. Ibid., vi–vii, 6.

110. On joke structures, see further, e.g., Arthur Koestler, *The Act of Creation* (London, 1964), 35–37.

111. See further Schorske, *Thinking with History*, 125–56 and passim.

112. Famous nineteenth-century narratives about losing one's shadow include Adalbert von Chamisson's *Peter Schlemihls wundersame Geschichte* (1814) and H.C. Andersen's *Skyggen* (1847).

113. 'Zur bevorstehenden Wurstelprater-Regulirung', *Der Floh*, 6 June 1869.

114. 'Abschied vom Wurstel-Prater', *Kikeriki*, 16 March 1890.

115. See 'Wenn das Glacis in Folge der Neubauten verschwinden muss, was soll alsdann mit allen Denen geschehen?', *Figaro*, 28 August 1858. See also Harald Robert Stühlinger, *Der Wettbewerb zur Wiener Ringstraße* (Ph.D. diss., Zürich, 2013), 77.

116. 'Das Trauerspiel vor dem Burgthore', *Figaro*, 8 December 1866; 'Aus dem Stadtpark', *Figaro*, 8 July 1876 / *Wiener Luft* No. 28; 'Im Volksgarten', *Figaro*, 22 April 1876 / *Wiener Luft* No. 17; 'Dandy: Ist der Platz hier frei, Fräulein!', *Der Floh*, 4 November 1888.

117. E.g. *Kikeriki*, 12 December 1861. For more on the construction of the Stadtpark and how it was discussed in the press in general, see Masanz and Nagl, *Ringstraßenallee*, 83–87; Springer, *Geschichte und Kulturleben*, 205–16.

118. Harvey, *Paris*, 113–15; Berman, *All That Is Solid*, 150–51; Springer, *Geschichte und Kulturleben*, 616.

119. Masanz and Nagl, *Ringstraßenallee*, 2, 97–133.

120. E.g. Schottenring, 1875. Blickfänge einer Reise nach Wien – Fotografien 1860–1910. Ausstellungskatalog des Wien Museums, 2006.
121. 'Unsere Ringstraße-Alleen', *Kikeriki*, 29 March 1866.
122. Das erste, was Einem auf der Ringstraße in die Augen fällt, ist – der Staub. Die schattenloseste Schattenseite der Stadterweiterung sind bekanntlich die Platanen-Alleen. Die armen Platanen, die nicht ein früher Tod von ihren Leiden befreit, sollen in nächsten Sommer mit Sonnenschirmen versehen werden, um sich wenigstens einigermaßenßen gegen die fürchterliche Hitze schützen zu können. Franz Masaidek, *Staberl als Fremdenführer in Wien und Umgebung* (Vienna, 1868), 48.
123. 'Der Commune Wiens geht so schlecht, dass sie gezwungen ist die Bäume zu versetzen', *Kikeriki*, 5 February 1863; 'Letztes Mittel', *Kikeriki*, 14 April 1872; '1100 Ailanthusbäume', *Kikeriki*, 24 June 1880; 'Todeslied des ersäuften Ailanthus', *Kikeriki*, 11 July 1880; 'Ringstraße', *Kikeriki*, 30 June 1881; 'Ersatz der Ringstraßenbäume', *Figaro*, 30 April 1881 / *Wiener Luft* No. 18; 'Die neue Baumpflanzung auf der Ringstraße', *Kikeriki*, 19 March 1882.
124. One of the most famous observations of this time was Immanuel Kant's widespread argument from the *Critique of Judgement* that humour is based on strained expectations that dissolve into nothing. 'Laughter is an affection arising from the sudden transformation of a strained expectation into nothing.' Cited in John Morreall, *The Philosophy of Laughter and Humor* (Albany, 1987), 47. On the early incongruence theories, see further ibid., 45–82; Critchley, *On Humour*, 5; Wickberg, *Senses of Humor*, 54–64; Billig, *Laughter and Ridicule*, 57–76.
125. Renate Banik-Schweizer and Gerhard Meißl, *Industriestadt Wien: Die Durchsetzung der industriellen Marktproduktion in der Habsburgerresidenz* (Vienna, 1983), 22–33, 120. See also Bertrand Michael Buchmann, 'Die Epoche vom Ende des 18. Jahrhunderts bis um 1860: Wirtschaft und Finanzen', in Peter Csendes und Ferdinand Oppl (eds), *Wien – Geschichte einer Stadt: Von 1790 bis zur Gegenwart* (Vienna, 2006), 134–35.
126. Masanz and Nagl, *Ringstraßenallee*, 99–133.
127. Cf. Salmi, *Nineteenth-Century Europe*, 12–13.
128. 'Neueste Verschönerungs Vorschläge', *Kikeriki*, 2 July 1863.
129. 'Wieder ein Prächtiger Vorschlag des Kikeriki', *Kikeriki*, 18 August 1864; 'Zur Baumfrage', *Kikeriki*, 24 July 1871; 'Ringstraßen-Bepflanzung', *Kikeriki*, 28 April 1872: 'Unsere Ringstraßen-Alleen', *Kikeriki*, 24 April 1881.
130. 'Glacisbäume', *Kikeriki*, 4 August 1864.
131. Cf. 'Das Malheur des Sonntagreiters', *Der Floh*, 21 September 1979; Bergson, *Nauru*, 28–35.
132. Schorske, *Thinking with History*, 11, 125–36. On the critique of Schorske's thesis, see Beller, 'Introduction', 11–18.
133. Wolfgang Maderthaner, 'Von der Zeit um 1860 bis zum Jahr 1945', in Csendes and Oppl, *Wien – Geschichte einer Stadt*, 249–55; Janik, 'Vienna 1900 Revisited', 40–41.

Chapter 4

KNOWING THE CITY

(Mis)Reading the City and the Deception of Sight

Since the contributions of Walter Benjamin and Georg Simmel, studies of modernity and modern experience have emphasized the interconnection between change in the urban environment and shifts in perception in trying to decipher this new kind of spatial surroundings. Life in the modern city did not merely create new kinds of rhythms of life, but it shaped and remodelled the sensory experiences through which urbanity was lived and reflected. Walter Benjamin is one of the most famous theorists to have paid attention to the fragmentation of experience, arguing that in the modern environment, long, integrated experience (*Erlebnis*) was increasingly being transformed into streams of momentary and isolated experiences (*Erfahrung*).[1] According to the body of work written on modernity since the 1980s, especially, the foundations of modern experience thus lie in the city environment and in its fragmented and simultaneous nature, expressing a new kind of rhythm, continuous change and movement.[2]

Furthermore, the research tradition on modernity has emphasized the role of visuality in the new urban surroundings. Mass print culture created a vast number of texts and images that circulated in the growing European metropolises, creating a discursive environment that constantly reimagined the city, giving meanings and values to the continuously changing urban life. According to the widely influential studies of Peter Fritzsche, reading was an essential part of understanding the nineteenth-century city. Urban representations shaped the ways in which the modern metropolitan environment was encountered and conducted.[3]

The Viennese humorous texts and illustrations provided a self-conscious meta-perspective to this growing presence of texts and images in urban space.

Texts were depicted as a fundamental part of the new modern city, and the growing presence of textuality in urban space was an important component in many comical scenes.[4] Encounters with prohibition signs and advertisements, especially, were presented in comical situations, in which passers-by and incidental strangers stop in front of the signs to discuss them.[5] Often the presence of the texts, and ads in particular, was portrayed as unnerving or even suppressive. Their increasing visibility in urban space was confronted with irony: texts were depicted as haunting people, as literally pressing and squashing them in the city.[6]

Kikeriki, especially, made fun of the ways in which ads were situated in urban space. On many occasions, the humour derived from transforming the original message of the commercial text. For example, in 1873 it published a cartoon on the practice of putting ads on the benches on the Ringstraße. It showed an old veteran with both legs amputated, sitting next to an ad that says: 'No more corns!'[7] The caption makes it clear that the target of the joke was not the veteran, but advertisers, who were taking over the city with their commercial ads. The caption pointed out that the ads were able to make a classical travesty of the innocent passers-by.

This ability to see humour in the contrast between texts and the urban reality was a typical characteristic of the Viennese nineteenth-century *Witzblätter*. Being themselves part of the textual environment, the humorous magazines were extremely conscious of the practices of writing the city, and they constantly rewrote different kinds of texts and parodied the conventions, political discourses and worn-out phrases in which journalistic writing and other popular texts tried to capture the urban reality.[8] Moreover, by using visual means, the magazines were able to juxtapose the presence of texts with situations that somehow undermined their authority: a sign states 'Keep off the grass', for example, in a place used by the military as a parade ground; 'An interesting cattle show', reads an advertisement covering one side of an omnibus carrying ordinary Viennese from Schottenring to Prater.[9] The humorous magazines were thus interested in disruptions in discursive coherence. The humour highlighted incongruities between the lived reality and the discursive level, thus revealing an insightful contemporary awareness of the gaps between the city as a text and the city as a lived place.[10]

In addition to the contrast between texts and their changing contexts, humour also arose from misreading these texts or detecting their errors or internal contradictions.[11] One humorous text in *Kikeriki* described an incident during which an anonymous narrator, probably O.F. Berg himself, saw the words 'MÖBEL SPORT (FURNITURE SPORT)' on a cart parked on the street. The narrator was so baffled by the text that he went to ask several university professors to explain what it meant. The professors came up with imaginative explanations, like an idea of a new 'American entertainment', in which normal pieces of furniture such as chairs and tables would be used in fitness training and competitive sports. However, there was a logical conclusion to the puzzle after all. It turns out that the text was actually 'MÖBEL TRANSPORT (FURNITURE TRANSPORT)' written on a furniture cart.[12]

The jokes about misreading and misspelling the city were based on humour's ability to intensify awareness of cultural rules by breaking them. The contemporary collapse of a rule or a structure, such as grammatical correctness, made them visible.[13] Consequently, joking about misspelling the city demonstrates the significance of reading as a vital competence in the nineteenth-century city. Living in the city required the ability to read the city: timetables, guides, signs and advertisements were essential in orienting oneself in the urban surroundings.[14] Misreading the city was funny, because it represented an error in the competence that was vital for the citizens. On the other hand, the jokes also revealed a sense of uncanniness and discomfort at being surrounded by a growing number of both authoritarian and commercial texts.

Reading the city correctly was also a sign of belonging to the city. There was a fine line between playing with errors and making errors, such as struggling with the German language or taking texts too literally. In most cases, the people being confused by the city's texts were somehow subordinate to the bourgeois Austrian-German identity: they came from the lower classes, or they were visitors or foreigners. Tourists struggled with German texts, and beggars misspelt their pleas for charity, writing on their pitiful placards that they were 'Plint durch Gepurt' ('born blind', misspelt).[15] For example, in *Der Floh*, a watchman finds a Saxon visitor standing in the Rathauspark. The man explains that he has been protecting the park for three hours, because the sign says: 'This area is under public protection'.[16] The Saxon had taken the sign too literally, as an order instead of an announcement. Again, the joke is all about neglecting the context, and mocking the inability to correctly interpret urban texts. The ridicule of those misspelling and misreading the city meant excluding certain groups, such as the lower classes and visitors from abroad, outside the Viennese middle-class urban community that shared certain codes of urban existence.[17]

Yet these shared codes were not unproblematic; they seem to have undergone a crisis parallel to the urban renewal. The vast popularity of jokes dealing with all kinds of mistakes, errors, confusions and puzzles gives us reason to believe that humour did not merely confirm the belief in a detectable solid reality, but it also revealed profound doubt about the possibility of conceiving and mastering the new urban reality. The city was often presented as a source of riddles instead of a lucid and easily understandable place.[18] Like the modern detective stories, such as the Sherlock Holmes stories in the 1890s, Viennese popular humour depicted the modern city as a complex puzzle, a mystery to be solved.[19]

In addition to these riddles and puzzles, the humorous magazines also published various typographical experiments, visual gags and illusions that demanded curiosity and mental flexibility, and challenged conventional ways of understanding things. *Der Floh* and *Figaro* made typographical experiments as well, but not on the same scale or with the same enthusiasm as *Kikeriki*, which made exploring the full potentiality of print media its trademark.[20] Visual illusions were part of this experimentation.

Puzzle pictures and visual illusions inspired turn-of-the-century psychologists in their interest in the cognitive processes of the human mind. The American psychologist Joseph Jastrow used a famous cartoon from the German magazine *Fliegende Blätter* from 1892 in his famous duck-rabbit illusion, based on a figure that resembled both a duck and a rabbit, depending on how the image is perceived.[21] Printed illusions were thus interrelated with the growing interest in perception in the late nineteenth century. The Viennese humorous magazines, too, expressed great interest in perception as a way of gaining knowledge of the urban environment.[22]

There were a large number of cognitive gags, based on lived situations in which the senses, and the eyes in particular, were somehow insufficient in rendering the surrounding reality. In these jokes, the city is somehow deceiving the human eye. Things are not what they seem. For example, in one cartoon from 1871, a stranger is admiring an unusual latticed fence on the Burgplatz, but on a closer look it turns out that the fence is actually a line of Bohemian workers on a construction site.[23] A special type of joke was offered by caricatures depicting how short-sighted persons would see the city. These caricatures were based on a shift of perspective, revealing that things are not what they at first seem to be.[24]

This dual close/far perspective is explicitly present in the caricature 'From a distance – From close-to' ('Aus der Entfernung – In der Nähe') (Figure 4.1), published in 1874. In the first picture, the short-sighted man is saying: 'This avenue of fence-posts' ('Diese Allee von Barrierestöcken'); in the second picture, the Kikeriki rooster replies: 'But my dear sir, these are the pure cream of society' ('Aber lieber Herr, das sind ja lauter Spitzen der Gesellschaft').

This 'avenue of fence-posts' probably refers to the Praterallee, a boulevard reconstructed for the World Exhibition site in 1873. Another possible site could be the Ringstraße, but the width of the street, together with the blooming treeline, does not match the contemporary image of the Ringstraße as a treeless and barren street, as discussed in the previous chapter.

Here the Kikeriki figure is, again, helping to see the city correctly, explaining that the 'posts' are actually members of high society. The German dialogue contains an ironic wordplay (*Spitzen*: 'peak, apex') that cannot be fully translated into English. However, the context of the cartoon can shed some light on its meanings. The Praterallee was one of the meeting places for the *crème de la crème* of society. Furthermore, by the 1870s, upper-class dandies known as 'Gigerls' were spending their days strolling on the boulevard.[25] It seems that the 'posts' here are these high-class dandies, associated with the modern boulevards such as Praterallee and the Ringstraße. The joke is based on the confusion of

Figure 4.1 'From a distance – From close-to', *Kikeriki*, 19 April 1874. Source: Austrian National Library.

something noble (the fashionable gentleman) with something low and laughable (a fence-post).

However, despite the multiple layers of meaning in the cartoon, it is the error of sight that lies at the core of the joke. This kind of humour recalls our attention to the importance of seeing in the nineteenth century. The fact that deception of the eyes was considered to be the most fatal failure of the sensory capacity highlights the significance of looking as a way of gaining information and knowledge in the urban surroundings. Although much humour related to disruptions in other sensory data as well – disturbing sounds, smells and confusing bodily experiences[26] – it seems that in the world of jokes, seeing was considered to be the most important epistemological tool to rely on for gaining knowledge of the city. Most of the caricatures dealing with misreading the city were based on visual errors.[27]

The idea of visual errors and confusion fascinated the Viennese bourgeois audience for decades. For example, in a cartoon from *Der Floh* from 1891, a man confuses the brightly lit dial of the new Rathaus clock with the moon, and thinks that he must be seeing things double, despite having had only three beers.[28] The title of the image, 'An Understandable Mistake' ('Begreiflicher Irrthum'), is ambiguous. On the one hand it refers to the drunken state of the observer after three large beers (the *Krügel* is the largest size for a beer glass, just under an English pint and just over a US pint). On the other hand, the reference may be to the space. The caption 'A scene in the City Hall Park' ('Eine szene vor dem Rathauspark') places the event at a particular location in the city, and the joke could actually refer to a lived experience of the site, which was finished in 1883. The (new) bright light of the tower clock would have been recognizable for the Viennese. Thus, it is perhaps this lived experience of the city itself that underlies the joke, and renders 'understandable' the mistake made by the man in the cartoon.

Using the theme of the deception of sight as a topic of humour suggests that the relationship between the perceiving body and the urban environment preoccupied the Viennese nineteenth-century middle-class audience. The idea of losing the ability to perceive correctly was seen as fatal in late nineteenth-century discourses. The body was seen as a source of knowledge, and perceptual disorders were dangerous, because the collapse of the integrity of perception was believed to cause disorders such as hysteria and other nervous disorders. As Julian Brigstocke has observed, in the nineteenth century perceptual disorders were seen above all as a social problem, because it was the milieu of the body – the modern city – that changed its sensory experience of reality. In other words, the senses became overwhelmed by the city.[29]

In the examples we have seen so far, the relationship between the body and the city has been twofold. On the one hand, failures in vision resulted from a quality or feature of the perceiver (short sight, drunkenness, being a stranger) that prevents them from perceiving and understanding the city properly. These features also associate the errors with the realm of the comical rather than serious medical conditions. On the other hand, the failures also reference the idea that the city itself was becoming more baffling and confusing, due to the rapid growth and transformation of the urban space. What supports the latter explanation is the fact that jokes about deception of the eyes were often, though not always, placed at sites that were part of the new urban fabric created in the urban renewal, such as the Ringstraße zone (including the Burgplatz and Rathauspark) or the regulated Prater area. In other words, the problem might not only be in the individual's ability to perceive the world, but the world itself was becoming harder and harder to comprehend. However, by mapping the new zones in the inner city and other upper- and middle-class neighbourhoods, the bourgeois *Witzblätter* stayed on safe ground; they did not venture into the suburbs, where there was a real danger of getting lost in the unfamiliar urban labyrinth.

Deep down, these jokes about the deception of sight seem to reflect a post-mid-century loss of confidence in both texts and the human body as a source of knowledge. Most of the examples studied in this section are from the 1870s and 1880s, at a time of crisis in liberalism after the triumph of the 1860s.[30] The following decades were a period of economic depression and political crisis. This ongoing turmoil, which shook the basic values and ideas of Austrian liberalism, could be seen as the source of a cultural uncertainty that undermined the trust in solid truths, and led to a growing interest in the human psyche, which became the main focus of artistic and intellectual endeavours in *fin-de-siècle* Vienna.[31]

In addition to the context of political events and cultural atmosphere, the humour on deception of the senses should also be analysed in the context of Austrian nineteenth-century scientific debate.[32] Recently, there has been a growing interest in the history of science and its implications for Viennese cultural history. Deborah R. Coen's study *Vienna in the Age of Uncertainty: Science, Liberalism and Private Life* (2007) criticized the Schorskean research tradition for neglecting the Austrian scientific debate, which played a vital role in shaping cultural expression and political thought. Coen claims that the crisis of liberalism was not merely a crisis of politics and culture, but an epistemological crisis as well; in the second part of the nineteenth century, the absolute claims of science and law were challenged. Furthermore, Coen argues, tolerance of uncertainty and resistance to determinism were strengths of Austrian scientific thought. Viennese tolerance of uncertainty and less-than-certain knowledge distinguished it from, for example, contemporary France (positivism) or Prussia (study of causality), and created growing interest in the theory of probability.[33]

Coen suggests that the ability to see things from different viewpoints, a 'many-sidedness' (*Vielseitigkeit*), was the main goal of the Austrian liberal mindset. Many-sidedness was considered to be a high compliment for a person. It implied an ability for self-conscious reflection and mental flexibility, highly valued by the educated Viennese *Bürger*.[34] As Coen puts it: 'Learning not just to tolerate but to find beauty in the unpredictable was part of cultivating a liberal character'.[35]

In my view, displaying a good sense of humour was very much related to this agenda. In fact, the idea of wit resonates strongly with the Austrian bourgeois ideal of many-sidedness. As scholars like Michael Billig and Daniel Wickberg have noted, from the eighteenth century onwards, wit meant a special ability to bring together contradictory ideas in an intelligent and agreeable manner. Wit was also a sign of mental flexibility, the ability to change perspective and combine incongruous or contradictory ideas. A witty gentleman was quick and clever.[36]

Moreover, as Michael Billig has shown, the idea of wit had since the eighteenth century been closely associated with the European coffee house culture. Coffee houses were centres of intellectual discussion in European cities in general, and in Vienna in particular. Human intellectual capacities and cognitive processes gained a new kind of philosophical attention in these highly stimulating surroundings, where members of society gathered together in order to engage in intellectual discussion and political debate. In the discussion on humour, the focus of interest shifted from emotions and social hierarchies (superiority theories) to cognitive processes (incongruence theories). At the same time, the philosophical discussions revolved increasingly around the perceptual basis of knowledge.[37]

What distinguished Vienna from other cities was the Jewish character of the Viennese coffee house culture. Jewishness does not mean here an ethnicity or religion, but a cultural heritage and intellectual tradition that continuously challenged established conventions of logic and language.[38] As Harold B. Segel has noted, Jewish coffee house clients, even if they did not necessarily bring a special Jewish awareness or self-consciousness to the coffee house, certainly contributed important characteristics of the Jewish liberal bourgeois intelligentsia of the period, such as intellectual curiosity, argumentativeness, and enthusiasm for exploring the resources of language.[39]

Popular culture and popular humour were thus part of a larger cultural matrix in multicultural and heterogeneous late nineteenth-century Vienna. As the humorous magazines such as *Figaro*, *Kikeriki* and *Der Floh* were read in the Viennese coffee houses, they should be seen as part of this wider coffee house culture, which focused increasingly on discovering the meanings of human cognition and intellectual activity. Although far more simple and vulgar than the sophisticated feuilleton writings, popular jokes and cartoons nonetheless expressed the same kind of interest in the question of perception as the contemporary intellectual discussions and scientific discourses.

One illuminating example of the connection between nineteenth-century scientific discussion and popular humour are the Viennese parodies of Charles Darwin's (1809–82) theory of evolution, introduced in the volumes *On the Origin of Species* (1859) and *The Descent of Man* (1871). The latter book caused a sensation by introducing the idea of human evolution.[40]

As seen in Figures 4.2–4.5, the same cartoon was imitated from one humorous magazine to another and finally lost the original reference to Darwin and continued as an example of a visual trick, based on juxtaposing two different objects that look similar. This visual trick had its origins in the tradition of political cartoons, and it is a variation of the famous French cartoon depicting King Louis Philippe I as a pear.[41] The Viennese late nineteenth-century humorous magazines thus consciously used the earlier tradition of political cartoons to comment on modern contemporary phenomena. Yet the original political attack was transformed into a more abstract reflection on questions of perception and causality,[42] and these jokes and visual conventions transferred across the political borders from one magazine to another, carrying with them a more or less loose relationship to contemporary scientific discussion.

The example above illustrates the creative potential of the printed forms of popular humour in Vienna. Arthur Koestler has argued that humour is above all creative, and actually works quite similarly to scientific thought; it challenges traditional patterns of thought and unconventional ways of thinking, offering original insights that defy common sense. Koestler's famous theory of 'bisociative' thinking posits that humour involves working on more than one mental plane, and discovering relationships between different intellectual systems.[43]

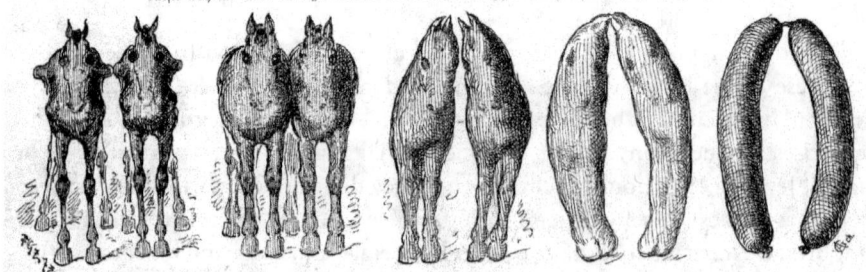

Figure 4.2 *Kikeriki*, 8 May 1873. Source: Austrian National Library.

Figure 4.3 *Der Floh*, 23 September 1877. Source: Austrian National Library.

Figure 4.4 *Der Floh*, 24 November 1878. Source: Austrian National Library.

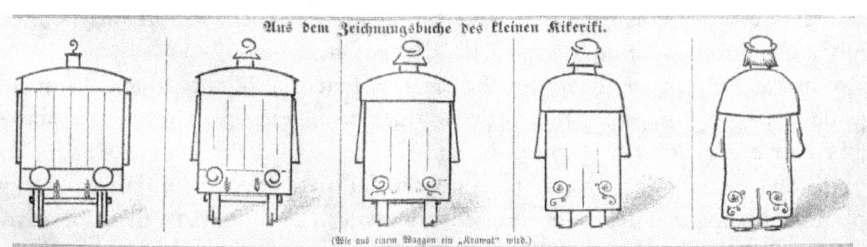

Figure 4.5 *Kikeriki*, 6 February 1879. Source: Austrian National Library.

Since Koestler, the relationship between humour and knowledge has been scrutinized in a number of studies on humour and laughter. For example, in her study on satirical magazines in Wilhelmine Germany, Ann Taylor Allen approached humour as a symbolic form of communication and an imaginative model used in order to interpret unfamiliar conditions and create new meanings in an age of cultural crisis.[44] The folklorist Seppo Knuuttila, on the other hand, has suggested in his research on Finnish jests that humour involves an epistemological interest: it is one way of testing and producing knowledge.[45]

In late nineteenth-century Vienna, the question of knowledge was central, due not only to the transformation of the material environment, but also to shifts in the ways of understanding the relationship between the mind and reality. As Coen has noted, not only the city itself, but also the scientific conception of the world was far from stable. Humour was borne out and operated in this state of instability. Looking at the city through the lens of humour was a special way of approaching the changing urban environment through the defamiliarization of the familiar and looking at it from unexpected perspectives.[46] Normal, reliable experience was turned into something unexpected and surprising. The puzzle of the city temporarily made sense, not through serious judgement, but through comic insight.

I would therefore suggest that the significance of the physical, material space was essential for understanding this comic insight and 'getting the joke'. The lived experience of the city was the very base of jokes and cartoons which transformed experiences of material spaces into representations that were, in turn, read in the physical city space. The humorous magazines continuously played with this ongoing reciprocity between perception and representation. In order to understand this circle, one has to look at the city space itself.

Jokes and cartoons did not only rely on cultural meanings and values associated with specific places in Vienna, but the lens of humour also enabled a challenge of the traditional cultural hierarchies embedded in the urban space. To give an example, in 1882 *Figaro* published a cartoon of a statue 'sketched *in situ* by a short-sighted person' (Figure 4.6). This cartoon was published in a section set aside for 'dilettantes', which indicates that it had been sent in by a reader, an amateur humourist.[47] The statue in question here is probably the equestrian statue of Archduke Karl (1771–1847) on the Heldenplatz, erected in 1860 (Figure 4.7).[48]

Here the established visual hierarchy is challenged through a humorous perspective from below, which subverts the cultural and political authority of the statue of a national hero (*Held*; hence *Heldenplatz*). Traditionally, the perspective from an elevated point of view has been seen as the perspective of power and control, described in such terms as 'panoptic gaze' and 'celestial eye'.[49] Whereas looking at monuments and equestrian statues from a distance acknowledges their authority and prestige, a change of perspective enables a

Figure 4.6 A statue sketched by a short-sighted person. *Figaro*, 10 June 1882. Source: Austrian National Library.

Figure 4.7 The monument of Archduke Karl (1860) at the Heldenplatz. Photo: Heidi Hakkarainen.

humorous counter-reading of the narrative of heroism and power. When the power represented by a monument in the city space is looked at from 'too close', this reveals it as ridiculous. What makes this case even more interesting is that this perspective was actually possible in the city space. Seen from close to, instead of from a distance, the proportions of the statue do change.

Thus, while the cartoons worked as self-contained representations on one level, the direct reference to the physical space added another level to the humour. Lived experiences of the city were crucial in order to get the joke on both levels. Accordingly, the humorous magazines clearly presupposed that their readers were familiar with the physical places of Vienna and had first-hand bodily and sensory experiences of the urban surroundings in which the cartoons were situated. It was the continuous movement between perception and representation that created the dynamics of humour in these examples. What was most radical about this approach was that the humour did not remain merely in the world of texts and pictures, but the humorous magazines created alternative ways of depicting the physical city itself.[50] What was seen in print inevitably moulded the ways of seeing und understanding the material reality. Could the serious message of the statue of Archduke Karl ever be the same again after one had seen it from 'too close'? Perhaps the most radical potential of the humorous magazines lay in the fact that they did not just make jokes about the city, but they made the city a joke.

In his book *The Life of the City* (2014), Julian Brigstocke contested the established idea that nineteenth-century urban culture was dominated by abstract discourses and representations. In his study, Brigstocke suggests that humour enabled an interruption of urban visibilities and representations by means of error and counter-display. 'Points of error' were an ongoing quest of surviving, adapting and establishing a relationship with the new environment based on the authority of lived experience. Brigstocke argues that humour was a way to 'test and transgress established discourses concerning the "life of the city"'. Like Brigstocke's, my work draws attention back to the embodied lived experience in the city in the nineteenth-century urban reality. However, I would not go so far as to suggest that Viennese popular humour was solely based on the vitality of lived experience aiming at challenging urban representations. After all, jokes and cartoons as humorous expressions were themselves urban representations. In my view, the humorous magazines, as printed publications, rather investigated the unbridgeable gap between the city as a discourse and the city as a lived place. Although the topics varied, this gap was somehow present in all the examples studied in this section. Popular humour could be seen as a way of testing knowledge about the city. This process of challenging established knowledge was, at the same time, an act of creating new knowledge about the city.

Nostalgia for *Alt-Wien*

As the city became increasingly unfamiliar for the Viennese audience, there was a growing interest in popular stereotypes and narratives about the vanishing old city. The lost, pre-modern *Alt-Wien* became a central topos for the discussion on modernity. It was an imaginary place, a culturally constructed counterpoint to the modern city, representing qualities that were seen to be absent from the contemporary capital: cosiness, security and a sense of community.[51] As the 'new' was interpreted in contrast to the 'old', the juxtaposition between past and present evoked not just intellectual curiosity, but also emotional responses to the change. Nostalgia, especially, played an important role in humour concerning the transformation of the city.

The term *nostalgia* derives originally from the Greek words for homecoming (*nostos*) and pain (*algos*). The Swiss doctor Johannes Hofer (1669–1752) coined the concept in the seventeenth century, to refer to the homesickness (*Heimweh*) of Swiss soldiers away from their home country.[52] Karin Johannisson has explored nostalgia as a historical emotion, especially symptomatic for the nineteenth century. She suggests that nostalgia was inextricably related to the experience of modernity, as it changed in meaning from a medical state into a cultural phenomenon, signifying a feeling of sentimentality and an incapacity to adapt to a new space and time. In the nineteenth-century context, nostalgia came to mean longing for something that had been lost. It signalled a constant desire to return to one's (idealized) past, which was, however, impossible. Nostalgia thus expresses irreversible separation, in a certain bittersweet tone.[53]

In this section, the nostalgia for *Alt-Wien* is investigated through two forms of humorous expressions. First, I explore visual and narrative juxtapositions between the old and the new city. Second, I look into jokes and caricatures based on personifying places in the city; buildings like the Stephansdom and landmarks such as the River Wien were presented as living creatures with feelings, thoughts and memories of their own.[54] My aim is to show that both of these examples are based on simulating affective experiences such as the feeling of loss. Popular humour was thus intimately interlinked with emotions evoked by change in the city, and it was used to mobilize affective experiences related to the modernization process. This section thus seeks to demonstrate how sharing a certain sense of humour was linked with the formation of an 'emotional community', which, as Barbara H. Rosenwein has suggested, organizes systems of feelings that sustain and endorse cultural attitudes and ideas.[55]

At the centre of all this was the concept of *Alt-Wien*, which the humorous magazines and popular literature used when referring to the vanishing/vanished older Vienna. Through this concept, the humorous discourse actively participated in a larger discursive framework concerning the modernization of the city. *Alt-Wien* was a key concept in the late nineteenth-century discourses on urbanization and modernization, referring to the demolished old city that had existed before the Ringstraße development. Yet *Alt-Wien* was not merely a name for Vienna before the urban renewal; it was a *modern* construction involving a range of ideas and ideologies about past and present, tradition and modernity.

Lutz Musner has argued that the newly emerging popular culture in late nineteenth-century Vienna was important for the canonization of the cultural imaginaries of *Alt-Wien*, which were constantly re-established in popular songs, theatre performances and print culture. Musner suggests that popular culture was a significant site of memory (*Gedächtnisort*)[56] for *Alt-Wien*, incorporating not only the historical heritage of the earlier architecture in the city centre, but also a nostalgic perspective for the pre-modern modes of everyday life; *Alt-Wien* stood for an idealized conception of humanity, comprehensiveness and a sense of community.[57]

The popularity of these nostalgic popular imaginaries of *Alt-Wien* has usually been located in the *fin-de-siècle* era between 1890 and 1914. The cultural valorizations of *Alt-Wien* related, on the one hand, to the fierce architectural debates in Vienna from the 1890s onwards, and especially to the dispute between the architects Otto Wagner (1841–1918) and Camillo Sitte (1843–1903).[58] On the other hand, the turn-of-the-century interest in *Alt-Wien* was also a reaction to the rapid population growth. The influx of new incomers triggered sentimentality for the vanishing *Alt-Wien* and a demand for familiar stereotypes: traditional Viennese 'types' (*Wiener Typen*) such as the *Fiaker*, or the *Schusterbuben* or *Stubenmädl*, who were cultural stereotypes representing the idealized *Volk*.[59] The associations of the *Volk* were an important part of the growing modern urban consumption culture and they were evoked not just in humorous publications but also in the theatre and various styles of popular music, including waltzes and songs such as 'Fiakerlied', famously sung by Alexander Girardi (1850–1918).[60] Although these nostalgic representations of Old Vienna certainly flourished at the turn of the century, the roots of this popular imaginary ran deeper in nineteenth-century culture. Dichotomies between Old and New Vienna had already emerged by the late 1850s, when the rebuilding of the city began.

Der Humorist and *Figaro*, which appeared during the early phase of the urban renewal in the 1850s, published ironic goodbyes to the old places and created a comical contrast between the old and the new city.[61] For example, a humorous text titled 'Alt-Wien contra Neu-Wien', published in *Figaro* in 1860, presented the urban development as a battle between old and new materials and places.[62] The ideas of destruction and forgetting inspired narratives of *Alt-Wien* right from the very earliest stage of the transformation process.[63] The mid nineteenth century was seen as a watershed between the past and the future Vienna. In 1858, when the demolition of the city wall had just begun, the humorous magazine *Jörgel Briefe* wrote about the situation as follows:

> Precisely at a time when Old Vienna and its walls are sinking down, but of the Phoenix of New Vienna which is to arise out of the ashes of the past nothing is yet to be seen, it seems to me understandable that the Viennese should turn their eyes towards the past – half in pleasure, half in nostalgia – and let the past of their beloved home city parade before them in review, looking back reflectively on what has been experienced and what has been told, and take their emotional leave.[64]

Yet, although the nostalgic rhetoric about the loss of *Alt-Wien* seemed to come to life after the city renewal began in the 1850s, it is also important to note that juxtapositions between 'once' and 'nowadays' were already a well-established humorous convention dating from the early nineteenth century. For example, Moritz Gottlieb Saphir's *Humorist* had already frequently used these juxtapositions during the *Vormärz* era.[65] The convention was so established that readers of the humorous magazines even used pen names like 'Then and Now' ('Einst und Jetzt'),[66] and, for example, *Kikeriki* informed its readers in 1876 that the juxtapositions between now and before were so common that they were getting worn out.[67]

Using contrasts between past and present was thus already by mid century an established way of constructing meanings for the old and the new. As such, it was related to the larger nineteenth-century understanding of living in an era of inevitable change, a watershed between past and future.[68] Yet, as the urban renewal proceeded in Vienna, popular culture took on an increasingly vital role in expressing a symbolic conflict between the old and the new city. In addition to the *Witzblätter*, other forms of popular culture such as theatres and other performances also participated in interpreting the change through the idea of transition from one world into another. For instance, in 1860, the entertainment venue Elysium organized an exhibition, 'What can we keep from Alt-Wien; what does Neu-Wien bring us?' ('Was behalten wir von Alt-Wien; Was bringt uns Neu-Wien?'). This was an imaginary world in which visitors were able to go through the transition from the old to the new city by moving bodily through the showrooms.[69]

However, the contribution of the illustrated *Witzblätter* in visualizing the contrasts between Old and New Vienna was significant, just as popular periodicals played a major part in depicting urban change in other European cities as well.[70] The transformation of the city was interpreted through humorous conflicts between past and present, between two temporal horizons inextricably joined in a paradox. Humorous conflicts between past and present continued to be popular during the transformation process and beyond.[71] In most of these cases, the comic effect is born out of the contrast between an idealized past and a ridiculous present. Although the idyllic visualizations of *Alt-Wien* could also be read in an ironic light, in these humorous juxtapositions it was, as in most cases discussed in this study, the modern city that was presented as comical and ridiculous. The comparison between past and present almost without exception showed the present city as inferior to the past. By depicting the old city as more affluent, fair and humane, the humorous representations satirically criticized the present state of conditions in Vienna.[72]

As the urban renewal slowly came to completion, the concept of *Alt-Wien* was not lost, but continued to feature increasingly in turn-of-the-century journalistic discussions. In the 1890s, especially, the term occurred frequently in the press, partly related to the fact that a model of *Alt-Wien* was showcased at the Chicago World Exhibition in 1903. Meanwhile, humorous narratives and representations of the old city continued to be popular, in a variety of forms and expressions.[73] Entire humorous books, such as Vinzenz Chiavacci's *Stories from Alt-Wien* (*Geschichten aus Alt-Wien*, 1884), were published depicting Vienna before the urban renewal.

My aim here is not to trace the humorous usage of the concept *Alt-Wien* from the nineteenth into the twentieth century, a task that would simply be too vast for the scope of this study. Yet what I would like to demonstrate is that a certain language for humorous nostalgia came to life in the late 1850s and early 1860s when the urban renewal began, using conventions from the *Vormärz* era and continuing in various forms into the twentieth century. The conceptual opposition between the old and the new city, suggests David Frisby, was a vital element in understanding and discussing modernity in *fin-de-siècle* Vienna. Especially after 1890, when anti-modernist movements started to gain a stronger foothold in the city, the dichotomy between old and new began to shape the ways of understanding of the urban fabric and city structure. The old was increasingly associated with the historical city centre, whereas the expanding suburbs represented the new.[74] The rebuilding of the city stimulated nostalgic literature about pre-Ringstraße Vienna, especially after the 1890s, when the *Groß-Wien* project came to completion.[75]

What has not been thoroughly explored so far is that the cultural valorizations of Old Vienna or *Alt-Wien*, both before and after 1890, were very often characteristically *humorous* representations of the lost pre-modern city life. For example, the turn-of-the-century *Wiener Skizzen*, which Frisby sees as examples of nostalgic literature, were known for their light humorous tone and use of local dialect. Therefore, it seems worthwhile to pay more attention to the element of humour in these valorizations between the past and present, tradition and modernity. Why humour? What special value did humour add to these representations dealing with the change?

It seems that the answer has much to do with emotions. This brings us to the affective element of humour, which forms a major challenge for the historical study of humour, because it is so hard to pinpoint and analyse. Yet the affective aspects of humour can help to explain what makes humour so powerful as a mode of social communication and interaction. As humour often relates to practices of exclusion and inclusion, the emotions play a vital part in creating in-groups and establishing affective bonds between people. On the other hand, humour can also be used to ridicule and diminish other social groups. Precisely humour's ability to construct social hierarchies by creating or reducing emotional bonds between people makes it a significant means for creating collective identities and a sense of community. As Julian Brigstocke argues, in order to gain a better understanding of the affective aspect of humour, research should be 'attentive to its corporeal dynamics, its ability to affect bodies in ways that are not reducible to its discursive content'.[76] This means recognizing the corporeal, embodied element of humour that is so vital for expressing and mobilizing the affective energy that can be tapped into for various political or social purposes. Furthermore, Brigstocke suggests that it is precisely the affective potential of humour that makes it so important in spatial politics, as humour is used, in various ways, in negotiations about urban space.[77]

In order to understand humour's role in creating and transmitting affective experiences in late nineteenth-century Vienna, one has to look into the history of middle-class humour, which had its roots in the comedies of the *Alt-Wiener Volkstheater* at the beginning of the century. Playwrights Ferdinand Raimund (1790–1836) and Johann Nestroy (1801–62) had a massive impact on nineteenth-century popular humour, as they had created dramatic figures, verbal sayings, forms, melodies and conventions that influenced various forms of popular humour well into the twentieth and twenty-first centuries.[78] In addition to these beloved comic writers, a generation of humorous journalists were actively working both before and after the 1848 revolution, including names such as Moriz Gottlieb Saphir, born Moses Saphir (1795–1858),[79] whom the next generation of writers admired as pioneers of the humorous-satirical press and champions of press freedom.

In his talk 'Aus Alt-und Neu-Wien' for the Viennese students' club on 28 January 1882, for example, Friedrich Schlögl suggested that it was the combination of intensity of feeling and sharp wit that distinguished the humour of the old masters, such as Raimund, Nestroy and Saphir, from contemporary trivial entertainment, which he sarcastically called 'Hamur' instead of 'Humor'. Speaking to the young hopes of the future sitting in the audience in 1882, Schlögl expressed his concern over the transformation of humour from thought-provoking training of the mind into superficial and lifeless entertainment.[80]

This idea of the disappearance or deterioration of humour due to the modernization process was prevalent among other humourists as well. At the same time as humour was conceived as a bridge to the pre-modern past, to the idealized *Alt-Wien*, there was a constant fear that the humour and laughter would disappear from the city.[81] Accordingly, humour was not just a means of expression for nostalgia, but also itself a subject for nostalgia.

Humour's affective role was attested to by discourses that linked it to the *Lokalgefühl*, 'local feeling', that lay at the heart of the mythical Viennese substance

(*Wienerthum*).[82] Since popular humour had a history of its own, intertwining with the history of the city, there were conventions that tied humour and the city closely together in the minds of the middle-class audience. Humour had already been used to depict urban life and express subjective experiences before the city renewal process.[83] There was a long tradition of mapping the physical and mental characteristics of the city with humour through imaginary walks in the urban landscape. For example, Heinrich Walden's[84] *Wien und seine Bewohner humoristisch geschildert auf einem Spaziergang über die ganze Bastey* (*Vienna and Its Inhabitants, Humorously Illustrated on a Stroll through the Entire Bastion*, 1834) tells us how the author shows the city to a friend who has come to visit from the country. The book opens with a narrator's note expressing his aim to create a 'humorous topography' (*humoristische Topografie*) of Vienna.[85]

Similarly, throughout the century, the theme of walking through the city appeared time and again in humorous narratives, leading the way to feuilleton literature such as Daniel Spitzer's famous *Wiener Spaziergänge*.[86] On the other hand, humorous books on Vienna were part of a larger wave of urban literature from the early nineteenth century focusing on exploring and promoting the capital to the growing literate public both within the empire and abroad.[87] In the 1870s and 1880s, a new genre of humorous travel guides emerged, and booklets like the *Humoristischer Fremdenführer für Wien und Umgebung* (*Humorous Guidebook for Vienna and its Environs*, 1880) guided their readers around the streets of Vienna, and parodied the conventions of expanding travel literature.[88]

Consequently, popular humour in Vienna was spatially and locally oriented. Viennese humour and the local environment were interconnected; they were inseparable and shaped each other.[89] Two important factors came into play in the construction of *Lokalgefühl* through humorous expressions: first, the use of Viennese dialect (*Wienerisch*), which was fundamental for Viennese popular humour, and second, references to the past, the commemoration and reimagination of the city's history.

In order to illustrate the importance of these aspects, I will proceed by taking a brief look at jokes and caricatures representing places as alive, and lending a voice to the city environment. In the magazines there were many different but recurrent patterns of jokes in which inanimate material places and inhuman actors become personified and depicted as living creatures. Personified places, specifically, often offered a voice for satirical critique,[90] but they also articulated memories of the past and feelings regarding the future. Since the juxtaposition between *Alt-Wien* and *Neu-Wien* depended on a comical conflict between the past and the present, humorous texts and images presenting places as alive could articulate the break with an even stronger emotional charge. The destruction of the old spatial surroundings was compared to the death of a living organism. Moreover, the aspect of memory was crucial for the imaginaries of living places. Old places connected the past with the present because they embodied memories of events and experiences from bygone times. Furthermore, when places spoke about their memories of the past, they did so in a distinctive Viennese tone, using dialect and verbal expressions that gave their message an emotional and intimate feel. For instance, in the following example from 1858, the city wall cried out his last goodbye before being demolished in the face of a new era:

> … Oh ungrateful world, is this your disdainful reward,
> This sneering laughter, as I am dethroned?
> I, who alone defended Christendom,
> As a hundred thousand Turks attacked me;
> I, who not with the quill but with the sword,
> Victorious defeated the crescent moon.
> O beautiful nation of today, hideously modernized,
> You know no mercy for that which once flourished.[91]

As the city renewal started, with the demolition of the old city wall, there was a strong sense that the disappearance of the old city also meant the extinction of memories associated with it. Although the demolition work was reflected in other forms of popular culture as well, most famously in Demolirer-Polka, op. 269 (1862) by Johann Strauss Jr.,[92] popular humour in particular voiced the nostalgia and the feeling of loss caused by the rebuilding process. Already in the late 1850s, the demolition work on the wall and other old parts of the city that stood in the way of the city renewal created a sense of loss that manifested itself in numerous jokes and puns wishing farewell both to the old city and to the old times as well. For example, Saphir's *Der Humorist* wrote eulogies for every demolished bastion, which had protected the city from the army of the Ottoman Empire in the Siege of Vienna in 1529 and in the Battle of Vienna in 1683, but could not survive modern bureaucracy.[93] This strong attachment to the city wall reflected the fact that the people had been shielded behind it for centuries. Moreover, in addition to giving shelter against foreign enemies, the city wall had literally defined the limits of the city.[94] As both the physical and mental boundary of the city, the wall had played a significant part in constructing the Viennese identity. Tearing down the wall therefore disrupted not only the physical city space but also the mental world of its citizens.[95]

This personification of the city reveals a strong attachment to the environment threatened by the urban renewal. The imagery of the old city as a living creature expressed a close bond between the city and its inhabitants. Furthermore, it also suggested a relationship with the past that was very similar to living memory. These places had experienced the events of the past; they had seen and heard the great battles of history. Therefore, preserving the places meant preserving the memory.

For example, in 1857 in *Der Humorist* the spire of the medieval cathedral of St. Stephen (Stephansdom) appealed to the audience against its renovation. The

Catholic cathedral was the most prestigious place in the city, and it becomes clear that the intention was not merely to make light fun, but to take part in the public discussion on what the city should be like, and to make a stand for the preservation of old marks of its history:

> I have survived many dark times;
> My ears bore the sound of thunderous cannons
> Of the wild fanatic Osman army,
> And my granite walls have repulsed
> Many cannonballs of the enemy;
>
> But in the storm of the centuries I remained standing,
> A worthy monument to German strength.
> But then they started to complain
> That my appearance was not young enough,
> And decorated me with new curls
> And embellished my tip with spikes,
> So that I would like to sink from embarrassment.
> Then I started to believe myself
>
> That I had become too old for this world
> And the awareness of aging
> Is a gloomy foreboding of death …[96]

As can be seen in both of these examples, the Turkish sieges played an important role in the nineteenth-century historical imagination.[97] The heroic past offered a mirror for the present, commenting through imaginary authoritative voices from the past.

In fact, the Stephansdom had a very distinctive symbolic role in the humorous publications, and is by far the most popular place to be depicted as alive: talking, moving and even singing.[98] As an emblem of the capital of the Habsburg Empire, the Stephansdom is also set against the landmarks of other European cities. In *Wiener Luft*, the cathedral was in correspondence with the Eiffel Tower in Paris.[99] *Der Floh* published a dialogue between the Stephansdom and its 'colleague' in Pisa.[100] Clearly, the Stephansdom had a special role as a site in Viennese culture embodying local patriotism and city identity.[101] As a commentator on modern urban development, moreover, the Stephansdom figure often spoke with a heavy local dialect, highlighting its association with the Viennese past.[102]

There are several aspects that contribute to the humour of depicting the Stephansdom as alive. First, the cathedral was a very serious place, and an institution symbolizing the conservative and indeed reactionary Catholic culture, which the liberal and democratically oriented humorous magazines repeatedly mocked and ridiculed.[103] As Michael Mulkay and Daniel Wickberg among other scholars have noted, the tensions and contradictions of the serious world are vital for the realms of humour, and those things especially that bear the most prestige and cause the greatest anxiety are also most often the subject matter for humour.[104]

Moreover, the perspective of the Stephansdom provided a distanced perspective to the city, which gained authority through its long history and vertical height – the Stephansdom was for a long time not just one of the oldest, but also the tallest building in Vienna.[105] As already pointed out in the previous discussion, the humorous magazines often made use of an elevated viewpoint on the city, a 'mocking bird's-eye view' (*Spottvogelperspective*), from which the foibles and follies of human life in a great city were observed. The Stephansdom enabled a perspective on the contemporary city that had both vertical height and historical depth.

Finally, the humour relating to picturing the Stephansdom as alive was related to an intimate, personal relationship with the old city environment. Imagining the old places, such as the Stephansdom, as alive signalled a strong attachment to these places. It meant knowing them on a personal and intimate level, as if it might be possible to know how they would think and feel. This intimate relationship made the disappearance of old places seem like wishing farewell to old friends. This association was sustained by humorous expressions that used the conventions of friendship and intimacy in the context of the old places. For example, in 1888 *Wiener Luft* published an imaginary correspondence between two places facing renewal and destruction, the River Wien and the outer fortifications of the city:

> I
> The River Wien to the Fortifications.
>
> My dear old friend!
> Since you enquire about my health, I am happy to inform you that I continue in the same state as formerly. Other than a new lunette that was recently driven into my side, I have no particular pains to complain of. How is it with you, my dear old friend? – Yours, &c., the River Wien.
>
> II
> The Fortifications to the River Wien.
>
> My respected Neighbour,
> I thank you for your concern. I am still to be found in the same place, and am happy to let the grass grow in peace over the various rumours of impending elevation, realignment, etc. Like yourself, I have survived many an onslaught, and I look forward to the future in contentment. I remain, my dear companion, your servant, etc. – The Fortifications.[106]

Imagining places as alive expressed an intimate and personal connection to the material surroundings. Notably, it was almost without exception old places that were given a voice on the pages of humorous publications. I have found only one example in which the new Ringstraße had a voice: in 1863, in *Kikeriki*, the street demanded that the city expansion commission should speed up the construction works in order to be finished on time.¹⁰⁷ So, here too, the Ringstraße was a symbol of the new era, not associated with the past.

This viewpoint expressed a historical consciousness that was very different from the idea of the Ringstraße as a synthesis of different historical styles. Traditionally, the Ringstraße has been seen as a manifestation of the nineteenth-century culture of history, intended as a 'total work of art', a *Gesamtkunstwerk* that brought together different historical periods. This spatial historical synthesis was constructed in a series of monumental buildings representing different historical styles from the neo-gothic to the neo-baroque. The synthesis of the city space was to be comprehended as one moved along the street from one building and one period to another.¹⁰⁸ The Ringstraße thus became an intentionally and institutionally constructed place that combined the material, symbolic and functional aspects of embodied memory.¹⁰⁹

In Viennese popular humour, however, a contradiction was seen between the Ringstraße as an institutionally constructed place of memory and *Alt-Wien* as a topos for the local historical consciousness. In the humorous-satirical magazines, the Ringstraße was seen as part of New Vienna, representing novelty, not memory. It was considered to be part of the new era instead of bearing memories from the past.

This idea was made explicit in a humorous short story by Eduard Pötzl, in which he writes that the old houses of Vienna have a soul because of the generations who have inhabited them, whereas the new houses are mere mute and lifeless puppets:

> ... The old houses have a soul, you see. Not just because they have a smell, which some half-baked philosopher might consider to be evidence of a soul, but because the departed generations who over the centuries have dwelt there have passed on to them something of their own spirit. The new houses, on the contrary, are lifeless puppets, dull and blank, without memories, without a soul.¹¹⁰

This section has looked into the ways in which the old city, destroyed in the urban renewal, was commemorated and reimagined in popular humour. Humour played a vital and specific role in the cultural valorization of *Alt-Wien*, because humour was seen to be part of the same traditional way of Viennese life that was now threatened by the urban renewal process. In the discursive environment surrounding the transformation of the city, humour had a specific role because it enabled people to express and generate affective experiences and to create emotional bonds among the readers of the humorous magazines. Accordingly, it is important to recognize that such forms as irony and satire, traditionally viewed as intellectual forms of discourse, have affective motivations, contents and effects as well.[111] Emotions such as nostalgia were employed in the process of collective meaning-making and the construction of identities in the changing city. Understanding Vienna meant not merely exploring the new material surroundings, but sharing memories of the city's past as well. Knowing the city thus involved not only perception but also memory, emotions and imagination, which all entered into the contemporary understanding that humour required both sense and sensibility.

News from the Future

Viennese middle-class popular humour did not look only at the past, but was future-oriented as well. During the massive transformation of the city, Viennese humorous magazines published jokes, stories and caricatures depicting the future Vienna through satiric eyes. There was thus a constant interplay between visions of the past, present and future city, presented side by side on the pages of the humorous magazines.

An interest in the future also distinguished different genres of humour: whereas humorous novels, short stories and plays were usually placed in the present or past Vienna,[112] the future aspect was characteristic of the humorous magazines, in particular. *Der Figaro*, *Kikeriki* and *Der Floh* all published cartoons and jokes with such titles as 'Zukunftsbilder' and 'Zukuftsszenen', portraying amusing scenarios in the future Vienna.[113] Furthermore, humorous magazines also published imaginary news from the future, depicting how city life would look in ten or two thousand years.[114] These future newspaper reports illustrate the important role of the press in generating expectations, fears and hopes for the future in the second part of the nineteenth century. Furthermore, the press and contemporary fiction were closely interrelated, as newspaper articles inspired writers like Jules Verne (1828–1905), who, in return, often published their stories in newspapers.

In this section I address the relationship between satirical humour and the future aspect in the discussion of modernity. By looking at the humorous visions and news from the future, I seek to understand why the future aspect was so significant for discussing the transformation of Vienna. The reason I have chosen to discuss accounts of the future within the chapter 'Knowing the City' is that I want to demonstrate how important the future aspect was for late nineteenth-century discussions on modernity and urbanity. The rebuilding of the city nurtured fantasies, rumours and expectations about the future. During the second half of the century, middle-class citizens were preoccupied not only with understanding present-day Vienna, and commemorating its roots in the historical past, but the question of what the city would and could be after the urban renewal had also become a critical issue.

Two distinctive features of this material serve as a starting point for my analysis. First, these humorous accounts of the future were in most cases located in Vienna itself, and thus commented directly on the city renewal project and contemporary urban phenomena. In most cases the visions of future Vienna entailed a sharp satirical critique of contemporary phenomena, highlighted by the use of irony and comical exaggeration. Second, in order to understand the irony and satire hidden in these visions, one had to have intimate knowledge of the city: familiarity with all kinds of knowledge, experiences and memories from Vienna past and present was required in order to make and understand jokes about Vienna in the future. The satirical humour of the humorous magazines was closely linked to the contemporary press reporting of various municipal projects and city politics between 1857 and 1890. Furthermore, the predominantly middle-class readers of these magazines were also well equipped in understanding more or less subtle literary references to many different spheres of nineteenth-century bourgeois culture, from Jules Verne's novels to the nihilistic views of *fin-de-siècle* philosophy.

The readers of humorous magazines thus formed not only an 'emotional community', as explored in the previous section, but also a 'discursive community', able to communicate and interpret irony, and 'make it happen', as Linda Hutcheon has suggested, because of their shared knowledge, assumptions, values and beliefs that enabled a delicate balance between the said and the unsaid.[115] It is, of course, good to keep in mind that the group of people who read humorous magazines and published in them was not a cohesive entity, but more likely a diverse and porous population consisting of several overlapping communities. As noted in the previous chapters, *Figaro*, *Kikeriki* and *Der Floh* all had slightly different target groups, and even within one single *Witzblatt*, not all the jokes would make sense to, or be found funny by all readers.[116]

It would thus be wrong to assume that satirical humour about New Vienna was purely an intellectual affair, whereas humorous nostalgia for Old Vienna might be based solely on its emotional effect. On the contrary, discourses and emotions intermingle and constitute each other. They do not rule each other out, and irony, as well as nostalgia, is very much related to creating communities, in-groups and collective identities.[117]

In the following analysis, special attention is paid to comical dystopias, humoristic visions of decline and destruction, which were the dominant feature of jokes and caricatures set in the future Vienna. However, not all visions of the future fell into the category of comical dystopias, and I will start by looking at visions of flying, which were another distinctive feature of imaginations of the future.

The fantastic scenes of the future Vienna often involved an element of verticality or aviation; there were future trains circulating above the rooftops,[118] and people flying in balloons high above the city.[119] Balloons, especially, were a characteristic feature of cartoons depicting the future city. For instance, in 1872 *Figaro* published a cartoon 'Das Zukunfts-Wien', in which the city was covered with a massive number of commercial texts and newspapers. Above this bizarre city, air balloons are flying in the sky offering news from the moon (*Mond-Post*).[120]

The idea of intercelestial news from the moon illustrates well the nineteenth-century fascination with overcoming vast distances. This fascination was linked with the sense that the world was becoming smaller and smaller due to technological innovations and mass transportation. New technological discoveries such as the steamboat (1788), the train (1804) and the telegraph (1837) made it possible to link places together that had previously been far apart.[121] In the Viennese humorous magazines this led to more or less ironic fantasies of overcoming even greater distances in future. For example, as early as 1858 *Figaro* introduced an idea that in future the telegraph would connect Earth with the sun and the moon.[122]

In addition to the sense of annihilation of space, which previous research has seen as highly characteristic of nineteenth-century culture, Viennese popular humour also strongly reflects contemporary literary conventions, including a growing interest in the future. The nineteenth century saw a boom in narratives set in the future. The literary scholar Paul Alkon has suggested that whereas for fifteenth-century people it was impossible to construct narratives about things that had not yet happened, and the only way to look towards the future was by retelling history, the nineteenth century was characteristically interested in the aspect of temporality and in narratives set in the future. Accordingly, there was an important transition from spatial to temporal utopias. In contrast to the utopias of early modern times, such as Thomas More's *Utopia* (1516), which were often placed in distant locations such as far-away islands, the modern utopias set their imaginary places in the far future.[123]

The cultural historian Hannu Salmi, as well, has located the end of the nineteenth century as an era of rapid growth in utopian thought and literature, and relates this to the larger cultural framework of a sense of living in an age of transition, a watershed between past and future. Salmi suggests that modernity created a new kind of preoccupation with the future, which was seen as increasingly detached from and independent of the past. The rapid technological development nourished fantasies and speculations about different possible futures that current phenomena might lead to. Following the early temporal utopia in Louis-Sébastian Mercier's (1740–1814) *L'An 2440* from 1770, the fascination with temporal utopias and science fiction literature grew rapidly, leading to such famous narratives as H.G. Wells' *The Time Machine* (1895).[124]

In the humorous magazines, the World Exhibition of 1873, hosted by Vienna, gave rise to fantastic images of the future. *Der Floh* presented an account of the World Exhibition in 2073 in which participants came from Earth and the seventeen closest planets and their circulating moons.[125] World Exhibitions embodied the belief in progress, which has been seen as constitutive of European thought from the mid eighteenth century to the beginning of the twentieth century. After the scientific revolution in an increasingly modern, mundane society, belief in progress became the prevalent ideology.[126] The new modern notion of progress was interlinked with an idea of linear time and a radically new future.[127]

As a prevailing ideology, the belief in progress was also a subject for parody. For instance, *Der Floh* published a cartoon of the wonders of the World Exhibition, including Richard Wagner's 'Zukunftsmusik for the destruction of opera houses', and balloon transport routes from the Stephansplatz to Prater.[128] There is an air of fantasy in all of these visions that mingles with a sense of irony. A clash between creative hope and a belief in progress, with militarism, warfare and destruction, makes these wonders of the World Exhibition comical. Moreover, the balloons convey multiple ambivalent meanings here. On the one hand they were an important metaphor for optimistic expectations for the future. Balloons represent a trope for ascending and transcending the city, which, as already noted in chapter 3, subtly links with what Freud called the uplifting (*erhebend*) quality of humour.[129] Yet, on the other hand, the balloons were also a way to comment ironically on the great expectations associated with the World Exhibition institution.

Importantly, balloons had a very distinctive significance in seventeenth- to nineteenth-century European satirical literature. Following the first balloon voyage in 1783, near Paris, argues Steven E. Jones, balloons became associated with utopian thinking, which made them targets for satire: 'Balloons in the early nineteenth century were still strongly associated with the Enlightenment goals of the *previous* century: universal knowledge, scientific progress, and the Promethean conquest of nature by human reason'.[130]

Balloons symbolized the naive daydreaming and escapism that utopian writers were often ridiculed for.[131] Balloon travel and the associated utopian thinking were popular targets for satire in early nineteenth-century popular pamphlets and other published material.[132] Balloons were thus a well-established symbol for thinking that moved beyond the established rational limits of their own time.

The interest in balloon voyages was further increased by contemporary fiction, especially by Jules Verne, who was extremely widely read in Vienna. The major newspaper *Neue Freie Presse* published Verne's stories translated into German in the feuilleton section in the 1870s,[133] while the middle classes read Verne in the original French. For example, the *Wiener Zeitung* dedicated a long feature article to Verne in 1875 when his latest book, *L'Île mystérieuse*, came out:

> What remains for Jules Verne to write about? Where have his *voyages extraordinaires* not already taken us? In his 'Autour de la lune' he takes us in an aluminium balloon round the moon; in 'Tour de monde en quatre-vingt jours' around the earth; in his

'Voyage au centre de la terre' we have to follow him to the central point of the world, and in 'Vingt mille lieues sours les mers' we accompany him to the depths of the ocean and even to the South Pole ... but that is not enough; for even more amazing experiences we must spend five weeks with him in an air balloon.[134]

Viennese readers were thus used to exploring exotic spaces in fictional journeys to far-away places with the help of the latest technological innovations.[135] Verne's stories were also performed as plays. For example, the Wiener Carltheater performed the play *Reise um die Erde in 80 Tagen* more than 108 times in 1875.[136] Roland Innerhofer emphasizes Verne's influence on the emergence of science fiction literature in German in the late nineteenth century.[137] It seems that popular humour, too, was strongly inspired by Verne, and the humorous imaginaries of flying balloons owe much to Verne's book, *Five Weeks in a Balloon*,[138] which came out in 1863 and is referred to in the *Wiener Zeitung* article cited above.

In one cartoon, published in *Kikeriki* in 1867, the balloon was used ironically as an emblem of utopian thinking, depicted in a context of destruction and violence as the humorous magazine suggested that in future, when the old fortifications have been torn down, the enemy might attack the new 'open city'[139] from vehicles floating in the air.[140] This example illustrates how humorous visions were integrally incorporated with the contemporary process of urban renewal and urbanization, commenting on them directly. Thus, these humorous representations, like all cultural products, thoughts and ideas, were shaped by the social milieu in which they were produced. Moreover, the humorous representations were not just reflecting the social context, but also actively remoulding it, as humour and satire served as tools for criticism.[141]

It is important to note that utopian writing and satire have long gone hand in hand. As the literary scholar Paul Alkon has noted, early narratives set in the future were often written for satirical purposes, to correct human vices and follies and to improve society by revealing its internal flaws.[142] In Vienna, the future aspect was not used only by the humorous magazines, but was employed more widely as a tool for social satire and progressive agendas. For example, Bertha von Suttner (1843–1914)[143] published under the pseudonym 'Jemand' ('Someone') a book called *Das Maschinenalter: Zukunftsvorlesungen über unsere Zeit* (*The Machine Age: Future Lectures over Our Own Time*, 1889), which consisted of imaginary lectures held in the twenty-first century, looking back at the primitive conditions of the nineteenth century. Suttner's critique was aimed especially at wars, violence and the unequal status between men and women in marriage.[144]

The cultural historian Riikka Forsström has identified two modes of existence – how things are and how they should be – as a distinctive feature of both satirical and utopian literature. Forsström sees the contrast between an idealized, radically different kind of society, and that state of society out of which the utopia is projected, as the most important element in utopian thinking.[145] Dystopias, the opposite of idealized societies, also spring from a temporal contrast between the current social order and a radically different state of society. However, in contrast to utopias, dystopic imaginaries of a radically different kind of society serve as warnings for what might come in the future if mankind does not learn from its mistakes.

Most of the visions of the future offered by *Figaro*, *Der Floh* and *Kikeriki* were not optimistic accounts of a better city, but rather these kinds of comical dystopias, envisioning the future city as a warning. They were, at root, critical comments on the decisions made in the present.

The targets of satire, however, varied, and the objects of critique shifted over the period of urban renewal. In the early phase, in the 1850s and 1860s, the humorous magazines published imaginary news in order to criticize the slow building process. As already mentioned in chapter 1, after the imperial *Handschreiben* was published in *Wiener Zeitung* on 25 December 1857, discussion in the press was increasingly preoccupied with speculations about the future. Expectations for New Vienna were often accompanied by a sense of impatience. The future perspective was blended with an awareness of the passing of time, and a suspicion that the new city might not be finished in the lifetime of the contemporary generations. *Figaro*, for instance, mocked the slow building process in an article suggesting that the ceremonious laying of the foundation stone for the new City Hall would take place in 2734, and that the whole current City Council would attend the event as mummies.[146]

Many humorous accounts presented the urban renewal as an unending project, expanding to ridiculous proportions, such as all the way to the Great Wall of China.[147] For instance, *Kikeriki* published an imaginary article from *Wiener Zeitung* in 1963, suggesting that exactly the same problems would appear in the news in a hundred years' time.[148]

Later, in the 1860s and 1870s, the satirical critique shifted from criticizing the slow speed of the process to portraying the harmful results of change in the city. Two major sources of uncertainty, which paradoxically enough were seemingly contradictory, were satirically criticized: growing insecurity and increasing control. Humour was produced through exaggerating these contemporary tendencies and taking them to extremes.

A humorous 'news from the future' item illustrates well how the future Vienna was often depicted as a topsy-turvy world where no rules of logic apply:

> Order and security are being significantly re-established in our city. Yesterday, a mere fifteen murders linked to theft were reported, one attempted and four successful assassinations, sixteen robberies with violence, eight revenge homicides and six motivated by jealousy. The Detective Bureau could therefore be reduced to eight thousand officers …
>
> Today, the 12th of January, the first plums were on offer at the market. In contrast to yesterday's cold with minus 28 degrees, the temperature today was plus 36 degrees in

the shade. During the flurries of snow the day before yesterday, it was so warm that people were wearing short sleeves. The lightning struck over 20 times in the bright, dry weather.[149]

The idea of an upside-down future world was used in various forms of political and social satire, to ridicule themes like increasing control and greediness in the city,[150] the emancipation of women,[151] and to mock the City Council.[152] Sometimes these themes overlapped. For example, in 1869 *Kikeriki* published a cartoon titled 'In ten years' (Figure 4.8), predicting how the new Ringstraße would look in ten years if things went on in the same manner as now.

Here we again see a fantastic vision of the future Vienna, combining an element of general decline with a sense of elevation, symbolized by the flying balloons. The various fantastic elements of the image portray new aspects of urban life, such as technological development and the emancipation of women, and render them comical. Yet the image also had a very specific target, for the collapsing houses were a satirical comment on the greed of construction companies building low-quality housing for quick profits.[153]

Importantly, the phrase 'unsere Ringstraße' assumes a certain 'we', a community to which the space belongs. Accordingly, the caricature actively invokes a sense of community and consensus by using irony. Irony, like humour, is dependent on its context, on the situation in which an utterance or representation is produced. As Linda Hutcheon has pointed out, irony operates not only between said and unsaid meanings, but also between people. It is the discursive community, argues Hutcheon, that 'makes irony happen', that is, precedes and makes possible the comprehension of irony.[154]

The high expectations around the urban renewal, and belief in progress, formed the interpretative framework for irony that was a distinctive feature of the comical scenes and reports from the future Vienna. Without belief in progress, embedded in many ways in the urban renewal project, the irony of these comical accounts would not make sense. Whereas in the early phase the comical dystopias usually depicted a situation in which the urban renewal had turned into an unending megalomaniac project, later in the 1860s and 1870s the perspective of the future lent the satire a distanced perspective, from which the contemporary city was examined.

Furthermore, there was yet a third variation of comical dystopias, which portrayed New Vienna as a ruined and deserted ghost town. The idea that the brave new city would soon fall into ruins had various expressions in the *Witzblätter*. In a few cases the new technology was presented as the source of destruction, turning into uncontrollable monsters consuming the vitality of urban life.[155] In many cases, it was simply the passing of time that had made the great city ancient and obsolete.[156] Fascination with ruins and destruction grew in the 1880s, especially, and the *Figaro* appendix *Wiener Luft* offered several visions of future Vienna in

Figure 4.8 'In ten years', *Kikeriki*, 20 May 1869. Source: Austrian National Library.

which growth and progress had turned into their opposite, ruin and destruction. For example, one of these imaginary visions of future Vienna used the narrative form of an archaeological exploration: in the year 3886, a future archaeologist finds a long-lost city, which he believes to be Vienna:

> It seems that we have discovered the long sought buried city of 'Vienna'. The city is located on the bank of the River Danube, which once, as we know from the old legends, was beyond compare in its beautiful blue colour and stood out from all the other rivers on the continent. Now it is murky and slimy and the riverbanks have become deserted. There is nothing left to recall the great time when this place was buzzing with trade and activity ...[157]

Comical dystopias also related to the competition with other rival capitals, and the comicality of decline and destruction should be seen in the context of high aspirations for Vienna's future. It was precisely the high hopes for the imperial capital that made the comical dystopias deeply ironical. For instance, one humorous text presented itself as a future Baedeker travel guide, which informed foreign tourists visiting Vienna that this former centre of the vast Habsburg Empire had become an almost deserted town, with a population of only 150,000. The description of the town goes as follows: the administration is scattered in the suburbs, and the collections of the museums transported to Prague, Lviv and Kraków. The theatres are closed, with the exception of one production each winter, usually continuing for one month. The great palaces have been rented to the army for military barracks. The remaining inhabitants of the city belong to the working class and are occupied during the daytime in the suburban factories, which makes Vienna a totally empty and dead ghost city. There are no means of public transportation, and house doors are closed by 8 p.m. All in all, the text concludes sarcastically, there is nothing worth mentioning in the city except for a commission dedicated to attracting more tourists.[158]

A third comical dystopia, 'Das "Verödete Wien"', brought the pessimism to an ironical and morbid climax, introducing Vienna as totally deserted; all the prestigious areas are being taken over by grass, and the trees on the Ringstraße are dying off. On the city corners, half-frozen homeless bishops and civil servants (*Verwaltungsräthe*) are begging for charity. All the schools are empty, since almost every school-aged child has died of hunger. The dystopic text continues with other examples of decline and destruction, and at the same time comments ironically on the economic ambivalence of contemporary Vienna: all businesses are ruined, except for those few running pawn shops or writing horror stories.[159]

The literary scholar Karlheinz Stierle has traced back the metaphor of ruined cities in eighteenth- and nineteenth-century literature, seeing it as a topos of modern self-reflection. Stierle argues that it was precisely this contradiction between a simultaneous belief in linear progress and a fear of it becoming endangered that was one of the major paradoxes that shaped the modern consciousness.

The modern ability to imagine future worlds leads to a new awareness that in the future the present would also be past. Modern consciousness was thus saliently marked by an awareness of the transient nature of reality. The transient was crystallized in the idea that at some distant point in history the great modern metropolises, too, would face destruction and become antique ruins.[160] Marshall Berman has also located a paradox between urban vitality and destruction in the core of modern experience as cities, especially, encapsulated both the era's aspirations for constant progress and its fears of future destruction.[161] Satirical imaginary landscapes of dead and deserted urban spaces appeared not only in Vienna, but in other European capitals as well.[162] The idea of the destruction of the modern cities thus inspired multiple cultural expressions across national borders.[163]

These various visions of destruction, which emerged at the same time as the European capitals grew to massive proportions, were also related to cultural pessimism and a cyclical understanding of the rise and fall of cultures which began to characterize the *fin-de-siècle* era, starting from Friedrich Nietzsche's philosophy in the 1870s and 1880s and culminating after World War I in the cultural pessimism and civilization critique of Oswald Sprengler's (1880–1936) classic study *Der Untergang des Abendlandes* (1918–22).[164] Viennese literature, too, inclined increasingly towards pessimistic worldviews. The most famous expression of this Viennese critical pessimism was, of course, the satirical play *Die Letzten Tage der Menschheit* by Karl Kraus, published between 1915 and 1922 after the outbreak of the war.[165]

However, even before Kraus and his famous satirical magazine *Die Fackel*, Viennese humour seems to have begun to lose some of its mid-century optimistic innocence. Two of the most famous members of the 1848 generation, the founders and editors of the humorous magazines *Kikeriki* and *Figaro*, Ottokar Ebersberg and Karl Sitter, both suffered from increasing mental problems as they entered middle age. Ebersberg died in a mental institution in 1886; Sitter had passed away two years earlier in 1884, and was seen at the time as having become a bitter old man, unable to forget his struggles and captivity under the absolutist regime in the 1850s.[166] In her study of Friedrich Schlögl, one of the founding forces of the *Wiener Luft* appendix of the *Figaro* magazine, Ann Mitchell Fuess has observed that a constant balancing between a desire to improve society and pessimistic views on the future was characteristic of Schlögl's entire work as a journalist, and at the end of his career he too fell into deepening melancholy and pessimism.[167] The cultural turn to *fin-de-siècle* pessimism was thus closely linked with the experiences of the 1848 generation, as towards the end of the century they lost the political optimism of their youth and turned to pessimism, when the long-desired constitution of 1867 did not solve the political and social problems of the era, but the contradictions seemed only to grow and multiply within the Austro-Hungarian Empire as the nineteenth century neared its close.

Yet, since the new generation of journalists taking over the humorous magazines in the 1880s also produced increasingly dark and melancholy humour on the city, the simple generational aspect does not explain the gradual shift to darker and more violent humour in the last decades of the century.[168] It is thus necessary to look further into the wider cultural atmosphere of *fin-de-siècle* Europe.

The historical epoch of the *fin de siècle* is associated with a prevailing social and cultural pessimism, and a belief that Western culture was in decline. The major social and cultural changes, such as urbanization and industrialization, that were taking place in the second half of the nineteenth century created feelings of insecurity and uncertainty, leading to fears of what kind of phenomena might result from all the massive changes that were moulding people's lives.[169] At the turn of the century, illness was taken up as a cultural metaphor, for the whole era was seen as a sick body fading away.[170] The imaginaries of ruined cities were thus part of a wider cultural matrix revolving around ideas of destruction and death.

The turn of the century nourished all kinds of premonitions of a coming apocalypse.[171] In Vienna, too, the idea of the world coming to an end at the transition to the twentieth century surfaced in popular humour.[172] For instance, Vinzenz Chiavacci, who was famous for his humorous short stories, published a novel in 1897, *Der Weltuntergang: Eine Phantasie aus dem Jahre 1900*, which envisions an apocalypse as a comet pushes Earth out of its orbit, slowly floating away from the sun into outer space. This means a slow and agonizing death for the whole planet, due to the loss of light and warmth. However, in the end not all hope is lost. On its way to certain destruction, Earth meets Mars, representing an idealized and more developed society. The Martians explain to the people of Earth that they still have a chance to return to their original orbit. In the end, following the conventions of early utopian literature, it turns out that the apocalypse was nothing but a scientist's feverish nightmare. The dreamed experience of an apocalypse thus becomes a warning, a premonition of the coming war, expressing a desire for a second chance to create a better future.[173]

All this testifies that a certain pessimistic attitude about the future intensified towards the turn of the century. Moreover, humour did not merely reflect this new sense of the end of an era, but actively shaped and nourished it. Satirical and comical visions of the future affirm, in my view, the basic idea that middle-class popular humour did not reflect merely ideas and attitudes relating to the modernization of Vienna, but during the urban renewal process between 1857 and 1890 actively constructed the experience and understanding of modernity. This idea also implicates an understanding from previous research, that visual culture and media representations played a pivotal role in creating the experience of modernity and modern life.[174] Whereas previous studies have above all examined the relationship between representations of the 'present' and the experience of modernity, it is interesting to look further into the ways in which the future aspect was used to reimagine the city in untraditional and innovative ways: no matter how serious or comical the depictions of the future are intended to be, they are inescapably creative and novel by nature, expressing *poesis*, not *mimesis*.[175] This makes them characteristically modern cultural expressions.

This chapter has aimed to give insight into the strong sense of temporality that thoroughly permeated the humorous representations of the transformation of Vienna. Popular humorous publications were an important part of the Viennese middle-class nineteenth-century culture of history, increasingly preoccupied with the passing of time and finding a place on the historical continuum. At the same time as the great monumental buildings of the Ringstraße were creating a spatial narrative of different historical ages, all coming together in the city space, these humorous representations of the city investigated the relationship between past, present and future in other ways. Both city and knowledge of the city were distinctively temporal for the Viennese bourgeoisie. Memories of *Alt-Wien* and expectations for the future Vienna were inseparable from the present, which in turn seemed to have become more confusing and deceptive during the transformation process. However, all these levels of time gained their meaning in relationship to one another; jokes about present and past Vienna were published side by side with visions of future dystopias, and this simultaneous coexistence created an ironically detached yet affective framework within which the transformation process was interpreted.

Consequently, this chapter has aimed to shed light on the spatial and affective aspects of humour and to show that Viennese middle-class humour was locally oriented. The idea of a distinctive Viennese sense of humour was imbued with a sense of place and local identity.[176] For this reason it seems that humorous magazines played a major role in creating an emotional community able to laugh and mourn together in the changing city. In the field of the history of emotions, Barbara H. Rosenwein has referred to the fact that in the modern era, in particular, emotional communities are often textual, discursive communities, where people who do not otherwise meet are bound together by means of media representations.[177] Humorous media representations have special potential to tie people together, because of their strong affective element. In the late nineteenth century, in an age of urbanization and rapid population growth, imaginaries of the past became a way of constructing local identity. This kind of knowing the city, on both an intellectual and an emotional level, meant not only shared memories from the past but also mutual fears and hopes for the future.

At the same time, knowing the city increasingly meant owning the city: memories of the old city distinguished members of the mythical *Wienerthum* from newcomers; not only could they orientate themselves in the new urban surroundings better than strangers, but most importantly, they knew how the city had been before. Being Viennese meant knowing the city, intimately and personally. Because the processes of creating and understanding humour were based on shared tacit knowledge of the city, popular humour was important for creating a sense of community. The next chapter will study further the process of exclusion and inclusion in discussion of the city. In the last decades of the century, humour increasingly targeted marginalized groups encountered in the urban space, such as foreigners, emancipated women and members of the urban underclass.

Notes

1. See further Julian Brigstocke, *The Life of the City: Space, Humour, and the Experience of Truth in Fin-de-siècle Montmartre* (Surrey, 2014), 59. Cf. David Frisby, *Cityscapes of Modernity: Critical Explorations* (Cambridge, 2001), 40.
2. See, for example, Brigstocke, *Life of the City*, 58–62; Frisby, *Cityscapes*, 2–5; Peter Fritzsche, *Reading Berlin 1900* (Cambridge, MA, 1998), 33, 43–45, 101; Marshall Berman, *All That Is Solid Melts Into Air: The Experience of Modernity* (New York, 1988), 16.
3. Fritzsche refers to this in the term 'word city'. Fritzsche, *Reading Berlin*, 1–11. Cf. Vanessa R. Schwarz, *Spectacular Realities: Early Mass Culture in Fin-de-siècle Paris* (Berkeley, 1999), 2.
4. See, e.g., 'Für solide Damen', *Kikeriki*, 5 December 1878; 'Die neueste Mode, die Sonnenschirme mit Sprüchlein zu bedrucken', *Der Floh*, 27 April 1884.
5. See, e.g., 'Was einem beim Annoncen-Pharus geschehen kann', *Kikeriki*, 25 December 1862; 'Halb überklebte Plakate', *Figaro*, 9 March 1878 / *Wiener Luft* No. 10.
6. See, e.g., 'Strassenkehrers Monolog', *Der Floh*, 1 September 1872; 'Recht appetitlich sind die Annoncen in den Tramway-Waggons', *Kikeriki*, 4 July 1878; 'Merkwürdig', *Kikeriki*, 21 May 1885; 'Spetziell Wienerisch', *Kikeriki*, 25 March 1886; 'Buchstabengeist', *Kikeriki*, 26 January 1888; 'Drei Inserate', *Kikeriki*, 13 January 1889.
7. 'Keine Hühneraugen mehr! Eine neue Reklame-Speculation', *Kikeriki*, 8 May 1873.
8. E.g. 'Druckstücke von Zeitungs-Notizen', *Kikeriki*, 22 October 1868; 'Kleine Anzeiger und Resultate', *Figaro*, 27 January 1877 / *Wiener Luft* No. 4.
9. E.g. 'Die Annoncentafeln', *Kikeriki*, 3 August 1873; 'Auf der Straße', *Der Floh*, 27 July 1884; 'Ein übles Beispiel', *Figaro*, 18 September 1886 / *Wiener Luft* No. 38.
10. Cf. Fritzsche, *Reading Berlin*, 1; Schwartz, *Spectacular Realities*, 2.
11. See, e.g., 'Irrthum durch Plakat-Aenlichkeit', *Kikeriki*, 6 July 1879.
12. 'Ein neuer Sport', *Kikeriki*, 4 July 1870. Jokes were also created by misspelling urban texts such as signboards and playing with their changing meanings. 'Zwei moderne Plakate', *Kikeriki*, 2 January 1871.
13. Cf. Terry Castle, *Masquerade and Civilization: The Carnivalesque in Eighteenth-Century English Culture and Fiction* (London, 1986), 87–88; Peter Stallybrass and Allon White, *The Politics and Poetics of Transgression* (London, 1986), 2–3 and passim.
14. Peter Fritzsche, 'Readers, Browsers, Strangers, Spectators: Narrative Forms and Metropolitan Encounters in Twentieth-Century Berlin', in Malcolm Gee and Tim Kirk (eds), *Printed Matters: Printing, Publishing and Urban Culture in Europe in the Modern Period* (Aldershot, 2002), 90–91; Fritzsche, *Reading Berlin*, 9–10.
15. 'Plint durch Gepurt', *Der Floh*, 8 February 1885.

16. 'Die Fremden in Wien', *Der Floh*, 26 August 1877.
17. Cf. Brigstocke, *Life of the City*, 109. On the idea of ridicule, see further Michael Billig, *Laughter and Ridicule: Towards a Social Critique of Humour* (London, 2012).
18. See, e.g., 'Rebus', *Figaro*, 12 May 1858; 'Unschuldige Räthsel', *Kikeriki*, 16 January 1861; 'Räthsel', *Figaro*, 6 February 1875. The materiality of the paper was often used as a vehicle for both creating the mystery and solving it. This happened so that the texts and images had to be turned upside down in order to get the joke and solve the puzzle.
19. On the nineteenth-century detective stories, see further Frisby, *Cityscapes*, 13–15, 24, 94, 98; Hannu Salmi, *Nineteenth-Century Europe: A Cultural History* (Cambridge, 2008), 138–39; Brigstocke, *Life of the City*, 31, 71, 109, 141. On the nineteenth-century idea of the city as a maze or labyrinth, see Elisabeth Wilson, *The Sphinx in the City: Urban Life, the Control of Disorder, and Women* (Berkeley, 1992), 3, 157.
20. See, for example, 'Pyramidale Wasserleitungsangst', *Kikeriki*, 20 May 1875.
21. Later Ludwig Wittgenstein studied the duck-rabbit illusion in his *Philosophical Investigations*. See further Linda Hutcheon, *Irony's Edge: The Theory and Politics of Irony* (New York, 1995), 59–60.
22. Cf. Brigstocke, *Life of the City*, 136.
23. 'Auf dem äußeren Burgplatze', *Kikeriki*, 8 May 1871. See also 'Das Mißverständnis auf der Wiener Ringstraße', *Kikeriki*, 5 April 1866.
24. See, e.g., 'Fluch der Kurzsichtigkeit', *Kikeriki*, 13 September 1885.
25. See further section 'New Clothes of Vindobona: Modernity and Gender' in chapter 5.
26. The uncanny bodily experiences resulted often from drunkenness. See, for example, 'Auf dem Heimwege', *Figaro*, 19 February 1881 / *Wiener Luft* No. 8.
27. The theme of visual errors included faults in representations as well. See, for instance, 'Die Amateur-Photographien des "Floh"', *Der Floh*, 7 October 1888; 'Optische Täuschung', *Der Floh*, 15 September 1889.
28. 'Merkwürdig, ich hab' doch nur drei Krügel getrunken, wie kann ich denn da den Mond schon doppelt seh'n?' 'Begreiflicher Irrthum', *Der Floh*, 11 October 1891.
29. Brigstocke, *Life of the City*, 159. On the contemporary notions of the modern city as a source of spatial illnesses and maladies, see further the section 'Desiring order' in chapter 2.
30. The 1860s were a time of radical political changes. The constitutional monarchy was born and the liberals gained power in the City Council of Vienna.
31. Carl E. Schorske, *Fin-de-siècle Vienna: Politics and Culture* (Cambridge, [1961] 1981), passim, especially 146.
32. See further Steven Beller, 'Review of Coen, Deborah R., *Vienna in the Age of Uncertainty: Science, Liberalism and Private Life*', HABSBURG, H-Net Reviews, January 2010. An earlier work combining cultural history and scientific thought is the classic study *Wittgenstein's Vienna* (Chicago, [1973] 1996) by Allan Janik and Stephen Toulmin.
33. Deborah R. Coen, *Vienna in the Age of Uncertainty: Science, Liberalism and Private Life* (Chicago, 2007), 2, 12–15. Coen relates this Austrian tradition also to the birth of applied logical positivism of the Vienna circle after World War I.
34. Coen, *Vienna in the Age of Uncertainty*, 23–24.
35. Ibid., 30.
36. Billig, *Laughter and Ridicule*, 63–65. Daniel Wickberg, on the other hand, has argued that being witty and having a good sense of humour were valued by the nineteenth-

century bourgeoisie. Daniel Wickberg, *Senses of Humor: Self and Laughter in Modern America* (Ithaca, 1998), 58, 74 and passim.
37. Billig, *Laughter and Ridicule*, 58–61. On Viennese coffee house culture, see further Harold B. Segel, *The Vienna Coffee House Wits, 1890–1938* (West Lafayette, 1993); Charlotte Ashby, Tag Gronberg and Simon Shaw-Miller (eds), *The Viennese Café and Fin-de-Siècle Culture* (New York, 2013).
38. Cf. Billig, *Laughter and Ridicule*, 164. Yet, as Steven Beller reminds us, it is important to challenge the myth of one essentially Jewish mind or consciousness and remain attentive to the fact that the Jewish presence in the social strata and cultural life of late nineteenth-century Vienna was a multifaceted and convoluted phenomenon, meaning that there was a huge variety of Jewish thought and experience. Yet the desire for assimilation, which was however denied by the main Austrian-German population, was characteristic of the educated middle-class Jewish population. See further Steven Beller, *Vienna and the Jews 1867–1938: A Cultural History* (Cambridge, 2003), 40–41, 73–74, 78–82 and passim.
39. Segel, *Vienna Coffee House Wits*, 12.
40. *On the Origin of Species by Means of Natural Selection, or the Preservation of Favoured Races in the Struggle for Life* was translated into German in 1860 and *The Descent of Man, and Selection in Relation to Sex* was translated into German in 1871.
41. Daumier's cartoon was published in the satirical journal *La Caricature* in 1831.
42. The political edge and the original reference to Darwin did, however, return later in 1895 when the social democratic *Glühlichter* used this convention to mock the leader of the Christian Social Party by publishing a caricature, 'Frei Nach Darwin'schen Theorie', in which the head of a donkey 'evolves' into the head of Karl Lueger. 'Frei Nach Darwin'schen Theorie', *Glühlichter*, 12 April 1895.
43. Arthur Koestler, *The Act of Creation* (London, 1964), 35–37.
44. Ann Taylor Allen, *Satire and Society in Wilhelmine Germany: Kladderadatsch & Simplicissimus 1890–1914* (Lexington, 1984), 8.
45. Seppo Knuuttila, *Kansanhuumorin mieli: Kaskut maailmankuvan aineksena* (Helsinki, 1992), 12, 275–276.
46. Cf. Billig, *Laughter and Ridicule*, 158; Simon Critchley, *On Humour* (New York, 2002), 10.
47. The so-called 'Dilettantenmappe' was published in *Wiener Luft* in the 1880s. There were special instructions for readers who wished to send their contributions for publication in this section.
48. Archduke Karl defeated Napoleon in the battle of Aspern in 1809.
49. Ole Frahm, 'Every Window Tells a Story: Remarks on the Urbanity of Early Comic Strips', in Jörn Ahrens and Arno Meteling (eds), *Comics and the City: Urban Space in Print, Picture and Sequence* (New York, 2010), 33.
50. Cf. Brigstocke, *Life of the City*, xi, 98, 144–45.
51. Cf. Lutz Musner, *Der Geschmack von Wien: Kultur und Habitus einer Stadt* (Frankfurt am Main, 2009), 188–214; Frisby, *Cityscapes*, 18, 168–82. See also Sandor Békési, 'The Attraction of Heimat: Homeland Protection in Vienna around 1900, or the Preservation and Reform of the City', in Arnold Bartetzky and Marc Schalenberg (eds), *Urban Planning and the Pursuit of Happiness* (Berlin, 2009), 72–76.
52. See further Karin Johannisson, *Nostalgia: En känslas historia* (Stockholm, 2001), 17–18, 51; Pertti Grönholm and Heli Paalumäki, 'Nostalgian ja utopian risteyksessä.

'Keskusteluja modernin kaipuun merkityksistä ja aikaulottuvuuksista', in Heli Paalumäki and Pertti Grönholm (eds), *Kaipaava moderni: Nostalgian ja utopian kohtaamisia Euroopassa 1600-luvulta 2000-luvulle* (Turku, 2015), 11–15.

53. Johannisson, *Nostalgia*, 10–11, 28. See also Svetlana Boym, *The Future of Nostalgia* (New York, 2001), 7, 16, 511–13.
54. 'Die letzte Hoffnung: Der alte Steffl singt', *Der Floh*, 24 April 1887; 'Loblied der Wien an die Wiener', *Figaro*, 8 June 1889 / *Wiener Luft* No. 23.
55. Barbara H. Rosenwein, 'Problems and Methods in the History of Emotions', *Passions in Context* 1(1) (2010), 19; Jan Plamper, 'The History of Emotions: An Interview with William Reddy, Barbara Rosenwein, and Peter Stearns', *History and Theory* 49(2) (2010), 253.
56. Cf. *lieu de mémoire*. Pierre Nora, 'General Introduction: Between Memory and History', in Pierre Nora (ed.), *Realms of Memory: Rethinking the French Past*, Vol. 1, *Conflicts and Divisions* (New York, 1996), 1–3, 6–7.
57. Musner, *Geschmack von Wien*, 188–89.
58. Wagner was a renowned pioneer of modern architecture and Sitte a well-known critic of modernist urban planning, who claimed in his book *Der Städte-Bau nach seinen künstlerischen Grundsätzen* (Vienna, [1889] 1901) that urban design should go back to organic forms. See further Schorske, *Fin-de-siècle Vienna*, 62–110; Frisby, *Cityscapes*, 215–17, 222–26.
59. Cf. Frisby, *Cityscapes*, 215.
60. Derek B. Scott, *Sounds of the Metropolis: The 19th-Century Popular Music Revolution in London, New York, Paris and Vienna* (Oxford, 2008), 35, 137–38; Marion Linhardt, *Residenzstadt und Metropole: Zu einer kulturellen Topographie des Wiener Unterhaltungstheaters (1858–1918)* (Berlin, 2012), 162–65, 176.
61. E.g. 'Gonzeibastei', *Der Humorist*, 27 February 1859; 'Illustrierte Wochenschau', *Figaro*, 10 December 1859; 'Abschieds-Scene am Glacis, Rührender Abschied zweier Bäume', *Der Humorist*, 24 September 1860.
62. 'Alt-Wien contra Neu-Wien', *Der Humorist*, 8 October 1860.
63. See, e.g., 'Blätter aus einer Chronist Wiens, aus unbestimmter Zeit, wie solche nach vielen Jahrhunderten unter einer Ruine Alt-Wiens werden aufgefunden werden', *Figaro*, 25 January 1857.
64. Grad in derselben Zeit, wo Alt-Wien in seinen Mauern niedersinkt und wo man natürlich von dem Phönix Neu-Wien noch nichts sehen kann, der aus dem Aschen der Vergangenheit aufsteigen soll, grad in dieser Zeit find i es begreiflich, daß der Wiener halb heiter, halb wehmütig das Aug nach rückwärts wendet, die Vergangenheit seiner geliebten Vaterstadt im Geist Revue passiren laßt [sic], Erlebtes und Erzähltes mit dem Erinnerungsperspektive anschaut und von Alt-Wien herzlichen Abschied nimmt. *Jörgel Briefe*, 26 April 1858.
65. E.g. 'Einst und jetzt', *Der Humorist*, 17 September 1838.
66. 'Briefkasten der Redaktion', *Figaro*, 7 June 1862.
67. 'Kleine Post der Redaktion', *Kikeriki*, 27 January 1876.
68. See further Salmi, *Nineteenth-Century Europe*, 5 and passim.
69. 'Blaubuch', *Der Humorist*, 3 December 1860.
70. See, e.g., Mary Gluck, *The Invisible Jewish Budapest: Metropolitan Culture at the Fin de Siècle* (Madison, 2016), 13, 18–20; Vanesa Galindo Rodriguez, 'Visuality and Practices of Looking in Nineteenth-Century Madrid: Representations of the Old and Modern

City in the Illustrated Press', in U. Krampl, R. Beck and E. Retaillaud-Bajac (eds), *Les cinq sens de la ville du Moyen Âge à nos jours* (Tours, 2013), 227–29; Taina Syrjämaa, 'The Clash of Picturesque Decay and Modern Cleanliness in Late Nineteenth-Century Rome', in Mark Bradley (ed.), *Rome: Pollution and Propriety. Dirt Disease and Hygiene in the Eternal City from Antiquity to Modernity* (Cambridge, 2012), 211; David Harvey, *Paris, Capital of Modernity* (New York, 2006), 17 and passim.

71. See, e.g., 'Wiener Wirthe einst und jetzt', *Der Floh*, 18 November 1877; 'Alt- und Neu-Wien', *Der Floh*, 12 March 1882; 'Der grabenstiegene Wiener', *Figaro*, 10 September 1887 / *Wiener Luft* No. 37; 'Mai Gespräche einst und jetzt', *Der Floh*, 1 July 1888; 'Einst und Jetzt', *Figaro*, 6 July 1889. Cf. Franz Ullmayer, *Wiener Volksleben: Ein humoristisches Bädecker bei der Weltausstellung* (Vienna, 1873), 7–12.
72. See, e.g., 'Humanität im "verschimpfirten" Alt-Wien, im "fortgeschrittenen" Neu-Wien', *Figaro*, 15 April 1876 / *Wiener Luft* No. 16.
73. 'Um das Interesse des Publikums', in 'Alt-Wien', *Kikeriki*, 26 June 1892; 'In Alt-Wien. (Im Ausstellungsplatze)', *Figaro*, 20 August 1892 / *Wiener Luft* No. 34; 'Aus Chicago', *Der Floh*, 21 May 1893. On the significance of *Alt-Wien* nostalgia in *fin-de-siècle* popular culture, see further Musner, *Geschmack von Wien*, 188–94.
74. Frisby, *Cityscapes*, 214–20.
75. Ibid., 18, 168.
76. Brigstocke, *Life of the City*, 25.
77. See further ibid., 24–26, 109–10.
78. See, e.g., Edward Timms, *Karl Kraus: Satiriker der Apokalypse. Leben und Werk 1874 bis 1918* (Berlin, [1986] 1999), 19.
79. For Saphir's publishing activities, see further Mary Lee Townsend, *Forbidden Laughter: Popular Humor and the Limits of Repression in Nineteenth-Century Prussia* (Ann Arbor, 1992), 35–41.
80. Friedrich Schlögl, *Aus Alt-und Neu-Wien (Nebst einen Stück Autobiografie)* (Vienna, 1882), 26–27. See also Jo Ann Mitchell Fuess, *The Cultural Crisis of Lower Middle Class Vienna 1848–1892: A Study of the Works of Friedrich Schlögl* (Lincoln, 1992), 8, 54, 136–43.
81. A nostalgic view on humour was typical for the humorous magazines. See, e.g., 'Altwiener's Schmerzenschrei', *Kikeriki*, 10 February 1884; 'Wiener Lieder', *Der Floh*, 17 August 1884; 'Wie man uns das Lachen abgewöhnt', *Kikeriki*, 9 November 1890.
82. For instance, according to Schlögl, the *Wienerthum* consisted of sensitivity, sharp wit and a joyous melody of high-spirited frivolity. Schlögl, *Alt-und Neu-Wien*, 4.
83. This aim of mapping both physical and mental characteristics of Vienna was a very distinctive element of Biedermaier-era humorous literature, featuring such titles as *Wien mit seinen Vorstädten humoristisch geschildert* (o.J.) and *Komische Gedichte über die Vorstädte Wiens* (1812–20). This tradition continued after the 1848 revolution as humorous urban texts continued to seek the characteristics of the city through subjective experiences; various incidents, encounters and phenomena related to the local urban environment were typical for humorous books and booklets dealing with the city. For example, a booklet titled *Eines kleinen Teufels humoristisch-satirische Spaziergänge durch Stadt und Land* was published in 1850. Also, Carl Sitter's *Modernes Wien: Humoristische Federzeichnungen* (Vienna, 1859) and Heinrich Ritter von Levitschnigg's *Wien wie es war und ist* (Vienna, 1860) carried on evolving this tradition of humorous narratives of the city.

84. Pseudonym for Joseph Alois (1772–1841).
85. Heinrich Walden, *Wien und seine Bewohner humoristisch geschildert auf einem Spaziergang über die ganze Bastey* (Vienna, 1834), 1, 8–9, 22–23.
86. See further Matthias Nöllke, *Daniel Spitzers Wiener Spatziergänge: Liberales Feuilleton im Zeitungskontext* (Frankfurt am Main, 1994).
87. See, e.g., Johann Babtist Weis, *Wien's Merkwürdigkeiten mit ihren geschichtlichen Erinnerungen: Ein Wegweiser für Fremde und Einheimische* (Vienna, 1834).
88. Julius Neidl, *Humoristischer Fremdenführer für Wien und Umgebung* (Vienna, 1880).
89. This notion supports the research on how humour was very much related to processes of making places, creating local identities in other growing nineteenth-century cities such as Paris or Berlin. Cf. Brigstocke, *Life of the City*, 108. On *Berliner Schnauze* and a sense of locality and urban identity, see, e.g., Jan Rüger, 'Die Berliner Schnauze im Ersten Weltkrieg', in Thomas Biskup and Marc Schalenberg (eds), *Selling Berlin: Imagebildung und Stadtmarketing von der preußischen Residenz bis zur Bundeshauptstadt* (Stuttgart, 2008), 147.
90. 'Monolog des Allgemeinen Krankenhauses', *Kikeriki*, 7 September 1876; 'Brunnröhren-Monolog', *Kikeriki*, 28 October 1877; 'Wenn die Häuser reden könnten', *Kikeriki*, 27 March 1881.
91. … Du undankbare Welt, ist dies dein schnöder Lohn, / Daß du noch lachest drob, wann man mich stürzt von Thron? / Mich, der die Christenheit alleinig hat beschirmet, / Als hunderttausend Türkhen wider mich gestürmet, / Mich, der die Feder nicht, sondern das Schwert gezuckt, / Und siegreich hat damit den Halbmond unterdrückt; / Du schönes Volk vom heut, gräulich modernisiret, / Kennst kein Erbahmnuß nicht mit dem, der einst floriret … 'Wiener Heroiden-Briefe II. Herr Bastionarus an Jungfer Vienna-Nova', *Figaro*, 4 January 1858.
92. See Scott, *Sounds of the Metropolis*, 8.
93. See, e.g., *Der Humorist*, 6 October 1858.
94. For the meaning of the wall in the Viennese past, see Michaela Masanz and Martina Nagl, *Ringstraßenallee: Von der Freiheit zur Ordnung vor den Toren Wiens* (Vienna, 1996), 5, 42–43, 65.
95. Cf. Musner, *Geschmack von Wien*, 183–87.
96. … Viel trübe Stunden habe ich durchlebt, / Zu meinem Ohr drang der Kanonendonner / Des wild fanatischen Osmanenheeres, / Und an den Panzer meiner Granitmauern / Ist manche Feindeskugel abgeprallt – / Doch blieb ich steh'n im Sturm der Aeonen / Ein würdig Denkmal deutscher Kraft. – // Da fing man an, an meinem Äußern / Die jugendliche Striche zu vermissen, / und zierte mich mit neuen Schnörkeln / Und bellerte an meinen spitzen Zinken / Daß ich derab vor Scham mocht' gern versinken, / Da fing ich endlich selbst zu glauben an, / Daß ich in dieser Welt zu alt geworden, / Und das Bewusstsein, daß man älter wird / Ist des Verscheidens ahnend' Vorgefühl … 'Monolog des Stefansthurmes', *Der Humorist*, 19 December 1857.
97. See, e.g., 'Die Wiener von 1683 an die von 1883', *Figaro*, 28 July 1883.
98. See, e.g., 'Die Letzte Hoffnung: der alte Steffl singt', *Der Floh*, 24 April 1887; 'Was der St. Stefansthurm dem Kikeriki ins Ohr flüsterte', *Kikeriki*, 10 July 1890.
99. 'Offener Brief des alten Steffels an den Eiffelthurm', *Figaro*, 19 January 1889 / *Wiener Luft* No. 3.
100. 'Gespräch zwischen zwei Thürmen', *Der Floh*, 10 February 1889.

101. Also reference point to other landmarks in European cities, at a time when the competition on vertical dimensions was accumulating.
102. E.g. 'Der alte Steffel. Wiener Lieder', *Der Floh*, 17 August 1884.
103. See further Carl E. Schorske, *Thinking with History: Explorations in the Passage to Modernism* (Princeton, 1998), 194.
104. Michael Mulkay, *On Humour: Its Nature and Its Place in Modern Society* (Cambridge, 1988), 79–84; Wickberg, *Senses of Humor*, 172. See also Critchley, *On Humour*, 56–57.
105. The cathedral was built in 1160 and it has been renovated many times since it was first completed in the twelfth century.
106. I. Der Wienfluß an den Linienwall. Lieber, alter Freund! Da Sie sich nach meinem Befinden erkundigen, theile ich Ihnen mit, daß ich mich noch immer in meinem alten Zustande befinde. Abgesehen von einer frischen Sunette, die mir unlängst wieder gestochen wurde, kann ich über keine besonderen Schmerzen klagen. Wie geht es Ihnen, lieber Alter? Ihr ec. Wienfluß. II Der Liniewall an der Wienfluß. Geehrter Herr Nachbar! Ich danke der Nachfrage. Ich stehe noch immer auf dem alten Fleck und lasse über die verschiedenen Gerüchte von bevorstehender Aufhebung, Hinausschiebung u.s.w. ruhig das Gras wachsen. Ich habe gleich Ihnen manchen Puff ausgehalten und blicke lebensfroh in die Zukunft. Servus alter Spezi! Ihr Linienwall. 'Intimer Briefwechsel zwischen mehreren alten Bekannten', *Figaro*, 13 October 1888 / *Wiener Luft* No. 41.
107. *Kikeriki*, 4 June 1863.
108. Schorske, *Fin-de-siècle Vienna*, 33–36.
109. Nora, 'General Introduction', 14.
110. … Alte Häuser haben nämlich eine Seele. Nicht weil sie riechen und ein grobwollener Philosoph in dieser Äußerung die Seele erkennen will. Sie haben ein Seele, weil von dem Geiste der abschiedenen Geschlechter, die in ihnen während der Jahrhunderte hausten, ein Weniges auf sie selbst übergangen ist. Neue Hauser dagegen sind leblose Puppen, fad und nüchtern, ohne Erinnerungen, ohne Seele. Eduard Pötzl, 'Das ausgegrabene Haus', in *Rund um den Stephansthurm* (Vienna, 1916), 35.
111. Cf. Plamper, 'History of Emotions', 259. On humour and affective experiences, see further Brigstocke, *Life of the City*, 108–11.
112. One exception is Vinzenz Chiavacci's *Der Weltuntergang: Eine Phantasie aus dem Jahre 1900* (Stuttgart, 1897), which I will discuss later in this chapter.
113. See, e.g., 'Die neue Fiakertaxe. Eine Zukunftsszene', *Kikeriki*, 29 October 1868; 'Nach hundert Jahren', *Figaro*, 17 July 1869; 'Ein Zukunftsbild', *Figaro*, 21 October 1871.
114. 'Aus einer Zukunftszeitung des Jahres 1895', *Kikeriki*, 29 April 1875; 'Aus der k.k. Wiener Zeitung 1976', *Figaro*, 29 April 1876;'Ein wahrscheinlicher Bericht der "Medizinischer Wochenschrift" im Jahre 2881', *Figaro*, 12 February 1881. Cf. Gluck, *The Invisible Jewish Budapest*, 34–35.
115. Hutcheon, *Irony's Edge*, 57–58, 95.
116. Cf. chapter 1.
117. See Hutcheon, *Irony's Edge*, 54.
118. 'Nach der Vollendung der auf Säulen und Traversen gebauten Zukunfts-Gürtelbahn', *Kikeriki*, 11 September 1881; 'Das neue Stadtbahnprojekt', *Kikeriki*, 11 October 1888.
119. 'In zehn Jahren', *Kikeriki*, 20 May 1869. See also 'Neueste Erfindung des Kikeriki', *Kikeriki*, 9 January 1862; 'Neuer Omnibusverkehr für Wien', *Kikeriki*, 30 June 1864.
120. 'Das Zukunfts-Wien', *Figaro*, 30 March 1872.

121. Salmi, *Nineteenth-Century Europe*, 33–42.
122. 'Welche unausbleiblichen Fortschritte der Telegraf in nächster Zukunft machen dürfte', *Figaro*, 15 May 1858.
123. Paul K. Alkon, *Origins of Futuristic Fiction* (Athens, 2010), 3–4.
124. Salmi, *Nineteenth-Century Europe*, 5–6, 140–45. On the history of the term *utopia* and Mercier's utopian thought, see further Riikka Forsström, *Possible Worlds: The Idea of Happiness in the Utopian Vision of Louis-Sébastien Mercier* (Helsinki, 2002), passim, especially 46–47.
125. 'Wiener Weltausstellung vom Jahre 2073', *Der Floh*, 30 March 1873.
126. Forsström, *Possible Worlds*, 17.
127. Cf. Reinhart Koselleck, *Futures Past: On the Semantics of Historical Time* (New York, [1979] 2004).
128. 'Wunder der Weltausstellung', *Der Floh*, 10 May 1873. On the parody of Wagner's theories on art in the future, see also, e.g., 'Lohengrin oder ein Zukunfts-Comfortable, oder die bestrafte Neugierde', *Figaro*, 21 August 1858.
129. Sigmund Freud, *Der Humor* (Frankfurt am Main, [1927] 2006), 254. See also Wickberg, *Senses of Humor*, 90–91; Critchley, *On Humour*, 95.
130. Original emphasis. Steven E. Jones, 'Balloons. An Essay on Mary Shelley's *The Last Man*', Romantic Circles (1997).
131. Forsström, *Possible Worlds*, 30–40.
132. See, e.g., Marion Fulgence, *Wonderful Balloon Ascents or the Conquest of the Skies: A History of Balloons and Balloon Voyages* (London, 1870), 127.
133. 'Jules Verne und seine Schriften (Feuilleton)', *Neue Freie Presse*, 3 October 1874. On the Viennese reception of Verne, see further Roland Innerhofer, *Deutsche Science Fiction 1870–1914: Rekonstruktion und Analyse der Anfänge einer Gattung* (Vienna, 1996), 58–59.
134. Worüber hätte Jules Verne aber noch nicht geschrieben? Wohin hätte seine Voyages extraordinaires uns noch nicht geführt? In seinem Werke: 'Autour de la lune' führt er uns in einem Luftballon aus Alluminium um den Mond, in seinem „Tour de monde en quatre-vingt jours' um die Erde, in seinem Buche: 'Voyage au centre de la terre' müssen wir ihn zum Mittelpunkt der Erde, in 'Vingt mille lieues sours les mers' in die Tiefen auf den Grund der Meere und bis zum Südpol begleiten … nicht genugt daran, müssen wir ihm fünf Wochen in einem Luftballon zubringen und die wunderlichsten Dinge erleben. 'Ein neues Buch von Jules Verne', *Wiener Zeitung*, 29 April 1875.
135. On the colonial utopias in the late nineteenth-century Habsburg Monarchy, see further Ulrich E. Bach, *Tropics of Vienna: Colonial Utopias of the Habsburg Empire* (New York, 2016), 2 and passim.
136. Innerhofer, *Deutsche Science Fiction*, 52.
137. See further ibid., 29–84.
138. *Cinq semaines en ballon*.
139. The so-called 'open city' was a modern ideal that replaced the old function of cities as forts. Masanz and Nagl, *Ringstraßenallee*, 10.
140. 'Die Befestigung von Wien', *Kikeriki*, 7 March 1867.
141. Cf. Forsström, *Possible Worlds*, 12.
142. Alkon, *Origins of Futuristic Fiction*, 4, 18–19.
143. Bertha von Suttner was an Austrian pacifist and novelist who received the Nobel Peace Prize in 1905.

144. Jemand (pseudonym for Berttha von Suttner), *Das Maschinenalter: Zukunftsvorlesungen über unsere Zeit* (Zurich, 1889), 4. On Suttner's publishing activities, see further Harriet Anderson, *Utopian Feminism: Women's Movements in Fin-de-siècle Vienna* (New Haven, 1992), 143.
145. Forsström, *Possible Worlds*, 11–12, 59–61.
146. 'Kommunales', *Figaro*, 7 October 1871. See also Heidi Hakkarainen, 'Humor, Satire und Karikatur: Das humoristische Imaginarium der Wiener Ringstraße', in Harald R. Stühlinger (ed.), *Vom Werden der Wiener Ringstraße* (Vienna, 2015), 228; Marianne Bernhard, *Die Wiener Ringstraße: Architektur und Gesellschaft 1858–1906* (Munich, 1992), 222.
147. 'Beiträge für den Altertumsverein. Ein Plan von Neu-Wien', *Figaro*, 24 November 1860. Cf. 'Zukunfts-Journal-Notizen', *Der Humorist*, 3 September 1860; 'Zukunfts-Journal-Notizen', *Der Humorist*, 17 September 1860.
148. 'Die Wiener Zeitung von Jahre 1963. Ein Phantasie-Bild', *Kikeriki*, 21 May 1863.
149. In unsere Stadt ist nun wieder so ziemlich Ordnung und Sicherheit eingekehrt. Gestern kamen nur mehr fünfzehn Raubmorde, ein versuchter und vier vollbrachte Meuchelmorde, sechzehn Raubanfälle, acht Todschläge aus Rachsucht und sechs solche aus Eifersucht vor. Das Detektivkorps konnte somit auf achttausend Mann reduziert worden ... Heute, am 12. Jänner wurden die ersten Zwetschken auf dem Markte feilgeboten. Es herrschte im Gegensatz zu der gestrigen Kälte von 28 Graden heute eine Hitze von 36 Graden im Schatten. Während des vorgestrigen Schneegestöbers war es auf der Straße so schwül, daß viele Leute in Hemdärmeln gingen. Der Blitz schlug bei heiterem, trockenem Wetter über 20 Male ein. 'Zukunfts-Journal-Notizen. (Gefolgert aus den Vorkommnissen der Jetztzeit)', *Kikeriki*, 1 February 1874.
150. 'Die neue Fiakertaxe. Eine Zukunftsszene', *Kikeriki*, 29 October 1868; 'Der Zukunfts-Hausherr', *Kikeriki*, 19 March 1868; 'Zukunftsbild', *Kikeriki*, 31 March 1872; 'Zukunfts-Szene', *Kikeriki*, 27 January 1876; 'Zukunftssteuer', *Der Floh*, 3 April 1887.
151. 'Zukunftsbild', *Der Floh*, 28 February 1886.
152. 'Bericht über eine Bezirks-Ausschuss-Sitzung (Von einem Zukunfts-Berichterstatter)', *Kikeriki*, 24 April 1871; 'Aus einer Zukunfts-Zeitung des Jahres 1895', *Kikeriki*, 29 April 1875; 'Aus der k.k. Wiener Zeitung 1976', *Figaro*, 29 April 1876; 'Wiener Zukunftsbild', *Der Floh*, 14 October 1888.
153. Cf. the section 'Desiring order' in chapter 2.
154. Hutcheon, *Irony's Edge*, 57–58.
155. See, e.g., 'Das Gas- und Wasserröhrennetz der Stadt Wien', *Kikeriki*, 2 May 1875; 'Der Niedergang Wiens', *Kikeriki*, 10 June 1883.
156. See, e.g., 'Neueste Ausgrabungen der Pumpej-Schonwissen', *Der Floh*, 31 May 1873.
157. Es scheint, daß wir es hier mit der lange gesuchten, tiefgesunkenen Stadt 'Wienöda' zu thun haben. Die Stadt liegt an dem Flusse Danubis, der sich ehemals, wie aus alten Inschriften ersichtlich, durch seine schöne Bläue vor allen anderen Flüssen des Erdtheiles ausgezeichnet hat. Jetzt ist er trüb' und schlammig, seine Ufer sind verödet und nichts erinnert mehr an den großartigen Handel und Wandel, der sich einst auf seinen Ufern abgespielt ... 'Bericht des Dr. Mauerkratzer über eine von ihm entdeckte, ausgestorbene Stadt (Im Jahre 3886)', *Figaro*, 24 July 1886 / *Wiener Luft* No. 30.
158. 'Wien und der Zukunfts-Bädeker', *Figaro*, 7 July 1883 / *Wiener Luft* No. 27.
159. 'Das "verödete" Wien. Ein Nachtbild von Dr. Schreckeles', *Figaro*, 18 May 1889 / *Wiener Luft* No. 20.

160. Karlheinz Stierle, 'Der Tod der großen Stadt. Paris als neues Rom und Karthago', in Manfred Smuda (ed.,) *Die Großstadt als >Text<* (Munich, 1992), 101–3. See also Ritva Hapuli, *Nykyajan sininen kukka. Olavi Paavolainen ja nykyaika* (Helsinki, 1995), 44–55.
161. Berman, *All That Is Solid*, 15–19, 98–101.
162. See further Brigstocke, *Life of the City*, 147–51; Fritzsche, *Reading Berlin*, 12–15.
163. Later, in the twentieth century, dystopias of the modern city continued in the new global and post-socialist context. However, even in the more recent cases, dark, dystopic representations of cities often serve as a means of urban criticism, animated by an implicit hope for improvement. Gyan Prakash, 'Introduction: Imagining the Modern City, Darkly', in Gyan Prakash (ed.), *Noir Urbanisms: Dystopic Images of the Modern City* (Princeton, 2010), 2.
164. Hapuli, *Nykyajan*, 44–45.
165. On the satirical work of Karl Kraus, see further Timms, *Karl Kraus*.
166. *Lebenslauf des Wiener Schriftstellers und Redakteur des 'Figaro' Karl sitter*, Wienbibliothek im Rathaus; Nachrufe auf Karl Sitter aus verschiedenen Zeitungen, Wienbibliothek im Rathaus. *Kikeriki*'s turn to antisemitism has been explained through Berg's personal problems. Ernst Scheidl, *Die humoristisch- satirische Presse im Wien von den Anfängen bis 1918 und die öffentliche Meinung* (Ph.D. diss., Vienna, 1950), 166. See also O.F. Berg, *Kikeriki*, 21 January 1886. Yet, in my view, the more general cultural atmosphere played a much more important role here.
167. Fuess, *Cultural Crisis*, 34–35.
168. See also chapter 5 in this book.
169. The term *fin de siècle* emerged for the first time in France in the 1880s, but is better known from the newspaper *Le Fin de Siècle* by Édouard Dujardin between 1890 and 1909. See further Salmi, *Nineteenth-Century Europe*, 6, 124–25.
170. Ibid., 133.
171. Ibid., 124–39.
172. See, e.g., 'Nach dem Weltuntergangstag', *Der Floh*, 11 May 1890.
173. Chiavacci, *Der Weltuntergang*, 64–93. On the conventions of using dreams within utopian literature, see further Alkon, *Origins of Futuristic Fiction*, 117–25, 221. Roland Innerhofer has discussed Chiavacci's novel in more detail in his study on early German science fiction. Innerhofer, *Deutsche Science Fiction*, 380.
174. Cf. Prakash, 'Introduction', 2.
175. Cf. Alkon, *Origins of Futuristic Fiction*, 7.
176. On the relationship between place and identity, see further Markus Reisenleitner, 'Tradition, Cultural Boundaries and the Construction of Spaces of Identity', *spacesofidentity* (1.1)(2001).
177. See further Plamper, 'History of Emotions', 253.

Chapter 5

URBAN TYPES AND CHARACTERS

New Clothes of Vindobona – Modernity and Gender

In Viennese late nineteenth-century popular humour, discussion of modernity was closely connected with discussion of gender.[1] Not only did women appear in the humorous magazines and other publications in various roles, from innocent family girls to coquettes, bluestockings and spinsters, but the relationships between men and women, and moreover a constant playing with the fluid limits of the masculine and the feminine, were recurrent themes in late nineteenth-century middle-class popular humour. Understanding and discussing modernity was thus linked with the discourse about gender and the status of gender roles in the changing city. The humorous magazines focused especially on changes and breaks in traditional gender relationships. The humorous visions sprang from and were able to portray variations and deviations in the rules for gender, and were often based on playing with the boundaries between the feminine and the masculine. In the topsy-turvy world of humour, the rules for gender could be crossed both internally and externally; a rational young girl could have a shy and sentimental beau, and a man could be mistaken for a woman on the street.[2]

Breaking the rules of gender was funny, because sex and gender were both delicate and important issues in contemporary public debates. The transformation of the city and the modernization of society also threw the gender system into transition, and the second half of the century was a time for the first wave of the women's movement in Vienna.[3] Laughter was thus not mere trivial fun, but was at the same time a way of raising questions on changing gender roles.[4] Furthermore, discussing modernity through gender was a distinctively Viennese feature. As Elisabeth Wilson has noted, at the turn of the century modernity was understood and discussed in terms of gender and sexuality in Vienna especially.

Intellectuals such as Sigmund Freud and Otto Weininger placed sexual difference at the centre of their theories of modern life.⁵

In order to illustrate how profoundly the talk about modern urbanity was related to the talk about gender, I will start by exploring the observation that in the humorous magazines the city of Vienna itself was often portrayed as a female figure called 'Vindobona', after the name of the Roman camp that served as a basis for the city around 15 BC.⁶ The city renewal project, which in fact was very much linked to a masculine public sphere and political power, was interpreted as a feminine metamorphosis, of an older woman into a fashionable young beauty. From the start, the humorous magazines developed an image of the new Vienna as a young woman who is making herself beautiful through fashionable new clothes.

The first example is a poem from *Figaro* in January 1858. It was published barely a fortnight after Christmas Day 1857, when the *Wiener Zeitung* brought the Viennese the proclamation of the city renewal as a Christmas present from their ruler, Emperor Franz Joseph.⁷ The poem presents an alternative interpretation of the renewal project. The newly planted idea of the radical transformation of the city is turned into the story of a man who wishes to exchange his older wife for a younger one. The city of Vienna is portrayed as an old coquette, with the Stephansdom as her loyal admirer:

> We're all of us familiar with the old city coquette
> With her bastion bodice and Ringwall attire;
> The dress she wears is a counterscarp,
> And ever since Roman times she's been called our 'Old Vindobona'.
> Similarly, we all know the gentleman called Stephansdom,
> Her sweetheart and faithful admirer in the olden style;
> Who now (since in his life of luxury he's lost his greying hair)
> Wears an iron coronet ...⁸

The two of them have lived together happily for centuries. However, when the Stephansdom is renovated, he starts to look down on his old bride, who is taken by this rejection with grief and heartache. Then a medicine man with a magic wand turns up at Christmas and rips away the girdle that is confining the body of Vindobona: from the weak and crippled body of *Alt-Wien* is born the 'blühend, stolze Weib Jung-Wien' ('proud and blooming lady of Young Vienna'). At the end, she and the Stephansdom celebrate their golden wedding day. A happy end for the male cathedral and a conclusion that could almost be understood as a Freudian concealed wish for sexual renewal.

As the urban renewal project went ahead, the relationship between the masculine past and the feminine present became more tense and problematic. Rebuilding the city was compared to a battle between the sexes, a struggle between an older man and a young woman. What made this struggle both uneasy and comical was that in a reversal of the hierarchies of power characteristic of contemporary Viennese bourgeois social life, in the world of humour the girl was triumphing over the old man. The feminine young Vienna was conquering the old masculine Vienna. She was the winner, representing the future.

In 1858, *Figaro* published an imaginary correspondence between *Alt-Wien* (Herr Bastionarus) and *Jung-Wien* (Jungfer Vienna Nova). Here the old city is portrayed as an old man, who has experienced the great battles of the past but now has to retreat in the face of a new time. His wistful letter to the young lady is also a sentimental love letter from the noble past to frivolous modernity.[9]

> ... And in my anguish, now I turn to you,
> My only solace, Viennese maid, (Hopefully) well built;
> And although my voice may sound stony, muffled, and raw,
> Regard not my words, but look kindly
> And with pride on your ancient partisan!
> Do not withhold the apple of your favour;
> Be a gentle Venus to my banished Mars!
> And when my wheel of fortune takes its final turn,
> My final hour approaches in clouds of dust,
> And you see me (dreadful sight!) tumble into the moat,
> But for *you*, my pretty maid, the new spring is fragrant with violets,
> And you wander round ... not bulwarks, but boulevards ...
> A soft heart then forbid, and not a hard
> Think then with pleasant memories
> Of me, your old friend, Herr Bastionarus![10]

This letter to the young Vienna is not only a love letter, but a testament as well. The name Herr Bastionarus refers to the old fortifications (*Bastions*), which were to be demolished for the construction of the Ringstraße. This imaginary letter written in 1858 by the soon-to-be-demolished fortification wall thus foreshadows its own death. The letter ends with a request: Herr Bastionarus asks the young lady to remember him when he is dead and she wanders in the boulevards, entering the new spring full of the scent of violets.

Notably, not only does this text reveal a sense of nostalgia and emotional attachment to Old Vienna, facing destruction, but it also does this in terms of gender hierarchy. The boulevards were new city spaces, characterized as feminine, associated with young girls' keenness for fashion, entertainment and commercialism. Furthermore, the frivolous nature of this modern femininity becomes especially clear in the reply that Herr Bastionarus receives from Young Vienna, published in *Figaro* a couple of weeks later:

> The bombardment of heavy words from your iron mouth
> Has made a serious breach in my weak heart:
> In the middle of my maiden heart! – From the edge of the Alservorstadt

All the way to the Schottentor, a great breach!
But please rest assured, old iron-eater, I would have written to you ages ago,
Had I not been busy with my ... attire;
The land-surveyors' fashions for me are continually changing,
And my dressmakers the architects won't leave me in peace![11]

Young Vienna is so preoccupied with all the new clothes, such as 'Galerien-Strümpfe mit Museums-Zwickeln' ('gallery stockings with museum pleats'), that she cannot find any sympathy for the old gentleman, but mocks him mercilessly:

For the death of ancient cannon come no wreaths and no bouquets;
So, old soldier, leave the girls alone.
'The old falls, and the times change, but out of the ruins flowers the new'
[adapted quotation from Schiller];
Bastionarus falls into rubble, and New Vienna blossoms.[12]

The correspondence between Herr Bastionarus and Jungfer Vienna Nova shows the basic dichotomy that runs through the popular humour during the era of urban renewal: whereas the old city and the past were masculine, the new city was essentially feminine. The new Vienna was often portrayed as a coquettish young woman, constantly chasing after the new and fashionable. She enjoyed her new places and monuments as if they were new exciting clothes. This narrative of a young woman who wants to update her wardrobe with new clothes was used in varying ways in all the humorous magazines studied here. The humorous imaginary made use of the old allegory of a city as a human body, functioning as one harmonious totality.[13] However, in the case of Vindobona, an opposition was made between the body and the new modern places that do not actually belong to the body, but are presented as clothes rather than body parts. Instead of substance and naturalness, modernity was associated with artificiality and surface. In 1873, for example, when Vienna hosted the World Exhibition, the Rotunde – the main site for this massive event – was pictured as a parasol (Figures 5.1 and 5.2). In addition, the persistent competition with other cities was described in terms of female jealousy:

Frau Vindobona had gradually acquired new clothes; one piece after another of her old stuff was removed and replaced with new fashion, and she was even given the ornament of a *magnificent ring*. All of this flattered her vanity, and so she was forced to note with dismay that she still had no parasol. Furthermore, after her neighbours, Madame France and Lady Britannia, had already adopted the new fashion, her jealousy grew from day to day, and since ladies always get their way, now she really has one![14]

Vienna was not the only city where the contradictory and elusive nature of urbanity was discussed in terms of femininity. Change and changeability have traditionally been seen as feminine features, associated with wanton frivolity. Moreover, in Western culture there has been a long tradition of comparing the

Figure 5.1 'The elegant Vindobona'. *Kikeriki*, 3 April 1873. Source: Austrian National Library.

city to a woman. For example, nineteenth-century Paris was often compared to a prostitute: the city was an unattainable and deceptive object of desire, sexualized and essentially female.[15]

Yet it seems that in Vienna the aesthetic culture, which distinguished the city from other contemporary metropolises, played an important part in the cultural imagination of the Vindobona figure. In Vienna, the city renewal project was called the expansion of the city, *Stadterweiterung*, but also simultaneously *Stadtverschönerung*, the beautification of the city. The transformation of the city space was thus conducted in terms of aesthetic values, and this emphasis on the ideal of beauty made the urbanization process in Vienna different than in contemporary Paris or Berlin, for instance. In my view, the Vindobona figure expressed one variation of the clash between aesthetic and moral values that was so typical for Vienna. On the one hand, romantic language and imagery enabled the expression of the emotions associated with the city space, and showed passion and devotion

Figure 5.2 The Rotunde was the main site for the 1873 World Exhibition. Source: Wikimedia Commons.

to her much like that to an admired beautiful lady. On the other hand, comparing the rebuilding of the city to dressing up in new clothes as a vain and pampered young girl was a way of criticizing the city renewal for focusing only on appearances and neglecting the internal troubles and moral questions of urban life.[16]

There was thus a multifaceted historical background for imagining the city as female. However, the Vindobona figure was a unique Viennese expression for the local tensions relating to the transformation of the city. It was created in a highly intermedial environment, in which the humorous printed publications intersected with other forms of popular culture such as theatre comedies. As noted in the previous discussion, many of the journalists contributing to the field of humorous magazines, such as O.F. Berg, Karl Sitter and Friedrich Schlögl, wrote for the stage as well. In spring 1876, for example, a play by O.F. Berg called *Vindobona* was played in the k.k. Carl Theater, with the famous actress Josefina Gallmeyer (1838–84) starring in the leading role.[17] In humorous magazines, the feminine Vindobona figure became a conventionalized way of commenting on the rebuilding of the city for decades.

For example, in 1888, thirty years after the urban renewal project had begun, *Der Floh* portrayed the city as an aging Vindobona, who is restricted by her tight corset and wants to get rid of it. This was a statement in support of the construction works, which aimed at transforming the outer Linienwall fortifications into a Gürtelstrasse much in the way of the Ringstraße decades earlier. Vindobona speaks a casual Viennese dialect, which gives the agony of the corset (Linienwall) pressing her body an even more intimate feel:

> ... Well now, I'm getting to the age when the corset bothers me, and gets tighter every week –
> it's a real trouble! I bend and twist, full of pain;
> I can't get enough air; 'cos in the girdle I can't gasp, I can't breathe ...[18]

Here the expansion of the city is interpreted as the bodily experience of a woman who wants to get rid of her corset, but protests that abandoning the suffocating undergarment does not imply a loss of virtue. This symbolic image illustrates well the intimate relationship in the humorous discourse between the rebuilding of the city space and the emancipation of women.

What is also striking here is that the voice of the city is the voice of a woman. Or to be more precise, she has multiple voices, over the decades, as these examples show. Interestingly, however, Vindobona's voice was also sometimes used as the voice of authority. In the 1870s and 1880s, the female figure of Vindobona appeared occasionally criticizing the city planners and complaining about city politics.[19] She was used as a matriarchal authority figure, mocking the male politicians with female wit. The Roman name Vindobona emphasized the city's connection to the historical past; it was her old age that was the key to her authority, although she had gone through a metamorphosis and become young again.

So it seems that the question of age was crucial when talking about gender. Where Vindobona as an old woman could have matriarchal authority, as a young woman she often turned to mere triviality. The popular imagery of the city as a woman was dominated by the theme of a rejuvenating metamorphosis, which meant outer beautification but inner degeneration. Consequently, it was the combination of youth and femininity that was somehow unnerving and threatening to the cultural atmosphere of the *Gründerzeit*. As we will see later, the modern women ridiculed in the humorous magazines were also distinctively young women.

The problem of young women seems to resonate with the population patterns in the second half of the century, when the growing city was actually becoming younger. The historian Karl Vocelka notes that in 1880 as much as 29 per cent of the population were under fourteen years old, and 26.9 per cent were aged between fifteen and twenty-nine.[20] This means that more than half of the population were under thirty years old. The city was inhabited by young people, which meant, of course, great markets for humour, but also tensions between the generations. This generation gap, which Carl E. Schorske has placed at the heart of his thesis about the breakthrough of the modernist culture in Vienna, has previously been viewed as a struggle between liberal fathers and their aesthetic sons.[21] The humorous allegory of the battle between an old man and a young girl shows that the clusters of ideas and values related to gender played a major part in this cultural crisis as well.

Laughter and humour lead to points of rupture and uncertainty in culture. Not only in Vienna, but in Western European thought in general, the drastically changing gender relations were considered to be a fundamental symptom of modernity. Moreover, talk about these changes was an important way of defining and understanding modernity, and the role of women in the cities was a theme that circulated in the public discussions well after the turn of the century.[22] Thus, as scholars like Elisabeth Wilson, Rita Felski and Ute Frevert have shown, the male–female dichotomy was an essential element in the discussion on modernity.[23] Because the gender issue was closely connected with hierarchies and power relations, the gendered talk about modernity also reveals emotions and attitudes relating to the change. Anti-modernism was linked to anti-feminism, and the modern city was often viewed as a threat to the patriarchal order.[24]

The nineteenth-century city was viewed with suspicion, suggests Elisabeth Wilson, because it allowed middle-class women a new kind of freedom.[25] In the second half of the nineteenth century, European urban renewal projects created new city spaces, such as department stores and boulevards, that were both accessible and attractive for middle-class women. Accordingly, modern cities have been viewed as places in which middle-class women became visible in the urban surroundings as never before.[26] Although there were no department stores on the Ringstraße,[27] the boulevards and other new urban spaces made it possible to depart from old rules of social life. However, this transition from older spatial and social structures was far from painless and straightforward; as scholars like Elisabeth Wilson and Judith Walkowitz have argued, in nineteenth-century cities the presence of women was an ongoing source of threatening ambiguity, constantly broached in the contemporary debates. Contemporary fact and fiction, such as novels and newspaper reports, frequently revolved around the problem of female sexuality, creating an image of the city as a place of threat and desire.[28]

What has thus been argued is that modern urbanity, both as a physical and imaginary environment, entails underlying assumptions of gender that are embedded both in material places and in the representations of these places. Elisabeth Wilson has described the modern city as an ongoing struggle between masculine order and feminine disorder: 'The city – as an experience, environment, concept – is constructed by means of multiple contrasts: natural, unnatural; monolithic, fragmented; secret, public; pitiless, enveloping; rich, poor; sublime, beautiful. Behind all these lies the ultimate and major contrast: male-female; culture, nature; city, country'.[29] It seems that the Vindobona figure enabled the articulation of some of the crucial tensions and contrasts that the modernization process triggered in Vienna. Humour was used as a way of unveiling and exploring dichotomies that were meaningful in the process of comprehending the transformation of city space: the contrast between young and old, man and woman, past and future.

Modern Women

In addition to the Vindobona figure, the *Witzblätter* also constantly reproduced and circulated a popular imaginary of new kinds of women who were somehow threatening the old order in society. Next, I will focus on these comical female figures, because of their connection to defining and understanding modernity. These women were usually referred to as 'modern women' (*moderne Frauen*), but there were differing and even contradictory characterizations of what *modern* meant. The word 'modern' entailed two kinds of novelty: on the one hand there were frivolous and vain modern women interested only in fashion and love affairs; on the other hand, the humour often targeted emancipated women, who were associated with women's movements.

Characterizing new urban women under these stereotypes was part of a wider imagery reinforced and legitimized in popular humour. Harriet Anderson has documented the earliest feminist movements in *fin-de-siècle* Vienna, and finds that the Viennese conservatives made use of two kinds of stereotypic images of new women: the masculine 'emancipated woman', and the 'modern woman' who was a senseless and vain creature, a symbol for the cultural decline of the times.[30] The comic figures of the Viennese *Witzblätter* thus did not belong only to the sphere of the humorous, but were initially created in serious discourse addressing the social and cultural changes of the nineteenth century, when the position of women was changing radically, due to urbanization, industrial capitalism and the emergence of modern civil societies.

In the second half of the century, women entered not only new urban spaces but also new domains in society. In Austria, women were allowed to take the matriculation examination (*Matura*) in 1878, but could not proceed to university studies until the end of the century. During the second half of the century, women's movements started to mobilize women to claim a better status in society; in Vienna, the middle-class women's movement, which became active in the 1860s and 1870s, demanded rights to higher education and professional occupations. Simultaneously, the proletarian women's movement, which was created together with the labour movement and the Social Democratic Party, fought for better conditions for women workers and servants. Both movements demanded the right for women to vote, which they finally gained in Austria in 1918.[31]

The popularity of jokes and caricatures on new modern women shows that in late nineteenth-century Vienna humour was a crucial way of dealing with the changing presence of women in the city. Along similar lines, Ann Taylor Allen has discovered how in Wilhelmine Germany humour and satire became an expression of the period's reaction to the changing position of women in a manner that was a 'compound of rebellion and inhibition, wishful fantasy and anxiety'.[32]

Interestingly, when it came to the question of gender, the popular humour of the Viennese bourgeois *Witzblätter* echoed the conservative imaginary, notwithstanding the liberal and democratic tendencies that they showed on other issues. Humour was deployed as a means of resistance to changes in gender relations. Accordingly, especially when talking about gender, *modern* was used as an evaluating term that entailed judgement about the worth of those phenomena or persons that it was associated with.[33] This reflects the fact that in many cases *modern* equalled a break with the old order: both the emancipated women and the fashionable frivolous women somehow challenged traditional gender roles and expectations for women. Just like the city of Vindobona, the women were changing as well; they smoked, wore daring attire and men's clothes and were (potentially) more sexually free.[34]

This concern about modern women was related to the understanding of the corruptive nature of the modern city, considered to be especially dangerous for young women. The city was seen as a new dangerous environment to grow up in, full of temptations and bad influences. Young modern girls, spoiled by the city, were often ridiculed. They were reading dangerous novels and press scandals, as well as taking dance lessons and visiting questionable exhibitions, even murder trials. The point of the joke was often an ironic moral lesson: despite all the entertainment and flirting, they would end up as solitary spinsters.[35]

This mocking of modern women was thus to a large extent a disciplinary form of social control. The aim was to put women back in their place, by frowning upon and ridiculing their free behaviour through humour. As Michael Billig has argued, humour has traditionally been one of the most important modes for social discipline and punishment.[36] Furthermore, modern women were also used as a way of commenting on society. They stood for modern decadence, which manifested itself in feminine boredom, superficiality and amorality.[37] This moral disapproval was expressed in a light mocking tone. For instance, in the text 'Eine moderne Frau muss' published in *Kikeriki* in 1873, the modern woman is described as follows: instead of sorting linens, she learns how to skate. Instead of teaching her children how to pray, she studies the latest fashion. Instead of supervising the household tasks, she tries out new hair colours. She lies in bed until 11 instead of getting up at 6 in the morning, and is through and through a 'Frau nach der Mode'.[38]

The word *Mode*, fashion, appeared frequently in connection with modern women, and it is therefore necessary to continue with a brief look at the interrelationships between fashion, sexuality and modernity. The topic of fashion was not a distinctively modern phenomenon, but it has been a problematic subject and a topic for humour for centuries. Even in the early modern period, as Anu Korhonen has pointed out, following fashion was seen as a sign of vanity and pride in women, which was to be punished. Fashion was also a problem of gender, and control over women has traditionally been a problem for the maintenance of patriarchal order.[39] In the late nineteenth century, the industrial revolution and capitalist consumer culture reinforced the acceleration of new styles and fashions. Following the latest fashion meant keeping up with the pace of the city. It was a skill of renewing and reconstructing oneself, a talent of being modern.

Fashion not only expressed a craving for novelty, but was also a central way of displaying the self in public. Georg Simmel described modern fashion as an ongoing struggle between individuality and social coherence; with their clothes, people try to distinguish themselves from the masses and at the same time to blend in to obtain social acceptance.[40] Clothes were an essential part of constructing modern individuality and urban identity. As Richard Sennett has argued, members of the nineteenth-century bourgeoisie were trained in reading the meanings of clothes, which became an important feature of the new secular public life of industrial capitalism. In the city environment, surrounded by strangers, the new urban middle classes were trying to discern other people's status and character by reading their clothes.[41]

This might explain the Viennese preoccupation with clothes: much of the popular humour about gender and the city revolved around the idea of dressing up and changing clothes. Just like the city of Vindobona, the women – meaning bourgeois women – were depicted as almost possessed with the need to change clothes constantly, and this desire for and promise of change had a distinctively modern urban character, which in the countryside could only be envied.[42] This constant desire for new clothes was ridiculous because it mirrored both vanity and falling into the mercy of the consumer culture. However, on the other hand there was a more profound concern related to the metamorphoses performed by dressing up. Going through a transformation through clothes, like the Vindobona figure, was simultaneously exciting and unnerving, because it indicated that appearance was something fluid and changing, not to be trusted.

In addition, fashion and clothes were closely related to the status of women. Allen Janik and Stephen Toulmin have seen the women's fashion of the *Gründerzeit* as a symbol of their restricted place in society; women needed help to get into and out of their clothes, which forced them into artificial movements and made it impossible to breathe freely.[43] Mary L. Wagener has drawn attention to the fact that a fashion reform became part of the feminist movement in *fin-de-siècle* Vienna. Whereas in the 1860s and 1870s middle-class women's attire was often designed to express the wealth of their husbands, and was often so tight it made moving and breathing difficult, at the turn of the century the

Secession movement created a completely new ideal for freely hanging clothes, which enabled free movement.[44]

Fashion thus moulded and regulated the body and was deeply involved in the process of displaying and constructing gender.[45] Viennese popular humour was fascinated by breaks and disruptions in the coherent display of gender through clothes. At the same time, there were humorous accounts that pointed out the artificial aspects of the construction of gender. In 1885, for example, *Der Floh* published a cartoon suggesting that little girls could be used as bustles to educate them for the role of the lady.[46] In addition, the *Witzblätter* created humour by showing variations of gender roles and behaviour that were otherwise unimaginable. In 1876, for example, a cartoon in *Wiener Luft* ridiculed the latest women's fashion by suggesting that women could solve the problem of moving with a tight hemline by bouncing as if they were kangaroos or taking part in a sack race.[47]

This kind of humour sprang from imagining actions in space that were somehow surprising, improper or abnormal.[48] In addition to actions and movements, the humour about fashion also paid attention to the comicality of the body, by reimagining its proportions, shapes and forms.[49] Fashion gave a pretext to picture the female body and it involved enjoyment in combining intellectual and sexual curiosity.[50] But most importantly, fashion was enthralling and dangerous because it had the ability to upset the traditional lines of gender. By far the most common theme of cartoons dealing with modern fashion was that clothes made men more feminine and women more masculine. In 1862, for example, *Kikeriki* published its 'Neuester Modebericht aus Paris', featuring the 'Herren-Krinoline', an apparatus to widen the trousers in full splendour, much like women's dresses.[51] Similarly, in 1873, *Kikeriki* commented on the latest fashion, which made men look suspiciously feminine and might lead in turn to more masculine fashion for women.[52]

The variety of these jokes was wide, but they all revolved around the same topic: how clothes blurred traditional gender distinctions.[53] Most of these jokes boil down to the fear of losing masculinity. This fear came to the surface also in numerous jokes about men running after the latest fashions. In Vienna, especially from the 1880s onwards, the Ringstraße was associated with the male *Gigerl*, who came to show off their latest fads on the boulevard. Unlike the famous English 'dandies', the *Gigerl* was not striving for masculine ideals of perfection and self-control, but was ridiculous because of his obsession with the crazes and fashions of mass culture.[54] This craving for novelty was regarded as a feminine feature and therefore threatening to masculinity.[55] A loss of masculinity was dangerous because it meant redistributing power to women. Consequently, despite their speculative nature, these humorous visions and ideas expressed and commented on actual attitudes and fears concerning modern fashion and its implications for issues of gender.[56]

The close relationship between fashion, gender and the body seems to be at the core of this persistent concern about masculine women and feminine men. Cross-dressing was disruptive because clothes had essential meaning in constructing and displaying gender. Thus, jokes about cross-dressing were a way of drawing attention to gender difference. They expressed a multilayered ridicule that aimed explicitly at punishing those crossing the lines of the prevailing gender system, but implicitly also took pleasure in depicting them. Humorous representations thus simultaneously tried to uphold lines of gender and enjoyed crossing them.

By attacking the borders of gender distinctions, the jokes about cross-dressing unravelled the seemingly natural bond between clothes and gender. Henri Bergson saw at the end of the century that the comicality of fashion relates to a natural incongruity between a person and his or her clothes. A living human being and the inanimate wrappings he or she is using in order to cover the naked body are two separate things. Normally this difference goes unnoticed: a person and his or her clothes are seen as the same. However, the comicality of fashion becomes visible when the clothes somehow do not match their wearer, and the person seems to be masking him or herself in the clothes.[57]

The idea of masking leads us to the theme of masquerades, which were not just a major part of late nineteenth-century Viennese bourgeois social life, but also a way of exploring the carnivalesque aspects of modern urban living.[58] The city environment enabled a new kind of anonymity and the possibility to create subjectivities that were not fixed but fluid and constantly changing. Playing with clothes and dressing up thus seems to refer to a wider tradition of carnivals, transferred into a device for discussing the changing gender roles in the modern city. In their study *The Politics and Poetics of Transgression* (1986), Peter Stallybrass and Allon White suggest that Western thought has carried for centuries a ritual strategy of hierarchy reversal, 'turning the world upside down', which has been used in order to broach the symbolic hierarchies through which a culture constructs itself. Stallybrass and White suggest that the carnival – a persistent ritual feature of European culture – continued in the bourgeois eighteenth and nineteenth centuries in new forms. Whereas in early modern Europe the carnival was an epistemological tool, a mode of understanding cultural hierarchies and binary structures through shared imaginary repertoires, bourgeois culture created more alienated forms of investigating cultural boundaries by transgressing them.[59]

Thus, the humorous images of cross-dressing are to my mind intelligible in the context of the bourgeois culture of balls and masquerades, which derived from the old tradition of carnivals, an inherited part of the Catholic culture of medieval and early modern Europe.[60] Different kinds of masquerades were highly popular among the bourgeoisie and were one manifestation of the Viennese passion for the theatre and the theatrical.[61] Carnival time (*Fasching*), the festival season immediately before Lent, was the ball season of the bourgeoisie, a tradition highly visible in nineteenth-century Vienna, and claiming much space in the realms of humorous print culture. In addition to the humorous short stories set at the masquerades,[62] the ball season was closely followed and commented on each year in the humorous magazines. *Der Floh* and *Figaro*'s appendix *Wiener Luft*, especially, described the bourgeois masquerades and translated them into print.[63]

Cross-dressing was not predominant, but it was an integral feature of the caricatures depicting masquerades. Masquerades provided a cultural framework that partly explains the fascination with clothes and legitimized playing with gender. The topsy-turvy world of carnivals made it possible to transgress the boundaries of gender roles and hierarchies.

Along similar lines to Stallybrass and White, the literary scholar Terry Castle has argued in *Masquerade and Civilization: The Carnivalesque in Eighteenth-Century English Culture and Fiction* (1986) that masquerades were a particular stylized way of broaching the problematic concept of the self. As the modern understanding of the individual gradually took shape, masquerades served the function of collective mediation of the self and the other and investigating their relationship. Masquerades were a play on self-presentation and self-concealment, their magic based on the duality of the self and the other that were both simultaneously present.[64]

The masquerade thus projected an upside down world based on the pleasurable reversal of everyday social, sexual and intellectual hierarchies.[65] Masquerades assaulted cultural categories much like laughter and a substantial part of the tradition of the carnivals and masquerades was to process the fundamental divisions of class and gender; women dressed up as men, rich as poor, and so on.[66] As Castle notes, there had to be a conceptual clash between the costume and its wearer; in other words, the relationship between costume and wearer was ironic.[67]

In the case of cross-dressing, the two-in-one, the man-woman, was a joke recognizable and familiar to the Viennese audience. In addition to the carnival culture of misrule, the theme of cross-dressing had appeared in European plays and comedies for centuries.[68] The cultural meaning of the images might, however, relate above all to the fact that in the context of nineteenth-century culture, the idea of a woman dressed as a man had become more dangerous and unnerving, due to the emancipation of women. A humorous booklet, *Die Neuzeit in Elysium oder das lustige Wien* (*Modern Times in Elysium, or Fun in Vienna*, 1862–63) pointed to the danger of women getting used to the male role not merely in the carnival but in normal life as well:

> Here's another piece of modern Vienna! As the ladies get more and more emancipated, they'll start to want men's clothes, and to wear trousers. If this carries on, it'll put an end to male rule, and it'll change the course of history. But until now, the fair sex only has the right of lordship during Carnival – though in many houses, admittedly, it's gone further, and the woman wears the trousers all year round![69]

As nineteenth-century women started entering previously solely male domains in society, they adopted masculine attributes in order to break out of the old gender roles. George Eliot (1819–80) and George Sand (1804–76) used male pen names because they wanted to be taken seriously as writers. Sand also dressed as a man in order to stroll more freely in the streets of Paris. Cross-dressing became part of the urban bohemian lifestyle, which stood in a counterposition to the bourgeois way of life. Wearing male attire, notes Elisabeth Wilson, was an essential feature of late nineteenth-century lesbian scenes.[70] In Vienna, cross-dressing was part of the urban subcultures and the world of the demimonde. The historians Wolfgang Maderthaner and Lutz Musner note that the suburban inns organized masked balls in which women, mostly young prostitutes, disguised themselves as men.[71]

Women in drag were thus not merely an act of carnival misrule, but had become a marginal and unnerving part of the modern urban reality, echoing the wider cultural imaginary of the European middle classes. Thanks to the new print culture, the global and local were able to merge in a new way in the minds of the nineteenth-century European reading public. Radical emancipated women writers such as George Sand were undoubtedly known among educated Viennese readers,[72] but in addition, the local popular culture of the urban lower classes inspired the bourgeois imagination as well. Musner and Maderthaner note that middle-class humourists such as Friedrich Schlögl frequently visited *Volkssänger* shows and other performances in the suburban inns in search of inspiration for their accounts of modern city life.[73] Perhaps the Viennese tolerance of and even fondness for ambivalence explains why it was possible to simultaneously present and frown upon images of women who were socially and sexually suspect in their various ways.

The theme of cross-dressing was thus not just about wearing clothes, but it had much to do with gender roles. Changing clothes and turning gender roles upside down were closely interlinked, and offered similar kinds of fun in reversing the rules and categories of everyday life.[74] There were numerous jokes about women acting like men. The idea was to show how ridiculous it would be if the gender hierarchy were reversed: what if young girls were to engage in serious thinking and the world of science, while boys were allowed to think only about love?[75]

This kind of humour also actively commented on the sexual power relations embedded in the prevailing bourgeois gender hierarchy. Sexual hypocrisy and double standards of morality for men and women were typical features of the Viennese bourgeois culture. At the same time as family girls were expected to be chaste and ignorant of sex, prostitution was widespread in the city. Chasing women on the streets, a practice called *Nachsteigen*, was a characteristic amusement for bourgeois men.[76] Many jokes dealt with women brushing off strange men who were trying to make a pass at them in the city.[77] The new Ringstraße, where members of society came to display themselves in public, was especially favoured by officers and gentlemen trying to inspect and seduce young beauties.

In humour, this model was turned upside down in images of women in the city pursuing men, actively seducing shy men in the streets, at the opera or in the parks.[78] The sexualizing gaze to which women were so vulnerable was turned at men instead. At the same time, these jokes validate the suggestion that sexual unease and uncertainty shaped nineteenth-century modern city life.[79] The urban culture in Vienna, especially, has been seen as pronouncedly sexualized.[80]

Turning gender roles upside down offered a strategy for commenting on the emancipation of women and the goals of the women's movement by rendering them comical.[81] Defining the limits of the serious and comical simultaneously meant (re)defining the limits of gender. The entrance of women into the domains of education or working life was made ridiculous by suggesting that women, being sexual creatures by nature, would inescapably bring sex into the serious realms of the professions, education and politics. The idea of uncontrollable sexuality was made visible, for example, in a cartoon from *Der Floh* in which an imaginary female doctor says to a patient: '… und nun reichen Sie mir die Hand', and the patient replies in admiration: 'Angebeteter Doctor, für's Leben!' ('… And would you now give me your hand?' 'Yes, my dear Doctor – for life!').[82] This situation is supposed to be funny because the gender roles have been reversed, and the man assumes that the woman is asking for his hand in marriage.

This recurrent preoccupation with sex relates to the fact that in the contemporary discussions, the women's movement was primarily conceived and discussed in terms of unnatural sexuality. Emancipated women were seen as sexually abnormal, although the perspective did vary according to political standpoint. The conservatives saw female supporters of women's rights as over-sexed and believed it was their degenerate sexuality that drove them to the unnatural desire for power. The progressively oriented artists and intellectuals, on the other hand, argued that the concern within the women's rights movement for sexual morality was at root due to sexual envy and represented an alienation from femininity.[83]

It seems symptomatic that in Vienna, where their claims for legal, economic and political rights were neglected in serious political discussion, women were given so much space in the world of humour. The ridicule of the emancipation of women sheds light on the anti-feminist values and attitudes that were confirmed and reinforced in popular humour. The conservative atmosphere of Catholic Vienna made it difficult for women to enter the field of political action, and the early women's movements encountered hostility and resistance from the forces of anti-feminism. Consequently, in Vienna the emancipation of women did not gain such a firm foothold as it did, for example, in contemporary England.[84]

Humour was part of the struggle between genders, and one central way of diminishing and deprecating women. Marianne Hainisch (1839–1936), the leader of the middle-class women's movement and creator of the League of Austrian Women's Associations,[85] mentioned in her early lecture 'Die Brodfrage der Frau' (1875), for example, sneering laughter (*belachen, belächeln*) as an obstacle to the liberation of women from their old delimiting roles as merely wives and mothers.[86] Thus, popular humour was a crucial arena for the cultural negotiation of the place of the woman in society. The male-dominated popular humour of the humorous magazines was born out of and actively shaped the conservative attitudes of the time.

In late nineteenth-century Vienna, popular humour had serious aims and consequences in real life. It sprang from and actively shaped the social reality of the *Gründerzeit* and its discussions on the role of women in society. Studies on humour and gender suggest that humour is profoundly linked with power and the practices of exclusion and inclusion. Humour is based on shared experiences, attitudes and values, and it actively shapes their meanings, creating in-groups and out-groups, those who are laughing at you and those who are laughing with you.[87] Feminist researchers have pointed out that humour is not just a way of interpreting the reality, but it is also a form of communication that enables statements about that reality. Humour makes it possible to say things that are otherwise impossible to speak of. When it comes to issues like ethnicity, gender or class, which, as many studies of humour show, are issues that constantly trigger uncertainty and laughter, it is important to ask who is laughing at whom and why. Humour has a long tradition as a form of social control, and laughter has been used to reinforce social rules and norms by punishing aberrations from the rules.[88] As Anu Korhonen has pointed out, humour can be used to question and strengthen hierarchical social structures such as gender.[89]

What we have seen so far is the image of modern women and emancipated women as a target of jokes, which fits quite nicely with the existing understanding of humour as a male domain, which has been restricted for women for centuries. However, the Viennese humorous magazines prove to be more complex and gender-nuanced than that. What makes the situation more confusing is the fact that women also read humorous magazines and even wrote for them.

Women Readers

Next I will discuss several indications which suggest that the humorous magazines were read by women as well. It seems that middle-class women actually had more opportunities to take part in public joking than has been thought previously. First of all, the editorial responses to readers' letters refer repeatedly to feminine pseudonyms. In *Kikeriki*, *Figaro* and *Der Floh*, readers communicated with the editors using pen names such as 'Wienerin' ('Viennese [lady]'), 'Fräulein Emma' ('Miss Emma'), 'Verehrerin' ('[female] Admirer') or 'Aufmerksame Leserin' ('Attentive [female] Reader').[90] To give some examples, *Kikeriki* wrote to the pen name 'Eine Dame' ('A Lady') in the issue of 15 November 1866 as follows: 'You will find that your excellent ideas have been used in the present issue'.[91] When going through the magazine, however, where all contributions were published anonymously, one can only guess which topic the pen name 'Eine Dame' had written on: the freedom of nations, fire safety, or the status of the Kingdom of Hungary in the empire.

There were also other successful female pen names that received positive feedback from the otherwise harsh editors. The pen name 'Monika' sent something 'very funny' to *Kikeriki* in 1879, and in 1881 an 'Eifrige Leserin' ('Devoted [female] Reader') was given feedback from the editors of *Figaro* that they 'admired her sharp wit'.[92] Not all female pseudonyms were successful. 'Frau H.', for example, who persistently tried to offer her contributions to *Figaro* for at least nine years, between 1881 and 1890, was for the most part rejected.[93] However, the persistence of 'Frau H.' confirms the impression that at least some female pen names tried to produce humour for publication systematically rather than randomly.[94] So, although it is wise to stay alert with pen names and remember that some of these female pseudonyms might not in fact have been women, but men pretending to be women,[95] it is very unlikely that all of the contributors writing under female pseudonyms were men.

A second feature that further indicates a female readership is the fact that all the humorous magazines published advertisements directly aimed at women, including fashion magazines, sewing machines, beauty products, dresses and accessories.[96] In fact, whereas the jokes and humorous material were often oriented to political and social satire, the advertisements emphasized bourgeois private life, selling everyday products from toothpaste to children's clothes. The humorous magazines were not only read in public spaces such as coffee houses, but they were also read in private homes via mail subscription. Thus, in addition to coffee house culture, the humorous magazines were also related to a new kind of bourgeois family life and entertainment culture that began to take shape in the nineteenth century. In the comprehensive German research project *Geschichte des Deutschen Buchhandels im 19. und 20. Jahrhundert*, literary scholars Andreas Graf and Susanne Pellatz have linked the German *Witzblätter* together with a larger corpus of family and entertainment magazines, which became immensely popular during the era of the German Empire from 1871 to 1918.[97] There is reason to believe that the development followed similar lines in Vienna, and thanks to the subscription system women had access to the humorous magazines as well.

Thirdly, in addition to *Floh*, *Figaro* and *Kikeriki* themselves, I have found one text example that offers not only further evidence but also an interesting metalevel to the question of female readership. This text is a play called *Floh: Localer Scherz*, written and published under the pseudonym Fritz Mai[98] in 1869, the same year the *Witzblatt* started its publication. The play, dedicated to the editorial staff of *Floh*,[99] revolves around this humorous magazine. The protagonist Knauser is a bureaucrat in the Ministry of Finance. His wife, Gabriele, is a smart woman with a sense of humour who likes to read the press and humorous magazines. Gabriele asks her female servant, who is going out with a cartoonist at *Floh*, to bring her a confiscated number of the magazine. The two women manage to smuggle the humorous magazine into the house and hide it from Knauser, who, however, finds out what is going on and is horrified at the possibility of being caught with such incriminating material under his roof. However, when his superior, Regierungsrat Zopfer, does indeed find the magazine, the poor Knauser is not ruined as he feared, but it turns out that the high officer himself enjoys reading the *Witzblatt*, claiming that Austria is a constitutional state and in a constitutional state everybody can read *Der Floh* as they wish.[100] The comedy thus ends well with a celebration of freedom of speech, which echoes the bourgeois exultant atmosphere of the late 1860s following the achievement of a constitutional monarchy after centuries of absolutist rule.[101]

Here we have a fictional example of a bourgeois woman reading one of the humorous magazines studied in this book. Although the text seems rather marginal, and there is no information on whether or not this play was ever performed on stage or how it was received by contemporaries, it does shed light on the boundaries of what was thought possible and impossible with reference to women and humour. What is interesting is that the forbidden humorous magazine is here acquired, hidden and read by women. The following quote is from the scene in which Gabriele has finally got the confiscated issue of *Floh* in her hands and starts reading it:

> Gabriele (sits). So – Now we can concentrate on reading this – Hahaha! – I have to laugh when I think what a face my husband would make if he found me with this. That often makes me quite angry that there are some things I can only read furtively, like a small child – He doesn't like it when I get a letter from my childhood friend, 'cause she always writes so wittily; just recently he informed me that I ought rather to read pastoral circulars: that is much more patriotic. (Opens the magazine) Gosh, even these drawings on the first page, they're quite something! Well, if they ever decided to draw me in the magazine, I'd be curious to see what kind of a caricature that would be! (Knock at the door) Good heavens, someone's coming. (Quickly hides the magazine) All right, that's nice and tidy, as if there were nothing amiss. (Annoyed) Come in![102]

This example shows that women were seen as able to both create and appreciate humour, and in addition, it shows contemporary awareness of the boundaries through which men tried to restrict women's entrance to the humorous domain. Gabriele has to enjoy the humorous magazine secretly, in much the same fashion as her childhood friend's letters, which are presented as highly amusing and thus show the female capacity to be funny. The emotional charge of the scene shifts from liberated laughter to timidity, however, when somebody enters the room where Gabriele has been reading and she tries to hide the magazine. Yet the transformation of the female protagonist from a curious and courageous woman into an obedient wife shows her capacity to strategize and adapt her role, much like an actress balancing between social demands and individual will.

With this example, my aim is to demonstrate that for Viennese contemporaries it was not unimaginable that women could read humorous magazines and appreciate them. Furthermore, because Mai's play was clearly favourably inclined towards *Der Floh* and perhaps even set out to advertise it to the public, choosing a female reader as a central figure reveals a bias in favour of understanding the reading of the humorous magazines as something shared by both sexes.[103]

There is thus ample evidence that women also took part in creating and reading popular humour in late nineteenth-century Vienna. The further questions of why women were reading the humorous magazines, what they thought of them and to what extent they found the jokes funny are too broad to be answered in terms of this study. However, the reason I have paid so much attention to the evidence of women reading humorous magazines is simple. Women readers change the composition: we do not have just men laughing at women, but a situation that is more complex and nuanced.

If women actively read humorous magazines and even wrote contributions to them, the imaginary of the female city, and the allegory of clothes and fashion, take on yet another angle. Many of the jokes, such as the city wanting to get rid of her corset, open up to a different, empowering reading, in which the female city is an active subject, designing her own destiny. Consequently, humour was not just a means to put women down, but it also had a radical and innovative side, allowing ideas and images to surface that otherwise were repressed in the official culture. Like humour in general, jokes and cartoons dealing with gender and modernity were ambivalent and provided many different interpretations.

Behind the ridicule and suppression, therefore, there were possibilities for emancipated readings as well. Moreover, the frequent jokes and cartoons about modern women and emancipated women look slightly different when seen through the eyes of a supposed female audience. After all, in many ways these female figures challenged and transcended traditional gender roles and hierarchies; they dressed like men, acted like men, even bounced like kangaroos. Perhaps seeing these alternative and confusing variations of gender did not merely intensify the awareness of the existing gender structures and limitations, but also had potential to create completely new ways of perceiving oneself as a woman.

(De)Constructing the *Weltstadt*

In addition to modern and emancipated women, strangers and foreigners were also popular types in the humorous magazines. Vienna was often looked at through the eyes of foreign tourists visiting the city. Comical encounters between strangers and the Viennese were a standard feature in popular humour. In the humorous publications, tourists and visitors from the imperial provinces exploring the city without knowing it properly easily led to comical errors, misunderstandings and mistakes.[104] Moreover, the perspective of the strangers was employed to reveal comical or ridiculous aspects of Viennese everyday life.[105]

This stranger's perspective enabled an alienated view on the city's life; in the eyes of outsiders, ordinary everyday practices and experiences suddenly became curious and unfamiliar. In addition, foreign visitors themselves embodied unfamiliarity and were therefore auspicious targets for humour. Humour research has paid much attention to the fact that humour and laughter often relate to dealing with strangeness and unfamiliarity.[106] Already in the nineteenth century, the German word *komisch* meant 'funny-amusing' and 'funny-peculiar' at the same time. For example, Grimm's dictionary from 1873 reported that *komisch* meant not only 'foolish' or 'senseless' but also 'strange, peculiar or bizarre'. Moreover, the dictionary noted that when talking about a person, the word had an insulting tone.[107]

Because of its ability to degrade or elevate symbolic status positions, humour was used to divide people into various hierarchical categories, even before the modern era. Various comical encounters between different social groups were part of the European tradition of humour well before the nineteenth century. In the early modern English jest books, for example, the jests and anecdotes are often based on an encounter between different kinds of people: a man and a woman, a young person and an old person, a city dweller and a peasant, a fool and a wise man.[108] Modern mass print culture reclaimed and revitalized this old tradition.

However, comical encounters between individuals representing different ethnic and national groups tell us not merely about continuities in persisting joking traditions, but also about changes in social reality. Mass tourism started in the nineteenth century, and the growing metropolitan cities became transnational meeting places for people of highly varied origins, living close to each other in a new urban environment. Simultaneously, nationalism and new racial doctrines shaped the ways in which differences between people of various ethnic origins were perceived and categorized in nineteenth-century social, political and medical discourses. The division and segregation of people according to their nationality and ethnicity was above all a nineteenth-century invention, followed by an explosion of ethnic jokes in the modern era.[109]

The research on nationalism has shown that the ideas of a nation and nationhood were profoundly modern concepts, which shaped nineteenth- and twentieth-century history in a fundamental way. Moreover, the research into nationalism has emphasized the imaginary aspects of nationalism as an ideology that connects people together who otherwise would not be in touch.[110] Benedict Anderson has referred to nation states as 'imagined communities', and suggested that the nineteenth-century nation, as an imagined community, depended on cultural representations and material culture such as flags and urban architecture, which supported a national imaginary that tied people together and gave them a shared identity.[111]

When looking at the history of the comical press in nineteenth-century Europe, it seems that humour and satire played an important role in maintaining and circulating cultural stereotypes on nations and nationalities in a seemingly trivial and harmless form. Humour and laughter can thus be conceived as powerful instruments for banal nationalism, which Michael Billig has described as everyday public discourses that create and sustain collective identities and imagined communities. Billig emphasizes routines of thinking and using language as well as other unnoticed social habits as crucial for constructing and sustaining ideas on nationhood and national identity.[112] The recent discussion on humour has emphasized its role in the politics of identity, as humour is often used in order to form social groups and a sense of togetherness, by including some and excluding others.[113]

In the late nineteenth-century Viennese *Witzblätter*, humour was incorporated into the ongoing competition between nations and their capitals. The humorous magazines actively shaped the understanding of nations as having special characteristics such as a distinctive sense of humour. Furthermore, humour was seen not merely as a national characteristic, but different cities were attributed with their own peculiar type of humour. As noted in the previous discussion, humour was strongly associated with ideas of the Viennese way of life and city identity. Comparisons with other cities were made to strengthen the idea of an authentic and original Viennese sense of humour. For instance, at the beginning of its publishing activities in 1857, *Figaro* explicitly situated itself in an international context among other European humorous magazines, but with a sense of pride and superiority:

> Leave 'Punch' on the banks of the Thames, and 'Charivari' by the Seine,
> Let 'Kladderadatschen' pursue its nonsense by the Spree!
> 'Let each man look to his own': Goethe said it so, –
> So keep the River Wien for Figaro![114]

The era of rising nationalism was also a time for increased social interaction between people from different parts of the world. The mobility of people, thoughts and artefacts increased in the nineteenth century thanks to the technological innovations in mass transportation. New vehicles made it possible for people to move faster from one place to another. Accordingly, travelling became conceivable for more people than ever before.[115]

The World Exhibition in 1873 especially attracted visitors from abroad to Vienna, and tourism continued to grow through the following decades.[116] This new mobility created uncertainty among the authorities, who had traditionally kept an eye on foreign visitors coming to the city.[117] This general interest in and suspicion of visitors became visible in popular humorous publications, which featured visitors and tourists as comical outsider figures. Often the humorous magazines used only the term *Fremder* when referring to visitors from abroad. In addition, foreign tourists were frequently portrayed as national stereotypes: the English were dry but polite, the French sensual and the Italians loud. The Prussians preferred order and discipline, even on a holiday.[118] These national characteristics of foreigners were then depicted and mocked in imagined encounters with Viennese.

What all these visitors had in common was that they typically failed to understand the city correctly, misinterpreting the people, places and phenomena they encountered in Vienna.[119] This made the visitors strange and ridiculous in the eyes of the Viennese, since as seen in the previous chapter, knowing the city correctly was crucial for belonging to the Viennese urban community. Because tacit knowledge of the city was crucial for belonging to the city, jokes about misinterpretations and errors functioned as a strategy for inclusion and exclusion. At the same time as these jokes and cartoons about strangers repeatedly created a boundary between 'us' and 'them', they also reinforced shared meanings associated with particular places in the city. For example, the *Graben* in the city centre was habitually associated with prostitution, especially at night.[120] Consequently, making strangers unfamiliar in the humorous publications meant at the same time making Vienna familiar, as shared meaning and associations were constantly reawoken.

The comical encounters between strangers and the Viennese often involved themes of exploring and interpreting the great metropolis. The *Witzblätter* presented scenes in which Viennese characters show foreign visitors around their home city.[121] In addition, humorous travel guides parodied the conventions of travel literature and 'misguided' their readers to pay attention to the trivial, inappropriate and disturbing rather than the fine and presentable.[122] In Franz Masaidek's *Staberl als Fremdenführer* (1868), for example, Staberl, a Viennese citizen, is guiding Prussian Herr Piefecke around the city. The two men get into various comical adventures that both reveal the pitfalls of Viennese everyday urban life and make Herr Piefecke look ridiculous, as he does not blend in, but continually collides awkwardly with people, places and practices that to the Viennese were so familiar.[123]

Strangers did not only misinterpret the Viennese people, but also failed to read correctly the meanings of city spaces.[124] The emergence of European nation states and chauvinism shaped nineteenth-century urban history, as urban planning and city management were subjected to new kinds of competition and comparison. In Vienna, as in many other capital cities, the symbolic and representative value of city space was deployed to build an image of national identity. The symbolic aspects of the Ringstraße became dominant due to the fact that rising nationalism intensified the competition between emerging nation states.

The era of rising nationalism was especially difficult for the multi-ethnic Habsburg Empire, whose population consisted of eleven national groups that had to be bound together in order to prevent the disintegration of the empire. This task was demanding, since identification with the empire had to overcome both local identities and several borders of language and ethnicity. Paradoxically, the Habsburg Empire, which was a multi-ethnic nation, had to make use of the same strategies for creating a shared identity as the nation states. As a survival strategy, the role of Vienna as a concrete and symbolic centre of the Habsburg Empire was strongly emphasized, and the city renewal offered a perfect opportunity to reshape and reinforce the imaginary of a uniform imperial nation and its shared past.[125]

In addition to this symbolic function relating to domestic affairs, the growing European capitals were embarking on a competition for the leading position. In the turn-of-the-century urban theories, a distinction was drawn between the concepts of metropolis (*Großstadt*) and world city (*Weltstadt*).[126] From the 1860s onwards, the discussion on urbanity in Vienna revolved around the concept of *Weltstadt*.[127] A true world city or *Weltstadt* would express the progress and superiority of the whole nation. In order to be a world city, an urban centre had to have over one million inhabitants, influence over a large region, and an international atmosphere.

The humorous press expressed an ambivalent attitude towards this *Weltstadt* ideal. On the one hand, jokes and cartoons expressed national pride and a wish to make Vienna a real competitor with other capital cities. On the other hand, there was a fear that international influences would destroy Viennese originality and its local characteristics.[128] *Kikeriki*, especially, inclined towards parochial local patriotism, and created humour that attacked 'foreign' influences in Viennese spaces and culture. According to the magazine, the loss of Viennese identity was manifested in the disappearance of local dialect and local characteristics.[129] As Marion Linhardt has shown, the same kind of rhetoric was used in the 1880s in the discussion on French operettas that were seen to threaten traditional Viennese *Volkstheater*.[130]

This paradox between appropriation of and resistance to international influences was highlighted in humour concerning the World Exhibition that was hosted by Vienna in 1873. The urban renewal project was strongly motivated by a desire to make the city attractive for foreign visitors and compete with other nations in progress. The World Exhibition was an important part of the modernization process in Vienna. The transformation of the city space was driven by the competition with other European capitals, and in addition, international influences and models played a vital role in the discussion on urban planning in the late nineteenth century. For example, the special magazine for architects, the *Allgemeine Bauzeitung*, published travel accounts as early as the 1850s and 1860s, and focused in the following decades on the urban development in other European cities, which had a major influence on attitudes towards the urban renewal in Vienna.[131]

All humorous magazines, and *Kikeriki* especially, published humorous texts and cartoons dealing with the World Exhibition, and one often-repeated theme was that the city had been turned into an artificial landscape for foreign visitors and not for the Viennese themselves.[132] The investors built new hotels and impressive palaces in the city, instead of new apartments to ease the housing shortage. In 1872, *Kikeriki* published a cartoon in which the whole of Vienna had been turned into hotels, and the citizens had to flee the city to make room for the foreign visitors.[133]

Der Floh and *Figaro* looked at the World Exhibition from a different point of view: their jokes, cartoons and humorous anecdotes entailed more self-irony and ridicule towards the Viennese themselves, who were often the butt of humour rather than the foreigners.[134] Fellow citizens were mocked for taking advantage of the visitors. The humour targeted the greediness of the hotel and restaurant owners who were robbing the tourists with high prices and greedy scams.[135] These comical accounts often aimed at unveiling a gap between the sublime rhetoric of how the nations were meeting at the World Exhibition in peace and harmony, and the greedy desire for profit underlying the noble cause.[136] On the other hand, humorous magazines were not entirely detached from these economic interests themselves, as they published advertisements for the hotels during the exhibition.[137] The expensiveness of Vienna was in many ways ridiculed. For example, in *Figaro* a businessman from New York appealed for funding for visitors who had used up all their money in staying in Vienna and could not afford to travel back home after the World Exhibition.[138] *Der Floh* published a joke titled 'On parle Français', which portrayed a comical encounter between a French visitor and the staff at a Viennese hotel. This particular example, like many other humorous texts in the middle-class humorous magazines, required knowledge of French in order to be appreciated:

> Franzose. Combien conte une chambre au premier?
> Kellner. Trente florins.
> Franzose. Par mois?
> Kellner. Oui Monsieur, pour Vous.
> Franzose. Est-il bète!
> Kellner. Bett? – oh, comme il faut![139]

Using French can be interpreted here as a sign emphasizing the educated cosmopolitanism of the assumed readership of the magazine. In fact, the bourgeois humorous magazines often used different languages such as French, English, Italian and Hungarian in their repertoire.[140] This indicates that not only wittiness and a good sense of humour, but also educated language skills were seen as an important part of the modern metropolitan mindset.

Whereas wit and amiability were implicitly praised as desirable metropolitan qualities, satirical laughter was explicitly used to criticize those aspects of city life that were considered inadequate or unworthy for a *Weltstadt*. The closing of the theatres during summer, and the practice of closing the gates of the city at 10 in the evening (the *Sperrstunde*), were found especially embarrassing: as a result, Vienna had no cultural nightlife, as a metropolis should.[141] Vienna was often ridiculed as a miserable one-horse town (*Krähwinkel*) instead of a real major city.[142] For instance, an ironical text published in the *Wiener Luft* appendix of *Figaro* in 1882 suggested measures to keep tourists away from Vienna: all the gates should be closed at 8, lighting reduced in the most visited areas, and the bad smell of the River Wien would certainly drive away any other unsuspecting visitors.[143]

The ambivalent mixture of a sense of superiority and inferiority was especially visible in the way humorous magazines dealt with Western visitors. There was a striking difference between visitors from other European capitals and those from more exotic far-away countries such as China or Iran. As a rule, non-Western visitors from the Middle or Far East were depicted as more ridiculously clueless about the Viennese way of life.[144] This distinction between visitors depending on their origin shows how nineteenth-century humour maintained and reinforced racist and xenophobic tendencies in joking that have deep roots in the early modern era. The new printing technologies and means of mass production came together with new racial doctrines in the 1870s to bring about an increased prominence of racist imaginaries in popular printed publications. The humorous magazines made exotic strangers from other countries unfamiliar and laughable by imitating their errors in German and especially by visually exaggerating their physical features into racial stereotypes.[145] Furthermore, as will be further discussed in the following section, in the 1870s antisemitic representations started to proliferate in the *Witzblätter*, intermingling with racist imaginaries about foreign visitors.[146]

Moreover, the response to the World Exhibition was impacted by the international stock market crash in 1873, which created a unique context for the Viennese exhibition: the belief in progress suffered a severe blow. In Vienna, the boom in new building projects had led to speculation, which contributed to the crash on the Vienna stock market in May 1873, almost simultaneously with the opening of the World Exhibition site at Prater. *Der Floh* wrote ironically:

> Paris has, as is well known,
> Lost the World City throne,
> And since then, at one fell swoop,
> All countries now to Vienna look up –
> Treat our joke with respect –
> When our Stock Exchange goes crashin',
> America follows our new fashion![147]

All in all, in the humour around Vienna's aspirations of becoming a *Weltstadt*, the focus was not on the success or the glory, but on the faults and downsides of

Viennese urban life.[148] The themes of disorder and comicality in the transformation of the city's physical space, for instance, that were analysed in chapters 2 and 3, were also explored using the depiction of foreign visitors. For example, in one joke from 1871 a visitor asks how to get to the city district of Josefstadt, on the other side of the unfinished Ringstraße construction zone. When the Viennese citizen has given him instructions, which involve climbing over various planks and jumping over large pits, the foreign visitor comments that he will need to write a farewell letter to his family before setting off on such a dangerous journey.[149]

The eyes of visitors, and the perspective they offered on the changes in Vienna, enabled self-irony and social satire on many of the aspects of urbanization that have been discussed in previous chapters. Yet the foreign visitors' perspective set the flaws and problems in urban life into a wider framework of national competition.[150] The transformation of Vienna was motivated by and interpreted through an international context, as the competition between European capital cities and their symbolic prestige took on new meanings in an era of rising nationalism. The popularity of foreign visitors as comical outsider figures draws attention to the fact that modernization meant the growing presence of international influences in Viennese everyday life.[151] There were new international models for a modern city in urban planning and city architecture, and a new internationally oriented press, which followed and commented on the urban renewal from the very beginning. Furthermore, new means of transport increased tourism and brought more foreign visitors to the city. The World Exhibition highlighted the *Weltstadt* ideal as a determining factor in the ambition to rebuild the city to match new modern demands. Accordingly, the late nineteenth-century discussions on modernization and urbanization were fundamentally cosmopolitan in nature, and the new mixtures of local and global were part of the experience of modernity.

Yet it is necessary to look further into the specific Viennese context for humour about foreign visitors to the city. In addition to foreigners, the transformation of Vienna was examined through the eyes of ethnic minorities either visiting or settling in the imperial capital. This role of the city as a location for multicultural encounters added a special layer of meaning to the discussion of urban renewal in the Viennese comic press. The fact that Vienna was not the capital of a nation state, but the centre of a multi-ethnic state (*Vielvölkerstaat*), created a special context for the Viennese urban history and for the contemporary discussion on modernity.

In the nineteenth century, Vienna was the centre of the multinational Habsburg Empire, which encompassed over fifty million inhabitants. The population of the capital rose rapidly from around 476,000 in 1857 to over two million by 1910. The heavy migration to the capital made Vienna a unique multicultural metropolis that attracted in-migration from all the provinces of the empire. In 1800, as much as 90 per cent of the population was originally

Viennese, but by 1891 only 35 per cent of the citizens were born in Vienna.[152] The newcomers represented various traditions and cultures, from Eastern Central Europe to the Balkans and North Italy: Germans, Hungarians, Czechs, Poles, Serbs, Croatians, Romanians, Ruthenians, Slovaks, Slovenes and Italians.[153] In addition, as the next section will show, the number of Jews increased rapidly, as the new liberal laws gave them full civil rights and the right to move around the empire freely.

Nationalism affected both the domestic and foreign policy of the state. Whereas foreign policy was influenced by competition with other European superpowers, domestic policy was dominated by the constant need to balance different intra-imperial national interests. In the 1867 *Ausgleich*, for instance, the empire was remodelled into a dual monarchy sharing the same Emperor, with the western part, Cisleithanien, dominated by Austria, and the eastern part, Transleithanien, dominated by Hungary. The interests of the two dominant populations were thus recognized, but the less powerful ethnic minorities were not given the same recognition. Half a century later, the atmosphere of national tensions led to the outbreak of World War I when the Bosnian-Serbian separatist Gavrilo Princip shot Archduke Franz Ferdinand in Sarajevo in 1914.

Vienna had a special role as the capital city in this era of growing internal and external controversies. Alongside other urban centres within the empire which fostered an active intellectual and cultural life, such as Budapest, Prague and Bratislava, Vienna became a significant meeting place for different nationalities, cultures and languages. With its liberal and heterogeneous population, Vienna formed a cosmopolitan island in the empire, in contrast to the parochial narrow-mindedness and intolerance of the rural provinces.[154] This heterogeneity of the capital nourished dynamic and innovative intellectual and cultural thinking, leading to the famous cultural flowering of *fin-de-siècle* Vienna.[155] On the other hand, the recurrent language and national controversies that shook the whole empire culminated in the capital city of Vienna, which *Figaro* ironically compared to the Tower of Babel as early as 1865.[156]

Humorous magazines and satirical journals were an important forum for dealing with these national and language controversies.[157] In *Figaro*, *Kikeriki* and *Der Floh*, immigrants were portrayed as comical characters who, like the foreign visitors, did not know the city properly and misread it.[158]

As Ulrich E. Bach has noted, in comparison to powers like England and France, the Austro-Hungarian Empire did not pursue overseas imperialism, but had colonies and 'inland foreigners' within its own borders.[159] Accordingly, the humour about ethnic minorities contained a strong hierarchic element; laughter not only divided the German population from the other ethnic groups, but these groups were also presented as inferior, and were marked as outsiders in Vienna. Moreover, the relation between provincial immigrants and the Austrian-German Viennese was part of a multifaceted hierarchy: whereas foreigners (*Fremde*) represented competing nations, the ethnic minorities and immigrants came from the provinces of the empire. In the eyes of the Viennese middle classes, they were rustic, backward and uneducated.[160]

National costumes played an important role in identifying and depicting ethnic minorities. The rustic dress and appearance of the ethnic minorities, in particular, were portrayed as comical. Cartoons repeatedly established categorical differences between the appearance of different ethnic groups and nationalities, and played with these differences.[161] For instance, *Kikeriki* published a cartoon in which a man starts to follow a beautiful young girl on the street but discovers to his horror that the girl is actually a man dressed in national costume.[162] Such insinuations about the femininity of men from different ethnic backgrounds than the Austrian-German majority were a strategy of ridicule. Jokes about race and ethnicity often involved sexual connotations, and particularly popular were jokes about encounters between immigrant men and Viennese women. For example, *Der Floh* presented a character of a 'gallant' Hungarian who tries to act like a gentleman towards the women, but ends up insulting them horribly.[163]

Language issues surfaced in humour based on the comicality of different dialects and grammatical mistakes made by non-native German speakers. The German *Witzblätter* enjoyed playing with different languages and dialects, spoken by comical figures representing the empire's ethnic minorities. The non-native German speakers mixed up their own native tongue with German, and struggled to understand the city correctly, misreading various urban texts, from advertisements to official orders.[164]

The national pride, prejudices and local chauvinism of provincial visitors, especially, was ridiculed in the German-language magazines.[165] In addition, jokes and cartoons relating to ethnic minorities within the Habsburg Empire typically involved themes of 'race' and ethnicity more than the humour relating to foreign tourists from other European countries (France, Prussia, England). Different ethnic minorities, and the Czechs in particular, were presented as negative stereotypes, both stupid and aggressive.[166] This reflected the friction between Slavic groups and the German population, which struggled to maintain its dominant position in the empire.[167]

All these examples show that a tension between assimilation and separatism was characteristic of Viennese popular humour. This resulted from the specific context for Viennese urbanization in the nineteenth century, as the metropolitan capital city became a meeting place for different cultures and ethnic traditions. The Viennese modernization was strongly influenced by these tensions between different population groups, yet on the other hand everyday life in late nineteenth-century Vienna inescapably entailed encountering people of different origins. Vienna was characterized by cultural diversity, mixing and cross-cultural influences. Modernity meant increasing internationality, cosmopolitanism, but also dissent and frictions between different ethnic groups and nationalities.

Modernity and Jewishness

The ethnic minorities' nationalism, and their desire to distinguish themselves from the main population, were subject to laughter. Assimilation was often presented as a positive aspect of modernization. In humorous texts and images depicting the Jewish population, however, their aims of assimilation were ignored and, instead, the difference between Jewry and the Gentile population was constantly reiterated. One explanation for this is that, as previous research has suggested, the antisemites identified the Jews as a common enemy against whom multicultural Vienna was able to unite.[168] Moreover, in contrast to the foreign visitors and provincial immigrants, assimilated Jews were involved in many ways in creating the new Vienna. Wealthy Jewish dynasties such as the Ephrussi and Todesco families built their palaces on the Ringstraße and financed the building of public monuments.[169] Moreover, the emerging modernist culture in the Habsburg capital was in many ways shaped and created by Jewish thinkers, artists, journalists and scientists.

The history of Jews in the Habsburg Empire, and Jewish influence on Viennese cultural history, have been much explored and well covered by previous research.[170] The same applies to the history of antisemitism and political radicalization in late nineteenth-century Vienna.[171] It is impossible to ignore the Jewish influence in the urban history and cultural life of *fin-de-siècle* Vienna, but the relation between modernity and Jewishness remains highly problematic. As the cultural historians Scott Spector and Mary Gluck have noted, the association of Jews with the ambivalence of modernity has become a cliché that needs to be critically interrogated by further contextualization of primary sources and by new readings that do not take the discourse on Jewish modernity for granted, but unravel the ways in which it has been historically constructed to serve various cultural functions.[172]

In this study I will address only a small fragment of the Jewish issue by focusing on the question of how the discourses of Jewishness and of the modern city were linked in the popular humour of the *Gründerzeit*. My main point is that the humorous publications were a major cultural forum in which modernity and Jewishness became associated. The *Witzblätter* played a central role in creating popular imaginaries of Jews and circulating them in public. Moreover, these representations were open for various political and social agendas as popular humour became a central cultural arena for fierce debates on the status of Jews in the capital and their role in shaping its culture. The humorous expressions of the Viennese *Witzblätter* thus shed light on the ways in which the transformation of the city was interwoven with the rise of modern antisemitism in Austria-Hungary.

This process had its origin in the context of Austrian liberalism. During the reign of Franz Joseph, Jews had gained new opportunities to participate in social life, after hundreds of years of exclusion. The emancipation of Jews started after the 1848 revolution. The new liberal laws granted the Jewish population the right to vote, to own land and property, and to choose their place of abode. Full civil rights were guaranteed by the constitution in 1867.[173] Before the emancipation of Jews in 1860, there were 6,200 Jews in the city, 2.2 per cent of the population. By 1880, the number of Jews had risen to 72,600, or 10 per cent, and by 1890 to 118,500. In addition, there were a large number of assimilated Jews who had converted to Christianity, which means that the number of people with Jewish origin was substantially higher.[174]

The economic crisis of the 1870s, however, changed attitudes towards Jews, at the same time as new racial doctrines started to spread in Europe. Consequently, at the same time as the Jewish population was attempting to assimilate into society and find their place in the capital, antisemitism was growing, both inside and outside Vienna. In humorous discourse, the New Vienna, associated with rich Jewish speculators and investors, was in many ways ridiculed and distanced. While the Jewish middle-class intelligentsia and entrepreneurs were trying to assimilate in the city by funding and participating in the urban renewal project, popular humorous representations reiterated and underlined the difference between the Jewish and Gentile populations. Jews were made into strangers within their own city, responsible for turning Vienna into something alien and unfamiliar.[175] In *Kikeriki*, in particular, the Ringstraße was portrayed as a 'Jewish' street, and the presence of wealthy Jews on the main boulevard was a continual source of hate and bitterness.[176]

The Jewish topic in popular humour was, however, a complex and multifaceted phenomenon, as Jews were at the same time ridiculed and defended in the humorous magazines. In the 1860s, *Kikeriki* and *Figaro* defended the Jewish population by satirical attacks against antisemites,[177] but started to publish more negative caricatures and jokes about Jews in the 1880s. In the final decades of the century, *Kikeriki* turned to fierce antisemitism. *Der Floh*, on the other hand, was even more ambivalent in its humorous representations of Jews; despite publishing negative and stereotypic images of Jews,[178] in the 1880s this humorous magazine also violently attacked the antisemites with mockery and ridicule.[179] One joke under the pen name 'Russian and Polish Jews' called antisemitism a curious disease: when some become infected, it is others that have to suffer.[180] Another joke from 1887 stated: 'Antisemitism is a contradiction in itself, because it only strikes at kosher targets'.[181] Moreover, *Der Floh* also showed a more general inclination towards Jewish humour as it often published jokes and cartoons with themes and situations very similar to the Jewish anecdotes that Sigmund Freud used in his famous study.[182]

It is thus important to note that in the field of humour, especially, representations of Jews were open to a variety of different cultural and political agendas. The difficulty in separating 'good' or 'positive' from 'bad' or 'negative' images of Jews,[183] and the overlapping borders of irony and self-irony, make the Jewish issue extremely challenging, as negative visual stereotypes of Jews, and crude jokes underlining their ethnic and religious difference, were produced and consumed by people of Jewish descent as well.[184] After all, many of the famous nineteenth-century humourists, such as Daniel Spitzer, who wrote for *Figaro*, were themselves Jews. Also, as the scholars Mary Gluck and Jefferson S. Chase have reminded us, nineteenth-century German culture was strongly influenced by the tradition of the Jewish joke (*Judenwitz*), advocated by talented writers such as Moritz Gottlieb Saphir or Heinrich Heine, who had an enormous influence on the era's journalistic practices and literary culture.[185]

Chase has suggested that the tradition of the *Judenwitz* was increasingly seen as destructive and dangerous in nineteenth-century German discourse, set against the ideal of humour associated with the wholesome native society and positive connotations of *Gemütlichkeit*, *Kultur* and the literary tradition of Goethe and Schiller.[186] This tension between different cultural meanings related to *Witz* and *Humor* in the German-speaking world might explain the ambivalence in the Viennese humorous magazines, which proclaimed themselves on the outside as humorous magazines (*humoristische Blätter*) but certainly understood themselves as *Witzblätter*: *Kikeriki*, *Figaro* and *Der Floh* did not use the term *Witzblatt* in their titles, but more in their internal discussion,[187] which suggests that the Viennese comical press was a point of intersection for different traditions of humour, both Jewish and Gentile, the former being an implicit underlying thread running through these popular publications.[188]

In addition to such qualities as subversiveness and intellectual creativity, self-deprecation and self-irony have also been seen as characteristic of the Jewish joke.[189] The cultural significance and political consequences of Jewish self-deprecating humour and self-irony have been discussed from various angles in the previous research. Peter Jelavich has suggested in his study on the turn-of-the-century cabaret scene in Berlin that the intentions of Jewish humourists and their audience failed to meet, as their ironic self-deprecating jokes generated antisemitic laughter.[190] Ann Taylor Allen has seen the negative Jewish stereotypes in the satirical press of Wilhelmine Germany as an example of the breakthrough of the racial doctrines that made the Jewish minority see themselves through the eyes of the majority.[191] Other studies, as well, have addressed the ways in which the assimilated Jews in German-speaking Europe used humorous strategies in order to distinguish themselves from the Jewish migrants from the East, who were fleeing from pogroms in Russia and other places in Eastern Europe.[192] Most recently, Mary Gluck has suggested that the tradition of the *Judenwitz* expressed above all the cultural competence of the Jews, who used it as a strategy to navigate the complex discursive environment surrounding the 'Jewish question', as well as in pursuing a new radical and unstructured sense of the self in the face of the collapse of established political and social structures and traditional identities.[193]

The *Witzblatt* as a medium highlighted this crisis in many ways. The Viennese humorous magazines not only took part in the fierce debates concerning the 'Jewish question', but also more comprehensively gave expression to the crisis of narrative structures and cultural meanings that had sustained traditional social structures and identities. Instead of solid meanings and coherent identities, the *Witzblätter* offered their readers a world full of incoherence, ambivalence and multiple perspectives. Their ironic and parodic rhetorical devices, and constant playing with fake identities and pen names, made their humorous representations not only of the Jews but also about other issues discussed in this study overwhelmingly ambivalent.

Consequently, not only the subject matter of the magazines, but also the journalistic practices through which the humour was created, link the discussion on comical modernity with the discourses surrounding Jewishness and humour. This relates to a wider debate on how the liberal press was accused by the antisemites of being a 'Jewish press'. Jews were seen to dominate public opinion, due to their major role as owners and editors of all the major daily papers of the liberal press: the *Neue Freie Presse, Neues Wiener Tagblatt, Wiener Allgemeine Zeitung* and later the *Arbeiter Zeitung*. Accusations of Jewish predominance in the press lay at the heart of the debate on Jewish modernism.[194] It is notable that the Jewish influence on the cultural life of Vienna was seen especially in terms of discursive power. Jewish journalists were accused of creating a nihilistic cultural atmosphere with fragmented subjectivism and impressionistic narrative strategies and ironical distance.[195] As the antisemitic populists proclaimed a return to simple meanings and uniform identities in terms of race and nationality, the long projects of Jewish assimilation and Austrian liberalism both went into severe crisis.

Towards the turn of the century, popular humour was increasingly utilized to serve antisemitic purposes, and cartoons, especially, played an important role in depicting Jews as ethnically different and laughable. Viennese antisemitism was dominated by the idea of the omnipresence of Jews in Viennese public life. Jews were seen as controlling the press, theatres and the economy of the city. *Figaro* actively reinforced this imaginary in its jokes and cartoons. For example, in a cartoon published in *Wiener Luft* in 1890, a stranger asks where the Judengasse is and the Viennese answers: 'Can you tell me where it isn't?'[196]

The cartoon sheds light on how the discussion on Jews in the city was conducted in a trivial and seemingly harmless way, which nonetheless was extremely effective in creating a virulent antisemitic atmosphere that nourished new political mass parties and political movements such as the Christian Social movement of Karl Lueger, the pan-Germanism of Georg von Schönerer and later the Nazi Party[197] of Adolf Hitler. Lueger's antisemitic politics united the middle classes by 'creating the Jews of Vienna as a single monolithic enemy with international connections against which all Christians had to unite'.[198] Similarly, John Boyer has seen antisemitism as a complex defence mechanism against the massive social change that had taken place in Vienna in the second part of the century.[199]

In *fin-de-siècle* Vienna, humour and antisemitism were strongly linked, as humour was used as a means of expressing and legitimizing aggression against the Jews. As the further discussion will show, the number of antisemitic cartoons and jokes exploded in the humorous press after the 1873 stock market crash. Jews were attacked with other forms of humour as well: in the puppet show performances at the Prater in 1885, for example, the traditional *Hanswurst* figure was seen beating Jews to death while the audience was laughing.[200] Furthermore, humour, jokes and wittiness were a major part of the political antisemitic rhetoric; both Karl Lueger and Georg Schönerer frequently used jokes and humorous remarks in their speeches. It has been suggested that Lueger's ability to use the local Viennese dialect and the *Wiener Schmäh* was a major component in his charisma and popularity.[201] Humour thus played a major role in the cultural and political debates of the time, and popular culture became one key arena for the scorn and ridicule of political opponents.[202]

Although the reasons for the antisemitic atmosphere were social and political, humour as a symbolic form of speech offered an affective and powerful medium for aggression against Jews. The social and economic inequality that characterized late nineteenth-century Viennese urban living conditions played a major role in the history of modern Austrian antisemitism. The following section continues investigating the ways in which antisemitism, social problems and anti-capitalism intermingled in the late nineteenth-century Viennese *Witzblätter*.

Discussing Class and Capitalism: Fantasies of the Underclass

This section pursues the relation between the city space, urban poverty and humour by scrutinizing the symbolic use of the underclass, meaning the lowest societal stratum, in the discussion of modernity. Although the presence of the poor has always been part of life in towns and cities,[203] nineteenth-century urbanization created a whole new scale for human misery. As life in cities throughout Europe was increasingly shaped by industrial capitalism, the results of capitalism in the modes of living and experiencing the world were increasingly discussed in spatial terms.[204] Furthermore, as the renewal of the old spatial fabrics meant encountering poverty in new *modern* urban spaces, representations of the urban pariah population offered a significant way of discussing these spaces and giving them meaning.[205] In Vienna, the poor were present in the humorous representations of the new city in many ways. They were encountered on the Ringstraße and next to the beautiful palaces of the wealthy upper classes. Encounters between poor beggars and rich millionaires were a standard topic for jokes and cartoons during the *Gründerzeit*.

The humorous imaginaries of the poor uncover a nexus between capitalism and the modern city. As a vast body of scholarly literature has shown, concern about borders and distinctions between classes living close together was a major theme in nineteenth-century discussions of urbanity. The problem of urban poverty surfaced again and again in texts concerning urban planning, hygiene, morality and sexuality. The issue of the poor permeated both fact and fiction, ranging from police regulations and newspaper reports to novels by Charles Dickens in London or Émile Zola in Paris.[206] The historian Scott Spector has investigated how cultural fantasies of urban decay proliferated in Vienna and Berlin at the turn of the century: at the same time as these capital cities expanded on an unprecedented metropolitan scale, discourses addressing crime and poverty exploded in scientific, philosophical and popular debates.[207]

This section seeks to demonstrate that humour and laughter were important means of dealing with uncertainties relating to capitalism, social problems and class distinctions in Vienna, before the *fin-de-siècle* era, when narratives on society's margins became such an important part of the discourses surrounding urban modernity. In humorous magazines of the *Gründerzeit*, beggars and the so-called *Lumpenproletariat* were not merely an integral part of the city, but a central topos for modernity. This crucial role resulted not from a homogeneous or coherent understanding of the underclass, but from a dynamic ambivalence: the issue of the poor was an unresolved question and in that sense an important topic for humour. Whereas the famous figures of Viennese nineteenth-century popular culture such as the *Schusterbuben* (shoemaker's boy) or *Stubenmädchen* (maid) represented the idealized 'Volk', the beggars, vagabonds and petty criminals were not seen as traditional Viennese types surviving in the changing city, but modern figures of a new kind, created and shaped by the city.[208] The beggar, especially, was an urban type that embodied the crisis between bourgeois identity and the urban underclass.[209]

This crisis became visible in two contradictory ways of dealing with the poor, corresponding with two contradictory ways of understanding humour. On the one hand, especially in the early stage in the 1850s, there was a strong effort to improve the city by satirical humour. As we will soon see, the idea of satire was strongly associated with concepts of moral sense and social consciousness. On the other hand, however, this endeavour of improving the city with humour was balanced by an objective of enduring the city with humour. Towards the turn of the century, popular humour took on notably darker colours, and the concepts of modern and modernity were increasingly associated with morbid topics like violence, murder and suicide, all topics strongly associated with the underclass. There were two points of rupture that clearly influenced this change of mood: the stock market crash in 1873, and the case of the serial killer Hugo Schenk in 1884, which gained huge publicity in Vienna just four years before Jack the Ripper shocked Victorian London in 1888. Macabre topics and *fin-de-siècle* melancholia had thus already appeared in middle-class popular culture before the catastrophic Mayerling incident,[210] and they were strongly associated with attitudes and ideas relating to the underclass. Humour enabled the ventilation of both fascination with and fear of the urban pariah through cultural fantasies and imaginaries. Consequently, the two strands – of social critique concerning the conditions of the poor and emotional detachment from the suffering of the poor – formed one major paradox in middle-class popular humour dealing with the modern city. Next, I will look further into this paradox and its implications for how the understanding of humour changed during the three decades studied in this book.

Satire, Social Consciousness and Sympathy for the Poor

Social critique of the condition of the poor was at its strongest at the beginning of the urban renewal, in the late 1850s. In the early stage of the project, the issue of the housing shortage in the city (*Wohnungsnot*) was a major theme in the discussion on urban renewal, in both satirical and serious press discourses on urban planning.[211]

In the second part of the nineteenth century, the gradual population growth of previous centuries turned to rapid expansion. This increase further accelerated towards the end of the century, and in 1894 a study revealed that 47.3 per cent of the inhabitants of Vienna were living in one- or two-bedroom apartments without kitchens.[212] By 1910, the average number of persons in an apartment was 4.4, meaning approximately 1.24 persons per room, including all spaces such as bathrooms and kitchens.[213] Lack of space was a familiar problem in Vienna, as it also was in other late nineteenth-century growing metropolises. This led to high housing costs. In Paris in 1870, for example, workers might spend as much as 30 per cent of their income on housing, while in Vienna rents could take 25 per cent of a worker's income.[214] As space was becoming extremely expensive, speculation and rackrenting became common in Vienna as well as in other European capitals.

Many people were homeless. In Vienna there was a system of renting beds in private apartments for people who wandered around the city without a permanent residence. These homeless people looking for a place to sleep at night were called *Bettgeher*, and as we will see later, they appeared frequently in the bourgeois humorous magazines. In addition to seeking a place to sleep indoors, the poor were often forced to sleep outdoors in the city. As the housing shortage radically worsened in the 1850s, the homeless and vagrants were camping out in public squares and vacant green spaces in the city, and the police had to put them up in stables and municipal jails. Even in the early twentieth century the homeless continued to camp in urban wasteland, such as the Prater meadows; Franzens Bridge and the Ferdinand Bridge were also used as places where people came to sleep, cook and wash themselves. Many young girls turned to prostitution because they had no place to sleep.[215]

Although *Figaro* criticized the housing conditions in the city, it did not maintain the same level of interest in the issue as *Kikeriki*, which addressed the housing problem repeatedly over the decades. Here the basic distinction between the magazines becomes visible; as noted in previous chapters, *Figaro* and *Der Floh* followed the predominant liberal *Weltanschauung* of the era, whereas *Kikeriki* clearly took a more aggressive counterposition against liberal city politics. *Kikeriki* was clearly aimed at the lower middle classes, and the awareness of flaws in housing conditions therefore presumably reflects the fact that the readers of *Kikeriki* were more affected by the problem.[216] Nonetheless, although *Kikeriki* touched upon the poor housing conditions in the city, it did so from a middle-class point of view.

It is important to bear in mind that this humorous treatment of the misery of the lower classes appeared in a situation in which the suburban masses were marginalized not only in urban planning and municipal politics, but also in bourgeois discourses about the city. Only after 1890 did the conditions of the underclass receive increasing attention in the mass press, urban studies and municipal politics.[217] The liberal politicians of the *Gründerzeit* neglected the social aspects of urban planning. Whereas the liberal city fathers focused on the symbolic aspects of the city space, they turned a blind eye to the material conditions of the poor in the expanding capital. It has been suggested that the Christian Social Party gained popularity in the 1890s precisely because it took up a position against the liberals, proclaiming the protection of the rights of the petit bourgeoisie and improving the resources and infrastructure for urbanization.[218] In addition, the conditions of the underclasses went predominantly unmentioned in liberal papers like the *Neue Freie Presse*. As Lutz Musner and Wolfgang Maderthaner have commented, even novelists tended to avoid dealing with contemporary social problems; realism and naturalism did not gain a similar foothold in Austrian literature as in contemporary England, Russia or France. Consequently, there was no Viennese author to raise social consciousness by depicting urban conditions in the same manner as Charles Dickens in London, Fyodor Dostoevsky in St. Petersburg or Émile Zola in Paris.[219]

Humorous magazines thus seem to have provided one significant forum for ventilating the issue of the inequality of living conditions within modern capitalism. However, popular humour tended to reduce the misery of the poor to a relatively allegorical form, rather than providing a concrete depiction of inadequate living conditions and their structural causes. Accordingly, humour was not so much a means to address the problem, but rather a means to deal with the emotional baggage relating to it. The humorous fantasies about the underclasses and the dark side of the city shed light above all on the bourgeoisie's complex emotional responses to the presence of the neglected underclass in urban space. In the early phase, the satirical humour was characterized by a certain ethos of social consciousness: cartoons and other humorous representations tried to create a sense of sympathy and to express benevolence for the poor.

The historian Daniel Wickberg connects the modern idea of a sense of humour with the middle-class 'culture of sensibility' of the eighteenth and nineteenth centuries. The values of sentimentality and benevolence were harnessed as a counterbalance to capitalist society based on a supposed rational calculus. The concept of humour, argues Wickberg, was strongly incorporated with the middle-class values of sensibility. This new understanding of humour was related to a distinction between wit and humour, the former being associated with the aristocracy and the latter with the bourgeoisie. In the process of absorbing the idea of humour into the middle-class way of life, it became associated with positive values of sympathy and moral sense, an intuitive judgement of seeing the difference between right and wrong.[220]

One of the best-known nineteenth-century articulations of the close connection between humour and moral sense is William Hazlitt's (1778–1830) proposal from the *Lectures on English Comic Writers* (1819): 'Man is the only animal that laughs and weeps; for he is the only animal that is struck with the difference between how things are, and what they ought to be'.[221] This early nineteenth-century middle-class understanding of humour as a form of sympathetic imagination with a moral ethos explains, to some extent, why humour was employed in the contemporary discussions as a tool for social critique.

This social critique highlighted the contrast between wealth and poverty in Vienna.[222] In caricatures, for instance, encounters between the rich and the poor were often based on a visual contrast, accompanied by a poem or dialogue highlighting the gap between two realities living side by side in the city. This composition of rich and poor was extremely popular in nineteenth-century print culture, which broached the issues of economic inequality and social differences by means of a range of juxtapositions between the wealthy and the underprivileged sectors of society. The rich and the poor thus met each other, not only in physical city spaces, but also in texts and narratives about the cities.[223]

In Vienna, popular humour was employed as a means of constructing an idealized and romanticized image of the hardworking poor, and expressing sentimental sympathy towards them. The figures of the lower 'dangerous classes' and unfamiliar urban masses were transformed into harmless types and characters that fitted into existing bourgeois discourses about the city as a place where the rich and the poor lived side by side.[224] This kind of laughter was intended to express the moral sense and goodwill of the middle-class audience, who positioned themselves between extreme wealth and extreme poverty. *Kikeriki*, especially, promoted a sentimental image of the respectable poor.[225] A reactionary social conscience was awakened, especially at Christmas time, and social problems were dealt with in a Dickensian tone, showing goodwill for the unprivileged poor who had to survive in the hard city.[226]

Images of children and families were a typical motif in the conservative sympathetic imaginary about the poor.[227] For example, in a caricature from 1871, a lower civil servant is standing with his little children gazing at all the abundant food displayed in the Sacher shop window, and comments, full of melancholy: 'Don't you think, my dears, that fasting must taste better there inside?'.[228] Whereas, as we shall soon see, adult beggars were usually depicted as hideous and grotesque, and thus ridiculous, child beggars were not located beyond the reach of mercy, but were depicted in sentimental terms. This sympathetic attitude towards poor children encapsulated the middle-class understanding of humour as something that expressed a social conscience and moral sense.

Moreover, sympathy with the imaginary and idealized poor was often expressed in the form of ridicule and scorn of those seen as profiting from their misery. Humorous representations created a simple polarity between the hardworking poor trying to make a living in the harsh city, and greedy and lazy capitalists lacking a moral sense. Stock market speculators and greedy millionaires were a butt of humour in all the humorous magazines studied in this book. Notably, the speculators and greedy millionaires were often identified as Jewish. These sympathetic fantasies about the underclasses, and the idea of moral conscience, were thus harnessed to the growing antisemitism in Vienna.

As the previous section has shown, the history of antisemitism in Vienna has been approached from various perspectives.[229] Usually the rise of the antisemitic movements has been contextualized in the social and economic history of the era: in the 1860s, the new liberal laws gave the Jewish population of the monarchy full civil rights, including the right to choose freely their place of abode, and freedom of occupation. When the construction of the Ringstraße began, Jewish investors were important sponsors for the project, buying land on the boulevard for their town palaces and in this way funding the monumental public building projects such as the new Opera House. However, the stock market crash in 1873, together with other misfortunes such as defeat in the wars against Italy (1859) and Prussia (1866), created increasing insecurity, which led to envy, anger and discontent directed against the Jewish population, and especially against the self-confidence and well-being of the rich Jewish capital owners, labelled as 'rich capitalist Jews'. Ridicule of the 'Ritter der Ringstraße' ('knights of the Ringstraße') was a prevalent feature in the late nineteenth-century Viennese press,[230] and the topic of many caricatures.[231]

In the 1870s, hostility towards rich Jews and stock market speculators increased significantly, and the topics for jokes and tendencies in humour followed the economic situation in the *Gründerzeit* closely. Whereas the 1850s and 1860s were a time of economic upswing, the stock market crash on 9 May 1873 caused a great shock for the economy, leading to an economic downturn in the 1880s and 1890s.[232] Laughter was especially directed against Jewish speculators, who were seen as the culprits of the disaster.[233] Antisemitic attitudes

Auf dem Ring.

— Was, zehn Kreuzer! das is mir zu theuer, was kost denn, liebes Kind, das Riechen zu diese Veigerl.
— O bitte, gnä Herr, gar nix.
— Dann riech dazu Leonoreleben, s'is billiger!

Figure 5.3 Flower girl on the Ringstraße. *Der Floh*, 28 March 1874.
Source: Austrian National Library.

were thus increasingly generated and legitimized in popular humour from the 1870s onwards.

Consequently, the gap between the rich and the poor became symbolically linked with the gap between the Jewish and the Gentile population. For instance, in the caricature shown in Figure 5.3, an apparently rich Jewish couple encounters a poor flower girl on the Ringstraße. Instead of showing generosity, the man tries to bargain over the price of a flower.[234] The humorous press played a pivotal role in creating and circulating such negative stereotypes of Jews, excluding them from the 'main' population.[235]

In the last decades of the century, the meanings associated with the Ringstraße were predominantly about money, capitalism and Jewishness, and the linking of the Ring with financial greed continued in Viennese jokes and cartoons well into the turn-of-the-century period.[236] Popular humour was thus neither harmless nor trivial fun, but actively structured and legitimized the rise of modern antisemitic worldviews and prejudices that later culminated in the rise of Adolf Hitler and the Nazi Party in Weimar Germany.

Disgust and Detachment: Grotesque, Greedy Beggars

As the previous discussion has shown, different motifs and objectives intersected in the urban imagery of the underclasses. The problem of urban poverty was much too complex to be solved simply through romanticized and idealized images of the lower social strata. Whereas the sympathetic image of the poor had been based on the idea of hard work and nobility of character, criminals, beggars and vagabonds did not fit into this idealized imagery. The presence of the underclasses in the city created laughter that expressed more negative aspects of the bourgeois consciousness: disgust, fear, aggression and guilt. As the urban masses multiplied in the Habsburg capital towards the turn of the century, Viennese bourgeois popular humour started to show a new kind of tendency, serving emotional detachment from the misery of the poor rather than a moral conscience.[237]

In the 1870s and 1880s, in particular, the humorous magazines dealt extensively with urban pariahs encountered in the city. Whereas *Kikeriki* defended the little people of the city in an increasingly antisemitic tone, *Figaro* and *Der Floh* published jokes about grotesque and greedy beggars. With their alienated representations, these jokes and cartoons helped to deal with the hidden life of the city, and address the unfamiliar lower classes 'living so close to and so far from the bourgeoisie'.[238] Bourgeois popular humour succeeded in dealing with these disturbing topics by using a strategy that detached members of the lower class from their social setting: as an urban type, the beggar was disassociated from the suburbs as social space.[239] Rather than depicting them in the working-class districts or suburbs, the beggars were transposed to the prosperous parts of the

Figure 5.4 'To live like a god'. *Der Floh*, 31 October 1886. Source: Austrian National Library.

city, to the baroque city centre and to the new Ringstraße. This decontextualization detached these figures from their social reality and placed them in the more fictive setting of an imaginary Vienna. Furthermore, this act of disassociation made the beggars not pitiable but comical. In these imaginaries of mixtures of high and low, it was precisely the contrast between luxurious spaces and shabby urban pariahs that provided the major source for humour.

In the caricature shown in Figure 5.4, for example, two vagabonds meet by an elegant fountain, the Donnerbrunnen in the prosperous Neuer Markt in the city centre. The first man asks the second where he is currently staying. The other replies that during the day he doesn't need anywhere to stay, but during the night he sleeps next to the god statues of the fountain; if the watchmen should see him in the dark, they will think that he is a god as well.[240] This dialogue takes place in a strong vagabond argot,[241] and its colloquial tone intensifies the contrast between the two tramps and the classical background of the famous fountain, dating from 1739.

This cartoon constitutes a clear symbolic polarity between high and low, classical and grotesque, which was highly characteristic of the bourgeois imaginaries of the members of the urban underclass. Here the low is manifested in the vagabond's body, which provides a comical contrast with the expectations relating to representations of the gods in classical art. Stallybrass and White have noted that the grotesque body was typical in imaginaries of the lower social strata, constructing an opposite to the ideal classical body, which incorporates a certain ideology of being.[242]

The Viennese liberal bourgeoisie thus used the aesthetic hierarchy between beauty and the grotesque in order to distinguish themselves from the lower classes. This recurrent need to define the low as grotesque and ugly may relate to the fact that in Vienna the urban renewal was blurring the line between different social spaces, and disguising the class distinctions in urban space.

Wolfgang Maderthaner and Lutz Musner have noted that the use of decorative façades in suburban architecture significantly differentiated Vienna from other contemporary European metropolises. Although the material living conditions of the overpopulated tenement buildings in suburbs like Ottakring or Neulerchenfeld were miserable, their outward appearance followed the style of the Ringstraße architecture, creating an image of a uniform and homogeneous urban landscape. The liberal city fathers of the *Gründerzeit* aimed at creating a harmonious façade for the whole city, disguising the division of its social space in architectural aesthetics. The decorative beauty of the *Gründerzeit* architecture was thus not only a symbolic disguise for urban misery, but it also served a political function. The idea was to defuse the internal conflict between lower classes and the bourgeoisie, without abolishing the social difference between the two:[243] 'At first glance no great differences are notable. Architecture thus celebrates an identity inscribed on the façades, whereas functionality cements difference. The lower social strata are given the impression that there is not an absolute and deliberate distinction between them and the bourgeoisie, but simply a gradual one, which can be bridged at least in imagination'.[244]

Yet, whereas architecture was thus used to defuse the social differences in the wider city space, middle-class humorous representations of the beggars constantly reconstructed the class difference through an aesthetical hierarchy between the beautiful and the ugly. In the humorous magazines, the coherent narrative of a uniform beautiful city space is disrupted by beggars and vagabonds who embody grotesque ugliness, and make the social division between high and low clearly visible.[245] In these Viennese caricatures, the ugliness of the poor, which has been associated with the comical for centuries, from antiquity to the present day,[246] was highlighted and exaggerated: shabby, grotesque beggars were often shown next to an elegant representative of the middle classes.

One cartoon published in *Figaro* in 1879 portrayed a typical situation, in which a beggar asks a middle-class woman for food. The negative attitude towards the poor becomes clear in the beggar's response to the middle-class woman offering him a piece of bread: 'What? A piece of bread! You'll have to look for another beggar for that, thank you very much!'[247] The comicality of this scene is based on the suggestion that since the poor man is so picky about his food, he cannot really be hungry at all. Various other humorous representations of greedy and confident beggars also rest on the same kind of composition, in which pity for the poor was transformed into irritation and resentment.[248]

Later, after the turn of the century, Freud provided a famous example of a joke in which a poor man borrows money from a wealthy acquaintance, who then the same day sees him eating salmon and mayonnaise at a restaurant. When the benefactor scolds the man for spending his money on such luxury, the poor man replies: 'When I don't have money, I cannot eat salmon with mayonnaise. When I have money, I'm not allowed to eat salmon with mayonnaise. So when exactly am I supposed to eat salmon with mayonnaise?'[249] In Freud's interpretation, this joke is based on a conflict between the moral indignation of the rich man and the hidden cynicism of the poor man. The idea that the poor were exploiting their well-to-do benefactors was a wider and characteristically new feature of late nineteenth-century culture, and a result of the vast population increase and urbanization. Between the 1840s and the 1860s, says Olive Anderson, attitudes in Britain towards the poor changed as sentimental radicalism and social conscience gave way to disillusionment and emotional detachment. The poor were no longer seen as victims of society, but as its parasites.[250]

In Vienna the new emotional detachment towards the poor became particularly visible in the masquerade culture, which translated the sorrows and dangers of the metropolis into harmless bourgeois bonhomie. In the earlier section, 'New Clothes of Vindobona: Modernity and Gender', I examined how the hierarchies of gender were examined and reinforced in masquerades, using strategies like cross-dressing and transgressing gender borders. I would now like to draw attention to one special kind of masquerade, the *Lumpenball*. Jokes and cartoons relating to the *Lumpenball* offer an interesting perspective on the humour relating to class borders in Vienna.

The *Lumpenball* was a ball organized from 1872 onwards in the entertainment venue 'Schwenders Kolosseum' at Mariahilferstrasse 15. It was a charity event and a masquerade where middle- and upper-class participants dressed up in rags (*Lumpen*). The *Lumpenball* was a topsy-turvy world *par excellence*. The disturbing mixture of high and low, respectable members of society in rags, clearly fascinated the middle-class audience, creating humour around disguised identity and mixing different classes together. *Der Floh* and the *Figaro* appendix *Wiener Luft*, especially, published cartoons showing people in costumes going to or coming from the ball.[251] One joke was based on an idea of a real beggar turning up at the event and winning first prize.[252] In another cartoon, a group of men looking like beggars ask the watchman to do them the honour of escorting them to the ball as if they had been arrested – this would create the most brilliant entrée.[253]

The *Lumpenball* seems like a Viennese ritual simultaneously reinforcing and transgressing the boundaries between high and low, bourgeoisie and *Lumpenprotelariat*.[254] The enthusiasm of the respectable upper middle classes to dress up as beggars is baffling, and can perhaps be explained by the ambiguous mixture of disgust and fascination, which has been seen as constitutive in the bourgeois production of desire for the low and the other. In any case, the

Lumpenball clearly was one important expression for the middle-class fantasies of the underclasses. Furthermore, it seems plausible that as a cultural and social practice, the *Lumpenball* had a lot to do with the bourgeoisie's fear of losing status and becoming ruined, during an era in which the stock market crash of 1873 literally turned millionaires into beggars. The jokes and topics of humour can be highly revealing. As Elliott Oring has shown in his compelling study *The Jokes of Sigmund Freud* (1984/1997), Freud paid special attention to jokes revolving around money, and this, Oring suggests, had much to do with Freud's own financial struggles and shame at his constant lack of money.[255]

Despite the potentially mixed feelings raised by the *Lumpenball*, middle-class humorous literature usually viewed this institution positively, seeing it as a celebration of Viennese *Gemütlichkeit*. For example, the humourist Eduard Pötzl wrote about the *Lumpenball* in 1885 in a very positive manner:

> ... Overall, there was an unprecedented crush, so that the most magnificent persons found themselves ignored, and were lost among the thousands in the turmoil. Here were the famous models from the Academy of Fine Arts, dancing their Napolitan tarantella to the bagpipes; over there, the robber and murderer Hugo Schenk – always immaculately elegant – inviting elderly ladies with savings books to follow him into the Schmelz; here a troop of the homeless marched by, with banners and badges and a deafening noise, while over there Bastian, the spiritualist medium in tailcoat and woollen socks, was being evicted from his corner; here was the famous Hanswurst of the suburbs, Rante-Potante, turning out his pocket games; over there was someone in startlingly badly cut trousers begging for donations for his tailor; and so on and so on. The oddest were the lonely beggars, with their serious, thoughtful expressions and heavy sacks on their backs, traipsing around for hours without knowing why they were giving themselves so much trouble. The noise was considerably increased by the sellers of the imaginatively illustrated magazine *Der Lump*, much appreciated among the peddlers. And in all this deafening uproar and confusion, all this unbridled freedom enjoyed by those attending the *Lumpenball* – the police were joining in smiling at such nonsense – nothing offensive took place; not even two of the ten thousand got into a fight; even in the densest crowd, when poked in the ribs, everyone had a jest on their lips. Wherever one looked, there were laughing faces, cheerful considerateness, a quiet drink or effervescent good spirits – no drunkenness, no coarseness, no meanness. Several foreigners, having been brought to see the *Lumpenball* by Viennese friends from the best society, commented that the people of Vienna displayed a kindly charm, benevolence and goodwill unparalleled in the world; and may they never lose these qualities, cherished over the centuries; may they never be taken away. And thus even the *Lumpenball* helps to spread the reputation of the Viennese people, in the mouths of strangers.[256]

Here the panorama of the misery and dangers of the suburbs, from beggars to the serial killer Schenk, is re-enacted by the bourgeoisie and turned into a jolly charade, which according to Pötzl had nothing *anstößig*, inappropriate or offensive in it, thus representing the amiability of the Viennese at its best. As far as I can see, Pötzl's account has no irony, but expresses a genuine enjoyment of the carnival topsy-turvy world in which the most horrible and tragic things could be turned into safe, amusing and civilized fun. Notably, as Pötzl points out, in this fantasy world the civilized light-heartedness of the 'finest society' has replaced negative attributes such as drunkenness or the coarseness associated with the lower classes. The grim social reality was turned into something theatrical, and the urban population groups and actual historical figures were transformed into fictional characters floating in the collective imaginary of the middle-class participants who entered this fantasy world, in which unsettling lower-class phenomena could be encountered safely in the realms of bourgeois masquerade.

Although there was more critical satire against the *Lumpenball* and other similar charity balls in the humorous magazines,[257] Eduard Pötzl's account demonstrates how the Viennese middle classes used the realms of humour in order to address urban poverty in alienated forms based on emotional detachment from the suffering of the poor. Furthermore, Pötzl's account of the *Lumpenball* also shows how in the bourgeois imagination urban poverty was associated with ideas about anonymity and criminality.[258] The masquerades did not feature only beggars and *Bettgeher*, but infamous petty criminals and notorious murderers as well. Violence and criminality played a vital role in imagining and defining modernity in the Viennese discourses on urbanity.

Towards the end of the century, the humorous magazines offered a strikingly vast quantity of jokes, anecdotes, poems and caricatures on topics relating to death and violence. Popular humour was increasingly fascinated by sensational and spectacular topics such as crimes and suicide, and these were often attributed as 'modern'. Murders, in particular, came to be seen in the last decades of the century as a symptom of modernity, an expression of a decline in morals and decency in the city. The urban surroundings were seen as generating criminal characters and undermining morality.[259] Urban poverty was thus increasingly incorporated into ideas of rootlessness and crime.[260] There was an important shift in the attitudes towards the underclasses, who were no longer idealized and made harmless through humorous imagination, but increasingly associated with danger, violence and death.[261]

This new fascination with death and morbid topics was related to a wider cultural turn, the emergence of *fin-de-siècle* melancholia, in which the optimism of the previous decades gave way to cultural pessimism and growing anxiety concerning the future. The turn of the century also introduced new interpretations of humour, as in 1905 Freud connected jokes with the unconscious, and in 1899 Henri Bergson argued that humour requires an 'anaesthesia of the heart', freedom from the sense of pity and compassion.[262] This new emphasis on emotional detachment was very different from the former idea that humour was connected to the ideas of sympathy and moral sense. In fact, the idea of emotional detachment did not merely transform the understanding of humour, but it became a distinctive feature in contemporary discussion on modern city life. Early urban sociologists such as Georg Simmel saw that the metropolitan environment, crowded by millions of lives, demanded a certain ironical distance and blasé attitude from the individuals living in it.[263] The cities had simply grown too big for people to care about each tragedy and human destiny within the great urban fabric. As the cultural historian Hannu Salmi has suggested, the *fin-de-siècle* culture should thus be seen in the context of those social processes that created major pressure in urban centres, while the old structures of class society nonetheless remained intact. This conflict became visible as moral panic in the face of the growth of the lower social strata.[264]

This clash created humour that mixed together different elements. On one hand, the press was often criticized for sensationalism.[265] On the other hand, humour was produced with an increasingly callous tone, as beggars were not presented as sympathetic and pitiful but shabby and greedy. Humour about violence and death of the lower classes related not only to the new demography of the growing metropolis, but also to the narrative patterns of the contemporary press, which brought the hidden side of underprivileged Vienna into bourgeois homes by reporting on brutal murders and other sad stories from the suburbs and lower-class districts.[266] Major Viennese newspapers like the *Neue Freie Presse*, *Die Presse* and *Wiener Zeitung* all reported on a range of criminal cases within and outside Vienna in great detail.[267] Members of the middle classes were thus confronted in their daily papers with a different kind of urban reality than that in which they themselves lived.

The cheap press, and especially the *Illustriertes Wiener Extrablatt*, which came out between 1872 and 1928, were mocked for feeding the hunger of the mass public.[268] Notably, the *Extrablatt* was founded by Ottokar Franz Ebersberg together with Franz Josef Singer. Ebersberg, who was the chief editor of the humorous magazine *Kikeriki*, also worked as editor of the *Extrablatt* during its first year of publication in 1872. *Extrablatt* started as a political-satirical magazine, but turned in the direction of the yellow press, offering sensational reports of murder cases and other scandalous incidents.[269] The paths of the humorous and sensational press in late nineteenth-century Vienna were thus intertwined on a very concrete level.

The situation in Vienna was very similar to other European capitals, as the press radically changed with the rise of the cheap press and yellow papers, which attracted the public's attention with the new, the spectacular and the scandalous.[270] The historian Gregory Shaya has suggested that in Paris in the second half of the nineteenth century the cheap press shaped a new understanding of the mass public, defined by sensations, emotions and curiosity, displacing the earlier, more abstract ideal of 'public opinion', which had been the constitutive concept in the late eighteenth and early nineteenth century – a tendency which

Jürgen Habermas has famously described as the decline of the public sphere.²⁷¹ In Vienna, the humorous magazines generally held the press responsible for creating fears through scandalous reports of disasters, wars, accidents, crimes and other misfortunes.²⁷²

Especially in the 1880s, murders and suicides were strongly associated with this modern urban experience. As mentioned earlier in this chapter, the case of the mass murderer Hugo Schenk was particularly extensively covered in the humorous magazines.²⁷³ In 1883, Hugo Schenk (1849–84), with his companion Karl Schlossarek (1858–84), murdered four female servants. Schenk entrapped his victims with romantic announcements in the newspapers, claiming to be looking for a marriage companion, when in fact he was after the savings of the maids, who fell for him in the hope of a respectable marriage. In committing his crimes, Schenk took advantage of the anonymity of the great city by adopting various fake identities, claiming to be a wealthy civil servant, an engineer and a Polish prince.²⁷⁴ Schenk's case became public in 1884 after he was caught and sent to trial, and it encapsulated many of the fears relating to the vast, labyrinth-like city. The sensational details of the horrible crimes, involving fake identities, newspaper ads and innocent single women lured in under the spell of a beautiful stranger, accentuated the fear of the city as a place of sexual danger and hidden violence.²⁷⁵

One way in which the *fin-de-siècle* pessimism that spread in the cultural atmosphere of the turn of the century became visible was in an increasing preoccupation in popular humour with the theme of suicide. Suicides were seen as reflecting the modern lack of joy in life.²⁷⁶ The way in which the press handled suicides was also criticized.²⁷⁷ This boom in morbid humour on suicides was not only a response to the narrative culture of the press, but the roots of this humour cycle were also in social reality, since, according to the historian Karl Vocelka, suicide rates peaked in Vienna in the years after 1873 following the stock market crash.²⁷⁸

This nineteenth-century black humour was typical not only of Vienna; similar morbid topics were popular in other cities as well. Olive Anderson notes that suicides were a frequent topic for jokes in Victorian London, where it was common practice to use wordplay and parody in creating humour about the most severe and tragic topics.²⁷⁹

Nonetheless, black humour and gallows humour have been particularly associated with Vienna, and a morbid trait has traditionally been seen as a highly constitutive part of Viennese mentality. Fascination with death was a fundamental feature in the Viennese way of thinking, with its roots in the baroque *memento mori* mentality. This fatalist melancholy has often been described as the counterpoint to Vienna's frivolous and joyful culture. William Johnston identifies a fascination with death as an essential feature of the aesthetic culture of *fin-de-siècle* Vienna, and associated with a certain urban sense of life marked by temporality and changeability. In a way, death was a symbol for the ephemeral nature of urban life.[280]

There was a long tradition of morbid stories and anecdotes in Vienna, and the seventeenth-century story of the poor man Augustin, who fell drunk into a plague grave, but survived because of his merry sense of humour, especially pleased the nineteenth-century humourists. Vinzenz Chiavacci, for instance, saw Augustin as a forefather of the later Viennese *Volkssänger*. Accordingly, although the story of Augustin, who overcame death with jolly merriment, dates from the seventeenth century, the famous song 'Ei, du lieber Augustin', celebrating Viennese humour that drives even the plague and death away from the city, was composed only in the nineteenth century.[281]

Towards the turn of the century, humour was increasingly seen as a way of overcoming distressing and frightening aspects of city life. This new understanding of humour was related to humour's new role in enduring the city rather than improving it. In the 1870s, as city life came to be perceived more and more through the cool colours of sorrow and misery, the humour magazines began to advertise themselves as medicine for the modern melancholy. *Figaro*'s motto for its first twenty years, for example, was 'Es wird alles Besser, durch Seife und Messer' (Everything is getting better, through soap and knife); from 1878 onwards, however, the new motto was:

> Only cheeky jokes
> Can free you from all your worries,
> Not only honest,
> But also cheerful will last longest![282]

Kikeriki and *Der Floh* did not have mottos, but in the 1880s these humorous magazines, too, set themselves the task of 'keeping up a cheerful spirit' in increasingly serious times, and this was their selling point when they tried to win new subscribers.[283]

There were, however, some topics that were considered too terrible to make fun of, such as the Mayerling tragedy in 1889, or the fire at the Ringtheater in 1881. *Kikeriki*, for instance, commented after the fire at the Ringtheater that humour was impossible in the face of such a disaster.[284] These were catastrophes that touched the whole empire, and the bourgeoisie itself; here, therefore, death was no laughing matter, as it had been in the tragedies of underclass Vienna.

Consequently, the meaning of humour changed between 1857 and 1890. In the early phase of the urban renewal, satirical humour was seen as a means of improving the city, but from the 1870s it was increasingly defined as a way of enduring the city. This shift can be explained in relation to various social and economic processes, such as population increase, the stock market crash of 1873, and the rise in the last decades of the century of the mass press and a new kind of sensational reporting that revolved around crimes and violence. By the turn of the century, humour lost its intimate connection with ideas like social conscience and moral sense, and increasingly meant an emotional distance and detachment from the distressful aspects of urban life, such as poverty and crime. These aspects were characteristically associated with the underclass, which links the change in the understanding of humour with a new kind of relationship to the urban underclass. The middle-class fantasies about the underclass changed from a sympathetic and idealized image of the 'respectable poor' to the idea of the 'grotesque and potentially dangerous' poor. The transformation of Vienna shaped the way in which the middle classes saw the urban pariahs of the city. And conversely, through humorous visions of the underclass, the bourgeoisie addressed change in the city. What the beggars on the Ringstraße, Hugo Schenk's murdered maids, and suicide victims in the suburbs all had in common was that they came from the unprivileged parts of society, and their sorrows were symptoms of larger social problems in Vienna, where the uncontrolled expansion of the city led to miserable conditions on the 'other side of Vienna', outside the upper- and middle-class districts. The press, however, brought these problems to the bourgeois consciousness, and humour and laughter transformed them into imaginative cultural fantasies.

Towards the turn of the century the Viennese humourists focused more enthusiastically than ever before on the new kinds of urban groups, characters and subjectivities created by the contemporary, modern Vienna.[285] This chapter has analysed the meanings of three comical figures associated with the modern city: the modern woman, the stranger and the beggar. These figures featuring in jokes and caricatures were distinctive, modern characters that did not belong to the assemblage of traditional Viennese types, as discussed, for example, in the volume *Wiener Typen: Klischees und Wirklichkeit* (2013).[286] In contrast to the pre-modern comical characters, these new types were related directly to the changing city space in the second half of the century.

As the closer examination of these comical characters has shown, in the Viennese humorous magazines modernity was associated with femininity, internationality, Jewishness and economic inequality. Accordingly, anti-modernist attitudes mingled with anti-feminism, antisemitism and anti-capitalism. Humour had an important role in creating and circulating clichés and stereotypes with a high affective potential, and the power to intensify or reduce emotional bonds between people.

The modern woman, the stranger and the beggar were in many respects unlike each other, but they had one common feature that connected them: they all represented some kind of marginality in relation to the middle-class male Austrian-German readers who were the main public for the humorous magazines discussed in this study.[287] Humour around marginal or otherwise borderline figures was related to middle-class concerns about the transformation of the city and to the pursuit of reinforcing a masculine, German-Austrian bourgeois ethos and culture in an era of radical changes. However, in contrast to the traditional Viennese comical types of the *Gründerzeit*, such as the *Blumenmädchen* (flower girl), *Stubenmädchen* (maid) or *Schusterbuben* (shoemaker's boy), who also represented the city's non-bourgeois groups, strangers, modern women and beggars were strongly associated with the city's transformation.

Through these figures, the middle-class audience addressed a range of distressful contradictions caused by the modernization process: tensions between locality and the global level, between nationalism and internationalization, between rising capitalism and urban poverty. In the liberal era, not only the absolutist rule of the Emperor, but also the traditional Catholic patriarchal order of the old regime, came to a turning point, as the old hierarchies and categories of social life lost power and validity. As the Jewish influence on Viennese *Witzblätter* and the case of women readers show, popular humour was not simply imprinted with the social prejudices of the era, but constituted a heterogeneous arena that enabled many kinds of voices to be heard. Yet the recurring patterns of jokes and cartoons strengthened awareness of contrasts rather than similarities between different urban groups; the encounters between the Viennese and strangers, or between the rich and the poor, were comical because their experiences of life were presented as radically incompatible. As the urban population became more and more dispersed and heteronomous, the humorous press relied on familiar stereotypes that stressed stereotypical differences between people of different class, gender or ethnic origin. Humour based on binary contrasts between different urban groups actively defined and excluded certain identities outside and in opposition to the middle-class community, and in this sense humour about urban types and characters was reinforcing cultural boundaries rather than challenging them.

Notes

1. Parts of this chapter have been previously published in Heidi Hakkarainen, 'Humor, Satire und Karikatur: Das humoristische Imaginarium der Wiener Ringstraße', in Harald R. Stühlinger (ed.), *Vom Werden der Wiener Ringstraße* (Vienna, 2015), 220–43; Heidi Hakkarainen, 'Koomisia kohtaamisia: Monikansallisen kaupungin ristiriidat 1800-luvun lopun wieniläisessä huumorissa', in Anne Ollila and Juhana Saarelainen (eds), *Kosmopoliittisuus, monikulttuurisuus, kansainvälisyys: Kulttuurihistoriallisia näkökulmia* (Turku, 2013), 106–31.
2. For example, *Der Floh*, 4 September 1887. See also 'Auf dem Ringstraßen-corso', *Der Floh*, 14 March 1886; 'Die Fatalen Moden', *Kikeriki*, 8 November 1869; 'Schrecklichen Folge der modernen Trachtenverwirrung', *Kikeriki*, 14 January 1875; 'Fluch der Kurzsichtigkeit', *Kikeriki*, 13 September 1885.
3. Harriet Anderson, *Utopian Feminism: Women's Movements in Fin-de-siècle Vienna* (New Haven, 1992), 25–38 and passim; Scott Spector, *Violent Sensations: Sex, Crime & Utopia in Vienna and Berlin, 1860–1914* (Chicago, 2016), 2.

4. On the research tradition on humour and gender, see, e.g., June Sochen, 'Introduction', in June Sochen (ed.), *Women's Comic Visions* (Detroit, 1991), 9–16; Gail Finney, 'Introduction: Unity in Difference?', in Gail Finney (ed.), *Look Who's Laughing: Gender and Comedy* (Philadelphia, 1994), 1–13; Joanne R. Gilbert, *Performing Marginality: Humor, Gender and Cultural Critique* (Detroit, 2004).
5. Elisabeth Wilson, *The Sphinx in the City: Urban Life, the Control of Disorder, and Women* (Berkeley, 1992), 87; Rita Felski, *The Gender of Modernity* (Cambridge, MA, 1995), 4–6; Spector, *Violent Sensations*, 173–74.
6. The name Vindobona derives from the Celtic: *windo* 'white' + *bona* 'ground or land-holding'.
7. 'Es ist mein Wille', *Wiener Zeitung*, 25 December 1857.
8. Uns Allen ist gar wohl bekannt / Die alte Stadtkokette / Mit Bastionen-Miederband / Und Ringwall-Toilette. / Sie trägt ein Kontre-Eskarpenkleid / Und heißt noch von der Römerzeit / Die 'alte Vindobona'. // Und item ist uns wohlbekannt / Herr Stephansdom, ihr Buhle / Und allezeit treuer Amant, / noch von der alten Schule; / Er trägt, weil ihm ein Saus und Braus / Die grauen Haare gingen aus, / Jetzt eine Tour von Eisen ... 'Wiens Herz-Erweiterung', *Figaro*, 3 January 1858.
9. See further the section 'Nostalgia for *Alt-Wien*' in chapter 4.
10. ... Drum wend ich mich anjetzt in meinem Herzenleid / An Dich als einziger Trost, du junge Wiener-Maid, / Du (mindestens in spe) gar wohl gebaute Jungfrau, / Ob auch mein Angstruf klingt (wie billig) steinern, dumpf, rauh, / Schau auff [*sic*] die Worte nicht, schau nur holdseelig an / Mit deiner stolzen Front mich alten Partisan! / Den Apfel deiner Gunst, halt ihn nicht allzufern, / Sei mit verbanntem Mars ein heller Venus-Stern! – / Und wann den letzten Schwung thut meines Glückes Rad, / Wenn unter Ziegelrauch mein letztes Stündlein naht, / Und man (graunvoll [*sic*] zu sehn!) mich in den Graben stürzt, / *Dir* aber neuer Lenz die Luft mit Violen würzet, / Und statt um Bollwerkh du ... wandelst um Boulevards ... / Ein weiches Herz sodann bewahr, und nicht ein hart's, / O denk dann immerdar treu in Erinnernuß / An mich alten Kumpan, den Bastionarus! 'Wiener Heroiden-Briefe. I Herr Bastionarus an Jungfer Vienna Nova', *Figaro*, 24 January 1858. Original emphasis.
11. Die Wort-Bomben, die gewichtig Deinem Eisenmund entflossen, / Haben eine starke Bresche in mein schwaches Herz geschossen; / Mittendrin in Jungfrauherzen – von der Alservorstadt Saum / Bis zum Schottentore – klafft der weite Breschen-Raum // Alter Eisenfresser, glaub mir, daß ich längst geschrieben hätte, / Wär ich nicht zu sehr beschäftigt jetzt mit meiner ... Toilette; / Katastral-Marschandemoden laufen bei mir ab und zu, / Und die Schneider Architekten lassen mir schon gar nicht Ruh'! 'Wiener Heroiden-Briefe. II. Jungfer Vienna Nova an Herrn Bastionarus', *Figaro*, 7 February 1858.
12. Für den Tod des 'alten Pfunders' wächst kein Kraut und wächst kein Kräutchen, / Drum Du alter Partisan, laß Dir vergeh'n das junge Bräutchen: / 'Altes stürzt im Zeitenwechsel ... Neues blüht aus dem Ruin', / Bastionarus stürzt in Trümmer und aufblüht Jungfrau Neu-Wien. Ibid.
13. See, e.g., Richard Sennett, *Flesh and Stone: The Body and the City in Western Civilization* (New York, 1996), 22–26.
14. Frau Vindobona hatte nach und nach neue Kleider bekommen; von dem alten Zeug wurde Stück für Stück abgelegt und durch neue Moden ersetzt, und auch ein *prachtvoller Ring* wurde ihr zum Schmucke verliehen; alles das schmeichelte ihrer Eitelkeit und

sie mußte daher mit Betrübniß wahrnehmen, daß ihr noch ein eleganter Schirm fehlte. Nachdem überdies ihre Nachbarinnen, die Madame France und die Lady Brittania die neue Mode bereits mitgemacht hatten, stieg ihre Sehnsucht von Tag zu Tag und wie die Damen immer ihren Wunsch durchsetzen – sie hat ihn richtig bekommen! 'Frau Vindobona', *Kikeriki*, 3 April 1873. Original emphasis. On the allegory between clothes and the representational function of city architecture, see also 'Festgewand und Werktagskleid', *Figaro*, 14 May 1881.

15. Wilson, *Sphinx in the City*, 47; Ritva Hapuli, *Nykyajan sininen kukka: Olavi Paavolainen ja nykyaika* (Helsinki, 1995), 110–15.
16. See especially 'Die Wahrheit auf Besuch bei der Madame Vindobona', *Kikeriki*, 6 October 1864.
17. AT-OeStA HHStA SB Sammlung Wagner Theaterzettel 1-5-22. In fact, theatre comedies seem to have been an important forum for discussing questions of modernity and gender; parallel to the discussion in the humorous magazines, plays were put on in the Theater an der Wien and the k.k. Carl Theater with titles like *Einen Jux will sie machen, Die Weiber wie sie nicht sein sollen, Die schlimmen Töchter* and *Die alte Jungfer*. AT-OeStA HHStA SB Sammlung Wagner Theaterzettel 1-5-10–1-6-41.
18. … Na ja, i komm' jetzt in die Jahre, / Wo mi die Schnürbrust arg schenirt, / Die mir, es is a Noth, a wahre, / Mit jeder Wochen enger wird. // I ruck' und dehn' mi voller Grausen, / I kann net Luft mehr kriegen gnua, / Weil in dem Mieder i net pfnausen / Und nimmer athmen können thua … Klage der Vindobona. 'In Linienwall-Angelegenheiten', *Der Floh*, 30 September 1888.
19. See, for example, 'Monolog der Vindobona', *Figaro*, 22 December 1866.
20. Karl Vocelka, *K.u.K. Karikaturen und Karikaturen zum Zeitalter Kaiser Franz Josephs* (Vienna, 1986), 17. The changing age structure and predominance of young people were characteristic of other growing metropolitan nineteenth-century cities as well. See further Wilson, *Sphinx in the City*, 48; David Harvey, *Paris, Capital of Modernity* (New York, 2006), 196.
21. Carl E. Schorske, *Fin-de-siècle Vienna: Politics and Culture* (Cambridge, [1961] 1981), 4–5, 212 and passim.
22. See, for example, Judith R. Walkowitz, *City of Dreadful Delight: Narratives of Sexual Danger in Late-Victorian London* (Chicago, 1992) on London; Harvey, *Paris* and Wilson, *Sphinx in the City* on Paris; Ann Taylor Allen, *Satire and Society in Wilhelmine Germany: Kladderadatsch & Simplicissimus 1890–1914* (Lexington, 1984) on Berlin. The cultural historian Ritva Hapuli has noted that after World War I, gender was an important discursive topic for broaching cultural fears related to modernity. Hapuli, *Nykyajan*, 76–77.
23. Wilson, *Sphinx in the City*, 8; Felski, *Gender of Modernity*, 1–10; Ute Frevert, *Mann und Weib und Weib und Mann: Geschlechter-Differenzen in der Moderne* (Munich, 1995), 24–29.
24. See Wilson, *Sphinx in the City*, 9.
25. However, recent research has emphasized that already in early modern cities women had a more visible role in public life than had been previously thought.
26. See further Wilson, *Sphinx in the City*, 5–11 and passim; Walkowitz, *City of Dreadful Delight*, 41–80; Hannu Salmi, *Nineteenth-Century Europe: A Cultural History* (Cambridge, 2008), 94–97.
27. David Frisby, *Cityscapes of Modernity: Critical Explorations* (Cambridge, 2001), 193–94.

28. Walkowitz, *City of Dreadful Delight*, 1–13 and passim; Wilson, *Sphinx in the City*, 6.
29. Wilson, *Sphinx in the City*, 8.
30. Anderson, *Utopian Feminism*, 9.
31. See further ibid., 57–63; Karl Vocelka, *Geschichte Österreichs: Kultur-Gesellschaft-Politik* (Munich, 2011), 228–31.
32. Allen, *Satire and Society*, 160, 167.
33. Cf. Felski, *Gender of Modernity*, 210.
34. See, e.g., 'Moderne Frauen', *Der Floh*, 4 July 1886.
35. 'Moderne Jugend', *Kikeriki*, 4 December 1873; 'Stundeneintheilung unserer modernen Jungfrauen', *Der Floh*, 13 October 1878; 'Und da wundern sich die Leut', *Figaro*, 14 June 1879 / *Wiener Luft* No. 24; 'Die moderne Jungfrau', *Kikeriki*, 22 February 1880; 'Die moderne Jungfrau', *Kikeriki*, 13 February 1881.
36. Michael Billig, *Laughter and Ridicule: Towards a Social Critique of Humour* (London, 2012), 236–43.
37. Along similar lines, the Austrian historian Karl Vocelka has noted that late nineteenth-century cartoons repeatedly made use of the class-specific image of middle-class women as brainless creatures, only interested in clothes, fashion and lovers. Vocelka, *K.u.K. Karikaturen*, 92.
38. 'Eine Moderne Frau muss', *Kikeriki*, 7 December 1873.
39. Anu Korhonen, *Silmän ilot: Kauneuden kulttuurihistoriaa uuden ajan alussa* (Jyväskylä, 2005), 98–103.
40. Georg Simmel, *Suurkaupunki ja moderni elämä: Kirjoituksia vuosilta 1895–1917*, trans. Tiina Huuhtanen, ed. Arto Noro (Helsinki, 2005), 100–102.
41. Richard Sennett, *The Fall of Public Man* (Cambridge, 1977), 19–22.
42. 'Naturzauber', *Der Floh*, 3 August 1884. On the intersection of fashion and modern urban culture in Vienna, see further Susan Ingram and Markus Reisenleitner, *Wiener Chic: A Locational History of Vienna Fashion* (Bristol, 2013), 10–15 and passim.
43. Allan Janik and Stephen Toulmin, *Wittgenstein's Vienna* (Chicago, [1973] 1996), 47.
44. Mary L. Wagener, 'Fashion and Feminism in "Fin de Siecle" Vienna', *Woman's Art Journal* 10(2) (1989), 30–31, 29–33. See also Hapuli, *Nykyajan*, 63, 164–65.
45. On the performative aspects of constructing gender, see further Judith Butler, *Gender Trouble* (New York, 1999), 9–11.
46. 'Modebild', *Der Floh*, 15 November 1885. On the theme of artificiality, see also 'Wiener Modezeitung', *Kikeriki*, 1 November 1869; 'Galant', *Der Floh*, 7 February 1886; 'Discrete Frage', *Der Floh*, 29 December 1889.
47. 'Neueste Damen-Moden', *Figaro*, 15 January 1876 / *Wiener Luft* No. 3; 'Die moderne Tournüre und ihre praktische Verwendung', *Der Floh*, 4 May 1884; 'Cule Betrachtung', *Der Floh*, 13 June 1886.
48. Cf. section 'Laughing at Chaos' in chapter 3.
49. E.g. 'Wiener Saison-Studien', *Der Floh*, 16 February 1873; 'Die neueste Mode', *Kikeriki*, 25 January 1880; 'Original-Gigerl-Modeblatt für das Jahr 1888', *Figaro*, 31 March 1888 / *Wiener Luft* No. 13. On the cultural imaginaries related to body shapes in the early modern period, see Korhonen, *Silmän ilot*, 49–72.
50. See, for example, 'Die neuesten Wiener Passage-Hindernisse', *Kikeriki*, 2 July 1862; 'Neue Erfindung für Damen bei Regenwetter', *Kikeriki*, 19 November 1863; 'Das Gewand wird immer weniger', *Kikeriki*, 29 July 1877; 'Zur Mode', *Figaro*, 24 April 1884 / *Wiener Luft* No. 21.

51. 'Neuester Modebericht aus Paris', *Kikeriki*, 4 December 1862.
52. 'Wiener Croquis fon Quiqueriqui', *Kikeriki*, 31 July 1873.
53. 'Sehen unsere modern angezogenen Fräuleins nicht den Rittern von anno Dazumal gleich?', *Kikeriki*, 7 January 1864; 'Kellner (zu dem abgehenden Paare)', *Figaro*, 12 July 1879 / *Wiener Luft* No. 28; 'Zur Mode', *Kikeriki*, 16 October 1879; 'Wiener Bilderbogen', *Der Floh*, 9 October 1887.
54. See, for instance, 'Der Gigerl und sein Ring', *Der Floh*, 28 April 1889; 'Der Gipfel Des Pschütt', *Der Floh*, 1 June 1890.
55. Cf. Simmel, *Suurkaupunki ja moderni elämä*, 105; Hapuli, *Nykyajan*, 169–76.
56. As Anu Korhonen has suggested, humour is always related to a specific historical, cultural and social context and laughter involves processes of apprehension and interpretation. Anu Korhonen, *Kiusan henki: Sukupuoli ja huumori uuden ajan alussa* (Jyväskylä, 2013), 11.
57. Henri Bergson, *Nauru: Tutkimus komiikan merkityksestä*. French original: *Le Rire. Essai sur la signification du comique* (1900) (Helsinki, 1994), 32–33.
58. For example Wilson, *Sphinx in the City*, 7, 89.
59. Peter Stallybrass and Allon White, *The Politics and Poetics of Transgression* (London, 1986), 6, 188–90.
60. See Mikhail Bakhtin, *Rabelais and His World* (Bloomington, 1984), 8–18; Stallybrass and White, *Politics and Poetics*, 6–26. On the carnival culture of the Viennese nineteenth-century urban lower classes, see Wolfgang Maderthaner and Lutz Musner, *Unruly Masses: The Other Side of the Fin-de-siècle Vienna* (New York, 2008), 80–94.
61. See, e.g., Ingram and Reisenleitner, *Wiener Chic*, 53. The humorous magazines also published announcements for coming balls in the famous Schwender's Kolosseum and other places of entertainment, as well as advertisements for costumes.
62. See, e.g., Carl Sitter, *Modernes Wien: Humoristische Federzeichnungen* (Vienna, 1859); Friedrich Schlögl, *Wiener Luft: Kleine Culturbilder aus dem Volksleben der alten Kaiserstadt* (Vienna, 1876); and Eduard Pötzl, 'Lumpenball', in *Jung-Wien. Allerhand wienerische Skizzen. Hochdeutsch und in der Muttersprach* (Berlin, 1885).
63. The themes of cross-dressing and turning gender roles upside down occur especially in *Der Floh* and *Figaro*, less so in *Kikeriki*. This may reflect the fact that *Kikeriki* was, especially from the 1880s, more conservative than the other two magazines. Another plausible reason is the fact that *Kikeriki* was aimed at the lower middle classes, who probably had less experience of the balls and merry-making of high society. Perhaps these two things combined made *Kikeriki* less experimental when it came to playing with gender roles and hierarchies. It had no similar kind of intimate relationship with the masquerades as the other two humorous magazines.
64. Terry Castle, *Masquerade and Civilization: The Carnivalesque in Eighteenth-Century English Culture and Fiction* (London, 1986), 4–5.
65. Ibid., 6. Compare humour's tradition of the reversal of the ordinary, serious world. Billig, *Laughter and Ridicule*, 4; Simon Critchley, *On Humour* (New York, 2002), 1.
66. Castle, *Masquerade and Civilization*, 5–6, 22.
67. Cf. Arthur Koestler, *The Act of Creation* (London, 1964), 56, 68.
68. See, e.g., Eric A. Nicholson, '"That's How It Is": Comic Travesties of Sex and Gender in Early Sixteenth-Century Venice', in Finney, *Look Who's Laughing*, 17–34.
69. Ist auch ein stuck vom neuen Wien! / Die Damen werden mehr und mehr emanzipirt, / Bis endlich sie ihr Wunsch zu Männerkleider führt / Und sie's gelüstet, Höschen

anzuzieh'n. / Geht das so fort, so hört die Männerherrschaft auf / Und es verändert die Geschichte ihren Lauf. / Doch hat bis jetzt das schönere Geschlecht / Im Karneval allein nur Herrenrecht – / In manchem Hause geht es freilich fortan, / Da hat die Frau durch ganze Jahr die Hosen an! Hilarius Jocosus Jocus (pseud.), *Die Neuzeit im Elysium oder das lustige Wien nebst einigen Umgebungen im allerneuesten rosenfarbigsten Humor tief unter der Erde* (Vienna, 1862–63), 5.

70. Wilson, *Sphinx in the City*, 52, 61–62. Later, after World War I, in the popular literature there emerged new kinds of modern and free female figures, such as *la Garçonne*, the *bachelor girl* and the *flapper*. See further Hapuli, *Nykyajan*, 74–77, 159–60.
71. Maderthaner and Musner, *Unruly Masses*, 85.
72. For example, the newspaper *Die Presse* published Sand's novel in the feuilleton section in the 1860s. *Die Presse*, 6 February 1862.
73. Maderthaner and Musner, *Unruly Masses*, 85.
74. Stallybrass and White, *Politics and Poetics*, 2–4.
75. 'Im weiblichen Zukunftsgymnasium', *Der Floh*, 29 April 1888.
76. William M. Johnston, *The Austrian Mind: An Intellectual and Social History 1848–1938* (Berkeley, 1983), 118. Double standards of morality for men and women were typical for Vienna. Anderson, *Utopian Feminism*, 2.
77. See, e.g., 'Zum Mozartsjubiläum', *Der Floh*, 30 October 1887; 'Abgeschlagene Attaque', *Der Floh*, 17 March 1889.
78. See, for example, 'Den Frauen das letzte Wort', *Der Floh*, 30 December 1888; 'Zur Frauen-Emancipation', *Der Floh*, 26 May 1889.
79. Wilson, *Sphinx in the City*, 87–88.
80. See, for instance, Johnston, *Austrian Mind*, 115–19.
81. 'Die Ausschließung der Damen von öffentlichen Besuche der Universität', *Der Floh*, 9 June 1878; 'Zum Kapitel "Frauen-Emanzipation"', *Figaro*, 5 February 1881 / *Wiener Luft* No. 6; 'Die Rechte der Frauen', *Der Floh*, 28 March 1886; 'Das Wahlrecht der Frauen', *Der Floh*, 30 December 1888; 'Weibliche Barbiere. Zum Capitel "Frauenarbeit"', *Der Floh*, 13 April 1890; 'Auf der Straße', *Kikeriki*, 26 October 1890.
82. 'Wenn die Frauen prakticiren werden', *Der Floh*, 19 May 1889.
83. Anderson, *Utopian Feminism*, 1–9.
84. Ibid., 1–2, 21.
85. Band Österreichischer Frauenvereine was founded in 1902.
86. Marianne Hainisch, *Die Brodfrage der Frau* (Vienna, 1875), 4, 30.
87. See, e.g., Gilbert, *Performing Marginality*, xv.
88. See further ibid., 8–9; Finney, *Look Who's Laughing*, 6–7.
89. Korhonen, *Kiusan henki*, 9–15.
90. See, for example, 'Eine Kikeriki Freundin. Kleine Post der Redaction', *Kikeriki*, 6 February 1862; 'Aufmerksame Leserin. Kleine Post der Redaction', *Kikeriki*, 24 March 1864; 'Philippine N. Kleine Post der Redaction', *Kikeriki*, 22 June 1865; 'Literarische Freundin. Kleine Post der Redaction', *Kikeriki*, 14 May 1868; 'Eifrige "Floh" Leserin. Korrespondenz', *Der Floh*, 28 November 1869; 'Verehrerin. Kleine Post der Redaction', *Kikeriki*, 29 May 1871; 'Langjährige Leserin. Kleine Post der Redaktion', *Kikeriki*, 10 November 1881; 'Frl. Emma', *Figaro*, 16 July 1881; 'Verehrerin des "Figaro"', *Figaro*, 17 June 1882; 'Wienerin', *Figaro*, 26 April 1890.
91. Eine Dame. Ihren vortrefflichen Gedanken werden Sie in der heutigen Nummer verwendet finden.

92. 'Monika. Sehr lustig', *Kikeriki*, 18 September 1879; 'Eifrige Leserin … Wir bewundern Ihren scharfen Geist', *Figaro*, 12 February 1881; 'W. … obwohl wir unter diesem W eine geistreiche Einsenderin vermuthen … Correspondenz der Redaktion', *Der Floh*, 15 January 1888.
93. 'Fr.H. Schreckliche Verse', *Figaro*, 12 March 1881; 'Fr.H. Vorsündfluthlich', *Figaro*, 4 February 1882; 'Fr.H. Warum sollen wir das abdrucken?', *Figaro*, 18 August 1883; 'Fr.H. Das Meiste leider veraltet. Eine Bildidee wird verwendet', *Figaro*, 29 March 1890.
94. See also 'Aufmerksame Leserin. Kleine Post der Redaktion', *Kikeriki*, 15 November 1863.
95. On fake identities, see further the section 'Censorship, Satire and the Public Sphere' in chapter 1. Cf. also the case of 'Mrs. Emma' in the Hungarian periodical *A Hét*. Mary Gluck, *The Invisible Jewish Budapest: Metropolitan Culture at the Fin de Siècle* (Madison, 2016), 190–201.
96. E.g. *Kikeriki*, 1 June 1865; *Der Floh*, 8 August 1869; *Der Floh*, 2 January 1870; *Der Floh*, 3 April 1870; *Figaro*, 28 January 1882; *Figaro*, 7 August 1886; *Kikeriki*, 1 April 1888; *Der Floh*, 20 January 1889.
97. Andreas Graf and Susanne Pellatz, 'Familien- und Unterhaltungszeitschriften', in Georg Jäger (ed.), *Geschichte des Deutschen Buchhandels im 19. und 20. Jahrhundert*. Band 1. *Das Kaiserreich 1871–1918* (Frankfurt am Main, 2003), 480–96.
98. Ferdinand Manussi von Montesole (1839–1908).
99. 'Sämmtlichen Gelehrten des "Floh" freundlichst gewidmet.' Fritz Mai, *Der Floh: Localer Scherz mit Gesang in Einem Akt* (Vienna, 1869), 2.
100. Mai, *Der Floh*, 5–32.
101. On the political development of the 1860s, see further Vocelka, *Geschichte Österreichs*, 216–20.
102. Gabriele (setzt sich). So – jetzt werd' n wir uns dieser Lektüre widmen – hahaha! – Ich muß lachen wenn ich das G'sicht denk', das mein Mann machet, – wenn er mich dabei treffet, – das macht mich oft recht ärgerlich, daß ich gewisse Dinge, wie ein klein's Kind, nur verstohlen lesen darf, – 's ist ihn nicht einmal recht, wenn ich Briefe von meiner Jugendfreundin krieg', weil die immer so lustig schreibt, neulich meinte er gar, so soll ich Hirtenbriefe lesen, das ist viel patriotischer. (Sieht in das Blatt) Nein, diese Zeichnungen auf der ersten Seite sind schon famos, wann's mich nur auch einmal h'neinzeichneten, – ich wäre sehr neugierig wie's karikirten. (Man klopft) Himmel, 's kommt wer. (Versteckt schnell das Blatt) 's ist rein, als ob's nicht sein sollt. – (Aergerlich) Herein! Mai, *Der Floh*, 9.
103. This notion, again, contradicts the prevailing nineteenth-century understanding of women lacking the ability to enjoy or produce humour. Defining women as lacking a sense of humour was a major part of making gender distinctions. Furthermore, defining women as humourless was also a way of excluding them from the realms of public life and justifying their social domination by men. Women were seen as emotional and non-intellectual, lacking the intellectual capacity to understand incongruity and ambiguous meanings. They were seen as too sensitive and not aggressive enough to make jokes. Daniel Wickberg, *Senses of Humor: Self and Laughter in Modern America* (Ithaca, 1998), 92–95. According to June Sochen, the nineteenth-century theorists of humour such as Henri Bergson and Sigmund Freud agreed, despite their different approaches to laughter, that women had no sense of humour. Sochen, 'Introduction', 9–10. The

nineteenth-century discussions reinforced and were part of a long tradition of separating women from the field of the humorous and defining their sense of humour as different from men's. See further Gilbert, *Performing Marginality*, 26–29; Korhonen, *Kiusan henki*, 27; Finney, *Look Who's Laughing*, 5. Debates on women's humour have gained academic interest in scholarly discussions, especially since the 1980s. Joanne R. Gilbert makes the distinction between 'women's' humour and 'feminist' humour, the latter having emerged in the 1960s by the second wave of the women's movement and aiming to challenge and reform the prevailing gender system. Gilbert, *Performing Marginality*, 30–31.

104. See, e.g., 'Irrthum eines Fremden', *Kikeriki*, 8 October 1868; 'Wien in der Fremdesaison', *Der Figaro*, 5 August 1876 / *Wiener Luft* No. 32; 'Irrthum eines Zugereisten', *Kikeriki*, 18 August 1881; 'Verzeichlicher Irrthum', *Der Floh*, 4 April 1886.
105. See, e.g., 'Was die Fremden über Wien sagen', *Figaro*, 29 July 1876 / *Wiener Luft* No. 31; 'Kikeriki als Fremdenführer', *Kikeriki*, 21 May 1885.
106. See, e.g., Susanne Schäfer, *Komik in Kultur und Kontext* (Munich, 1996), 16–17, 42–43.
107. Jacob and Wilhelm Grimm, *Deutsches Wörterbuch* (Leipzig, 1873), 1625. See also Hakkarainen, 'Koomisia', 112.
108. See further Korhonen, *Kiusan henki*, 22 and passim.
109. Cf. Christie Davies, *Ethnic Humour around the World: A Comparative Analysis* (Bloomington, 1990), 10.
110. Michael Billig, *Banal Nationalism* (London, 2004), 1–2.
111. Benedict Anderson, *Imagined Communities: Reflections on the Origin and Spread of Nationalism* (London, [1983] 1991), 1–7.
112. Billig, *Banal Nationalism*, 8–9.
113. See Julian Brigstocke, *The Life of the City: Space, Humour, and the Experience of Truth in Fin-de-siècle Montmartre* (Surrey, 2014), 24; Billig, *Laughter and Ridicule*, 236–43; Jefferson S. Chase, *Inciting Laughter: The Development of 'Jewish Humor' in 19th Century German Culture* (Berlin, 2000), 2.
114. Laßt den 'Punch' am Themsestrande, an der Sein' den 'Charivari', / An den Spree 'Kladderadatschen' treiben nur ihr Larifari! / 'Sehe Jeder, wie er's treibe': Anders ziemt sich anderswo, – / Doch die 'Wien' zu reguliren überlaßt dem Figaro. 'An das Publikum!', *Figaro*, 18 January 1857. See also 'Wir haben Humor', *Figaro*, 27 March 1875.
115. See, e.g., Salmi, *Nineteenth-Century Europe*, 52–62, 151.
116. The number of hotel guests in the city increased from 181,088 in 1882 to 363,691 in 1897 and to 443,713 in 1903. Frisby, *Cityscapes*, 193.
117. It was prohibited to stay in the city without permission. Everybody living in Vienna, permanently or as a visitor, had to be registered by the officials of the city district. See further Bertrand Michael Buchmann, 'Dynamik des Städtebaus', in Peter Csendes and Ferdinand Oppl (eds), *Wien - Geschichte einer Stadt: Von 1790 bis zur Gegenwart* (Vienna, 2006), 69–70.
118. See, e.g., 'Fremde in Wien', *Der Floh*, 13 August 1876.
119. 'Irrthum eines Fremden', *Kikeriki*, 8 October 1868.
120. See, e.g., 'Verläßlicher Wegweiser durch die belebtesten Gassen und Straßen der Stadt Wien', *Kikeriki*, 23 July 1868.
121. See, e.g., 'Ein Lohndiener zeigt einem Fremden Wiens Merkwürdigkeiten', *Figaro*, 23 September 1882 / *Wiener Luft* No. 38.

122. See Franz Masaidek, *Wien und die Wiener aus der Spottvogelperspektive: Wien's Sehens-, Merk- und Nichtswürdigkeiten* (Vienna, 1873); Franz Ullmayer, *Wiener Volksleben: Ein humoristisches Bädecker bei der Weltausstellung* (Vienna, 1873). The literary conventions of travel guides and handbooks were used as subtexts for humorous texts published in the *Witzblätter* as well. See, e.g., 'Kurzgefaßte Geographie von Wien', *Figaro*, 28 May 1887 / *Wiener Luft* No. 22.

123. Franz Masaidek, *Staberl als Fremdenführer in Wien und Umgebung* (Vienna, 1868). See also advertisement in the *Figaro* magazine on 1 August 1868. Notably, the two characters embody the competition between Vienna and Berlin on a symbolic level: whereas Piefecke (Piefke) is a traditional scoffing name for the Prussians, Staberl as a literary figure was originally invented for the Viennese popular theatre in the early nineteenth century. The name Piefke originates from composer Johann Gottfried Piefke (1815–84), who composed a victory march to celebrate Prussia's victory over Austria in the battle of Königgrätz. Peter Wehle, *Sprechen Sie Wienerisch? Von Adaxl bis Zwutschkerl* (Vienna, 1980), 29. Originally, the Staberl figure was created by Adolf Bäuerle (1786–1859) for his comedy *Die Bürger in Wien* (1813). Staberl continued to be a popular character in the nineteenth-century Viennese theatre (Alt-Wiener Volkstheater). This new rivalry composition between an Austrian-German and a Prussian was related to the Austro-Prussian War in the 1860s, in which Austria was defeated by Prussia in the battle of Königgrätz in 1866. The defeat separated Austrian-Germans from other Germans and buried the *grossdeutsch* idea when the German Empire united without Austria in 1871. On the pan-German movement in Austria, see further Schorske, *Fin-de-siècle Vienna*, 116–46; Alan Sked, *The Decline & Fall of the Habsburg Empire 1815–1918* (London, 1989), 226–31.

124. See, e.g., 'Kikeriki als Fremdenführer', *Kikeriki*, 29 January 1863.

125. Irit Rogoff, 'Gustav Klimt, a Bridgehead to Modernism', in László Péter and Robert B. Pysent (eds), *Intellectuals and the Future in the Habsburg Monarchy 1890–1914* (London, 1988), 32–33; Carl E. Schorske, *Thinking with History: Explorations in the Passage to Modernism* (Princeton, 1998), 109; Schorske, *Fin-de-siècle Vienna*, 24–62.

126. Frisby, *Cityscapes*, 134.

127. According to a word frequency search on the ANNO database, the word *Weltstadt* emerged in the press within the Habsburg Empire 1,575 times between 1833 and 1869 and 5,674 times between 1870 and 1906. Austrian Newspapers Online, Österreichisches Nationalbibliothek, www.anno.ac.at (accessed 26 August 2015).

128. See, e.g., 'Die neue Invasion', *Der Floh*, 2 March 1884.

129. 'Spaziergang durch den verschönerten Zukunfts-Prater', *Kikeriki*, 7 April 1872; 'Im Kaffeehaus', *Kikeriki*, 6 October 1872; 'Um Gottes Willen nicht wienerisch!', *Kikeriki*, 11 January 1877; 'Kein Wien mehr in Wien', *Kikeriki*, 23 October 1879; 'In der deutschen Stadt Wien', *Kikeriki*, 8 May 1881.

130. Marion Linhardt, *Residenzstadt und Metropole: Zu einer kulturellen Topographie des Wiener Unterhaltungstheaters (1858–1918)* (Berlin, 2012), 209, 33–34, 131–40.

131. Katharina Fóti-Roessler, *Theoretische Auseinandersetzungen mit der Wiener Stadterweiterung ab 1857 an Hand der Allgemeinen Bauzeitung* (Ph.D. diss., Vienna, 1992), 11–12.

132. 'Platz für die Fremden', *Kikeriki*, 7 April 1872; 'Ein Festzug', *Kikeriki*, 16 February 1873; 'Alles für die Fremden', *Kikeriki*, 27 April 1873.

133. 'Die Wiener und die Weltaustellung', *Kikeriki*, 25 February 1872.

134. See, e.g., 'Wiener Skizzen aus dem Tagebuche eines reisenden Engländers', *Figaro*, 8 January 1858; 'Die Wiener und die Weltausstellung', *Der Floh*, 10 May 1873.
135. 'Der Bakonnerwald auf dem Schottenring', *Kikeriki*, 8 December 1872; 'Welausstellungs-Bilder', *Figaro*, 3 May 1873; 'Zwecmäßige Situation', *Kikeriki*, 8 May 1873; 'Auf der Straße vor dem Bahnhof', *Kikeriki*, 22 May 1873; 'Der kleine Weltausstellungs-Rathgeber', *Kikeriki*, 13 March 1873; 'Fremde in Wien', *Der Floh*, 22 June 1884.
136. See, e.g., 'Willkommen! (Zur Eröffnung der Wiener Weltausstellung)', *Figaro*, 3 May 1873; 'Wiener Spaziergänge', *Figaro*, 10 May 1873.
137. *Der Floh*, 13 April 1873.
138. 'Eingesendet', *Figaro*, 17 May 1873.
139. *Frenchman:* What does a room on the first floor cost? *Hotel staff:* Thirty florins. *F:* For the month [mwa]? *H:* Yes, Monsieur, for you (confusing French *mois* 'month' [mwa] with *moi* 'me' [mwa]). *F:* Is he stupid? *H:* Bett? (confusing French *bête* 'stupid' [bet] with German *Bett* 'bed' [bet]). Of course! 'On parle Français', *Der Floh*, 10 May 1873.
140. See, e.g., 'English modesty!', *Figaro*, 16 December 1865.
141. 'Der Fremde in Wien', *Figaro*, 19 July 1879 / *Wiener Luft* No. 29; 'Alphabetisch geordneter Wiener Fremdenführer', *Figaro*, 2 July 1887 / *Wiener Luft* No. 27. On the differences in nightlife in Vienna and Budapest, see further Gluck, *Invisible Jewish Budapest*, 141.
142. 'Wien als Großstadt und als Krähwinkel', *Kikeriki*, 7 December 1879; 'Ladislaus Bubus', *Der Floh*, 15 August 1886.
143. 'Eine Weltstadt', *Figaro*, 8 July 1882 / *Wiener Luft* No. 27.
144. 'Aus dem Tagebuche des Schah', *Kikeriki*, 14 June 1874; 'Aus König Kalakaua's Notizen für die "Hawaiian Gazzette"', *Figaro*, 20 August 1881 / *Wiener Luft* No. 34; 'Aus dem Notizbuch eines chinesischen Gesandtschaft-Mittgliedes', *Figaro*, 10 September 1881 / *Wiener Luft* No. 37; 'Vom Indischen Prinzen', *Der Floh*, 17 July 1887.
145. 'Selige Erinnerung eines Ausstellers', *Kikeriki*, 20 April 1873; 'Die ersten Fremden am Ausstellungsplatze', *Kikeriki*, 1 May 1873; 'Bilder aus der Weltausstellung', *Figaro*, 10 May 1873; 'Welausstellungs-Gäste aus dem Osten', *Der Floh*, 13 April 1873.
146. 'Zwei Fremde', *Kikeriki*, 15 May 1873; 'Wehe uns allen', *Kikeriki*, 15 May 1873.
147. Abgesetzt, das ist gewiß / Ist als Weltstadt Paris / Und den Ton für alle Lande / Gibt seitdem – 's ist keine Schande – / Unser Wien und, ja, potz Blitz, / alles huldigt unserm Witz / Selbst den großen Börsenkrach / Macht America uns nach!' 'Wien als Weltstadt', *Der Floh*, 27 September 1873. Comparisons between the stock market crash and the World Exhibitions were also made by other satirical commentators. See, e.g., 'Wiener Volkstheater. Zum 1. Mal. "Ach und Krach"', *Figaro*, 17 May 1873.
148. 'An der blauen Donau', *Kikeriki*, 21 February 1870.
149. 'Der Weg über den Paradeplatz', *Kikeriki*, 2 October 1871.
150. 'Weltausstellung des "Floh". Österreichische Abtheilung', *Der Floh*, 3 May 1873; 'Was die Wiener auszustellen haben, was man aber auf der Weltausstellung nicht vorfindet', *Kikeriki*, 4 May 1873; 'In der Kärnthnerstraße', *Kikeriki*, 28 January 1875; 'Fremder', *Wiener Luft* No. 24, 1880; 'Im Prater', *Wiener Luft* No. 19, 1881; 'Wiener Sehenswürdigkeiten', *Wiener Luft* No. 30, 1882; 'Hebung des Nachtlebens', *Wiener Luft* No. 34, 1890.
151. I would like to thank Vanesa Rodriguez Galindo for drawing my attention to the innate relationship between modernization and growing international influences in the nineteenth-century European capitals.

152. Jo Ann Mitchell Fuess, *The Cultural Crisis of Lower Middle Class Vienna 1848–1892: A Study of the Works of Friedrich Schlögl* (Lincoln, 1992), 62. In 1880, over 60 per cent of inhabitants were born outside Vienna. Hans Fassman and Rainer Münz, 'BetweenMelting Pot and Ethnic Fragmentation: Historical and Recent Immigration to Vienna', in Curtis C. Roseman, Hans Dieter Laux and Günther Thieme (eds), *EthniCity: Geographic Perspectives on Ethnic Change in Modern Cities* (Lanham, 1996), 166. By 1900, the number of citizens born outside Vienna outnumbered the original population. Frisby, *Cityscapes*, 186. See also Maderthaner and Musner, *Unruly Masses*, 42.
153. On the division of nationalities in the empire, see further Sked, *Decline & Fall*, 278–79, 284.
154. Cf. Malachi Haim Hacohen, 'Popper's Cosmopolitanism: Culture Clash and Jewish Identity', in Steven Beller (ed.), *Rethinking Vienna 1900* (New York, 2001), 171, 173–75.
155. Cf. Steven Beller, *Vienna and the Jews 1867–1938: A Cultural History* (Cambridge, 2003), 3.
156. 'Wiener Gasflammen', *Figaro*, 7 October 1865.
157. On the building of national stereotypes in Viennese late nineteenth-century humorous magazines in general, see further Walter Peterseil, *Nationalen Stereotypen in der Karikatur: Die Magyaren, Polen, Serben, Slowanen und Tschechen in Wiener humoristisch-satirischen Zeitschriften (1895–1921)* (thesis, Vienna, 1991), 28 and passim.
158. 'Aus majnen Erlebnissen vom Wiener Sootenmarkt. (Mitgethajlt von Fekete Lajos aus Szamos-Ujvar)', *Der Floh*, 2 September 1888.
159. See further Ulrich E. Bach, *Tropics of Vienna: Colonial Utopias of the Habsburg Empire* (New York, 2016), 1–6.
160. On Parisian laughter at visitors from the provinces in French humorous literature, see Alain Corbin, 'Paris-Province', in Pierre Nora (ed.), *Realms of Memory: Rethinking the French Past* (New York, 1996), 427–64.
161. 'Die äußere Erscheinung verschiedener Nationalitäten auf ihre Grundformen zurückgeführt. (Eine Ethnografische Skizze)', *Figaro*, 10 August 1861; 'Ansicht jener Nationalisten', *Kikeriki*, 7 March 1880; 'Die Situationsveränderungen bei den Nationalitäten', *Kikeriki*, 26 February 1882.
162. See, e.g., 'Weltaustellungs-Irrthum', *Kikeriki*, 20 April 1873. See also 'Alles Magyarisirt!', *Kikeriki*, 11 April 1880.
163. 'Der galante Ungarn', *Der Floh*, 16 June 1889.
164. See, e.g., 'Ueber das Schlittschuhlaufen', *Kikeriki*, 12 March 1874. See also the section '(Mis)reading the City and Deception of Sight' in chapter 4.
165. 'Wien im croatischen Lichte', *Der Floh*, 24 August 1884.
166. See, e.g., 'Lustig immer lustig Czechen', *Figaro*, 10 August 1861; 'Selbstgespräch eines czechischen Nationalen in Prag', *Figaro*, 1 February 1868; 'Wie man die Keckheit der Czechen leicht begegnen könnte', *Kikeriki*, 7 July 1881.
167. Cf. *Der Floh*, 28 March 1886; *Kikeriki*, 13 June 1889.
168. Beller, *Vienna and the Jews*, 193.
169. Gabriele Kohlbauer-Fritz, 'Familiengeschichten: Die Ringstraßenpalais und ihre Bewohner', in Gabriele Kohlbauer-Fritz (ed.), *Ringstraße: Ein jüdischer Boulevard* (Vienna, 2015), 24–58. On the situation in Budapest, cf. Gluck, *Invisible Jewish Budapest*, 11–13.

170. See Hans Tietze, *Die Juden Wiens: Geschichte, Wirtschaft, Kultur* (Vienna, [1933] 2007); Robert S. Wistrich, *The Jews of Vienna in the Age of Franz Joseph* (Oxford, 1990); Beller, *Vienna and the Jews*; Elliott Oring, *The Jokes of Sigmund Freud: A Study in Humor and Jewish Identity* (Philadelphia, 1997); Marcus G. Patka, *Wege des Lachens: Jüdischer Witz und Humor aus Wien* (Weitra, 2010).
171. John W. Boyer, *Political Radicalism in Late Imperial Vienna: Origins of the Christian Social Movement, 1848–1897* (Chicago, 1981); Brigitte Hamann, *Hitlers Wien: Lehrjahre eines Diktators* (Munich, 1996).
172. Spector, *Violent Sensations*, 202–6; Gluck, *Invisible Jewish Budapest*, 4–5. See also Hamann, *Hitlers Wien*, 112–19.
173. Tietze, *Juden Wiens*, 193–96, 219; Johnston, *Austrian Mind*, 16; Hamann, *Hitlers Wien*, 467–72.
174. Tietze, *Juden Wiens*, 196; Wistrich, *Jews of Vienna*, 145; Hamann, *Hitlers Wien*, 468; Beller, *Vienna and the Jews*, 166.
175. See, e.g., 'Feuilleton', *Der Floh*, 24 November 1872; 'Moderne Logik', *Kikeriki*, 23 October 1873.
176. 'Moderner Ringstraßen-Dialog', *Kikeriki*, 2 January 1873; 'Die neuen Ringstraßenbarone', *Kikeriki*, 5 January 1873; 'Ringstraßen-Fatalitäten', *Figaro*, 29 July 1876 / *Wiener Luft* No. 31.
177. 'Zur Regelung der Nationalitätenfrage', *Figaro*, 14 September 1861; 'Juden – Hebräer – Israeliten', *Kikeriki*, 10 November 1864; 'Eine Judenpresse', *Kikeriki*, 26 August 1869.
178. See, e.g., 'Auf der Börse', *Der Floh*, 21 December 1884; 'Ein gefährlicher Hand', *Der Floh*, 8 April 1888.
179. 'Aus dem Jahresberichte', *Der Floh*, 6 January 1884; 'Von den Fünfgulden-Männer', *Der Floh*, 8 June 1884; 'Aus dem Lande der Nasen', *Der Floh*, 14 June 1885; 'Im Antisemitisten-Beisl', *Der Floh*, 7 November 1886.
180. 'Eine merkwürdige Krankheit', *Der Floh*, 28 September 1884.
181. Der Antisemitismus ist ein Widerspruch in sich selbst, denn er will ja nur denn treffen, was koscher ist. 'Anti-Antisemititistisches', *Der Floh*, 18 December 1887.
182. See, e.g., 'Kompromis', *Der Floh*, 24 February 1884; 'Die Macht der Gewohnheit', *Der Floh*, 23 October 1887. See also 'Im Poste-Restante Bureau', *Der Floh*, 27 March 1887. Cf. Sigmund Freud, *Der Witz und seine Beziehung zum Unbewussten* (Frankfurt am Main, [1905] 2006), 64, 66, 70. On jokes about the eastern Jews and cleanliness, see also Oring, *Jokes of Sigmund Freud*, 42–43.
183. Cf. Linda Nochlin, 'Introduction. Starting with the Self: Jewish Identity and its Representation', in Linda Nochlin and Tamar Garb (eds), *The Jew in the Text: Modernity and the Construction of Identity* (London, 1995), 12.
184. In some cases, the pen names of readers indicate a Jewish origin. See, e.g., 'Redactions-Correspondenz', *Der Floh*, 17 November 1872; 'Ein Wiener Jude. Briefkasten der Redaction', *Figaro*, 26 April 1890.
185. Gluck, *Invisible Jewish Budapest*, 104–38; Chase, *Inciting Laughter*, 1–2 and passim. See also Patka, *Wege des Lachens*, 98–103.
186. Chase, *Inciting Laughter*, 1–3.
187. Between 1862 and 1897 the word *Witzblatt* occurs in all the digitized humorous magazines 468 times, while the term *humoristisches Blatt*, for example, occurs only nineteen times between 1852 and 1899. ANNO Austrian Newspapers Online, ÖNB, http://

anno.onb.ac.at/ (accessed 14 October 2016). Furthermore, *Kikeriki*, *Figaro* and *Der Floh* regularly used the term *Witzblatt* when referring to their own publishing activities, as well as to other rival humorous magazines. See, e.g., 'Briefkasten der Redaktion', *Figaro*, 2 June 1860; 'Kleine Post der Redaktion', *Kikeriki*, 6 March 1862; 'An die Völker Österreichs!', *Figaro*, 30 September 1865; 'Offizielle Scherzfragen', *Figaro*, 20 October 1866; 'Kleine Post der Redaktion', *Kikeriki*, 26 September 1867; 'Kleine Post der Redaktion', *Kikeriki*, 23 April 1868; 'Oui et non', *Der Floh*, 1 May 1870; 'An unsere Leser!', *Der Floh*, 21 March 1875.

188. Cf. Gluck, *Invisible Jewish Budapest*, 5, 104–38.
189. Cf. ibid., 107; Patka, *Wege des Lachens*, 23–28; Elliott Oring, *Jokes and Their Relations* (Lexington, 1992), 122.
190. Peter Jelavich, *Berlin Cabaret* (Cambridge, MA, 1996), 200–209.
191. Allen, *Satire and Society*, 188–94.
192. Oring, *Jokes of Sigmund Freud*, 42–51; Hamann, *Hitlers Wien*, 119–21.
193. See further Gluck, *Invisible Jewish Budapest*, 124–31.
194. Beller, *Vienna and the Jews*, 38–39.
195. See further Chase, *Inciting Laughter*, 3–4; Gluck, *Invisible Jewish Budapest*, 107–9.
196. 'Wegweiser in Wien', *Figaro*, 1 March 1890 / *Wiener Luft* No. 9.
197. National Socialist German Workers' Party.
198. Wistrich, *Jews of Vienna*, 229.
199. Boyer, *Political Radicalism*, 40–88 and passim.
200. Beller, *Vienna and the Jews*, 188.
201. See further ibid., 198; Boyer, *Political Radicalism*, 185.
202. Cf. 'Was sich liebt, das neckt sich oder das ist der Fluch der bösen That', *Figaro*, 18 August 1888 / *Wiener Luft* No. 33.
203. See, for example, Riitta Laitinen, *Order, Materiality and Urban Space in the Early Modern Kingdom of Sweden* (Amsterdam, 2017), 87–107.
204. Frisby, *Cityscapes*, 3–4, 178; Edward Soja, 'History: Geography: Modernity', in Simon During (ed.), *The Cultural Studies Reader* (New York, 1993), 146. See also Judith Frigyesi, *Béla Bartók and the Turn-of-the-Century Budapest* (Berkeley, 1998), 49.
205. Marshall Berman, *All That Is Solid Melts Into Air: The Experience of Modernity* (New York, 1988), 147–55.
206. Peter Fritzsche, 'Readers, Browsers, Strangers, Spectators: Narrative Forms and Metropolitan Encounters in Twentieth-Century Berlin', in Malcom Gee and Tim Kirk (eds), *Printed Matters: Printing, Publishing and Urban Culture in Europe in the Modern Period* (Aldershot, 2002), 90; Wilson, *Sphinx in the City*, 29; Walkowitz, *City of Dreadful Delight*, 1–13.
207. See further Spector, *Violent Sensations*, 2–4 and passim.
208. I have chosen to use the term *underclass* instead of *lower classes* since the focus in this chapter is especially on the new urban pariah, and not on the servants and workers.
209. The beggar is also a figure that appears in various Western narrative traditions like fairy tales or jests. For example, the *Schnorrer* is a standard figure in Jewish jokes. On the *Schnorrer*, see Beller, *Vienna and the Jews*, 111; Oring, *Jokes of Sigmund Freud*, 13–26. On the other hand, urban theorists such as Walter Benjamin and Georg Simmel were interested in the beggar as an urban figure that reflected the transition into the new modern money economy. See further Frisby, *Cityscapes*, 10.

210. Crown Prince Rudolf von Habsburg shot himself and his lover Mary Vetsera in an imperial hunting lodge in Mayerling in 1889. This was a serious blow for Austria-Hungary, leading to an emerging uncertainty about the future of the empire.
211. See further Harald Robert Stühlinger, *Der Wettbewerb zur Wiener Ringstraße* (Ph.D. diss., Zurich, 2013), 96.
212. The situation in Vienna was worse than in other European capitals: in Berlin 36.5 per cent, in Paris 33.1 per cent and in London 7.2 per cent. The study by Eugen von Philippovich revealed also that in small dwellings 25 per cent of people had access to less than half of the minimum air space, 10 cubic metres, for each person over one year old. Frisby, *Cityscapes*, 229.
213. Janik and Toulmin, *Wittgenstein's Vienna*, 50.
214. Harvey, *Paris*, 198.
215. Maderthaner and Musner, *Unruly Masses*, 32, 48. Other growing metropolises faced the same problem. For example, in 1905 in Budapest thirty-five people were found living in trees in public parks. Janik and Toulmin, *Wittgenstein's Vienna*, 50–51.
216. E.g. 'Neueste, auf der Schmelz aufzustellende Erfindung des Kikeriki – zur Abhilfe der Wohnungsnoth', *Kikeriki*, 14 April 1872; 'Die Wohnungsnoth und unsere Wasserröhren', *Kikeriki*, 28 April 1872; 'Noch ein Rettungsmittel', *Kikeriki*, 19 May 1872. See also 'Einige Neue Häusergruppen', *Kikeriki*, 9 February 1873. In 1890, a cartoon observed that for decades poor people had been using the riverbanks of the Danube (*Donauregulierungsgründen*) as a substitute for cheap flats. *Kikeriki*, 6 April 1890.
217. See further Spector, *Violent Sensations*, 23–30.
218. Maderthaner and Musner, *Unruly Masses*, 5–6, 10; Wolfgang Maderthaner, 'Von der Zeit um 1860 bis zum Jahr 1945', in Csendes and Oppl, *Wien - Geschichte einer Stadt*, 215, 222–24.
219. In contrast to other European countries, in Vienna suburban settings were strikingly absent from contemporary 'high' literature and fiction. Maderthaner and Musner, *Unruly Masses*, 32–34, 44–67.
220. Wickberg, *Senses of Humor*, 50–65, 71.
221. Cited in John Morreall, *The Philosophy of Laughter and Humor* (Albany, 1987), 65.
222. 'Ich bedaure sehr', *Figaro*, 27 December 1879 / *Wiener Luft* No. 52; 'Die soziale Frage kann man am Besten auf der Ringstraße studiren', *Kikeriki*, 19 October 1882; 'Auf der Ringstrasse', *Der Floh*, 15 March 1885; 'Wiener Strassenbild', *Der Floh*, 12 April 1885; 'Gerechter Zweifel', *Der Floh*, 24 January 1886.
223. As William A. Cohen has suggested, encounters with the lower social strata, with the low and rough, were an important part of the bourgeois imaginaries about city life. William A. Cohen, 'Introduction: Locating Filth', in William A. Cohen and Ryan Johnson (eds), *Filth, Dirt, Disgust and Modern Life* (Minneapolis, 2004), xxi. See also Frigyesi, *Béla Bartók*, 45; Allen, *Satire and Society*, 154–55; Schorske, *Thinking with History*, 86–88.
224. Frisby, *Cityscapes*, 31–32.
225. See, e.g., 'Von der Neugierde der Massen', *Kikeriki*, 11 April 1875.
226. 'Der Engel und die Ringstraße', *Kikeriki*, 31 December 1868; 'Weihnachten der Armen', *Kikeriki*, 24 December 1874; 'Die Weihnachtsbetheilung der Armen', *Kikeriki*, 23 December 1875.
227. 'Wiener Strassenbild', *Der Floh*, 12 April 1885. Cf. 'Moderne Wohlthätigkeit', *Der Floh*, 19 July 1885; 'Zeichen der Zeit', *Der Floh*, 24 May 1885.

228. 'Der Weihnachtsabend des kleinen Beamten', *Kikeriki*, 25 December 1871.
229. See especially Boyer, *Political Radicalism*; Hamann, *Hitlers Wien*.
230. See further Albert Lichtblau, 'Im Visier der antisemitischen Populisten: Jüdische Reiche und die Wiener Rinstraße', in Kohlbauer-Fritz, *Ringstraße*, 270–84.
231. 'Ritter von Einst – Ritter von Jetzt', *Kikeriki*, 29 December 1872; 'Moderner Ringtrassendialog', *Kikeriki*, 2 January 1873; 'Auf der Ringstraße', *Figaro*, 3 May 1879 / *Wiener Luft* No. 18; 'Der Bank auf der wir hier sitzen', *Figaro*, 6 September 1879 / *Wiener Luft* No. 36.
232. Maderthaner and Musner, *Unruly Masses*, 23.
233. Hamann, *Hitlers Wien*, 472; Beller, *Vienna and the Jews*, 188–237. Hostility against the stock market and modern capitalism were intertwined with the growing antisemitism, not only in Vienna, but in other countries as well. Cf. Harvey, *Paris*; Allen, *Satire and Society*.
234. 'Auf dem Ring', *Der Floh*, 28 March 1874.
235. Cf. Julia Schäfer, *Vermessen – gezeichnet – verlacht: Judenbilder in Populären Zeitschriften 1918–1933* (Frankfurt am Main, 2004), 324–43.
236. See further ibid., 324–43. Cf. Freud, *Der Witz*, 66.
237. Cf. Fuess, *Cultural Crisis*, 66–69.
238. Wilson, *Sphinx in the City*, 27.
239. Cf. Maderthaner and Musner, *Unruly Masses*, 32–34, 44–67; Fritzsche, 'Readers, Browsers', 98.
240. '–Wo loshirst den, blader Schakerl? –No, dös fixt ja! Beim Tag brauch' i ka Loschi, und bei der Nacht leg' i mi da her unter dö Götter vom Donner-Brunn', da halten mi dö Sicherheiterer im Finstern a für an' Gott'. 'Ein Götterleben', *Der Floh*, 31 October 1886.
241. This slang seems like a middle-class imitation of the 'Rotwelsch' used by marginal social groups such as vagabonds, beggars and petty criminals. See further Maderthaner and Musner, *Unruly Masses*, 18, 150.
242. Cf. Stallybrass and White, *Politics and Poetics*, 16, 20–23.
243. Maderthaner and Musner, *Unruly Masses*, 2–5, 52–55. Cf. Harvey, *Paris*, 199.
244. Maderthaner and Musner, *Unruly Masses*, 56.
245. Cf. ibid., 30.
246. Umberto Eco (ed.), *Die Geschichte der Hässlichkeit*, trans. Friederike Hausmann, Petra Kaiser and Sigrid Vagt (Munich, 2010), 135. Cf. Wilson, *Sphinx in the City*, 34–37.
247. *Figaro*, 8 March 1879 / *Wiener Luft* No. 10.
248. 'Ein Talent', *Der Floh*, 21 September 1884; 'Praktisch', *Der Floh*, 11 January 1885; 'Coulance', *Der Floh*, 3 May 1885; 'Zeichen der Zeit', *Der Floh*, 24 May 1885; 'Moderne Bettler', *Figaro*, 24 December 1887 / *Wiener Luft* No. 52; 'Der gebildete Bettler', *Figaro*, 18 January 1890 / *Wiener Luft* No. 3.
249. My translation. Freud, *Der Witz*, 65–67.
250. Olive Anderson, *Suicide in Victorian and Edwardian England* (Oxford, 1987), 201–7.
251. 'Auf dem Lumbenballe', *Figaro*, 27 January 1883 / *Wiener Luft* No. 4; 'Auf dem Lumpenball', *Figaro*, 9 February 1884 / *Wiener Luft* No. 6; 'Typen für den Lumpenball', *Der Floh*, 10 February 1884; 'Auf der Südbahn', *Figaro*, 6 March 1886 / *Wiener Luft* No. 10; 'In der Nacht des Lumpenballes', *Der Floh*, 14 February 1886; 'Bei der Heimkehr vom Lumpenballe', *Figaro*, 2 March 1889 / *Wiener Luft* No. 9.
252. 'Ein großer Lump', *Figaro*, 27 January 1883 / *Wiener Luft* No. 4.

253. 'Konsequent', *Figaro*, 8 February 1890 / *Wiener Luft* No. 6.
254. Cf. Stallybrass and White, *Politics and Poetics*, 125–26.
255. Oring, *Jokes of Sigmund Freud*, 13–26. Freud's material includes many jokes involving *Schnorrer* (beggars), moneylenders, wealthy millionaires and impoverished relatives.
256. ... Ueberall herrschte ein beispielloses Gedränge, so daß die prächtigsten Figuren ohne rechte Beachtung zu finden, in dem Getümmel der Tausende verschwanden. Hier tanzten die bekannten Modelle von der Akademie der bildenden Künste zum Dudelsack ihre neapolitanische Tarantella, dort forderte ein nichts weniger als eleganter Raubmörder Hugo Schenk ältere Frauen mit Sparkassebüchern auf, ihm auf die Schmelz zu folgen; hier zog mit Fahnen, Emblemen und betäubendem Geschrei eine Truppe Obdachloser vorüber, dort wurde das Spiritisten-Medium Bastian, ein befrackter Herr in wollenen Strümpfen, aus einer Nische geworfen; hier produzirte der bekannte Vororte-Hanswurst Rante-Potante seine Taschenspielereien, dort schrie sich ein Individuum in merkwürdig defekten Beinkleider heiser nach milden Spenden für seinen Schneider u. dgl. m. Am drolligsten waren die einsamen Lumpe, die mit ernster, nachdenklicher Miene, einen schweren Sack auf dem Rücken, stundenlang herumzogen und nicht wußten, warum sie sich eigentlich solche Plage auferlegten. Wesentlich vermehrt wurde der Lärm durch die Austräger des von Schließmann schwungvoll gezeichneten Journals 'Der Lump', welches die Begünstigung der Kolportage genoß. Und in dem ganzen betäubenden Wirrwarr, bei der ganzen ungezügelten Freiheit, welche die Besucher des Lumpenballs genossen – die Polizei lächelte mit über den Unsinn – geschah nichts, was anstößig gewesen wäre, balgten sich nicht zwei von den zehntausend, hatte Jeder im dichtesten Gedränge ein Scherzwort auf den Lippen, wenn ihn der Nachbar in die Rippen stieß. Wohin man sah: lachende Gesichter, heitere Aufmerksamkeit, stiller Trunk oder sprühende Laune – keine Besoffenheit, keine Grobheit, keine Gemeinheit. Mehrere Fremde, welchen von Wiener Freunden aus der besten Gesellschaft der Lumpenball als eine Spezialität gezeigt wurde, erklärten, das Wiener Volk stehe in seiner Liebenswürdigkeit, Harmlosigkeit und Gutmüthigkeit einzig da auf der Welt. Möge es diese durch Jahrhunderte bewahrten Eigenschaften nie verlieren, mögen sie ihm nicht genommen werden. So dient selbst der Lumpenball dazu, den Ruf der Wiener Volkes durch den Mund Fremder hinauszutragen. Pötzl, 'Lumpenball', 110–16.
257. 'Zum Vortheil der Armen', *Kikeriki*, 24 November 1867; 'Galgenhumor', *Kikeriki*, 10 February 1881; 'Am früheren Morgen nach dem Narrenabende', *Kikeriki*, 9 March 1884; 'Pariser Ungemütlichkeit und Wiener Gemütlichkeit', *Figaro*, 14 February 1885 / *Wiener Luft* No. 7.
258. Cf. Allen, *Satire and Society*, 142.
259. See, e.g., 'Kriminalstudien des Kikeriki', *Kikeriki*, 19 March 1863; 'Das Testament des Raubmörders', *Kikeriki*, 24 August 1865; 'Unsere Zeit', *Kikeriki*, 22 March 1866; 'Heftige Erkrankung', *Kikeriki*, 8 February 1866; 'Moderne Neuigkeiten', *Kikeriki*, 3 September 1868; 'Moderne Moral', *Kikeriki*, 2 April 1874; 'Aus der Mordwoche', *Figaro*, 28 October 1876 / *Wiener Luft* No. 44.
260. Cf. Allen, *Satire and Society*, 142.
261. For a similar kind of situation in nineteenth-century England, see Anderson, *Suicide*, 201–7.
262. Bergson, *Nauru*, 9–10, 100.
263. Frisby, *Cityscapes*, 251.
264. Salmi, *Nineteenth-Century Europe*, 124–25.

265. 'Moderne Journal-Eindrücke', *Kikeriki*, 9 April 1879; 'In der Redaktion der Spektakel-Zeitung', *Wiener Luft*, No. 3, 1880; 'Muster, wie ein Wiener Volksblatt zusammengestellt wird', *Figaro*, 7 May 1881 / *Wiener Luft* No. 19.
266. According to a word frequency search on the ANNO database, words like 'Mord' and 'Selbstmord' expanded hugely in the second part of the century: 'Mord' 5,176 (1791–1841), 49,083 (1842–92); 'Selbsmord' 5,202 (1829–66), 70,019 (1867–1904). ANNO Austrian Newspapers Online, ÖNB, http://anno.onb.ac.at/ (accessed 22 May 2015).
267. See, e.g., 'Aus dem Gerichtssaale', *Neue Freie Presse*, 19 October 1868; 'Der Mord in Floridsdorf. (Orig.-Bericht der "Presse")', *Die Presse*, 28 January 1884; 'Locales (Mord und Selbstmord)', *Wiener Zeitung*, 20 June 1887.
268. See, e.g., 'Hüte dich beim Sylvesterpunch- das Extra-Blatt zu lesen', *Der Floh*, 29 December 1889.
269. See, e.g., *Illustriertes Wiener Extrablatt*, 1 January 1903.
270. On the similar situation in England, see further Anderson, *Suicide*, 194, 214.
271. Gregory Shaya, 'The *Flâneur*, the *Badaud* and the Making of a Mass Public in France, circa 1860–1910', *American Historical Review* 109(1) (2004), 42. Subsequently, there has been much criticism of Habermas's theory for idealizing the public sphere, and ignoring earlier forms of popular culture such as penny dreadfuls and early scandal sheets, resulting in an oversimplified image of the degeneration of the public sphere. Ibid.
272. See, e.g., 'Volksbildung durch die Presse', *Figaro*, 11 April 1874; 'Beilage: Journalistik als Mörderschule', *Figaro*, 11 July 1874; 'Moderne Journal Eindrücke', *Kikeriki*, 9 April 1879.
273. 'Aus dem Verhöre Mit Hugo Schenk', *Figaro*, 26 January 1884 / *Wiener Luft* No. 4; 'Aus dem "Memoiren" des Hugo Schenk. (Fragment)', *Figaro*, 22 March 1884 / *Wiener Luft* No. 12; 'Angedruckt erschienene Bücher: "Theorie und Technik des Raubmords" von Hugo Schenk', *Der Floh*, 20 January 1884; 'Was Hugo Schenk noch plante', *Der Floh*, 3 February 1884.
274. On Schenk's case, see further Spector, *Violent Sensations*, 167; Harald Seyrl, *Wiener Pitaval* (Vienna, 2000), 353–73; Theodor F. Meysels (ed.), *Schauderhafte Moritaten* (Salzburg, 1962), 63–64.
275. Cf. Walkowitz, *City of Dreadful Delight*.
276. 'Aviso für selbsmörder', *Kikeriki*, 7 June 1874; 'P.T. Selbsmörder', *Figaro*, 5 October 1872; 'Doppel-Selbstmord-Korrespondenzen', *Kikeriki*, 26 February 1874; 'Praktische Rettungs-Vorrichtungen', *Kikeriki*, 25 June 1874; 'Moderne Selbstmords-Ursachen', *Kikeriki*, 29 October 1876; 'Modernes Familienbild', *Figaro*, 13 August 1881 / *Wiener Luft* No. 33; 'Die Flucht aus dem Leben', *Figaro*, 26 July 1884; 'Moderne Frühlingslieder', *Der Floh*, 20 April 1890.
277. See, e.g., 'Ueber Selbstmordnotizen', *Kikeriki*, 25 June 1882.
278. Vocelka, *K.u.K. Karikaturen*, 14.
279. Anderson, *Suicide*, 207–13.
280. Johnston, *Austrian Mind*, 169. See also Fritzsche, 'Readers, Browsers', 97–98.
281. Johannes Kunz, *'Der Tod muss ein Wiener Sein': Morbide Geschichten und Anekdoten* (Vienna, 2009), 17–18.
282. Kecker Witz allein befreit / Euch von allen Aengsten, / Nicht nur ehrlich, sondern auch / Lustig währt am längsten! *Figaro*, 4 January 1879. See also Elfried Schneider, *Karikatur*

und Satire als politische Kampfmittel: Ein Beitrag zur Wiener satirisch-humoristischen Presse des 19. Jahrhunderts (1849–1914) (Ph.D. diss., Vienna, 1972), 253.
283. 'Heiter auch in ernster Zeit', *Kikeriki*, 24 April 1881; 'Zum 28. August', *Kikeriki*, 24 April 1881; 'Zur Saison (an unsere Leser)', *Der Floh*, 21 September 1884; 'Eine Conferenz der Conferenz', *Der Floh*, 3 August 1884; 'Kein Stoff', *Der Floh*, 30 August 1885; 'Sylvester', *Der Floh*, 2 January 1887; 'Weihnachtsmanifest des "Floh"', *Der Floh*, 23 December 1888; 'Die Zeitkrankheit', *Der Floh*, 31 March 1889.
284. 'An die Leser', *Kikeriki*, 15 December 1881.
285. E.g. Friedrich Schlögl, *Wiener Blut* (Vienna, 1873); Schlögl, *Wiener Luft: Kleine Culturbilder*, Vinzenz Chiavacci, *Wiener vom Grund: Bilder aus dem Kleinleben der Großstadt* (Vienna, 1888); Eduard Pötzl, *Stadtmenschen: Ein Wiener Skizzenbuch* (Vienna, 1895).
286. Wolfgang Kos (ed.), *Wiener Typen: Klischees und Wirklichkeit* (Vienna, 2013). 'Wiener Typen' played a significant role in late nineteenth-century Viennese popular culture. The established repertoire of Viennese types, such as *Schusterbuben*, *Waschmädl* or *Fiaker*, had their origins in the visual culture of the early modern era. These familiar 'types' were an important part of the Viennese nineteenth-century print culture, and their representations carried on into the twentieth century, evolving in new media forms such as cabaret, records, films and television. See further Lutz Musner, *Der Geschmack von Wien: Kultur und Habitus einer Stadt* (Frankfurt am Main, 2009), 18–19 and passim.
287. Later in the *fin-de-siècle* era, the cultural fantasies of the middle class revolved increasingly around marginal, liminal or 'border' figures that both evoked associations of sexual danger and violence and served to validate respectable bourgeois identities. See further Spector, *Violent Sensations*, 2–3 and passim.

CONCLUSIONS

In her study *The Gender of Modernity*, Rita Felski cites Carl E. Schorske's idea that the task of a historian approaching modernity should be the 'empirical pursuit of pluralities' rather than a search for a common denominator that would explain the characteristics of the age.[1] This study has addressed the pluralities of modernity by investigating various aspects of late nineteenth-century everyday life that were seen or described as 'modern' in the Viennese *Witzblätter*. The multiple, often contradictory voices of the humorous *Witzblätter* underline the notion that modernity is not a solid or coherent concept or experience, but rather is defined by multiple perspectives and intersecting strands and ideas. As an ambivalent, paradoxical, dynamic, elusive and changing era, it was searched, encountered and redefined in the constant act of (re)interpretation. This is also what makes modernity comical. In this study I suggest that the realms of humour were vital for investigating and discussing the innate instability of modernity.

The purpose of this study has been to gain new insight into the complex experience of modernity by reading empirical primary source material that has not previously been closely studied but articulates important cultural reactions to the changing city in Vienna between 1857 and 1890. Through my analysis I have explored the various ways in which humorous representations constructed the sense of the modern in late nineteenth-century Vienna. I have approached humour both as an interpretative tool that helped to recognize the inner contradictions and paradoxes of modernity, as well as a mode of communication that enabled discussion on points of friction in such a manner as otherwise was impossible. My aim has been to set the focus on the relationship between the material city and its representations. By reading cultural representations in the context of the social history of urbanization and the political history of the bourgeoisie, I have approached humorous texts and images as cultural products that can shed light on past experiences, in the rapidly and radically changing physical reality during the transformation of Vienna. Understanding humour required shared meanings, associations, experiences, memories and emotions. This makes humorous magazines a valuable source for understanding the processes through which the nineteenth-century Viennese middle classes interpreted and discussed the change in their everyday environment.

The emphasis of this study has been on the *popular*, which does not mean that I wish to diminish the work of the journalists and caricaturists working on the staff of the humorous magazines – on the contrary. Yet, whereas previous research has successfully achieved knowledge about the history of the Viennese humorous magazines and their creators, my interest has been elsewhere. The purpose of this study has been to find out if there was such a thing as a middle-class popular humour in Vienna, and if so, what kind of intellectual and emotional framework this created for the negotiation of the transformation of the city space between 1857 and 1890.

The main idea of this research is that although the humorous-satirical magazines were not *popular culture* in the prevailing traditional sense, being part of the bourgeois culture, they most certainly expressed *popular humour*, stemming from the late nineteenth-century Viennese urban experience and culture, combining elements from and shedding light on its various fields. I am using the term *popular* in the sense of 'what is commonly known or shared by many people'. One of humour's most important features is that it is profoundly social, and requires and depends on shared meanings. As Henri Bergson had already noted earlier, the comical does not exist without the communication of minds.[2] Similarly, Koestler emphasizes the collaboration between the joke teller and her/his listener or reader. Jokes and other humorous texts and images contain elements of riddles; they include gaps that have to be filled in order to get the joke. Therefore, the receiver is always compelled to cooperate, to recreate the joke in her or his imagination.[3] Consequently, in this study the attempt to understand popular humour means that I have constantly attempted to establish the various contexts, shared meanings and associations that made it possible to crack the joke.

This quest for shared meanings and associations has led me to acknowledge the strong intermediality that characterized the late nineteenth-century Viennese humorous representations. These included familiar comical characters from the theatre, well-known songs performed by popular singers, famous quotations from Goethe and Schiller, and references to respected public figures, such as politicians, architects and artists. The humorous magazines thus constantly combined elements of 'high' or 'learned' culture with the 'low' and 'popular', and the resulting state of creative split-mindedness between different associative worlds was the very essence of creating and understanding humour in a new literary mass form.

Taking this into consideration, I suggest that using humorous-satirical magazines as source material reveals a new perspective on the late nineteenth century, which has been seen through a strong juxtaposition between the emerging modern popular culture and bourgeois high culture. Middle-class humorous magazines challenge the idea of a rigid dichotomy between nineteenth-century popular culture and bourgeois high culture. Because the humorous-satirical magazines revealed voices that contradicted the ruling values and ideas of the liberal bourgeoisie, they undermine the understanding of the Viennese bourgeoisie as a homogeneous and united social class, and, instead, reveal the inner tensions, contradictions and heterogeneity of the middle classes, which split in various political directions before 1900. In humour, the multiple frictions between liberalism, nationalism, democratic aspirations and antisemitism became visible, and especially the attitudes leading to the triumph of the Christian Social movement were circulated and reinforced in popular humorous publications.

However, one of the paradoxes of late nineteenth-century Vienna was that although Jews were frequently targets of jokes and ridicule, the humour itself was imprinted with Jewish tradition. Previously, Steven Beller has charted the influence of the Jewish element in the Viennese cultural elite and high culture, and Lutz Musner has shown that Viennese popular culture, too, was a meeting point for various cultural streams and traditions. My study confirms the heterogeneity of late nineteenth-century Viennese culture, and highlights the role of humour as an intersectional point for competing ideas and ideologies. With reference to the Jewish element in the humorous magazines, I think it is safe to say that it was a mixture of different traditions of humour, both Jewish and Gentile. Yet antisemitic attitudes became much more prominent in the humorous magazines after the stock market crash in 1873. The question of the Jewish element in Viennese popular humour is thus a complex and multifaceted issue. It is nonetheless important to acknowledge that there was indeed a Jewish element in Viennese popular humour, and the tradition of the Jewish joke was carried on in popular humorous expressions made by non-Jewish writers as well. For example, the influence of Saphir and Heine was widely acknowledged in the late nineteenth-century *Witzblätter*.

Kikeriki, *Figaro* and *Der Floh* were all different, but influential humorous magazines, that had more in common than has previously been recognized. Whereas earlier research has focused on discovering differences between these magazines and their readerships, my work brings out similarities between the most widely read Viennese *Witzblätter*: certain ideas, themes, conventions and even individual jokes recurred and circulated in the repertoire of all of these magazines. This means that it is possible to speak of popular humour as a wider cultural framework within which the magazines operated and made sense to their readers. By examining how the transformation of the city and the new modernity were discussed within this interpretative framework, this study widens the understanding of late nineteenth-century Viennese popular humour as a multifaceted cultural phenomenon that had various functions in making sense of, orientating in and experiencing the late nineteenth-century city.

While conducting this study, it has become clear how the transition towards modernity entailed multifaceted simultaneous processes that, despite their various directions, all came together on the pages of the humorous magazines and in the minds of their readers. During the period of urban renewal, the Viennese middle classes lived amidst a complex and changing urban fabric, in which they reorientated themselves and navigated their way with a sense of humour; joking about the city generated myriad and varied expressions during the timespan between 1857 and 1890. This means that the popular humour was not always easy to understand, even for the contemporary readers and editors of the magazines, and certainly not for a non-Viennese cultural historian trying the get the jokes more than a hundred years later at a different point in space and time. By careful contextualization I have tried to open up the various multifaceted layers of fluctuating meanings that made the humorous texts and images potentially funny in the eyes of the Viennese audience. This process has led me to investigate not just the jokes and cartoons as such, but rather the mental world of their readers.

In concluding this study, I would like to suggest that popular humour was employed as a tool for understanding and discussing the experience of change. The timespan between 1857 and 1890 was an age of transition and a break from the past. The urban renewal changed the city in many ways, with a new spatial structure dominated by the Ringstraße zone. In addition, after Vienna was able to introduce autonomous municipal policy in the 1860s, the liberal era saw many technological innovations and urban projects to modernize the city, such as improved gas lighting, the horse tramway and the regulation of the Danube. Other aspects of urbanization, such as social problems and the management of population increase, however, were neglected by the Liberal city fathers. This created contradictions and discrepancy among the Viennese middle classes, who then released their fears, uncertainties and discontent in humour. In addition to the urban renewal project, the second part of the century was an era of larger social and cultural changes: the first women's movements started to appear, nationalism shook the foundations of the *Vielvölkerstaat*, and the belief in progress was overshadowed by the threat of wars, destruction and disasters. All of these points of friction, conflicts and ruptures were featured in the humorous publications, which constantly hit the painful spots of society, while at the same time structuring their readers' understanding of the crucial weaknesses and problems of their own age.

In this study I have divided the interpretations of modernity into two main categories. The first part of this book analysed humour relating to the change and use of material city space, while the second part analysed the ways in which jokes and cartoons were instrumental in constructing city identity and a sense of urban community. While the first chapters investigated the negotiations over city space between the Emperor, City Council, police authorities and citizens, the last two chapters focused on asking how humour became a means of sharing perceptions and memories of and expectations for the city, as well as turning the unfamiliar urban crowd into familiar stereotypes and comical figures. Laughter was not merely a way of making political claims on the urban space, but it also served for sharing experiences, emotions and ideas that reinforced the bourgeois sense of community and class identity.

This shift of focus from the city space to people in the space is also to a large extent chronological. Towards the turn of the century, the Viennese humourists became increasingly interested in comical urban types and characters, whereas satirical commentary relating to spatial issues gained less and less space in the pages of the *Witzblätter*. This observation leads to my main argument: that popular humour was not merely a significant tool for encountering and interpreting the experiences of urbanization and modernity between 1857 and 1890, but in the course of the *Gründerzeit* era it also changed significantly. As the urban renewal proceeded, both the topics of humour and the ways in which the humorous *Witzblätter* saw themselves altered considerably. During the early phase of the urban renewal, in the late 1850s, 1860s and early 1870s, the focus of humour was largely on the transformation of the physical space. Humorous-satirical writings and cartoons dealt with urban planning, with the political meanings of specific places, and with questions as to who had the right to oversee and regulate public spaces in the city. Laughter was directed bottom-up against those responsible for the design and management of the city, especially against the City Council's management of the urban system and against the police for their oversight and regulation of public space. In the negotiations over power and authority over urban space, the tension between order and disorder, rebellion and discipline was an important aspect of popular humour.

However, from the 1870s onwards, new urban groups and phenomena associated with the modern city gained more and more prominence in the *Witzblätter*. Accordingly, in the late 1870s and 1880s, laughter was often directed top-down, against social groups and individuals living outside the respectable bourgeois world. Scenes from fleeting urban life often portrayed encounters between people of different ethnic groups, class and/or gender, and thus implicitly underlined sharp contrasts between different ways of urban existence. In a city with an expanding population, popular humour thus took on a significant role in the practices of exclusion and inclusion. New urban types and characters, such as modern women, strangers, Jews and beggars, were strongly associated with the transformation of the city, embodying different elements that were seen as threats to the traditional Viennese way of life.

This change in the popular humour was related to the shifting position of the middle classes and the adjustments in the political system in the 1860s, as the dynastic power of the Habsburgs was challenged by the ascending liberal bourgeoisie, demanding a constitution and new structures for civil society, which were, to a certain extent, established in the *Ausgleich* of 1867. Yet the new constitutional monarchy did not solve all the problems; international conflicts, rising nationalism and growing social problems in the expanding urban population became more and more visible in the city. Popular humour thus reflected and shaped the meanings of a wide range of contemporary phenomena such as the emergence of the women's movement, international influences and growing social problems within the great city. Poverty, especially, was an issue that permeated the realms of humour in many ways. Between 1857 and 1890, satirical critique highlighting the miserable condition of the underclass gave way to morbid black humour, as themes of violence and death gained more and more attention in the *Witzblätter* at the beginning of the *fin-de-siècle* era.

If humour is always historically and culturally determined, meaning that each society produces its own humour, historically oriented research needs to be attentive to the changes and also to possible continuities in humorous expressions. Accordingly, one of the most significant discoveries of this study is that the understanding of humour altered at the time when the urban renewal came to completion. In the first phase of the urban renewal, in the late 1850s and early 1860s, humour was understood as an intellectual exercise, and clearly worked as a means of political and social critique. Having a good sense of humour was seen as necessary for cultivating the right kind of liberal middle-class individuality that incorporated reason and imagination with moral and social consciousness. Jokes and cartoons were marked by socially and politically enlightened intentions and interests. Satirical humour aimed at improving the city by deploying ridicule that worked as a punishment for the failures and errors in organizing and maintaining urban life.

The satirical tradition of late nineteenth-century Vienna has traditionally been associated with one individual, Karl Kraus, but this study shows clearly that Kraus did not emerge from thin air; there had already been a strong tradition of humorous magazines and satirical journals before he launched his magazine *Die Fackel*. However, whereas Kraus actively and explicitly attacked the moral and aesthetic corruption of turn-of-the-century Vienna, the earlier humorous magazines proved to be more complex and inconsistent in their agenda. This resulted partly from the fact that *Kikeriki*, *Figaro* and *Der Floh* all had multiple contributors.[4] Moreover, the changes in the political, social and cultural context played a vital part here. The humorous magazines faced and reacted to many different phases in the second half of the century, having started from a position of opposition during the absolutist regime, but needing by the last decades of the century to adapt to the new kind of commercial, mass-scale media landscape.

Consequently, during the three decades studied in this book, the understanding of humour also changed, in correspondence with how the humorous magazines saw the changes in their world. In the 1880s, the humorous magazines showed a new understanding of their role as a means of dealing with the anxieties and fears caused by modern life. Humour no longer meant merely a polemical intellectual stand against the authorities, but it also became a way to encounter and process distressful and disturbing contemporary phenomena. In addition to improving the city, humour helped to endure the city.

This change resonates interestingly with the major theoretical turn that took place in Vienna around 1900 when Freud moved the focus of humour research from social critique (playful judgement) to unresolved problems of the mind. Throughout this study I have drawn on Sigmund Freud's views on humour as an analytical tool that helps us to understand the meaning of humour in the late nineteenth-century Viennese context. Freud's insights are especially valuable in understanding the role of humour in a bourgeois Viennese society strictly controlled and regulated by cultural practices and regimes that required the repression of unsuitable desires and actions. Because of the restricted manner of the middle-class way of life, humour had a very different kind of function in late nineteenth-century Vienna than it has in the United States of the twenty-first century, for example.[5] Accordingly, especially those aspects of the contemporary city that were seen as difficult, problematic or oppressive were the most likely to be targeted as topics of jokes and cartoons.

Moreover, Freud's new approach to jokes and humour has guided the analysis of this study by reminding us that humorous expressions do not only work in terms of 'positive' social agendas, but are linked to 'negative' aspects as well, disguising such issues as cultural taboos or social aggression. Thus, two overlapping agendas – of 'speaking the truth' and disguising problematic issues in comical form – made the *Witzblätter* ambivalent in their discussion of modern city life. Popular humour not only unveiled conflicts and problems in urban life, but also masked them in an acceptable form. In addition to Freud's contribution, which revealed jokes as much more multifaceted and ambivalent than previously thought, Henri Bergson's theoretical writings, which highlighted emotional detachment in laughter, have also served this study as a means to understand the complexity of humorous expression.

The elements of disguise and detachment had many different manifestations in humorous representations. Cartoons often depicted the city from an elevated point of view, transcending above it in the plane of imagination. Furthermore, humour ventilated repressed fears and anxieties concerning modernity that found their expression in an alienated and disguised form, be it a talking cathedral or a woman in drag. Yet these surprising and unconventional representations were no mere passive reactions to the change; they had an active creative potential to shake the limits of expectations and traditional patterns of thought. Even when being conservative, humour had enormous radical potential. Precisely the fantastic, creative and innovative side of popular humour made it, in my view, an important vehicle for creating and constructing the experience of modernity. As the humorous magazines discussed over decades the changing experience of space and time, they actively shaped the understanding of modernity through a comic mode using strategies of incongruences, surprises, contradictions and shifting perspectives.

In closing this study, I suggest that the great popularity of humour as an interpretative framework and rhetorical device in the discussion on modern urban life was a significant part of the transition towards modernity. As the experiences of life became increasingly complex and contradictory, humour and irony gained a vital role in addressing these paradoxes in the realms of the comical. Looking at late nineteenth-century Vienna through the lens of humour meant an ability to constantly change perspective on the city and adopt different kinds of positions within it. Like Robert Musil's protagonist in *Der Mann ohne Eigenschaften* (1930–1943), who was determined by his lack of character, the modern individual was shaped by an ability to see things from a different perspective than his or her own, to step outside him- or herself and not to take him/herself or the surrounding world too seriously.[6] Humour meant, above all, an ability to change perspective and to laugh at everything, even at the most horrid and disgusting things that the city had to offer. As a source of mental flexibility, humour made it possible both to recognize conflicts and paradoxes, and at the same time to rise above them with a sense of detachment and elevation. In this sense, popular humour did not just ventilate anti-modernist attitudes, but it substantially shaped and cultivated new urban modern sensibilities. To laugh at the modern was to be modern.

Notes

1. Rita Felski, *The Gender of Modernity* (Cambridge, MA, 1995), 208. See also Carl E. Schorske, *Fin-de-siècle Vienna: Politics and Culture* (Cambridge, [1961] 1981), xxii.
2. Henri Bergson, *Nauru: Tutkimus komiikan merkityksestä*. French original: *Le Rire: Essai sur la signification du comique* (1900) (Helsinki, 1994), 10.
3. Arthur Koestler, *The Act of Creation* (London, 1964), 68, 86.
4. Kraus has been seen as a literary outsider. Robert S. Wistrich, *The Jews of Vienna in the Age of Franz Joseph* (Oxford, 1990), 493.
5. Modern Anglo-American humour has been extensively studied by, e.g., Alan Dundes, *Cracking Jokes: Studies of Sick Humour Cycles and Stereotypes* (Berkeley, 1987); Michael Mulkay, *On Humour: Its Nature and Its Place in Modern Society* (Cambridge, 1988); Daniel Wickberg, *Senses of Humor: Self and Laughter in Modern America* (Ithaca, 1998); and Joanne R. Gilbert, *Performing Marginality: Humor, Gender and Cultural Critique* (Detroit, 2004).
6. Robert Musil, *Der Mann ohne Eigenschaften* (Hamburg, 1937), 35. On Musil and modern reconceptualizations of human subjectivity, see Stefan Jonsson, *Subject without Nation: Robert Musil and the History of Modern Identity* (Durham, 2000), 1–17.

BIBLIOGRAPHY

Archive Sources

Österreichisches Staatsarchiv:
  Allgemeines Verwaltungsarchiv (AVA) Polizei-Ministerium. Oberste Polizeibehörde, Präsidium (Präs. II.)
  AT-OeStA HHStA SB Sammlung Wagner Theaterzettel 1-5-10, 1-5-22, 1-5-31, 1-5-62, 1-6-41. Retrieved 31 October 2016 from Österreichisches Staatsarchiv. http://www.archivinformationssystem.at/detail.aspx?ID=2692591.
Wienbibliothek im Rathaus:
  Lebenslauf des Wiener Schriftstellers und Redakteur des 'Figaro' Karl sitter. o.V. o. J. Druckschriftensammlung.
  Wehle, J.H. Feuilleton. Ein Witzblatt-Redacteur. Nachrufe auf Karl Sitter aus verschiedenen Zeitungen. o. J. Druckschriftensammlung.
Österreichische Nationalbibliothek:
  Wien 1, Ringstraße. Josefstädter Glacis: Prekärer Zustand der Wegverhältnisse zur Zeit der Stadterweiterung. Lithographie um 1865. Digitale Sammlung ÖNB Bildarchiv und Grafiksammlung. Retrieved 7 February 2019 from http://data.onb.ac.at/rec/baa1898821.

Law Texts and Statutes

Reichsgesetzblatt für das Kaiserthum Österreich. Jahrgang 1863. IV Stück 6. Pressgesetz vom 17. Dezember 1862. Österreichische Nationalbibliothek. ALEX-Historische Rechts- und Gesetzestexte Online. www.alex.onb.at.
N. Oe. Landesgesetze. 2 Bd. Wasserrechts-, Straßen, Bau- und Feuerpolizeivorschriften. Vienna: Manz'sche k.k. Hof-Verlags- u. Universitäts-Buchhandlung, 1887.
N. Oe. Landesgesetze. 3. Bd. Wasserrecht, Flußregulirungs- und Flußpolizei-Vorschriften. Vienna: Manz'sche k.k. Hof-Verlags- u. Universitäts-Buchhandlung, 1897.
Niederösterreichische Landes-Gesetze. Manz'sche Gesetz-Ausgabe. (Hrsg.) Freiherr von Hock. k.k. Bezirkshauptmann. 4 Bd. Straßen- und Eisenbahn-Vorschriften. Verkehrsanlagen in Wien. 2. Aufl. Vienna: Manz'sche k.k. Hof-Verlags- u. Universitäts-Buchhandlung, 1897.
Niederösterreichische Landes-Gesetze. Manz'sche Gesetz-Ausgabe. (Hrsg.) Freiherr von Hock. k.k. Bezirkshauptmann. 5 Bd. Bau- und Feuerpolizei. 2. Aufl. Vienna: Manz'sche k.k. Hof-Verlags- u. Universitäts-Buchhandlung, 1897.

Primary and Secondary Literature

Alkon, Paul K. *Origins of Futuristic Fiction*. Athens: University of Georgia Press, 2010.
Allen, Ann Taylor. *Satire and Society in Wilhelmine Germany: Kladderadatsch & Simplicissimus 1890–1914*. Lexington: University Press of Kentucky, 1984.
Anderson, Benedict. *Imagined Communities: Reflections on the Origin and Spread of Nationalism*. London: Verso, [1983] 1991.
Anderson, Harriet. *Utopian Feminism: Women's Movements in Fin-de-siècle Vienna*. New Haven: Yale University Press, 1992.
Anderson, Olive. *Suicide in Victorian and Edwardian England*. Oxford: Clarendon Press, 1987.
Ashby, Charlotte, Tag Gronberg, and Simon Shaw-Miller (eds). *The Viennese Café and Fin-de-Siècle Culture*. New York: Berghahn Books, 2013.
Assmann, Jan. *Moses the Egyptian: The Memory of Egypt in Western Monotheism*. Cambridge, MA: Harvard University Press, 1999.
Bach, Ulrich E. *Tropics of Vienna: Colonial Utopias of the Habsburg Empire*. New York: Berghahn Books, 2016.
Bakhtin, Mikhail. *Rabelais and His World*. Bloomington: Indiana University Press, 1984.
Balzer, Jens. '"Hully gee, I'm a Hieroglyphe": Mobilizing the Gaze and the Invention of Comics in New York City, 1895', in Jörn Ahrens and Arno Meteling (eds), *Comics and the City: Urban Space in Print, Picture and Sequence* (New York: Continuum, 2010), 19–31.
Banik-Schweizer, Renate, and Gerhard Meißl. *Industriestadt Wien: Die Durchsetzung der industriellen Marktproduktion in der Habsburgerresidenz*. Vienna: Franz Deuticke, 1983.
Békési, Sandor. 'The Attraction of Heimat: Homeland Protection in Vienna around 1900, or the Preservation and Reform of the City', in Arnold Bartetzky and Marc Schalenberg (eds), *Urban Planning and the Pursuit of Happiness* (Berlin: Jovis, 2009), 67–79.
Beller, Steven. 'Introduction', in Steven Beller (ed.), *Rethinking Vienna 1900* (New York: Berghahn Books, 2001), 1–25.
Beller, Steven. Review of Coen, Deborah R., *Vienna in the Age of Uncertainty: Science, Liberalism and Private Life*. HABSBURG, H-Net Reviews, January 2010. Retrieved 25 January 2019 from https://networks.h-net.org/node/19384/reviews/19886/beller-coen-vienna-age-uncertainty-science-liberalism-and-private-life.
Beller, Steven. *Vienna and the Jews 1867–1938: A Cultural History*. Cambridge: Cambridge University Press, 2003.
Berg, O.F. (pseudonym for Ottokar Franz Ebersberg). *Kikeriki im Arrest: Ernste und heitere Erinnerungen an meine Haft*. Vienna: Dirnböck, 1863.
Berg, O.F. *Der Modeteufel: Posse mit Gesang in 3 Akten*. Vienna: A. Schweiger, 1860.
Berg, O.F. *Tage-Buch des Kikeriki*. Vienna: Sommer, 1870. Retrieved 28 January 2019 from http://digital.onb.ac.at/OnbViewer/viewer.faces?doc=ABO_%2BZ22880030X.
Berger, Peter. *Redeeming Laughter: The Comic Dimension of Human Experience*. Berlin: Walter de Gruyter, 1997.
Bergson, Henri. *Nauru: Tutkimus komiikan merkityksestä*. French original: *Le Rire: Essai sur la signification du comique* (1900), trans. Sanna Isto and Marko Pasanen. Helsinki: Loki-kirjat, 1994.
Berman, Marshall. *All That Is Solid Melts Into Air: The Experience of Modernity*. New York: Penguin Books, 1988.

Bernhard, Marianne. *Die Wiener Ringstraße: Architektur und Gesellschaft 1858–1906*. Munich: Kremayer & Scheriau, 1992.
Billig, Michael. *Banal Nationalism*. London: Sage, 2004.
Billig, Michael. *Laughter and Ridicule: Towards a Social Critique of Humour*. London: Sage, 2012.
Blevins, Cameron. 'Space, Nation, and the Triumph of Region: A View of the World from Houston'. *Journal of American History* 101(1) (2014), 122–47.
Bögl, Günther, and Harald Seyrl. *Die Wiener Polizei im Spiegel der Zeiten: Eine Chronik in Bildern*. 2. edition. Vienna: Edition S., 1993.
Boyer, John W. *Political Radicalism in Late Imperial Vienna: Origins of the Christian Social Movement, 1848–1897*. Chicago: University of Chicago Press, 1981.
Boym, Svetlana. *The Future of Nostalgia*. New York: Basic Books, 2001.
Bremmer, Jan, and Herman Roodenburg. 'Introduction: Humour and History', in Jan Bremmer and Herman Roodenburg (eds), *A Cultural History of Humour* (Cambridge: Polity Press, 1997), 1–10.
Brigstocke, Julian. *The Life of the City: Space, Humour, and the Experience of Truth in Fin-de-siècle Montmartre*. Surrey: Ashgate, 2014.
Buchmann, Bertrand Michael. 'Dynamik des Städtebaus', in Peter Csendes and Ferdinand Oppl (eds), *Wien – Geschichte einer Stadt: Von 1790 bis zur Gegenwart*, Vol. 3 (Vienna: Böhlau, 2006), 47–84.
Buchmann, Bertrand Michael. 'Die Epoche vom Ende des 18. Jahrhunderts bis um 1860: Wirtschaft und Finanzen', in Peter Csendes and Ferdinand Oppl (eds), *Wien – Geschichte einer Stadt: Von 1790 bis zur Gegenwart*, Vol. 3 (Vienna: Böhlau, 2006), 129–48.
Buchmann, Bertrand Michael. 'Politik und Verwaltung', in Peter Csendes and Ferdinand Oppl (eds), *Wien – Geschichte einer Stadt: Von 1790 bis zur Gegenwart*, Vol. 3 (Vienna: Böhlau, 2006), 85–129.
Burke, Peter. 'Frontiers of the Comic in Early Modern Italy, c. 1350-1750', in Jan Bremmer and Herman Roodenburg (eds), *Cultural History of Humour: From Antiquity to the Present Day* (Cambridge: Polity Press, 1997), 61–75.
Burri, Michael. 'Theodor Herzl and Richard von Shaukal: Self-Styled Nobility and the Sources of Bourgeois Belligerence in Prewar Vienna', in Steven Beller (ed.), *Rethinking Vienna 1900* (New York: Berghahn Books, 2001), 105–31.
Butler, Judith. *Gender Trouble*. New York: Routledge, 1999.
Castle, Terry. *Masquerade and Civilization: The Carnivalesque in Eighteenth-Century English Culture and Fiction*. London: Methuen, 1986.
Chase, Jefferson S. *Inciting Laughter: The Development of 'Jewish Humor' in 19th Century German Culture*. Berlin: Walter de Gruyter, 2000.
Chiavacci, Vinzenz. *Geschichten aus Alt-Wien*. Vienna: Almathea, [1884] 1973.
Chiavacci, Vinzenz. *Der Weltuntergang: Eine Phantasie aus dem Jahre 1900*. Stuttgart: A. Bonz, 1897. Retrieved 25 January 2019 from https://archive.org/details/derweltuntergan01chiagoog/page/n6.
Chiavacci, Vinzenz. *Wiener vom Grund: Bilder aus dem Kleinleben der Großstadt*. Vienna: Verlag von k.k. Hofbuchhandlung Karl Prochaska, 1888.
Coen, Deborah R. *Vienna in the Age of Uncertainty: Science, Liberalism and Private Life*. Chicago: University of Chicago Press, 2007.
Cohen, William A. 'Introduction: Locating Filth', in William A. Cohen and Ryan Johnson (eds), *Filth, Dirt, Disgust and Modern Life* (Minneapolis: University of Minnesota Press, 2004), vii–xxxvii.

Colomina, Beatriz. *Privacy and Publicity: Architecture as Mass Media.* Cambridge, MA: MIT Press, 1998.
Corbin, Alain. 'Paris-Province', in Pierre Nora (ed.), *Realms of Memory: Rethinking the French Past*, Vol. 1, *Conflicts and Divisions*, trans. Arthur Goldhammer (New York: Columbia University Press, 1996), 427–64.
Critchley, Simon. *On Humour.* New York: Routledge, 2002.
Darnton, Robert. *The Great Cat Massacre: And Other Episodes in French Cultural History.* New York: Vintage Books, [1985] 1999.
Darnton, Robert. 'History of Reading', in Peter Burke (ed.), *New Perspectives on Historical Writing* (Cambridge: Polity Press, 1995), 140–68.
Davies, Christie. *Ethnic Humour around the World: A Comparative Analysis.* Bloomington: Indiana University Press, 1990.
Davies, Christie. *Jokes and Targets.* Bloomington: Indiana University Press, 2011.
Dundes, Alan. *Cracking Jokes: Studies of Sick Humour Cycles and Stereotypes.* Berkeley: Ten Speed Press, 1987.
Eco, Umberto (ed.). *Die Geschichte der Hässlichkeit.* Translated from the Italian by Friederike Hausmann, Petra Kaiser and Sigrid Vagt. Munich: Carl Hanser Verlag, 2010.
Ehmer, Josef. 'Zur sozialen Schichtung der Wiener Bevölkerung 1857 bis 1910', in Gerhard Melinz and Susan Zimmermann (eds), *Wien–Prag–Budapest: Blütezeit der Habsburgermetropolen. Urbanisierung, Kommunalpolitik, gesellschaftliche Konflikte 1867–1918* (Vienna: Promedia, 1996), 73–83.
Eines kleinen Teufels humoristisch-satirische Spaziergänge durch Stadt und Land. Vienna: Gedruckt von Edl. v. Schmidbauer u. Holzwarth, 1850. Retrieved 28 January 2019 from http://data.onb.ac.at/ABO/%2BZ202398006.
Eiterberger von Edelberg, Rudolf. *Die preisgekrönten Entwürfe zur Erweiterung der Inneren Stadt Wien: Mit sieben in der kaiserlich-königlichen Hof- und Staatsdruckerei in Farbendruck ausgeführten Plänen und einem erläuternden Texte von Prof. R.v.E.* Vienna: Keiserlich-königliche Staatsdruckerei, [1859] 1981.
Estermann, Alfred. *Die Deutschen Literaturzeitschriften 1850–1880: Bibliographien – Programme.* Munich: K.G. Saur, 1988.
Fassman, Hans, and Rainer Münz. 'Between Melting Pot and Ethnic Fragmentation: Historical and Recent Immigration to Vienna', in Curtis C. Roseman, Hans Dieter Laux, and Günther Thieme (eds), *EthniCity: Geographic Perspectives on Ethnic Change in Modern Cities* (Lanham, MD: Rowman and Littlefield, 1996), 165–86.
Feigl, Susanne. *Wiener Humor um 1900: Literarische Skizzen.* Vienna: Edition S. Verlag der Österreichischen Staatsdruckerei, 1986.
Felski, Rita. *The Gender of Modernity.* Cambridge, MA: Harvard University Press, 1995.
Finney, Gail. 'Introduction: Unity in Difference?', in Gail Finney (ed.), *Look Who's Laughing: Gender and Comedy.* Studies in Humor and Gender, Vol. 1 (Philadelphia: Gordon and Breach, 1994), 1–13.
Finney, Gail (ed.). *Look Who's Laughing: Gender and Comedy.* Studies in Humor and Gender, Vol. 1. Philadelphia: Gordon and Breach, 1994.
Forsström, Riikka. *Possible Worlds: The Idea of Happiness in the Utopian Vision of Louis-Sébastien Mercier.* Helsinki: SKS, 2002.
Fóti-Roessler, Katharina. *Theoretische Auseinandersetzungen mit der Wiener Stadterweiterung ab 1857 an Hand der Allgemeinen Bauzeitung.* Ph.d. dissertation. Vienna: Universität Wien, 1992.

Frahm, Ole. 'Every Window Tells a Story: Remarks on the Urbanity of Early Comic Strips', in Jörn Ahrens and Arno Meteling (eds), *Comics and the City: Urban Space in Print, Picture and Sequence* (New York: Continuum, 2010), 32–44.
Freud, Sigmund. *Der Humor*. Frankfurt am Main: Fischer, [1927] 2006.
Freud, Sigmund. *Moses and Monotheism*. Translated from the German by Katherine Jones. Published by the Hogarth Press and the Institute of Psycho-Analysis. Hertfordshire: Garden City Press, 1939.
Freud, Sigmund. *Die Traumdeutung*. Leipzig: Franz Deuticke, 1899, postdated 1900. Retrieved 28 January 2019 from https://archive.org/details/Freud_1900_Die_Traumdeutung_k/page/n0.
Freud, Sigmund. *Traumdeutung*. 3. extended edition. Leipzig: Franz Deuticke, 1911. Retrieved 28 January 2019 from https://archive.org/details/Traumdeutung3.VermehrteAuflage/page/n217.
Freud, Sigmund. *Der Witz und seine Beziehung zum Unbewussten*. Frankfurt am Main: Fischer, [1905] 2006.
Frevert, Ute. *Mann und Weib und Weib und Mann: Geschlechter-Differenzen in der Moderne*. Munich: C.H. Beck, 1995.
Frigyesi, Judith. *Béla Bartók and the Turn-of-the-Century Budapest*. Berkeley: University of California Press, 1998.
Frisby, David. *Cityscapes of Modernity: Critical Explorations*. Cambridge: Polity Press, 2001.
Fritzsche, Peter. 'Readers, Browsers, Strangers, Spectators: Narrative Forms and Metropolitan Encounters in Twentieth-Century Berlin', in Malcolm Gee and Tim Kirk (eds), *Printed Matters: Printing, Publishing and Urban Culture in Europe in the Modern Period*. Historical Urban Studies (Aldershot: Ashgate, 2002), 88–104.
Fritzsche, Peter. *Reading Berlin 1900*. Cambridge, MA: Harvard University Press, 1998.
Fry, William F. 'Humor and Chaos'. *Humor. International Journal of Humor Research* 3–5 (1992), 219–232.
Fuess, Jo Ann Mitchell. *The Cultural Crisis of Lower Middle Class Vienna 1848–1892: A Study of the Works of Friedrich Schlögl*. Lincoln: University of Nebraska, 1992.
Fulgence, Marion (pseudonym for Camille Flammarion). *Wonderful Balloon Ascents or the Conquest of the Skies: A History of Balloons and Balloon Voyages*. London: Cassel, Petter & Galpin, 1870. Retrieved 28 January 2019 from http://en.wikisource.org/wiki/Wonderful_Balloon_Ascents.
Galindo Rodriguez, Vanesa. 'Visuality and Practices of Looking in Nineteenth-Century Madrid: Representations of the Old and Modern City in the Illustrated Press', in U. Krampl, R. Beck, and E. Retaillaud-Bajac (eds), *Les cinq sens de la ville du Moyen Âge à nos jours* (Tours: Presses Universitaires François-Rabelais, 2013), 227–42.
Gates, Barbara T. *Victorian Suicide: Mad Crimes and Sad Histories*. Princeton: Princeton University Press, 1988.
Gewey, Franz, and Carl Meisl. *Wien mit seinen Vorstädten humoristisch geschildert*. Vol. 1. Vienna: Geistinger, n.d.
Gilbert, Joanne R. *Performing Marginality: Humor, Gender and Cultural Critique*. Detroit: Wayne State University Press, 2004.
Gilman, Sander. *The Jew's Body*. New York: Routledge, 1991.
Gluck, Mary. 'Afterthoughts about Fin-de-Siècle Vienna: The Problem of Aesthetic Culture in Central Europe', in Steven Beller (ed.), *Rethinking Vienna 1900* (New York: Berghahn Books, 2001), 264–70.

Gluck, Mary. *The Invisible Jewish Budapest: Metropolitan Culture at the Fin de Siècle*. The George L. Mosse Series in Modern European Cultural and Intellectual History. Madison: University of Wisconsin Press, 2016.

Goldstein, Robert Justin. *Censorship of Political Caricature in Nineteenth-Century France*. Kent: Kent State University Press, 1989.

Graf, Andreas, and Susanne Pellatz. 'Familien- und Unterhaltungszeitschriften', in Georg Jäger (ed.), *Geschichte des Deutschen Buchhandels im 19. und 20. Jahrhundert*, Vol. 1, *Das Kaiserreich 1871–1918* (Frankfurt am Main: MVB, 2003), 409–522.

Gray, David W.S. 'Gavarni's Parisian Population Reproduced', in Malcom Gee and Tim Kirk (eds), *Printed Matters: Printing, Publishing and Urban Culture in Europe in the Modern Period*. Historical Urban Studies (Aldershot: Ashgate, 2002), 48–70.

Green, Nicholas. *The Spectacle of Nature*. Manchester: Manchester University Press, 1990.

Grimm, Jacob, and Wilhelm Grimm. *Deutsches Wörterbuch*. K. 5. Band. Edited by Dr. Rudolf Hildebrand. Leipzig: Verlag von S. Hirzel, 1873.

Gröger, Hans Roman. *Schienen für die Ewigkeit: 113 Wiener Straßenbahnstrecken aus dem Österreichischen Staatsarchiv*. Innsbruck: Studien Verlag, 2011.

Grönholm, Pertti, and Heli Paalumäki. 'Nostalgian ja utopian risteyksessä: Keskusteluja modernin kaipuun merkityksistä ja aikaulottuvuuksista', in Heli Paalumäki and Pertti Grönholm (eds), *Kaipaava moderni: Nostalgian ja utopian kohtaamisia Euroopassa 1600-luvulta 2000-luvulle*. Historia mirabilis 11 (Turku: Turun Historiallinen yhdistys, 2015), 9–38.

Habermas, Jürgen. *Strukturwandel der Öffentlichkeit: Untersuchungen zu einer Kategorie der bürgerlichen Gesellschaft*. Neuwied am Rhein: Luchterhand, 1965.

Hacohen, Malachi Haim. 'Popper's Cosmopolitanism: Culture Clash and Jewish Identity', in Steven Beller (ed.), *Rethinking Vienna 1900* (New York: Berghahn Books, 2001), 171–94.

Hainisch, Marianne. *Die Brodfrage der Frau*. Vienna: G. Giestel, 1875. Retrieved 28 January 2019 from http://www.literature.at/alo?objid=12806.

Hakkarainen, Heidi. 'Aus der Nähe betrachtet. Figaro: Folgen der Stadterweiterung, 1858', in Harald R. Stühlinger (ed.), *Vom Werden der Wiener Ringstraße* (Vienna: Metroverlag, 2015), 244–45.

Hakkarainen, Heidi. 'City Upside Down: Laughing at the Flooding of the Danube in Late Nineteenth-Century Vienna', in Deborah Simonton and Hannu Salmi (eds), *Catastrophe, Gender and Urban Experience, 1648–1920*. Routledge Research in Gender and History (New York: Routledge, 2017), 157–76.

Hakkarainen, Heidi. 'Humor, Satire und Karikatur: Das humoristische Imaginarium der Wiener Ringstraße', in Harald R. Stühlinger (ed.), *Vom Werden der Wiener Ringstraße* (Vienna: Metroverlag, 2015), 220–43.

Hakkarainen, Heidi. 'Koomisia kohtaamisia: Monikansallisen kaupungin ristiriidat 1800-luvun lopun wieniläisessä huumorissa', in Anne Ollila and Juhana Saarelainen (eds), *Kosmopoliittisuus, monikulttuurisuus, kansainvälisyys: Kulttuurihistoriallisia näkökulmia* (Turku: K&H, 2013), 106–31.

Hakkarainen, Heidi. 'Menetetty Alt-Wien: Huumori ja nostalgia populaareissa pilalehdissä 1800-luvun jälkipuolella', in Heli Paalumäki and Pertti Grönholm (eds), *Kaipaava moderni: Nostalgian ja utopian kohtaamisia Euroopassa 1600-luvulta 2000-luvulle*. Historia mirabilis 11 (Turku: Turun Historiallinen yhdistys, 2015), 145–76.

Hamann, Brigitte. *Hitlers Wien: Lehrjahre eines Diktators*. Munich: Piper, 1996.

Hank, Rainer. 'Topik und Topografie: Seelenlandschaft und Stadtlandschaft im Wien der Jahrhundertwende', in Manfred Smuda (ed.), *Die Großstadt als >Text<*. Bild und Text (Munich: Wilhelm Fink Verlag, 1992), 217–38.

Hansen, Miriam B. 'The Mass Production of the Senses: Classical Cinema as Vernacular Modernism'. *Modernism/Modernity* 6(2) (1999), 59–77.

Hapuli, Ritva. *Nykyajan sininen kukka: Olavi Paavolainen ja nykyaika*. Helsinki: SKS, 1995.

Harvey, David. *Paris, Capital of Modernity*. New York: Routledge, 2006.

Harvey, Robert C. 'How Comics Came to Be: Through the Juncture of Word and Image from Magazine Gag Cartoons to Newspaper Strips, Tools for Critical Appreciation plus Rare Seldom Witnessed Historical Facts', in Jeet Heer and Kent Worcester (eds), *A Comics Studies Reader* (Jackson: University Press of Mississippi, 2009), 25–45.

Hobbes, Thomas. *Leviathan*. Revised student edition. Cambridge Texts in the History of Political Thought. Edited by Richard Tuck. Cambridge: Cambridge University Press, [1651] 1997.

Hohendahl, Uwe. 'Die Entstehung der modernen Öffentlichkeit im Zusammenhang mit der Entstehung des modernen Publikums', in Uwe Hohendahl et al. (eds), *Öffentlichkeit: Geschichte eines kritischen Begriffs* (Stuttgart: Verlag J.B. Metzler, 2000), 8–37.

Horel, Catherine. 'Austria-Hungary 1867–1914', in Robert Justin Goldstein and Andrew M. Nedd (eds), *Political Censorship of the Visual Arts in Nineteeth-Century Europe: Arresting Images* (London: Palgrave McMillan, 2015), 88–129.

Hutcheon, Linda. *Irony's Edge: The Theory and Politics of Irony*. New York: Routledge, 1995.

Ingram, Susan, and Markus Reisenleitner. *Wiener Chic: A Locational History of Vienna Fashion*. Bristol: Intellect, 2013.

Innerhofer, Roland. *Deutsche Science Fiction 1870–1914: Rekonstruktion und Analyse der Anfänge einer Gattung*. Vienna: Böhlau, 1996.

Jäger, Georg. 'Das Zeitschriftenwesen', in Georg Jäger (ed.), *Geschichte des Deutschen Buchhandels im 19. und 20. Jahrhundert*, Vol. 1, *Das Kaiserreich 1871–1918* (Frankfurt am Main: MVB, 2003), 368–89.

Janik, Allan. 'Vienna 1900 Revisited: Paradigms and Problems', in Steven Beller (ed.), *Rethinking Vienna 1900* (New York: Berghahn Books, 2001), 27–56.

Janik, Allan, and Stephen Toulmin. *Wittgenstein's Vienna*. Chicago: Elephant Paperbacks, [1973] 1996.

Jelavich, Peter. *Berlin Cabaret*. Cambridge, MA: Harvard University Press, 1996.

Jemand (pseudonym for Berttha von Suttner). *Das Maschinenalter: Zukunftsvorlesungen über unsere Zeit*. Zürich: Verlags Magazin, 1889. Retrieved 28 January 2019 from https://archive.org/details/bub_gb_M5UaAAAAYAAJ_2/page/n3.

Jenkins, Henry. *Confronting the Challenges of Participatory Culture: Media Education for the 21st Century*. With Ravi Purushotma, Margaret Weigel, Katie Clinton, and Alice J. Robison. Cambridge, MA: The MIT Press, 2009. Retrieved 28 January 2019 from https://mitpress.mit.edu/books/confronting-challenges-participatory-culture.

Jocosus Jocus, Hilarius (pseud.). *Die Neuzeit im Elysium oder das lustige Wien nebst einigen Umgebungen im allerneuesten rosenfarbigsten Humor tief unter der Erde*. Vienna: Eurich, 1862–63.

Johannisson, Karin. *Nostalgia: En känslas historia*. Stockholm: Bonnier, 2001.

Johnson, Bruce. 'Sites of Sound'. *Oral Tradition* 24(2) (2009), 455–70.

Johnston, William M. *The Austrian Mind: An Intellectual and Social History 1848–1938*. Berkeley: University of California Press, 1983.

Jones, Steven E. 'Balloons: An Essay on Mary Shelley's *The Last Man*'. Romantic Circles, 1997. Retrieved 28 January 2019 from http://www.rc.umd.edu/editions/mws/lastman/balloons.htm.

Jonsson, Stefan. *Subject without Nation: Robert Musil and the History of Modern Identity*. Durham, NC: Duke University Press, 2000.

Judson, Pieter M. *Exclusive Revolutionaries: Liberal Politics, Social Experience and National Identity in the Austrian Empire, 1848–1914*. Ann Arbor: University of Michigan Press, 1996.

Judson, Pieter M. *The Habsburg Empire: A New History*. Cambridge, MA: The Belknap Press of Harvard University Press, 2016.

Knuuttila, Seppo. *Kansanhuumorin mieli: Kaskut maailmankuvan aineksena*. Helsinki: SKS, 1992.

Koch, Ursula E. *Der Teufel in Berlin: Von der Märzrevolution bis zu Bismarcks Entlassung. Illustrierte politische Witzblätter einer Metropole 1848–1890*. Cologne: C.W. Leske Verlag, 1991.

Koestler, Arthur. *The Act of Creation*. London: Hutchinson, 1964.

Kohlbauer-Fritz, Gabriele. 'Familiengeschichten: Die Ringstraßenpalais und ihre Bewohner', in Gabriele Kohlbauer-Fritz (ed.), *Ringstraße: Ein jüdischer Boulevard* (Vienna: Almathea, 2015), 23–58.

Korabek, Sebastian. *Preß-Proceß des 'Kikeriki': Abgeführt vor dem k.k. Landesgerichte in Wien am 5. August 1862*. Vienna: Buchdruckerei von Alexander Eurich, 1862.

Korhonen, Anu. *Fellows of Infinite Jest: The Fool in Renaissance England*. Cultural History. Turku: University of Turku, 1999.

Korhonen, Anu. *Kiusan henki: Sukupuoli ja huumori uuden ajan alussa*. Jyväskylä: Atena, 2013.

Korhonen, Anu. *Silmän ilot: Kauneuden kulttuurihistoriaa uuden ajan alussa*. Jyväskylä: Atena, 2005.

Kos, Wolfgang (ed.). *Wiener Typen: Klischees und Wirklichkeit*. Vienna: Wien Museum und Brandstätter Verlag, 2013.

Koselleck, Reinhart. *Futures Past: On the Semantics of Historical Time*. Translated and with an introduction by Keith Tribe. New York: Columbia University Press, [1979] 2004.

Kunz, Johannes. *'Der Tod muss ein Wiener Sein': Morbide Geschichten und Anekdoten*. Vienna: Almathea, 2009.

Kunzle, David. *Father of the Comic Strip: Rodolphe Töpffer*. Jackson: University Press of Mississippi, 2007.

Kunzle, David. 'The Voices of Silence: Willette, Steinlen and the Introduction of the Silent Strip in the *Chat Noir* with a German Coda', in Robin Varnum and Christina T. Gibbons (eds), *Comics: Word and Image* (Jackson: University Press of Mississippi, 2001), 3–18.

Laitinen, Riitta. *Order, Materiality and Urban Space in the Early Modern Kingdom of Sweden*. Amsterdam: Amsterdam University Press, 2017.

Lefebvre, Henri. *The Production of Space*. Translated by Donald Nicholson-Smith. Oxford: Blackwell, [1974] 1991.

Levitschnigg, Heinrich Ritter von. *Wien wie es war und ist: Federzeichnungen*. Pest: Hartleben, 1860. Retrieved 28 January 2019 from https://archive.org/details/bub_gb_dTYuAAAAYAAJ.

Lichtblau, Albert. 'Im Visier der antisemitischen Populisten: Jüdische Reiche und die Wiener Rinstraße', in Gabriele Kohlbauer-Fritz (ed.), *Ringstraße: Ein jüdischer Boulevard* (Vienna: Almathea, 2015), 269–84.

Linhardt, Marion. *Residenzstadt und Metropole: Zu einer kulturellen Topographie des Wiener Unterhaltungstheaters (1858–1918)*. Berlin: De Gruyter, 2012.
Lutter, Christina, and Markus Reisenleitner. 'Introducing History (in)to Cultural Studies: Some Remarks on the German Speaking Context'. *Cultural Studies* 16(5) (2002), 611–30.
Maderthaner, Wolfgang. 'Von der Zeit um 1860 bis zum Jahr 1945', in Peter Csendes and Ferdinand Oppl (eds), *Wien – Geschichte einer Stadt: Von 1790 bis zur Gegenwart*, Vol. 3 (Vienna: Böhlau, 2006), 175–544.
Maderthaner, Wolfgang, and Lutz Musner. *Unruly Masses: The Other Side of the Fin-de-siècle Vienna*. New York: Berghahn Books, 2008.
Mai, Fritz (pseudonym for Ferdinand Manussi von Montesole). *Der Floh: Localer Scherz mit Gesang in Einem Akt*. Vienna: Verlag des Verfassers, Druck von J.B. Wallishausser, 1869.
Masaidek, Franz. *Staberl als Fremdenführer in Wien und Umgebung*. Vienna: Waldheim, 1868.
Masaidek, Franz. *Wien und die Wiener aus der Spottvogelperspektive: Wien's Sehens-, Merk- und Nichtswürdigkeiten*. Vienna: Waldheim, 1873.
Masanz, Michaela, and Martina Nagl. *Ringstraßenallee: Von der Freiheit zur Ordnung vor den Toren Wiens*. Vienna: Verlag Franz Deuticke, 1996.
McCloud, Scott. *Understanding Comics: The Invisible Art*. New York: HarperPerennial, 1993.
Meysels, Theodor F. (ed.). *Schauderhafte Moritaten*. Salzburg: Residenz-Verlag, 1962.
Mollik, Kurt, Hermann Reining, and Rudolf Wurzer. *Planung und Verwirklichung der Ringstraßenzone*. Die Wiener Ringstraße. Bild einer Epoche, Vol. III. Vienna: Steiner Verlag, 1980.
Morreall, John. 'Enjoying Incongruity'. *Humor. International Journal of Humor Research* 2(1) (1989), 1–18.
Morreall, John. *The Philosophy of Laughter and Humor*. Albany: State University of New York Press, 1987.
Mulkay, Michael. *On Humour: Its Nature and Its Place in Modern Society*. Cambridge: Polity Press, 1988.
Musil, Robert. *Der Mann ohne Eigenschaften*. Hamburg: Rowohlt Verlag, 1937. Retrieved 28 January 2019 from https://archive.org/stream/MusilDerMannOhneEigenschaften/Musil.
Musner, Lutz. *Der Geschmack von Wien: Kultur und Habitus einer Stadt*. Interdisziplinäre Stadtforschung. Frankfurt am Main: Campus Verlag, 2009.
Neidl, Julius. *Humoristischer Fremdenführer für Wien und Umgebung*. Vienna: Verlag des Verfassers, 1880.
Nicholson, Eric A. '"That's How It Is": Comic Travesties of Sex and Gender in Early Sixteenth-Century Venice', in Gail Finney (ed.), *Look Who's Laughing: Gender and Comedy*. Studies in Humor and Gender, Vol. 1 (Philadelphia: Gordon and Breach, 1994), 17–34.
Nochlin, Linda. 'Introduction. Starting with the Self: Jewish Identity and Its Representation', in Linda Nochlin and Tamar Garb (eds), *The Jew in the Text: Modernity and the Construction of Identity* (London: Thames and Hudson, 1995), 7–19.
Nöllke, Matthias. *Daniel Spitzers Wiener Spatziergänge: Liberales Feuilleton im Zeitungskontext*. Frankfurt am Main: Peter Lang, 1994.
Nora, Pierre. 'General Introduction: Between Memory and History', in Pierre Nora (ed.), *Realms of Memory: Rethinking the French Past*, Vol. 1, *Conflicts and Divisions*, trans. Arthur Goldhammer (New York: Columbia University Press, 1996), 1–20.

Olechowski, Thomas. *Die Entwicklung des Preßrechts in Österreich bis 1918: Ein Beitrag zu österreichischen Medienrechtsgeschichte*. Vienna: Manzsche Verlags- und Universitätsbuchhandlung, 2004.
Oring, Elliott. *Engaging Humour*. Champaign: University of Illinois Press, 2003.
Oring, Elliott. *Jokes and Their Relations*. Lexington: University Press of Kentucky, 1992.
Oring, Elliott. *The Jokes of Sigmund Freud: A Study in Humor and Jewish Identity*. Philadelphia: University of Pennsylvania Press, 1997.
Patka, Marcus G. *Wege des Lachens: Jüdischer Witz und Humor aus Wien*. Enzyklopädie des Wiener Wissens, Vol. XIII. Weitra: Bibliothek der Provinz, 2010.
Perloff, Marjorie. *Edge of Irony: Modernism in the Shadow of the Habsburg Empire*. Chicago: University of Chicago Press, 2016.
Peterseil, Walter. *Nationalen Stereotypen in der Karikatur: Die Magyaren, Polen, Serben, Slowanen und Tschechen in Wiener humoristisch-satirischen Zeitschriften (1895–1921)*. Thesis. Vienna: Universität Wien, 1991.
Plamper, Jan. 'The History of Emotions: An Interview with William Reddy, Barbara Rosenwein, and Peter Stearns'. *History and Theory* 49(2) (2010), 237–65.
Pötzl, Eduard. 'Das ausgegrabene Haus'. In *Rund um den Stephansthurm*. Vienna: Verlag von Robert Mohr, 1916.
Pötzl, Eduard. 'Gedanken eines Komfortablepferdes'. In *Gesammelte Skizzen*. 1. Volume. Vienna: Verlag von Robert Mohr, 1907.
Pötzl, Eduard. 'Lumpenball'. In *Jung-Wien: Allerhand wienerische Skizzen. Hochdeutsch und in der Muttersprach*. Berlin: Verlag von Wilhelm Friedrich, 1885.
Pötzl, Eduard. *Stadtmenschen: Ein Wiener Skizzenbuch*. 2nd ed. Vienna: Mohr, 1895.
Prakash, Gyan. 'Introduction: Imagining the Modern City, Darkly', in Gyan Prakash (ed.), *Noir Urbanisms: Dystopic Images of the Modern City* (Princeton: Princeton University Press, 2010), 1–15.
Rabus, A. *Vor fünfzig Jahren: Erinnerungen an Wien aus dem Jahre 1848*. Würzburg: Druck von Bonitas-Bauer, Kgl. Bayr. Hofdruckerei, 1898.
Rasocha, Ingrid. *Die humoristisch-satirische Presse im Vormärz und während der Revolution 1848*. Thesis. Vienna: Universität Wien, 1990.
Ratous, Olivier, and Martin Baumeister. 'Rire en ville: Rire de la ville. L'humour et le comique comme objets pour l'histoire urbaine contemporaine. Rire en ville à l'époque contemporaire'. *Histoire Urbaine* 2(31) (2011), 5–18.
Reddy, William M. *The Navigation of Feeling: A Framework for the History of Emotions*. Cambridge: Cambridge University Press, 2004.
Reisenleitner, Markus. 'Austria: To 1918', in Derek Jones (ed.), *Censorship: A World Encyclopedia*, Vol. 1 (London: Fitzroy Dearborn, 2001), 147–50.
Reisenleitner, Markus. 'Tradition, Cultural Boundaries and the Construction of Spaces of Identity'. *spacesofidentity* (1.1) (2001). Retrieved 28 January 2019 from http://www.yorku.ca/soi/Vol_1/_HTML/Reisenleitner.html.
Robb, David. 'Cities, Clocks and Chaos: A Modernist Perception of Time in the Comedy of Karl Valentin', in Susanne Marten-Finnis and Matthias Vecker (eds), *Berlin – Wien – Prag: Moderne, Minderheiten und Migranten in der Zwischenkriegszeit. Modernity, Minorities and Migration in the Inter-war Period* (Berlin: Peter Lang, 2001), 77–89.
Rogoff, Irit. 'Gustav Klimt, a Bridgehead to Modernism', in László Péter and Robert B. Pysent (eds), *Intellectuals and the Future in the Habsburg Monarchy 1890-1914* (London: Macmillan Press Ltd., 1988), 29–45.

Roschitz, Karlheinz. *Kaiserwalzer: Traum und Wirklichkeit der Ringstrassenzeit*. Vienna: Ueberreuter, 1996.
Rosenwein, Barbara H. 'Problems and Methods in the History of Emotions'. *Passions in Context* 1(1) (2010). Retrieved 25 January 2019 from https://www.passionsincontext.de/index.php/?id=557&L=0.
Rotenberg, Robert. *Landscape and Power in Vienna*. Baltimore, MD: Johns Hopkins University Press, 1995.
Rüger, Jan. 'Die Berliner Schnauze im Ersten Weltkrieg', in Thomas Biskup and Marc Schalenberg (eds), *Selling Berlin: Imagebildung und Stadtmarketing von der preußischen Residenz bis zur Bundeshauptstadt* (Stuttgart: Franz Steiner Verlag, 2008), 147–60.
Rumpler, Helmut. *Eine Chance für Mitteleuropa: Bürgerliche Emanzipation und Staatsverfall in der Habsburgermonarchie*. Österreichische Geschichte 1804–1914. Ed. Herwig Wolfram. Vienna: Ueberreuter, 2005.
Sachslehner, Johannes. *Wien: Geschichte einer Stadt*. Vienna: Pichler Verlag, 2012.
Salmi, Hannu. *Nineteenth-Century Europe: A Cultural History*. Cambridge: Polity Press, 2008.
Schäfer, Julia. *Vermessen – gezeichnet – verlacht: Judenbilder in Populären Zeitschriften 1918–1933*. Frankfurt am Main: Campus Verlag, 2004.
Schäfer, Susanne. *Komik in Kultur und Kontext*. Studien Deutsch, Vol. 22. Munich: iudicium Verlag, 1996.
Scheidl, Ernst. *Die humoristisch-satirische Presse im Wien von den Anfängen bis 1918 und die öffentliche Meinung*. Ph.D. dissertation. Vienna: Universität Wien, 1950.
Schivelbusch, Wolfgang. *Disenchanted Night: The Industrialisation of Light in the Nineteenth Century*. Translated from the German by Angela Davies. Berkeley: University of California Press, 1995.
Schivelbusch, Wolfgang. *The Railway Journey: The Industrialization of Time and Space in the Nineteenth Century*. Berkeley: University of California Press, 2014.
Schlögl, Friedrich. *Aus Alt-und Neu-Wien (Nebst einen Stück Autobiografie)*. A lecture given 28 January 1882 at Bösendorfer Hall in Vienna. Published by Viennese Students' Club. Vienna: Verlag von Carl Teufen, 1882.
Schlögl, Friedrich. *Wiener Blut*. Vienna: L. Rosner, 1873.
Schlögl, Friedrich. *Wiener Luft: Kleine Culturbilder aus dem Volksleben der alten Kaiserstadt*. Vienna: Rosner, 1876.
Schneider, Elfriede. *Karikatur und Satire als politische Kampfmittel: Ein Beitrag zur Wiener satirisch-humoristischen Presse des 19. Jahrhunderts (1849–1914)*. Ph.D. dissertation. Vienna: Universität Wien, 1972.
Schorske, Carl E. *Fin-de-siècle Vienna: Politics and Culture*. Cambridge: Cambridge University Press, [1961] 1981.
Schorske, Carl E. *Thinking with History: Explorations in the Passage to Modernism*. Princeton: Princeton University Press, 1998.
Schwartz, Vanessa R. *Spectacular Realities: Early Mass Culture in Fin-de-siècle Paris*. Berkeley: University of California Press, 1999.
Scott, Derek B. *Sounds of the Metropolis: The 19th-Century Popular Music Revolution in London, New York, Paris and Vienna*. Oxford: Oxford University Press, 2008.
Scott, Joan Wallach. 'Introduction: "Flyers to the Unknown". Gender, History and Psychoanalysis', in *The Fantasy of Feminist History* (Durham, NC: Duke University Press, 2011), 1–22.

Segel, Harold B. *The Vienna Coffee House Wits, 1890–1938*. West Lafayette: Purdue University Press, 1993.
Sennett, Richard. *The Fall of Public Man*. Cambridge: Cambridge University Press, 1977.
Sennett, Richard. *Flesh and Stone: The Body and the City in Western Civilization*. New York: W.W. Norton & Company. 1996.
Seyrl, Harald. *Wiener Pitaval*. Vienna: Edition Seyrl, 2000.
Shaya, Gregory. 'The *Flâneur*, the *Badaud* and the Making of a Mass Public in France, circa 1860–1910'. *American Historical Review* 109(1) (2004), 41–77.
Sheppard, Alice. 'Social Cognition, Gender Roles, and Women's Humor', in June Sochen (ed.), *Women's Comic Visions* (Detroit: Wayne State University Press, 1991), 33–56.
Simmel, Georg. *Suurkaupunki ja moderni elämä: Kirjoituksia vuosilta 1895–1917*, trans. Tiina Huuhtanen, ed. Arto Noro. Helsinki: Gaudeamus, 2005.
Sitte, Camillo. *Der Städte-Bau nach seinen künstlerischen Grundsätzen: Ein Beitrag zur Lösung moderner Fragen der Architektur und monumentaler Plastik unter besonderer Beziehung auf Wien*. Vienna: Verlag von Carl Kraeser, [1889] 1901. Retrieved 29 January 2019 from https://archive.org/details/derstdtebaunac00sittuoft/page/n4.
Sitter, Carl. *Modernes Wien: Humoristische Federzeichnungen*. Vienna: Waldheim, 1859.
Sked, Alan. *The Decline & Fall of the Habsburg Empire 1815–1918*. London: Longman, 1989.
Sochen, June. 'Introduction', in June Sochen (ed.), *Women's Comic Visions* (Detroit: Wayne State University Press, 1991), 9–16.
Soja, Edward. 'History: Geography: Modernity', in Simon During (ed.), *The Cultural Studies Reader* (New York: Routledge, 1993), 135–50.
Spector, Scott. *Violent Sensations: Sex, Crime & Utopia in Vienna and Berlin, 1860–1914*. Chicago: University of Chicago Press, 2016.
Spitzer, Daniel. *Wiener Spaziergänge*, Vol. 1. Munich: Georg Müller, 1912.
Springer, Elisabeth. *Geschichte und Kulturleben der Wiener Ringstraße*. Wiesbaden: Franz Steiner Verlag, 1979.
Stallybrass, Peter, and Allon White. *The Politics and Poetics of Transgression*. London: Methuen, 1986.
Stearns, Peter N. *American Cool: Constructing a Twentieth-Century Emotional Style*. New York: New York University Press, 1994.
Steinwender, Engelbert. *Von der Stadtguardia zur Sicherheitswache: Wiener Polizeiwachen und ihre Zeit. 1. Von der Frühzeit bis 1932*. Graz: Weishaupt Verlag, 1992.
Stierle, Karlheinz. 'Der Tod der großen Stadt: Paris als neues Rom und Karthago', in Manfred Smuda (ed.), *Die Großstadt als >Text<* (Munich: Wilhelm Fink, 1992), 101–29.
Strinati, Dominic. *An Introduction to the Theories of Popular Culture*. London: Routledge, 2004.
Stühlinger, Harald Robert 'Inundationen, miese Luft und wenig Wasser: Berichte über den Stadtzustand aus dem Wien von 1858', in Harald R. Stühlinger (ed.), *Vom Werden der Wiener Ringstraße* (Vienna: Metroverlag, 2015), 17–37.
Stühlinger, Harald Robert. *Der Wettbewerb zur Wiener Ringstraße*. Ph.D. dissertation. Zurich: ETH Zürich, 2013.
Syrjämaa, Taina. 'The Clash of Picturesque Decay and Modern Cleanliness in Late Nineteenth-Century Rome', in Mark Bradley (ed.), *Rome: Pollution and Propriety. Dirt Disease and Hygiene in the Eternal City from Antiquity to Modernity* (Cambridge: Cambridge University Press, 2012), 202–222.

Syrjämaa, Taina. *Constructing Unity, Living in Diversity: A Roman Decade*. Suomen tiedeakatemian toimituksia 344. Helsinki: Finnish Academy of Science and Letters, 2006.
Tietze, Hans. *Die Juden Wiens: Geschichte, Wirtschaft, Kultur*. Vienna: Mandelbaum Verlag, [1933] 2007.
Timms, Edward. *Karl Kraus: Satiriker der Apokalypse. Leben und Werk 1874 bis 1918*. Berlin: Suhrkamp, [1986] 1999.
Townsend, Mary Lee. *Forbidden Laughter: Popular Humor and the Limits of Repression in Nineteenth-Century Prussia*. Ann Arbor: University of Michigan Press, 1992.
Townsend, Mary Lee. 'Humour and the Public Sphere in Nineteenth-Century Germany', in Jan Bremmer and Herman Roodenburg (eds), *Cultural History of Humour: From Antiquity to the Present Day* (Cambridge: Polity Press, 1997), 200–221.
Ullmayer, Franz. *Wiener Volksleben: Ein humoristisches Bädecker bei der Weltausstellung*. Vols I-IV. Vienna: A. Wenedikt, 1873.
Vidler, Anthony. 'Psychopathologies of Modern Space: Metropolitan Fear from Agoraphobia to Estrangement', in Michael S. Roth (ed.), *Rediscovering History: Culture, Politics, and the Psyche* (Palo Alto, CA: Stanford University Press, 1994), 11–29.
Vocelka, Karl. *Geschichte Österreichs: Kultur-Gesellschaft-Politik*. Munich: Wilhelm Heyne Verlag, 2011.
Vocelka, Karl. *K.u.K. Karikaturen und Karikaturen zum Zeitalter Kaiser Franz Josephs*. Vienna: Jugend und Volk, 1986.
Wagener, Mary L. 'Fashion and Feminism in "Fin de Siecle" Vienna'. *Woman's Art Journal* 10(2) (1989–90), 29–33.
Wagner-Riegel, Renate. 'Einleitung', in Renate Wagner Riegel (ed.), *Die Wiener Ringstraße: Das Kunstwerk im Bild*, Die Wiener Ringstraße – Bild einer Epoche, Vol. I (Vienna: Verlag Hermann Böhlaus Nachf., 1969), 13–45.
Walden, Heinrich (pseudonym for Joseph Alois). *Wien und seine Bewohner humoristisch geschildert auf einem Spaziergang über die ganze Bastey; nebst einer Skizze der merkwürdigsten Gegenstände, deren malerisch-schöner Anblick sich hier darbietet*. Vienna: Verlag Franz Wimmer, 1834.
Walkowitz, Judith R. *City of Dreadful Delight: Narratives of Sexual Danger in Late-Victorian London*. Chicago: University of Chicago Press, 1992.
Wehle, Peter: *Sprechen Sie Wienerisch? Von Adaxl bis Zwutschkerl*. Vienna: Ueberreuter, 1980.
Weis, Johann Babtist. *Wien's Merkwürdigkeiten mit ihren geschichtlichen Erinnerungen: Ein Wegweiser für Fremde und Einheimische*. Vienna: Wimmer, 1834.
Wickberg, Daniel. *Senses of Humor: Self and Laughter in Modern America*. Ithaca: Cornell University Press, 1998.
Wilson, Elisabeth. *The Sphinx in the City: Urban Life, the Control of Disorder, and Women*. Berkeley: University of California Press, 1992.
Wistrich, Robert S. *The Jews of Vienna in the Age of Franz Joseph*. Oxford: Oxford University Press, 1990.
Wolf, G. *Geschichte der k.k. Archive in Wien*. Vienna: Wilhelm Braumüller, 1871. Retrieved 29 January 2019 from https://archive.org/details/geschichtederkk01wolfgoog.
Zweig, Stefan. *Die Welt von Gestern: Erinnerungen eines Europäers*. Frankfurt am Main: Fischer Taschenbuch Verlag, [1942] 2005.

Magazines

Die Bombe, Vienna. Österreichische Nationalbibliothek (ÖNB). ANNO Austrian Newspapers Online. www.anno.onb.ac.at.
Figaro. Humoristisches Wochenblatt, Vienna. Österreichische Nationalbibliothek (ÖNB). ANNO Austrian Newspapers Online. www.anno.onb.ac.at / MF 4786.
Der Floh, Vienna/Budapest. Österreichische Nationalbibliothek (ÖNB). ANNO Austrian Newspapers Online. www.anno.onb.ac.at.
Glühlichter. Humoristisch-satirisches Arbeiterblatt, Vienna, Jg. 1889–1895. Verein für Geschichte der ArbeiterInnenbewegung (VGA).
Der Humorist, Vienna. Österreichische Nationalbibliothek (ÖNB). ANNO Austrian Newspapers Online. www.anno.onb.ac.at.
Illustrierer Wiener Extrablatt, 1 January 1903. Österreichische Nationalbibliothek (ÖNB). ANNO Austrian Newspapers Online. www.anno.onb.ac.at.
Jörgel Briefe / Hans Jörgel von Gumpoldskirchen: Volksschrift im Wiener Dialekte, Vienna. Österreichische Nationalbibliothek (ÖNB). ANNO Austrian Newspapers Online. www.anno.onb.ac.at.
Kikeriki. Humoristisches Volksblatt, Vienna. Österreichische Nationalbibliothek (ÖNB). ANNO Austrian Newspapers Online. www.anno.onb.ac.at / MF 3039.
Neue Glühlichter. Humoristisch-satirisches Arbeiterblatt, Vienna, Jg.1895–1900. Verein für Geschichte der ArbeiterInnenbewegung (VGA).
Wiener Caricaturen, Vienna. Österreichische Nationalbibliothek (ÖNB). ANNO Austrian Newspapers Online. www.anno.onb.ac.at.

Newspapers

'Aus dem Gerichtssaale', *Neue Freie Presse*, 19 October 1868. Österreichische Nationalbibliothek (ÖNB). ANNO Austrian Newspapers Online. www.anno.onb.ac.at.
'Der Mord in Floridsdorf. (Orig.-Bericht der "Presse")', *Die Presse*, 28 January 1884. Österreichische Nationalbibliothek (ÖNB). ANNO Austrian Newspapers Online. www.anno.onb.ac.at.
'Die Familie Germandre. Roman von Georg Sand', *Die Presse*, 6 February 1862. Österreichische Nationalbibliothek (ÖNB). ANNO Austrian Newspapers Online. www.anno.onb.ac.at.
'Ein neues Buch von Jules Verne', *Wiener Zeitung*, 29 April 1875. Österreichische Nationalbibliothek (ÖNB). ANNO Austrian Newspapers Online. www.anno.onb.ac.at.
'Es ist mein Wille', *Wiener Zeitung*, 25 December 1857. Österreichische Nationalbibliothek (ÖNB). ANNO Austrian Newspapers Online. www.anno.onb.ac.at.
'Kleiner Wiener Chronik', *Die Presse*, 29 December 1857. Österreichische Nationalbibliothek (ÖNB). ANNO Austrian Newspapers Online. www.anno.onb.ac.at.
'Locales (Mord und Selbstmord)', *Wiener Zeitung*, 20 June 1887. Österreichische Nationalbibliothek (ÖNB). ANNO Austrian Newspapers Online. www.anno.onb.ac.at.
'Ueber die Neugestaltung Wiens', *Die Presse*, 28 October 1858. Österreichische Nationalbibliothek (ÖNB). ANNO Austrian Newspapers Online. www.anno.onb.ac.at.
'Ueber Nostalgie. Feuilleton', *Die Presse*, 1 May 1890. Österreichische Nationalbibliothek (ÖNB). ANNO Austrian Newspapers Online. www.anno.onb.ac.at.

Statistics

Statistisches Jahrbuch der Stadt Wien 1884, XVI. Bildungswesen. s.197: *Die periodische Presse in Wien in den Jahren 1875–1884*. Retrieved 29 January 2019 from http://anno.onb.ac.at/cgi-content/anno-plus?aid=sjw&datum=1884&size=45.

Visual Sources

Allerhöchst genehmigter Plan der Stadterweiterung. Holzstich. Vienna: K. k. Hof- und Staatsdruckerei. Retrieved 12 February 2019 from Wikimedia Commons. https://commons.wikimedia.org/wiki/File:Plan_Stadterweiterung_Wien_1860.jpg.

Rotunde, Weltausstellung 1873. Welt ausstellen. Schauplatz Wien 1873. Herausgeber Technisches Museum Wien. Retrieved 12 February 2019 from Wikimedia Commons, https://commons.wikimedia.org/wiki/File:Rotunde_Weltausstellung_1873.jpg.

Schottenring, 1875. Blickfänge einer Reise nach Wien – Fotografien 1860–1910. Ausstellungskatalog des Wien Museums, 2006. Retrieved 7 February 2019 from Wikimedia Commons, https://commons.wikimedia.org/wiki/Wiener_Ringstra%C3%9Fe#/media/File:Schottenring_Wien_1875.jpg.

INDEX

absolutism, 29, 40, 42–43, 59
Adler, Viktor, 78
advertisements, 12–13, 22n59, 78, 135, 196
aesthetic culture, rationality versus, 124
affect. *See* bodily experience; sensory experience
age, gender and, 185–86
aggression in humour, 57–58, 85n3, 86n3
agoraphobia, 83
Alkon, Paul, 159, 161
Allen, Ann Taylor, 10, 115, 143, 188, 210
Allgemeine Bauzeitung, 202
Alt-Wiener Volkstheater, 151
Anderson, Benedict, 199–200
Anderson, Harriet, 187
Anderson, Olive, 222
animals, personification of, 77–78
anti-modernism, 117, 123, 132n101, 150, 186
antisemitism, 204
  Kikeriki and, 12, 22n55, 27, 178n166, 209
  ridicule and, 208–12, 217–19
  stock market crash of 1873 and, 212, 217–19, 243n233, 249
architecture
  New Vienna competition and, 34–39, 52nn55–56
  symbolic nature of, 44–45, 108, 129n57
aristocracy, social rules and, 96
assimilation, Jewish, 208–11
Assmann, Jan, 113–14
Ausgleich, 206, 251

Austria-Hungary, 40. *See also* Habsburg Empire
authority, Vindobona figure and, 185
aviation, future Vienna and, 158–61, 163

Bach, Alexander, 36, 46
Bach, Ulrich E., 206
Bakhtin, Mikhail, 18
Baudelaire, Charles, 3
beauty, urban renewal, Vienna, emphasizing, 183–84
beggars, 212–13, 217–25, 228–29, 241n209
Békési, Sandor, 131
Beller, Steven, 6, 171n38, 249
Benjamin, Walter, 45, 134
Berg, O. F., 26–27, 62, 90n68, 99, 184. *See also* Ebersberg, Ottokar
Bergson, Henri, 224, 235, 248
  fashion and, 191
  laughter and, 17, 70, 95, 253
Berlin, 7–8
Berliner Schnauze, 8
Berman, Marshall, 3, 65, 100–101, 127n28, 166
Berührungsangst. See fear of touching
Bildung, 33
Billig, Michael, 14, 57, 61–62, 86n17, 87n23, 140
  nationalism and, 200
bisociative thinking, humour and, 141
Blevins, Cameron, 21n36
bodily experience, 81, 84, 85, 170n26, 173n83
  disorder and, 94–103
  humour, theories of, and, 95

Kikeriki and, 82–83, 98–99, 102–3, 120n20
Old Vienna and, 150–52
Der Bombe, 27
boulevards, 121
bourgeoisie, 2, 4–6, 41–45, 64, 127n28. *See also Bürgertum*; middle classes
  public sphere importance to, 37, 97
  revolution of 1848 and, 110, 113–14
  social rules and, 96
  underclass and, 215–16, 221–25, 228, 242n223
Boyer, John, 7, 41, 47, 211–12
Brigstocke, Julian, 139, 146, 151
Broch, Hermann, 107
Bürgertum, 18, 22n55, 46–47, 88n47, 96, 113. *See also* bourgeoisie; middle classes
Burke, Peter, 16

capitalism, 71–72, 75, 77–79, 127n28, 212
caricature, 27, 31, 152–57
carnival culture, 1, 191–93, 233n69
cartoons
  narrative, 98–99
  reader submissions of, 32
Castle, Terry, 192
cathedral of St. Stephen (Stephansdom), 153–55, 180
censorship, 11, 13, 25–33, 35, 37
Chase, Jefferson S., 210
Chiavacci, Vinzenz, 150, 167, 227
Christian Social Party, 76, 90n69, 171n42, 211, 215, 249
  monopolies ended by, 91n85
circulation, 13, 22n60, 32
City Council, Vienna, 41–42, 48, 170n30, 250–51
  Kikeriki and, 46–47, 55n108, 71, 117
  order, desire for, from, 72–75
  street lighting and, 79
class identity, social rules and, 96
Coen, Deborah R., 140, 143
coffee houses, 31–32, 140–41
Cohen, William A., 242n223
Colomina, Beatriz, 129n57
the comical, humour versus, 16–17, 23n70

comical modernity. *See also specific topics*
  twentieth century, 3
comics, United States and, 12
constitutional monarchy, 6–7, 40–41, 42–43, 170n30, 251–52
Constitution of 1867, 88n41
construction, 79, 110, 162
  Kikeriki and, 78, 92n103, 94, 107–8
contextualization of humour, 16
Corbin, Alain, 84
Counter-Reformation, 124, 128n46
Critchley, Simon, 70, 89n56, 95, 101
cross-dressing, 191–93, 198, 233n63, 233n69
cultural anxieties, humour responding to, 17–18, 23n65
cultural hierarchies in urban space, 143–46
cultural history, humour viewed via, 66
cultural pessimism, *fin-de-siècle* era and, 166–67

Darnton, Robert, 16, 32, 51n35
Darwin, Charles, 141–42, 171n42
Dickens, Charles, 213, 215, 217
disciplinary humour, 18–19
discursive community, humorous magazines forming, 158, 168
disorder, 94–103, 108–14
  Gründerzeit versus *fin-de-siècle*, 104–7
  modernity and, 100–101
Dundes, Alan, 86n3, 119
dystopias
  future Vienna as, 158, 162–68, 177n149, 177n157
  twentieth century, 178n163
  urban renewal, Vienna, and, 163–68

Ebersberg, Ottokar, 166, 225. *See also* Berg, O. F.
Eliot, George, 193
emancipation of Jews, in Habsburg Empire, 208–9
emotional community, 147, 168, 247–51
emotional detachment, 219–25, 253
Enlightenment, 124
ethnic minorities, 205–8, 207
etiquette. *See* social rules

evolution, theory of, 141–42
expansion of the city. *See* urban renewal, Vienna
experience. *See* bodily experience; sensory experience

fantasy, 69–71
fashion, modern women and, 187–91, 232n37
fear of touching (*Berührungsangst*), 82, 84
Felder, Cajetan, 45, 117
Felski, Rita, 247
femininity. *See* gender; Vindobona figure
Der Figaro, 11–12, 22n55
   antisemitism and, 211
   beggars and, 219, 221–22
   bodily experience and, 82, 84
   censorship and, 26–27, 31–32, 37
   circulation of, 13, 22n60
   construction and, 107–8, 162
   dystopias and, 163, 165–66, 177n157
   evolution, theory of, and, 141–42
   fashion and, 189–90
   future Vienna and, 159, 162–63, 165–66, 176n134
   masquerades and, 192, 222
   motto of, 227
   nationalism and, 200, 206
   New Vienna and, 33, 35–39, 52nn58–59
   Old Vienna and, 148–49
   parks and, 116, 131n96
   personified places and, 153–55, 174n91, 175n106
   reader submissions and, 171n47
   revolution of 1848 and, 107–8
   standardization of life and, 68
   urban space and, 47–48
   Vindobona figure and, 180–82, 230n8, 230nn10–12
   visual errors and, 143–46
   World Exhibition of 1873 and, 203–4
fin-de-siècle era, 124, 148, 150, 167
   antisemitism and, 212
   disorder in humour during, 104–7
   dystopias and, 166
   fashion in, 189–90

fin-de-siècle melancholia, 213–14, 224–27, 246n287
Der Floh, 19n1, 22n55, 56–57, 64, 85n1, 89n54
   advertisements and, 78
   antisemitism and, 209, 218
   beggars and, 218–20
   censorship and, 26–27, 29–30
   circulation of, 13
   evolution, theory of, and, 141–42
   fashion and, 190
   foreign visitors, 203, 238n139
   future Vienna and, 160–61
   masquerades and, 192, 222
   misreading and, 136
   Opera House, Vienna, and, 44, 54n96
   panoptic gaze and, 103–4
   personified places and, 154
   reader submissions and, 10, 32
   revolution of 1848 and, 114, 130n80
   Ringstraße and, 42–43, 103–5, 128n41
   sexuality and, 194
   shade, loss of, and, 117, 132n104
   standardization of life and, 56–57, 64, 68–69
   street lighting and, 80
   urban renewal, Vienna, and, 1, 54n91
   urban space and, 47–48
   Vindobona figure and, 184–85, 231n18
   visual errors and, 138–39
   women readers and, 196–98, 235n102
   World Exhibition of 1873 and, 203–4, 238n147
foreign visitors, 4, 198, 228–29, 236n117, 237n123
   Der Floh, 203, 238n139
   nationalism and, 199–205
   World Exhibition of 1873, 200–201, 203–5
Forsström, Riikka, 161
Frahm, Ole, 86n14
Franz Joseph (Emperor), 4, 36, 40, 109
Freud, Sigmund, 127n34, 180, 222
   aggression in humour and, 57–58, 85n3
   humour, theories of, and, 15–18, 24n81, 57–58, 78, 253

jokes and, 57–58, 87n27, 99, 101–3, 112–13, 223–24
Frevert, Ute, 186
Frisby, David, 131, 150
Fritzsche, Peter, 7, 39, 134, 169n3
fröhliche Apokalypse. *See* joyous apocalypse
Fuess, Jo Ann Mitchell, 69, 166

Gallmeyer, Josefina, 184
Gemeinschaft, *Gesellschaft* versus, 68
Gemütlichkeit, 8, 210, 233
gender, 193–94, 231n22. *See also* modern women
　ethnic minorities and, 207
　Vindobona figure and, 180–89
　World Exhibition of 1873 and, 182
Georges Haussmann (Baron), 3
Gesamtkunstwerk (total work of art), Ringstraße as, 156
Gesellschaft, *Gemeinschaft* versus, 68
Gesetz. *See* law
Gigerl, 137, 190
Gilbert, Joanne R., 236n103
Girardi, Alexander, 148
Glacis, Vienna, parks in, 116–21, 131n94
Gluck, Mary, 20n25, 208, 210
Glühlichter, 113
Goethe, Johann Wolfgang von, 1, 210
Goldstein, Robert Justin, 13, 30–31
Graf, Andreas, 196
Green, Nicholas, 115
Gründerzeit, 5, 20n16, 212
　disorder in humour during, 104–7
　fashion as symbol of restriction in, 189
　standardization of life and, 64

Habermas, Jürgen, 11, 226, 245n271
Habsburg Empire, 41–42, 53n79, 209
　censorship in, 28–31
　ethnic minorities in, 205–8
　nationalism and, 201–2, 205–7
　Press Laws in, 26, 29–30, 35
Hainisch, Marianne, 194
Hapuli, Ritva, 231n22
Harvey, David, 45
Hazlitt, William, 69, 216
Heine, Heinrich, 78, 131n86

high culture, popular culture versus, 5, 248–49
Hitler, Adolf, 211
Hobbes, Thomas, 15, 75, 91n80
Hofburg palace, 42–43, 96
Hofer, Johannes, 147
Hofmannsthal, Hugo von, 96–97, 107
homelessness, 214, 242n215
housing conditions, 214–15, 242n212
Der Humorist, 148–49, 153–54, 174n96
humorous magazines (*Witzblätter*), 8–9, 248. *See also specific magazines*
　discursive communities formed by, 158, 168
　sensory experience addressed in, 10, 157–58
　visual appearance of, 12
humour, theories of, 13–14, 23n81, 133n124, 141
　bodily experience and, 95
　Freud and, 15–18, 24n81, 57–58, 78, 253
　incongruence theories and, 15–16, 23n72, 86n3, 122
　relief theories and, 15–16, 62
　superiority theories and, 15, 57, 75, 91n80
humourists, 15, 23n69
Hutcheon, Linda, 158, 163

Illustriertes Wiener Extrablatt, 225
images, 51n35
　censorship and, 30–31
　New Vienna and, 37–39
　of urban space, 39, 53n75
imagination, 2, 14, 31, 39, 45, 69–71
imagined communities, nationalism and, 199–200
imagined geography, 9, 21n36
immigrants, Vienna and, 4
Imperial Commission, Habsburg, 41–42
incongruence theories of humour, 15–16, 23n72, 86n3, 122
individualism, 14
individuality, standardization of life as threat to, 68–69
industrialization, 122–23

Innenministerium. See Ministry of the Interior
Innerhofer, Roland, 161
intermediality, in humorous magazines, 248
irony, 61, 122–23, 156, 158, 160, 163, 210, 254. *See also* self-irony

Janik, Allan, 5–6, 107, 189
Jastrow, Joseph, 137
Jelavich, Peter, 87n26, 210
jest books, 199
Jewish assimilation, 208–11
Jewish culture, 141, 171n38, 249
Jewish joke (*Judenwitz*), 210
Jewishness, modernity and, 208–12
Johannisson, Karin, 147
Johnston, William M., 96–97, 226–27
joke cycles, 119–24
jokes, 32, 62, 248
    fantasy and, 70
    Freud on, 57–58, 87n27, 99, 101–3, 112–13, 223–24
Jones, Steven E., 160
Jörgel Briefe, 148–49, 172n64
Josefstädter Exerzierplatz, 60–62
joyous apocalypse (*fröhliche Apokalypse*), 107
Judenwitz. See Jewish joke

Kant, Immanuel, 133n124
Karl (Archduke), 143–46
Kikeriki, 11, 44, 87n24, 88n37, 88n46, 227
    advertisements and, 78, 135
    antisemitism and, 12, 22n55, 27, 178n166, 209
    bodily experience and, 82–83, 98–99, 102–3, 120n20
    censorship and, 26–27, 30
    circulation of, 13, 32
    City Council, Vienna, and, 46–47, 55n108, 71, 117
    construction and, 78, 92n103, 94, 107–8
    cross-dressing and, 233n63
    dystopias and, 162–64, 177n149
    ethnic minorities and, 207
    evolution, theory of, and, 141–42
    fashion and, 190
    future Vienna and, 161–64
    housing conditions and, 215
    misreading and, 135–36
    narrative cartoons and, 98–99
    nationalism and, 202
    nature and, 117–18, 123
    order, desire for, and, 71
    personified places and, 156
    police and, 59–61
    prohibition signs and, 58
    reader submissions and, 32–33, 196
    revolution of 1848 and, 107–8, 113, 130n85
    Ringstraße and, 123
    standardization of life and, 64–65, 66–67
    typographical experiments and, 137
    underclass and, 216
    urban space and, 45, 46–48
    Vindobona figure and, 182, 231n14
    visual errors and, 137–38
    World Exhibition of 1873 and, 203
k.k. Landesgerichte, 26
Knuuttila, Seppo, 143
Koestler, Arthur, 18, 23n81, 141, 143, 248
Korhonen, Anu, 13, 23n65, 189, 195, 233n56
Kraus, Karl, 107, 166, 252

laughter, 15, 23n65, 107, 233n56
    Bergson on, 17, 70, 95, 253
    as hierarchical, 75
    order, as threat to, 26, 87n18
    political meaning in, 25
    social punishment, humour as, and, 17, 70
law (*Gesetz*), bourgeoisie promoting, 64
Lefebvre, Henri, 8
liberalism, 4–5, 139–40, 208–9
    housing conditions and, 215
    lower middle classes alienated from, 6–7
Linhardt, Marion, 5
local feeling (*Lokalgefühl*), 151–52, 168, 174n89
Lokalgefühl. See local feeling
lower classes. *See also* underclass
    censorship and, 26
    revolution of 1848, 109–10

lower middle classes, 6–7
　City Council, Vienna, excluding, 46–48
　urban renewal, Vienna, and, 41
Lueger, Karl, 107, 211–12
Lumpenball, 222–24, 244n256

Maderthaner, Wolfgang, 71, 193, 215, 221
many-sidedness (*Vielseitigkeit*), 140
Maria Theresa (Empress), 50n19
Marx, Karl, 100
Märzlieder poems, 114
Masaidek, Franz, 121, 133n122, 201
masquerades, 233n61
　cross-dressing and, 191–92
　Lumpenball as, 222–24, 244n256
Mayerling incident, 214, 227, 242n210
Mecsery de Tsoor, Karl von, 26
melancholia, *fin-de-siècle*, 213–14, 224–27, 246n287
mental flexibility, humour as source of, 69–70, 254
Mercier, Louis-Sébastian, 159
middle classes. *See also* bourgeoisie; Bürgertum
　City Council, Vienna, relationship with, 46–48, 72
　heterogeneity of, 248–49
　moral sense and, 216
　urban space and, 44–49
Militär-Polizeiwache, 61
Ministerkonferenz, 28, 35–36
Ministry of Police, in Habsburg Empire, 28, 50n19
Ministry of the Interior (*Innenministerium*), 28
misreading, 135–36, 146
moderne Frauen. *See* modern women
modernism, 3, 107
modernism, Viennese, 5, 20n25
modernity, 3
　disorder and, 100–101
　gender and, 180–87, 231n22
　instability of, 247
　Jewishness and, 208–12
　order and, 58
　sensory experience and, 134

modernization, 3, 208
　humour, impact on, 151
　inner lives impacted by, 65
modern women (*moderne Frauen*), 186, 228–29, 231n25
　fashion and, 187–91, 232n37
　sense of humour and, 235n103
　sexuality and, 188, 193–95
monopolies, 76–77, 91n85
moral sense, 213, 216–17
More, Thomas, 159
Mulkay, Michael, 97, 154
Musil, Robert, 99, 254
Musner, Lutz, 148, 193, 215, 221, 249

narrative cartoons, *Kikeriki* and, 98–99
nationalism, 250, 252
　Habsburg Empire and, 201–2, 205–7
　imagined communities and, 199–200
　World Exhibition of 1873 and, 202–5
nature, 114, 118, 119–22, 124–25, 131n86
　anti-modernism and, 117, 123
neo-absolutism. *See* absolutism
Nestroy, Johann, 151
Neulerchenfeld, 110, 221
Neu-Wien. *See* New Vienna
New Vienna (*Neu-Wien*), 52nn58–59
　architecture competition for, 34–39, 52nn55–56
　censorship and, 35
　Franz Joseph and, 36
　gender and, 180–82
　images and, 37–39
　Jewishness and, 209
　public sphere and, 34–37
　Ringstraße and, 156
　satire and, 35–37
　urbanization, as response to, 33–34
Nietzsche, Friedrich, 166
Nöllke, Matthias, 22n55
nostalgia, 17, 114, 120, 131, 147–58, 181–82

Öffentlichkeit. *See* public sphere
Old Vienna (*Alt-Wien*), 125, 168
　anti-modernism and, 150

Old Vienna (*Alt-Wien*) (*cont.*)
   bodily experience and, 150–52
   fin-de-siècle era and, 148, 150
   gender and, 180–82
   local feeling and, 151–52
   nostalgia for, 147–58, 181–82
   personified places and, 152–57
   popular culture, as part of, 148–49
   urban renewal, Vienna and, 148–50, 153–57, 172n64
open city, 161, 176n139
Opera House, Vienna, 44–45, 54n96
order, desire for, 71–75
order, modernity and, 58
order, resistance to, 26, 87n18, 88n37, 127n24
   Freud on, 57–58
   police and, 59–63
   satire and, 58
   standardization of life and, 63–64
   theatre comedies and, 63
Oring, Elliott, 223
Ottakring, 9, 33, 109, 221

panoptic gaze, 61, 86n14, 128n39, 143, 155, 253
   Der Floh and, 103–4
Paris, urban renewal in, 3, 111
parks, 115–21, 131n94, 131n96
patriarchy, fashion as threat to, 189
Pellatz, Susanne, 196
personified places, 152–57, 174n91, 174n96, 175n106, 175n110, 253
place names, 42–43
police, 28, 50n19, 87n19
   order, resistance to, and, 59–63
   street lighting and, 80
poor. *See* underclass
popular culture
   high culture versus, 5, 248–49
   Old Vienna as part of, 148–49
popular humour, humorous magazines as, 248. *See also specific topics*
Pötzl, Eduard, 156, 175n110, 223–24, 244n256
Praterallee, 137–38
Die Presse, 34, 234n72

Press Laws, in Habsburg Empire, 26, 29–30, 35
prohibition signs, *Kikeriki* and, 58
pseudonyms, 32–33, 37–38, 193, 195–96
public sphere (*Öffentlichkeit*), 11, 225–26, 245n271
   bourgeoisie, importance to, 37, 97
   New Vienna and, 34–37
publishing licences, censorship and, 29–30
Der Punch, 26

racism, 204, 207
Raimund, Ferdinand, 151
rationality, 123
   aesthetic culture versus, 124
   capitalism and, 75
reader submissions, 10–11, 50n17, 171n47
   censorship and, 27–28, 31–33
   jokes as, 32
   pseudonyms and, 32–33
   women readers and, 195–96
rebellious humour, 18–19
regulations. *See* standardization of life
relief theories of humour, 15–16, 62
Residenz- und Reichshauptstadt, 40–41
revolution of 1848, 61, 129n64, 129n65, 129n67, 130n80, 130n85
   bourgeoisie and, 110, 113–14
   censorship and, 11, 28
   disorder represented through, 107–14
   Franz Joseph and, 109
   lower classes, 109–10
   street lighting and, 92n109
   urban renewal, Vienna, and, 107–12
revolutions, 19th century, urban space and, 108–9
ridicule, 44, 58–63, 72–76, 87n23
   antisemitism and, 208–12, 217–19
   of modern women, 188–95
   of underclass, 219–24
right to vote, women's movements and, 187
Ringstraße, 41–43, 103–5, 128n41, 131n88, 209, 217
   advertisements on, 135
   bourgeoisie, rise of, and, 4–5
   dead trees on, 121–24, 133n122
   as *Gesamtkunstwerk*, 156

modernism, Viennese, and, 5
    nature and, 121–25
    New Vienna and, 156
    opening of, 94
    as personified place, 156
    as spatial narrative, 45
    traffic on, 76
Rosenwein, Barbara H., 147, 168

Salmi, Hannu, 84, 159, 225
Sand, George, 193, 234n72
Saphir, Moriz Gottlieb, 151
satire, 9, 43
    censorship and, 25–26
    New Vienna and, 35–37
    order, desire for, and, 71–72
    order, resistance to, and, 58
    social consciousness and, 213–19
    utopias and, 161
Scheidl, Ernst, 22n55
Schenk, Hugo, 213, 223, 226
Schivelbusch, Wolfgang, 80
Schlögl, Friedrich, 27, 69, 112, 151, 166, 193
Schneider, Elfriede, 22n55
Schönerer, Georg, 211–12
Schopenhauer, Arthur, 69–70
Schorske, Carl E., 53n75, 66, 124, 126n15, 185–86, 247
    criticism of, 6
    Ringstraße and, 4–5, 41
    social rules and, 96–97
    urban renewal, Vienna, and, 40–41, 111–12, 119–20
Schwartz, Vanessa R., 7, 39
scientific thought, 19th century, uncertainty in, 140, 143
Scott, Joan Wallach, 70
script theories of humour, 89n63
Segel, Harold B., 141
self-irony, 203, 205, 210. *See also* irony
self-persuasion, jokes as, 62
self-reflection, dystopias and, 165–66
Sennett, Richard, 85, 189
sense of humour, 14, 89n48, 106, 171n36
    emotional community sharing, 147, 168
    women lacking, 235n103

sensory experience, 173n83
    humorous magazines addressing, 10, 157–58
    modernity and, 134
    of urban space, 82, 84–85, 134, 143–46
serious world, humour relationship with, 106–7, 154–55
sexuality, modern women and, 188, 193–95
shade, loss of, 117–21, 132n104
Shaya, Gregory, 225
Sicherheitswache, 61–62
Simmel, Georg, 67–68, 189, 225
Sitte, Camillo, 148, 172n58
Sitter, Karl, 26–27, 29, 166
Sochen, June, 235
social consciousness, 213–19
social control, modern women and, 188, 195
social punishment, humour as, 17, 62, 70, 75
social rules, 96–99, 120–21
Spector, Scott, 208, 213
Spencer, Herbert, 15
Spitzer, Daniel, 152
Sprengler, Oswald, 166
Springer, Elisabeth, 36–37, 41–42
Staberl figure, 237n123
Stadterweiterung. *See* urban renewal
Stadtrat, 46
Stallybrass, Peter, 191, 220
standardization of life, 56–57, 64–71, 112–13, 116–17, 120–21
Stephansdom. *See* cathedral of St. Stephen
Stierle, Karlheinz, 165
stock market crash of 1873, 20n16, 204, 238n147
    antisemitism and, 212, 217–19, 243n233, 249
Strauss, Johann, Jr., 153
street lighting, 79–80, 92n109
street sale of periodicals, prohibition of, 31
Stühlinger, Harald Robert, 34
suicide, 226
superiority theories of humour, 15, 57, 75, 91n80
Suttner, Bertha von, 161, 176n143

temporality, nature and, 119–20
textuality, urban space and, 7, 136
theatre comedies, 63, 231n17
Tönnies, Ferdinand, 67–68
total work of art. *See Gesamtkunstwerk*
Toulmin, Stephen, 189
Townsend, Mary Lee, 11, 26
traffic, 76–78
tramway, Vienna, 76–78, 91n82
Twain, Mark, 23n69
typographical experiments, 136–37

underclass, 241n208, 243n241, 252
    beggars as, 212–13, 217–25
    bourgeoisie and, 215–16, 221–25, 228, 242n223
    emotional detachment towards, 219–25
    Freud and, 222
    as grotesque, 219–21
    homelessness and, 214
    Lumpenball and, 222–24, 244n256
    social consciousness and, 213–19
    urban space and, 212–13, 221
United States, comics and, 12
urbanization
    New Vienna as response to, 33–34
    Simmel on, 67–68
urban renewal, Paris, 3, 111
urban renewal, Vienna (*Stadterweiterung*), 1, 54n91, 100–101, 249–51
    absolutism and, 40
    beauty emphasized in, 183–84
    bourgeoisie belief in, 97
    as break with past, 119–20
    capitalism and, 71–72
    constitutional monarchy and, 40–41, 42–43
    dystopias and, 163–68
    Franz Joseph and, 4, 40
    housing conditions and, 214–15
    lower middle classes and, 41
    Old Vienna and, 148–50, 153–57, 172n64
    revolution of 1848 and, 107–12
    Schorske on, 40–41, 111–12, 119–20
    Vindobona figure as representation of, 180–89
    visual errors caused by, 139
urban space, 8, 42–43, 250–51
    cultural hierarchies embedded in, 143–46
    fear of touching and, 82, 84
    foreign visitors misinterpreting, 201
    images of, 39, 53n75
    middle classes and, 44–49
    revolutions, 19th century, and, 108–9
    sensory experience of, 82, 84–85, 134, 143–46
    social rules displayed in, 97
    textuality and, 7, 136
    underclass and, 212–13, 221
utopia, 159–62

Verne, Jules, 157, 160–61, 176n134
Vielseitigkeit. See many-sidedness
Vienna, 1–2. *See also* future Vienna; New Vienna; Old Vienna; urban renewal, Vienna; *specific topics*
    as *Weltstadt*, 202–5, 237n127
Viennese dialect (*Wienerisch*), 152–54
Viennese types (*Wiener Typen*), 228, 246n286, 251
Vindobona figure, 180–89, 231n14, 231n18
visual errors, 137–39, 143–46, 170n18
Vocelka, Karl, 99, 186, 232n37
Vormärz, 25–26, 28, 61, 149–50

Wagner, Mary L., 189
Wagner, Otto, 148, 172n58
Walden, Heinrich, 152
Walkowitz, Judith, 186
Weininger, Otto, 180
Wells, H. G., 159
Weltstadt (world city), Vienna as, 202–5, 237n127
White, Allon, 191, 220
Wickberg, Daniel, 14, 23n69, 57, 89n48, 106, 140, 154, 171n36
    moral sense and, 216
Wienerisch. See Viennese dialect
Wiener Luft. See Der Figaro
Wiener Schmäh, 8, 212
Wiener Skizzen, 27, 150

Wiener Typen. See Viennese types
Wiener Zeitung, 160–61, 180
Wilson, Elizabeth, 18, 179–80, 186, 193
wit, 69–70, 106–7, 151, 171n36, 173n81
    coffee houses and, 140
    Counter-Reformation and, 128n46
    humour versus, 14
    many-sidedness and, 140
Witz, 14, 210. *See also* wit
Witzblatt, use of term, 241n187
Witzblätter. See humorous magazines
women readers, 195–98, 229, 235n102
women's movements, 187, 194–95, 250, 252
word city, 7, 169n3
workers' riots, in Vienna, 129n60
world city. *See Weltstadt*
World Exhibition of 1873, 46, 77, 159–60, 182, 200–205, 238n147

Young Vienna. *See* New Vienna

Zelinka, Andreas, 45
Zweig, Stefan, 99

www.ingramcontent.com/pod-product-compliance
Lightning Source LLC
Chambersburg PA
CBHW071151070526
44584CB00019B/2751